GROWING SPIRITUALLY

GROWING
SPIRITUALLY

E. STANLEY JONES

ABINGDON PRESS
New York • *Nashville*

GROWING SPIRITUALLY

Copyright MCMLIII by Pierce & Washabaugh

Standard Book Number: 687-15967-9

Library of Congress Catalog Card Number: 53-11338

Scripture quotations designated "R.S.V." are from *The Revised Standard Version of the Bible.* Copyright 1946 and 1952 by the Division of Christian Education of the National Council of Churches. Scripture quotations designated "Moffatt" are from *The Bible: A New Translation* by James Moffatt. Copyright 1922, 1935, 1950 by Harper & Bros. Used by permission. The quotation from *Modern Psychiatry* on p. 81 is used by permission of the C. V. Mosby Company. The poem on p. 152 is from *The Collected Poems of W. B. Yeats,* copyright 1950, and is used by permission of the Macmillan Company, the Macmillan Company of Canada, and Mrs. W. B. Yeats. The poem by Ella Wheeler Wilcox on p. 170 is used by permission of the W. B. Conkey Company. The poem on p. 296 is used by permission of Miss Erica Oxenham.

SET UP, PRINTED, AND BOUND BY THE
PARTHENON PRESS, AT NASHVILLE,
TENNESSEE, UNITED STATES OF AMERICA

INTRODUCTION

IN THE WRITING OF ALL MY BOOKS I HAVE TRIED FIRST TO SENSE a need and then have the book move in to meet that need, however inadequately. The need has been the call. This has been especially true of this one. One would have thought that, in view of the need, there would have been a spate of books on the subject of "Growing Spiritually." But when I asked my publishers about books on that subject, they replied, to my astonishment, that they could not think of any. Nor could I. Plenty of books on various phases of the subject of growth and development, especially in psychology, but few, if any, covering the subject from a definitely Christian standpoint. This book tries to step into that need and meet it.

And it tries to meet it at the place where spiritual growth is made or marred, namely, at the place of the devotional. It is at the place of the devotional that we go up or down spiritually. It is the crux. For in the devotional we expose ourselves to God's resources, we assimilate them and grow by them. But it must be an all-round growth of the total person—intellectual, emotional, volitional. If the devotional becomes merely the emotional, then decay sets in in the other parts, and that means a decay of the whole. We must grow totally or grow lopsidedly, which is not growth, except in the sense that a "growth" comes out on the body—an excrescence. It is a species of spiritual cancer—cells growing by feeding on the rest.

The necessity for spiritual growth is not merely our personal problem—it is that, but it is more: it is our world problem. At the center of almost every acute problem—personal, social, economic, political and international—is moral and spiritual immaturity. The problems and the possibilities in almost every situation have outgrown the persons. We are immature persons dealing with mature problems. Dr. Rebecca Beard says: "The consuming illness of our times is our immaturity—our refusal to grow up." We have on our hands powers and possibilities for mature people, but the people who handle those powers are immature. Here is a man who is supposedly the head of a home, in a situation demanding maturity, but he is emotionally immature. He creates havoc. The same thing happens in larger situations—the school, the church, business, the state, international relationships. Each time the area of possible havoc grows larger. Deficiency in our moral and spiritual growth means devastation around us. Our immaturity is costly—increasingly so. For larger and larger powers are put more and more into the hands of people morally and spiritually too immature to handle them for the collective good. As has often been said, our intellectual lives have outgrown our moral and spiritual lives. We have grown-up powers handled by half-grown persons. And that is serious. For the powers we now have are such that an irresponsible mistake by a few immature people can set the world on fire—literally.

Spiritual maturity is no longer a luxury for a few; it is a necessity for us all.

John Foster Dulles tells us how he was driven into being a Christian from seeing international conferences dealing with great issues break down because the people who took part in them lacked a spirit which would have made the conferences a success—the Christian spirit. Today we see all life around us being tangled and snarled because of a lack of an intangible something, and that something is Christian maturity. Through it anything can happen anywhere. It is the key—the master key to every situation.

Then to produce that Christian maturity must be the major business and endeavor of our race. It is that or chaos. So this book attempts to point the way to that maturity of character without which we will remain an infantile civilization. If it furthers that maturity only by inches, well—it will be something, and it will be something in the right direction.

Where do we begin? Where everything begins—with ourselves. "If religion doesn't begin with the individual, it does not begin. If it ends with the individual, it ends." The beginning must be within. We cannot point to the lack of spiritual maturity in others and leave it at that, for that may turn out to be what in psychology is called projection—a projecting on others the faults and lacks we find in ourselves and thus mentally escaping the responsibility.

But we must not leave the reader feeling the club of necessity to be spiritually mature hanging over his head. We cannot be scared or clubbed into maturity. It must be a beckoning instead of a bludgeoning. We must feel the call. Fortunately that call comes from above

INTRODUCTION

and from within. God wills our maturity. He has arranged the world and us with one thing in view, namely, our maturity. And fortunately we are made for maturity—for growth, for development, for perfection. Everything within us works toward that end, everything except one thing—sin, or evil. This is the unnatural intrusion throwing monkey wrenches into the machinery of human living. Except for this, all else—I repeat, all else—is made for spiritual maturity. We are destined to be mature, to be perfect. "Everything," says Tagore, "lifts up strong hands after perfection." It does. We can live against that destiny and cancel it. But it is our destiny, written into blood and tissue and nerve and cell and organ—written in us. All we have to do is to clear away hindrances and meet the conditions of growth, and we grow—grow out of an inner necessity. "The earth bears fruit of itself"—the earth—and we are a part of that earth and are made in our inner structure to bear fruit of ourselves.

God and nature and we can thus co-operate in our growth. And when we do, then nothing in heaven or on earth can stop us from growing.

But it all depends on our co-operation with God. Without this the nerve of our growth is cut. With it, then, anything can happen—the sky and beyond is the limit. "I am the tadpole of an archangel," cried an exultant soul, but we are more: we are made to be made in His likeness. "We shall be like Him for we shall see Him as He is." But it won't just happen. We have to will to grow and to create the conditions for growth. Not that growth is strain—it is not. It is receptivity, as we shall see. But we have to will to receive.

The most open time of receptivity is the devotional time. Here the pores of our being are open to God and life, and we are receptive to our fingertips. Hence I have linked growth with devotional exercises, following the plan of my other books, a page a day. But while this book is divided into a page a day, it follows a theme throughout. The page a day is not an isolated dab of unconnected ideas and suggestions. I have tried to make it all a consistent whole, going from the beginning stages on through to maturity. It tries to expound the possibility of the total growth of the total personality.

This book can be read a page a day; or, since it is divided into a week's complete thought, it can be used as a study book for group

INTRODUCTION

discussions; or, since one theme runs through the whole, it can be read straight through as an ordinary book.

Growth in life is life's greatest adventure. The business of life is to live and to live abundantly. But most people know everything about life except how to live it.

As one who has tried this business of living in every climate and in almost all conditions around the world and has found that it works, I would share my secret with you. It is not mine. I found it at the feet of Another—a gift. One night in India after a very hard week in which it seemed that everything adverse had piled upon me, I found myself awakening before daylight and saying to myself: "I can feel myself grow." I could. But it was all "in spite of." And it was not my own. I had learned a secret. I share that secret with you in this book. For it is "an open secret"—simple and learnable by anybody, by anybody who wants to grow and wants it enough to pay the price.

E. STANLEY JONES

CONTENTS

CONTENTS

CONTENTS

GROWING SPIRITUALLY

Mark 4:26-29 (R.S.V.) Week 1—SUNDAY

YOU ARE MADE TO GROW

You are made to grow. The creative God made you for creative growth. Growth is the law of your being. Violate that law, and you violate yourself. You are unfulfilled, hence frustrated and unhappy.

I grant that the body ceases to grow after a certain time, and the slow process of slowing down and eventual decay sets in. This process of slowing down and decay may be minimized and postponed by inner states of mind and soul, but in the end the body is destined to the dust. Not so the mind and the soul. They are not necessarily linked with this inevitable bodily decay. They may be. Many people are so closely linked with their bodies that the decay of the body means the decay of the person. They have lived to make the body comfortable—to ward off sickness and death from it, to satisfy the cravings and appetites—so that their very persons are bound up with the fortunes of the body. When it decays, they decay. Life's supreme tragedy is to watch the triple decay of body, mind, and spirit in yourself or in another. No tragedy can compare with this.

This decay of the person causes more unhappiness than all other causes combined. All other causes are marginal; this is central. For to know, consciously or unconsciously, that the central purpose of your being—the thing for which you are made—is unfulfilled, or worse, is being violated, is to cause a central and fundamental unhappiness to settle at the very center of your being.

No amount of marginal happiness or adjustment can atone for this central dissatisfaction. If you are not a creative and growing person, you are an unhappy person. This central frustration spreads its dissatisfaction through all marginal satisfactions and makes them curdle and sour. Dissatisfaction with life in general sets in.

On the other hand, when you are fulfilling the law of your being by being a growing personality, then this spreads its central satisfaction through all the marginal happenings of life. Whether these happenings are unhappy or not, you are centrally happy. Human happiness is a by-product of being a creative, growing personality.

O creative God and Father, help me to see the wonderful possibility of being a continuously growing person—now and forever. Amen.

AFFIRMATION FOR THE DAY: *I am made to grow. I will fulfill the purpose of my being.*

1

THE STAGE IS SET FOR GROWTH

If the end of human existence is to live creatively and growingly, then it is obvious that the stage on which this drama of life is set, namely the universe, had to be imperfect. It had to be the kind of universe that would not be perfect in itself, but would make possible our perfection. It would have to be such that, in striving to perfect it, we would help perfect ourselves. It couldn't be perfect.

Therefore the objection that people bring against God—that He created a universe in which there are earthquakes, tornadoes, volcanoes, germs that cause illness, snakes, weeds, and other things that have plagued the life of men, and therefore He cannot be a perfect God, for His universe is imperfect—misses the point. The end of life is not human happiness; it is human growth. Happiness is a by-product of that growth.

The end of life is not happiness, but growth in character and achievement. The universe therefore had to be a semi-hard universe—it had to be sufficiently hard to sharpen our souls upon. Were there no disease germs, we would not give ourselves to research to find remedies—we would not grow. Were there no earthquakes, we would not improve our building construction to withstand them—we would not grow. Were there no weeds, we would not improve our crops to outwit them, and we would not improve ourselves in the process. We had to be unfinished masters of an unfinished world. In finishing the unfinished world we help finish ourselves.

We have, then, the two things necessary for growth: first, an urge within us for development and growth, an urge for creation; and second, an environment which makes growth possible and which stimulates it. If we don't grow, then it isn't because God hasn't set the stage for growth. He has. The fault lies within us. We have stifled the urges within us and have muffed the opportunities around us. We are self-stunted. If you are a stunted and runted human being, it is because you have decided to be just that.

O God, I see that I have created my own lack of creation—I've decided against growth. Forgive me. Amen.

AFFIRMATION FOR THE DAY: *If my environment is rasping, I will use it to sharpen my soul.*

THE PROD TO PERFECTION

Yesterday we finished by saying that the stage is set for growth—we have the urge within us, and we have an environment, unfinished, therefore serving as an emery stone upon which to sharpen our otherwise dull souls and wits.

Yes, someone objects, this is true, but the real environment in which we live is more than physical. It is mental and spiritual. People make it up. And people can be as cruel as an earthquake and as devastating as disease germs and more persistent and cantankerous than weeds. What about this environment of people? Well, I'm persuaded that this too is a part of the prod to perfection. It's a part of the divine plan, apparently to make it possible that imperfect people should help to make perfect those who decide to grow and be perfect. Many grow on account of the resistances they receive from environing people. Not what happens to you, but what you do with it after it does happen, determines the result. You can decide whether it will make you bitter or better.

If we live with imperfect people who seem to do a perfect job of nagging and harassing our spirits, then this too can become a growing point. How we take it decides whether it will be a groaning point or a growing point.

Here was a woman who had entered an unfortunate marriage—the third marriage for the man. One woman had turned to drink to escape his torments, another to sex; this woman turned to God. "Is this tormenting of you hurting you?" I asked when we discussed divorce as the way out. "No, strangely enough," she said, "I'm growing under it." She is today a radiant, integrated personality, in spite of her mental and spiritual environment. In spite of? No, on account of! For she is making her environment make her.

As the airplane when taking off always rises against the wind, so we can rise against the adverse winds of an unfinished material environment and of an unfinished, and therefore resistant, mental and spiritual environment.

O God, I see that Thou hast conspired to make me grow. I am in the grip of a divine intention. Help me to yield to it. Amen.

AFFIRMATION FOR THE DAY: *My adverse winds shall be my advantage winds today.*

3

GOD CONSPIRES TO MAKE US GROW

We have seen: (1) that we are made in the inner structure of our being for creation, for growth; (2) that the unfinished, but malleable, world around us tends to make us as we try to finish it; (3) that the mental and spiritual environment in which we live is so made that it will further us if we know how to use it.

Suppose God had finished His creation—made it perfect, as some insist He ought to have done if He is a perfect God—then what would have happened to us? Would we, as imperfect beings, have grown in a finished and perfected environment? There is a story of a man who found himself in a position where every wish was immediately fulfilled. He wanted a house, and there it was with servants at the door; he wanted a Cadillac, and there it was with chauffeur. He was elated at the beginning, but it soon began to pall on him. He said to an attendant: "I want to get out of this. I want to create something, to suffer something. I would rather be in hell than this." And the attendant answered: "Where do you think you are?"

But if God has made a world of earthquakes and tornadoes, of snakes and scorpions, of disease germs and death, He has also hidden away the remedies for every one of these evils, awaiting our discovery of them. There are materials at hand for making cement and steel for earthquakeproof houses. There are remedies for snake bites and scorpion stings. There are the materials for the making of penicillin; if there is death for the body, then it can be postponed until the body is so worn out that we will welcome a change of clothing—a heavenly body.

And more important than all the above: if we are compelled to live in an environment in the home, in the office, in the factory, in the state—an environment which is hostile to our growth as moral beings, there have been provided by the foresight and love of a gracious God the resources to help us grow in any environment. These resources have become available to us in Jesus Christ. Jesus is God's latchstring hung so low that even a child can reach it and open the door—to everything!

Dear Father, Thou hast provided everything—everything for my growth. Teach me how to possess my possessions. Amen.

affirmation for the day: *Alongside my disability stands His ability. I shall exchange.*

A SECRET BUT AN OPEN SECRET

We saw yesterday that where there is a need in this world of ours, there is a supply to that need, also at hand, awaiting our discovery of it. But the remedy is never too obvious. It is tucked away, a secret—it has to be searched for—but it is "open"—open to all.

When it comes to *the* Remedy for *the* need, then we would expect that this Remedy would be not so clear that it would require no thinking about it, so available that no conditions would be required for its finding, or so close at hand that you wouldn't have to search for it. You would expect Christ would be hidden, and yet open.

He was hidden—hidden away in an obscure land, in an obscure family; He worked at an obscure occupation—carpentry, quietly dropped His message into the hearts of obscure people—mostly fishermen and ordinary folks. And then "God wrapped His heart in flesh and blood and let it break upon a cross," that in that breaking the heart of His resources might be revealed.

This hiddenness has been "unto the Jews a stumblingblock, and unto the Greeks foolishness"—religion and philosophy passed it by. But the simple of heart have found that here lie near at hand the resources—everything they need to grow and to become the persons they ought and long to be.

Jesus is God available and approachable. And in Him is uncovered the pattern of the man-to-be. "What we are to be is not apparent yet, but we do know that when he appears we are to be like him—for we are to see him as he is." (I John 3:2, Moffatt.) This is the breath-taking destiny we are headed for—to be remade into the image of Christ, the Divine. This puts back our shoulders. We are headed for big things—the biggest thing this planet knows; we are headed to be Christlike personalities. This cancels all inferiorities based on blood, all sense of failure based on past mistakes and sins, and all sense of unworthiness based on what we are. It sets our faces away from the past, toward this amazing future.

In order to be released from the *is* we must see the *to-be*. We see it—in Christ. He is the Possibility and the Way to that Possibility.

Gracious Father, my heart begins to sing in anticipation. There is a dignity stealing into my blood. I thank Thee. Amen.

AFFIRMATION FOR THE DAY: *I am made for the biggest thing that this planet knows. I shall not fall short.*

THE GOAL OF GROWTH

Before we go on to the steps in growth, we should see the goal of growth. This must be fixed. For as Harnack, the great church historian, once said to me when I asked him the Christian solution to a certain problem: "Christianity gives no solutions. It gives us goals and then gives us power to move on to those goals."

In one of my books, *The Christ of the Mount,* I said that the whole of the Sermon on the Mount revolves around one verse: "Be ye therefore perfect, even as your Father which is in heaven is perfect" (Matt. 5:48). The word "therefore" reaches back and puts into this perfection the meaning of the whole of the preceding forty-six verses. These verses describe the content of the perfection. The next two chapters of the Sermon describe the hindrances to that perfection. So the whole Sermon revolves around perfection as the goal of human living. And perfection of no mean type: "as your Father which is in heaven is perfect." The "as" could be translated "since"—since God is perfect as God, we are to be perfect as sons of God.

I now see that this interpretation, written in 1931, before the rise of the totalitarians, was inadequate. It was too individualistic—the goal of life was individual perfection. Events since then have forced us to rethink our positions and to discover, if possible, the perfected individual in a perfected society. It is there! In the same Sermon we read: "Our Father . . . , Thy kingdom come. Thy will be done in earth, as it is in heaven" (Matt. 6:9-10). Here was the coming of a new order on earth after no mean pattern—after the pattern of the heavenly order. The goal of human society, then, is the Kingdom of God on earth. There are thus two goals which are really one in the Sermon on the Mount, namely, a perfected individual in a perfected Society. And these two are after definite patterns. The individual is made after the pattern of God—he is to be perfect as his heavenly Father is perfect; the society is to be made after the pattern of the heavenly order: "as it is in heaven." Nothing higher could be conceived by God or man than that. It is the ultimate in goals.

Dear God, Thou hast conceived breath-taking goals for me. And more: Thou dost undertake to get me to them. I thank Thee. Amen.

AFFIRMATION FOR THE DAY: *There is a destiny in my blood—the perfect person in the perfect Society. I follow.*

A PERFECTED INDIVIDUAL IN A PERFECTED SOCIETY

We pause today to clarify the goal of the individual as perfection of character and life. This makes cheap the ordinary goal of human living—to get to heaven. In the New Testament, apart from the book of Revelation, heaven is spoken of twelve times as a place to which men go hereafter. But not once is it spoken of as the goal of life. But perfection is mentioned thirty-three times and always as the goal of life. Note:

And he gave some, apostles; and some, prophets; and some, evangelists; and some, pastors and teachers: for the perfecting of the saints, for the work of the ministry, for the edifying of the body of Christ; till we all come in the unity of the faith, and of the knowledge of the Son of God, unto a perfect man, unto the measure of the stature of the fulness of Christ (Eph. 4:11-13).

Here the total endeavor converges on one thing: "for the perfecting of the saints . . . unto a perfect man." And this after an astonishing pattern: "the measure of the stature of the fulness of Christ."

Again: "Whom we preach, warning every man, and teaching every man in all wisdom; that we may present every man perfect in Christ Jesus: whereunto I labour" (Col. 1:28-29).

The human personality is not to be suppressed or wiped out. It is to be affirmed and affirmed to perfection.

The philosophies in the East have, on the whole, been world-weary and personality-weary. The endeavor has been to escape both and to be merged into the Impersonal. This turns the power of religion to escape from the world and the transcendence of personality.

The Christian faith on the other hand turns its redemptive energy into transforming the individual unto perfection and into transforming the present world order into the Kingdom of God. The end of life is not negation, but affirmation. And affirmation where it counts—the character of the individual and society.

We have now set our sights. We know what we are aiming at: at nothing less than to be a perfected individual in a perfected society.

O Christ, Thou hast disclosed to us the Goal. Thou art the Goal, and Thou art the Way to that Goal. I thank Thee. Amen.

AFFIRMATION FOR THE DAY: *I am on the way to the Goal—and what a Way, and what a Goal!*

7

IS THIS "PERFECTIONISM"?

How can we rescue this perfection we are interpreting from psychological "perfectionism"? Will this not set the goal so high that it will end in discouragement and defeat? What are the saving factors?

The saving factors are four: First, in "perfectionism" you are the center of your endeavor to do everything perfectly. In the perfection Jesus presents, God is the center. In the one you work out from yourself; in the other you work from God. Since every self-centered person is automatically self-frustrated, so every perfectionist, always living in a state of self-reference, is automatically frustrated. Second, since God is the center of Jesus' perfection, He offers grace and power to move on to that goal. This grace and power save from the frustration that comes from depending on the limited resources of our own selves. Third, since this perfection will always be a relative perfection —relative to something higher than itself, God—it can be realized and yet not realized. The bud may be perfect as a bud, but not perfect as a flower. Ours is to be a growing perfection, growing forever. The finite will forever approach the Infinite but will never arrive. Fourth, since this perfection is primarily a perfection in love, it is consistent with imperfection in the manifestation of that love.

For instance, a father had been absent for a long time, and when he returned, his little boy was so happy he could scarcely contain himself. He wanted to show his love, so he asked: "Daddy, can't I do something for you?" The father asked him to bring a glass of water. The little fellow went pell-mell across the room, poured some of the water into the glass and some on the table, grabbed the glass, and put his two little dirty fingers inside the glass as he held it. And when the father took it from him, there were two little muddy streams trickling down on the inside of the glass. The father turned the glass around and drank every bit of it. The boy stood there rubbing his hands on his jacket saying, "Daddy, can't I do something else for you?" His love was perfect, but the manifestation of that love was imperfect.

Father, I thank Thee that Thou satisfieth me and yet forever unsatisfieth me. I have, and I yearn to have. I thank Thee. Amen.

AFFIRMATION FOR THE DAY: *I am the most satisfied, unsatisfied being on earth.*

GRACE IS THE SOIL

We have been trying to set the framework in which we are to grow. There are some frameworks in which it is next to impossible to grow.

If life is bounded by the narrow framework of an earthly existence, ending in the narrower framework of a coffin, then, of course, a stunted life is guaranteed. Moreover, if gaining a place in heaven by and by is the goal, then you cannot grow under that. All you can do is to pay the price of admission—faithfulness to your duty—and get in. But if life holds the possibility of an infinite growth after an Infinite Pattern, then that puts back my shoulders and fills me with an eagerness for the big, the significant, the perfect.

If this is the goal, how do we begin and where? A verse is often quoted at this point as the answer: "But go on growing in the grace and knowledge of our Lord and saviour Jesus Christ" (II Pet. 3:18, Moffatt). You are to begin to grow in the grace and knowlege—you begin to grow from where you are. I question that. You don't grow "into" grace; you grow when you are *in* it.

Then the real question is: How do I get "in" grace? It is by a new birth, a conversion, a changing of the center of your life from self to God by self-surrender. Planted in the soil of your self, you simply cannot grow. You are not made to grow as a self-centered being. If you try by self-effort to grow in the soil of your own self, then you will grow from tangle to tangle.

> O shepherd, guide thy people,
> thine own flock,
> so lonely, lonely like a wild patch
> within a garden.
> (Mic. 7:14, Moffatt)

If you are centered on yourself, then you are "so lonely, lonely like a wild patch within a garden." The universe is orderly, for it obeys God— it is a garden. But if you obey yourself, then you are a wild patch of disorderliness within that garden of orderliness.

O God, I am doomed to sterility if I'm planted in myself, but I'm destined to fertility if I'm planted in Thee. Amen.

AFFIRMATION FOR THE DAY: *I am the soul, God is the Soil. I shall grow!*

9

FROM THE SELF-CENTERED TO THE GOD-CENTERED

We saw yesterday that the first step in growing is transplanting—shifting from a self-centered life to a God-centered life.

This cuts across a great deal of modern emphasis which would find all the answers within ourselves. Discover yourself, cultivate yourself, express yourself—these are the slogans. And for awhile this emphasis works. It gives you a shot in the arm of positive assertion. It turns you away from negativism. So far so good. But only "so far." Beyond that initial boost it cannot go. It exhausts its resources very quickly. So the aspirant in self-discovery, self-cultivation, and self-expression turns to another cult for another "shot." The soil of self was never intended to be the seed-bed of eternal values.

Even the Divine comes under the law of self-surrender. The central thing in the Incarnation is: He "emptied himself" (Phil 2:7, Moffatt). But this follows: "Therefore God raised him high" v. 9). This is the law of life for God and man: lose your self and find it again. The law is inexorable. The seed, wrapped in itself, will die. But emptying itself into the earth, it lives in the growing plant.

A lady, very proper in appearance and outlook and who never talked to God except in the language of the King James Version, heard Christ saying to her while I was speaking: "This isn't for you. Come outside, I want to talk with you." She protested that she would have to climb over three people, one of them her husband, to get out, and they would consider her ill or unbalanced. The Voice persisted. So she went. "But suppose He wouldn't be there when I got out there?" He was there. "Let's take a walk," He said. They went up the hill to the chapel. There He seemed to impel her to pull out of her inner life resentments and self-centeredness and lay them before Him. She was ashamed and said limply: "What shall I do?" "Suppose we have a funeral," He replied. And they did. They buried that proud, resentful self, and when they walked down the hill, she was inwardly gay and free. A new birth had taken place. She was free to grow.

But we are called into the new life in many ways, by many means. It doesn't matter how we come, if we end up at His feet—changed.

O Christ, Thou didst empty Thyself. Help me to empty myself, especially of myself. Amen.

AFFIRMATION FOR THE DAY: *My biggest question: Whose am I? Why, I'm God's!*

FAIR WEATHER CULTS

There is a passage in Acts 27:8 which tells us of Paul on his journey to Rome coming to a Cretan harbor called "Fair Havens," but it was "badly placed for wintering in." It was a fair-weather harbor with a beautiful name, but it was badly placed—couldn't protect against winter winds and storms. Many people take refuge in cults and movements which bear lovely names like "Fair Havens," but they are "badly placed for wintering in." They can't stand up against the rugged facts of sin and death and disaster.

If the fair-weather cults are proving inadequate and leaving men homeless and wandering from one to the other, then the neo-orthodoxy of today leaves one in the lurch, strangely enough, for the same reason. They both turn you toward yourself—one to discover your goodness, your latent divinity; the other to discover your badness.

It is true that neo-orthodoxy preaches the gospel as a means of forgiveness from this pervasive sinfulness. It preaches the gospel, but as someone said of a leading exponent, "He preaches the gospel, but always as a postscript." The emphasis is on the sinfulness of man even after grace has taken hold of him. Someone has said that neo-orthodoxy reverses the verse of Paul: "Where sin abounded, grace did much more abound," and puts it: "Where grace abounded, sin did more abound." The emphasis is upon the sinful self.

Dr. A. J. Muste gives this penetrating comment:

In Neo-orthodoxy when we become obsessed with human helplessness and human corruption instead of being caught up in the transcending of them by the grace of God, we are still preoccupied with self, still self-centered and therefore still self-righteous. If we do not end with the experience of the grace and power of God as that which overcomes and blots out our preoccupation with our sinful selves, we are but giving another demonstration of the pretension and corruption of man, not of the grace of God.

We must end not with self-discovery, nor with self-condemnation, but with grace.

O Father, I thank Thee that where sin abounded, grace did much more abound. And that grace is for me. Amen.

AFFIRMATION FOR THE DAY: *I am a man of Grace. Therefore, I must be a gracious man. I will be.*

ARE WE MORE THAN FORGIVEN SINNERS?

We must pause a moment longer upon the neo-orthodoxy which says that there is "no difference between those in the Kingdom of God and those outside, except that those outside are unforgiven sinners and those inside are forgiven sinners. They are both sinners." Is that all? Has nothing more than that happened in conversion? I thought that Paul said: "Therefore if any man be in Christ, he is a new creature: old things are passed away; behold, all things are become new" (II Cor. 5:17). Something beyond forgiveness has happened—a new creation has taken place. The man who undergoes this new creation is as different from the ordinary man as the ordinary man is different from the animal.

Only a "forgiven sinner"? The emphasis here is on the final word, "sinner." Should it be? I prefer the last words of the saintly Bishop Oldham: "I am a sinner, saved by Grace." The last emphasis was on Grace. And grace transforms. It lifts the whole inner sense of guilt and estrangement and reconciles us to God, to ourselves, to life. We can view our past life as though it belonged to another person.

This saves us from a "guilt-ridden piety"—a piety that lauds one of the "fathers" who died with the words upon his lips: "O Lord, have mercy on me." Does a child of God go out with a sense of guilt, or a sense of gladness?

The whole thing leaves you with your eyes in the wrong direction—on your sinful self, instead of upon the saving Christ. This is psychologically unsound as well as morally unredemptive. For you are not saved from sin by becoming obsessed with it. You must become obsessed with the Saviour. It is not humility to be always talking about how sinful you are after redemption; it is a slur on the Redeemer. The redemption is only verbal—you are pronounced forgiven, but it is not vital; you are not redeemed from the guilt and fact of sin. It is all sub-Christian—a seventh chapter of Romans instead of an eighth chapter. It cannot sing: "the law of the Spirit of life in Christ Jesus hath made me free from the law of sin and death" (Rom. 8:1, 2). It is sin-centered instead of Saviour-centered.

O Jesus, I thank Thee that Thou dost stand between me and my past sins. I cannot see them. I see Thee. Amen.

AFFIRMATION FOR THE DAY: *My past buried, my present blessed, my future beckoning!*

"MY HANDS HAVE CORNS ON THEM"

We are looking at the fact that before we can grow in grace, we have to get into grace by self-surrender and faith. The steps are four: (1) failure, (2) faith, (3) freedom, and (4) future.

A student of dramatics heard a psychiatrist who had recently been transformed by the power of Christ, and she remarked to another student: "How is it that the Christians have sparkling eyes? I'd be a Christian too if I could get eyes like that." That thought must have dropped into her subconscious, and there it quietly worked. One day in a streetcar an invisible Someone sat beside her and asked: "Where are you going?" She knew He wasn't asking about her streetcar destination, so she said: "I wish I knew." He replied: "Turn around, and you will know." She said that inwardly she did turn around and was then and there soundly converted on the spot. She hurried to a Christian student and said: "I'm converted. What am I to do, now that I'm a Christian?" She was introduced to the Bible, the Quiet Time, and witnessing. She was in grace, and now she could grow in it.

A woman wrote: "My hands have corns on them working and trying so hard to be good." She was looking at her own hands and trusting them instead of looking at the nail-pierced hands of Christ. It was self-salvation instead of Saviour-salvation.

Here was an alcoholic who worked for six years getting hold of other alcoholics and really getting them to go straight, but he himself would fall into the habit again periodically. One day in his bed he was reading *Victorious Living*, when suddenly his faith took hold of Christ as Saviour. He got up, went to the telephone, called a friend, and said, "It's happened. I'm a new man." He was. Alcohol dropped away. He was free. He has won about twenty alcoholics to a new life.

This is what is meant by "grows with growth divine" (Col 2:19, Moffatt). It is not the result of human strivings, but a yielding to divine grace. This produces both humility and exultation—humility that it isn't our goodness, and exultation that grace has redeemed us.

O Christ, Thou hast thrown open to us the possibility of a growth divine. Help me to yield to this process with nothing held back. Amen.

AFFIRMATION FOR THE DAY: *God and I shall co-operate this day in this growth divine!*

WE RETREAT BEFORE WE ADVANCE

We have insisted that the first step in growth is a step backward. We have to reverse our values before we can get new ones. This verse expresses it: "For if we have grown into him by a death like his, we shall grow into him by a resurrection like his" (Rom. 6:5, Moffatt). "We have grown . . . by death." We have to go to a cross and there die to the kind of person we are—have to die to our self-centered preoccupation, our resentments, our pride, our jealousies, our fears, our guilts. Then a new man arises. "We shall grow into him by a resurrection like his."

Here was a girl who came to the mission field, well prepared, able, and devoted, and with an experience of God that was real and contagious. Then she slipped a cog. She got her eyes on everything except Jesus. For eight months she wandered amid her old fears— fears of the dark, fears of going places, fears of failure. Then came the moment when she knelt before the picture of Christ in a chapel and said very simply: "You've got me." An eight-months-long bondage was broken, and her fears dropped away. She arose the next day and said, "All day I have been throwing up windows and opening doors to let the fresh air and sunlight into the very musty and dingy house of my soul. I'm free again."

Now take another, the opposite of the above. Here was a woman who was as near distraction as she could be when she came to me. She and her husband were drinking and fussing their way to a divorce court. Oaths punctuated her distracted story. Then the prayer and the surrender. When she arose, she said, "Why I feel better already. Now I can take my head out from under my wing and look straight at life and everybody." When she returned home and her husband began fussing, for the first time she did not reply. It nonplused him. "Are you ill?" he asked anxiously. A friend saw her and said: "You look rested and happy for a change."

Conversion brings freedom from the past and the present and freedom to grow in the future.

O Father, I thank Thee that I need no longer be shackled by the past and by the present. Through conversion I can be free to grow. Amen.

AFFIRMATION FOR THE DAY: *Converted, I shall convert—myself and others!*

"A DART STRAIGHT TO THE HEART OF OUR PROBLEM"

The flower that kept its head turned down to look at its own roots would never grow. It has to look at something beyond itself—the sun.

The center of the Christian redemption is to save you from yourself. Not that the self in itself is evil, but it is evil if the self becomes the center of itself, becomes God. The First Commandment strikes at this: "Thou shalt have none other gods before me." And the biggest and most persistent of rival gods is the self.

So the first Beatitude in the opening verse of the Sermon on the Mount begins with: "Blessed are the poor in spirit: for their's is the kingdom of heaven" (Matt. 5:3). The word "poor" here is *"anav,"* "poor by choice." So it could be translated: "Blessed are the renounced in spirit," or "the surrendered in spirit." The first thing Jesus struck at in opening His Sermon was self-centered self-sufficiency. Shift the basis of your life from your self to God by self-surrender. Be a God-centered person instead of a self-centered person. God sends a dart straight to the heart of our problem—the problem of the self. That must be laid down before we can go on.

But the moment that is laid down, then the self is no longer a problem but a possibility. "The Kingdom of heaven belongs to you." You don't merely belong to it; it belongs to you. All its resources and powers are at your disposal. Having lost all, you gain all. If you are centered in the Kingdom, then whatever you need is yours whenever you need it. All you have to do is to reach out your hands and take it.

If the Kingdom of God, the perfect Society, is the goal, it is also the way to that goal. It offers you everything you need for body, mind, and spirit to move on to that goal. It supplies the End and then becomes the Means to that End.

The First Epistle of John seems to end on an anticlimax: "Dear children, keep clear of idols" (I John 5:21, Moffatt). But nothing could be more pertinent, for modern psychology would agree that the idol of self-preoccupation is the most deadly.

O Father, Thou hast me cornered. Art Thou the center or am I? I make Thee the center now by self-surrender. Amen.

AFFIRMATION FOR THE DAY: *I belong to the Kingdom of God; the Kingdom of God belongs to me, therefore everything else!*

15

THE THREE ENDS OF THE ATONEMENT

We cannot go on to the way to grow until we settle the question. To whom do I belong—to myself or to God? You are not primarily called to do, or to be; you are called to belong: "called to belong to Jesus Christ" (Rom. 1:6, Moffatt).

Yes, you say, but where do I get the strength and power to overcome the tyranny of self-preoccupation? "Who shall deliver me from the body of this death?" And the answer follows close on the heels of the question. "I thank God through Jesus Christ our Lord."

The three ends of the atonement could be named as: (1) "He gave himself for our sins"—redemption from what we have done, the past; (2) "to rescue us from the present evil world"—redemption from the dominance of the present evil herd (Gal. 1:4, Moffatt); and (3) "He died for all in order to have the living live no longer for themselves" (II Cor. 5:15, Moffatt)—redemption from our self-centered preoccupation.

The ends of the atonement then are three: to save us from the guilt and power of the past; to save us from the dominance of the surrounding herd—an evil social order; to save us from ourselves—from making the self the center and therefore God. Christ lays His redemptive hand on the past, on the environing present, on the within. This covers our need. For the three hindrances to growth come out of the haunting sense of past failure and guilt; out of the dominance of surrounding society, with its demands for conformity to its false standards; and most of all out of ourselves.

Can we be delivered from this threefold bondage? First, from the clinging past? A boy was told to drive a nail into a piece of wood every time he did some wrong. And then to pull out the nail when he confessed and was forgiven for the wrong. He triumphantly said, "The nails are all gone." "Yes," said the father, "but the marks made by the nails are still in the wood." The Carpenter of Nazareth can not only pull out the nails, but also plane the board and wipe out the marks too.

O Carpenter's Son, Thou canst not only forgive the past; Thou canst wipe it out too. I thank Thee. Amen.

AFFIRMATION FOR THE DAY: *God is counteracting my past by converting my present.*

THE PAST CAN BE USED

Yesterday we said that the past can not only be forgiven; it can be wiped out. You can remember it, but only as belonging to another person, a person who is dead. Therefore, its sting and shame are gone.

But while the past is blotted out, it comes back again—comes back redemptively. Even it can be used in the purposes of the new life. Our sins can be set to work saving others. We are so changed that when we tell others of the sins from which we have been saved, they wonder not at our sins but at the redemption. So our very sins form a background against which men can see the Saviour more clearly. A woman, marvelously saved, tremblingly told me of the past from which she had been saved. She told me tremblingly, lest she lose my friendship on account of the revelation of her past. Afterwards she said in wonder, "Your face never changed. It only lighted up the more:" It should have, for I saw not the greatness of her sin, but the greatness of her redemption. There are no skeletons in the Christian's closet, for they have all come out and are clothed in flesh and blood and walk as witnesses of the saving power of Christ.

Moreover, these past sins not only contribute to others in showing them the saving power of Christ; they contribute to us. For out of them we can rescue a lesson for the future. As a young Christian I stumbled and fell. As I got up and as I brushed off my spiritual clothes, I said to the tempter: "All right, Mr. Devil, you got me there, but I've learned a lesson. I'll remember." And I did. The learning of that lesson proved to be of value to me. It overbalanced the hurt from the fall. The fall was forgiven and wiped out, but the lesson lived on a part of me laid up against a future situation. Just as a bone broken becomes stronger at that place, when it heals, than the rest of the bone, so we can become strong by our very weaknesses.

A woman in great agony of spirit told me of her falls. It was a blow to me. But the Voice whispered: "If she has been so fine with this conflict, what won't she be now that the conflict is out?" We both saw the greater Open Door. When we stumble, we can stumble forward; when we fall, we can fall on our knees and get up stronger.

O Father, I thank Thee that when we belong to Thee, then everything belongs to us—even our past. It contributes. Amen.

AFFIRMATION FOR THE DAY: *No past can inhibit my glorious present and my more glorious future.*

A DELIVERANCE FROM THE PRESENT EVIL WORLD

We meditated yesterday on the first of the three deliverances in the atonement—deliverance from past sins. Today we come to the second—deliverance from the present evil world.

I question whether there is anything that keeps the Christian from growing so much as the present evil world—the herd. For growing means departure from the herd, a lifting of your head above it. This the herd tries to prevent. Society demands conformity. If you fall beneath its standards, it will punish you; if you rise above its standards, it will persecute you. It demands a dull, gray, average conformity. But the Christian is a departure upward. He gets out of step, for "he hears a distant Drummer." He is no longer an echo; he is a voice. He is not a thing; he is a person. The herd dominance is broken.

How? Not by running away from it, for now he goes more deeply into it. Not by fighting it, for now a new compassion for the herd comes over him. Not by incasing himself against it, for he is now more sensitive to its needs. He gets rid of it by surrendering the herd to God. Just as a man can be a self-centered man, so he can be a herd-centered man. He is a captive. There is only one way out—the surrender of the herd to God. Then God is God, not the herd. You no longer belong to the herd; you belong to God. But belonging to God, now the herd belongs to you. Delivered from it, you are free to go back into it emancipated and free to serve it.

The day after I was converted, I went to the barber shop where I had always played cards with "the gang." Instead of joining them I sat in the barber's chair, took out my New Testament, and began to read it. When I came across the passage "What shall it profit a man, if he shall gain the whole world, and lose his own soul?" I read it aloud. "Read it again. That's a good one," one of the gang remarked. I could now contribute to them, for I no longer belonged to them. The three steps I took past the card table to the barber's chair were three steps into freedom—freedom from the herd.

O Father, I thank Thee that when I belong to Thee, then everything, including the herd, belongs to me. I'm free. Amen.

AFFIRMATION FOR THE DAY: *The herd environs me, but God environs me more deeply and more intimately.*

"NO LONGER LIVE FOR THEMSELVES"

We come to the third end of the atonement—deliverance from self-centered preoccupation. "He died for all in order to have the living live no longer for themselves" (II Cor. 5:15, Moffatt).

Psychology would agree that the center of man's psychological problems is becoming immersed in oneself. Those in mental hospitals are suffering from one thing in various forms—self-centered preoccupation. When the superintendent of a mental hospital was asked if his patients weren't "beside themselves," he replied: "No, they are very much themselves. They have no interest beyond themselves. They are pickled in themselves. That's why they are here." I once suggested to people in a sanitarium the possibility of sewing for China relief, knowing they had a lot of time on their hands. I expected a rush at the close of the meeting to get the materials. Not a person came. Then I saw why they were there—they were bounded by their own problems and hence bound by them.

When a superintendent of a mental hospital was asked how so few officials were able to hold so many people in submission—wouldn't they organize and break out?—he replied: "It's very simple. The mentally ill never organize." They were made for outgoing love, made for co-operation and creative activity, and when they abandoned this for self-centered interest, they began to live against themselves, hence ended in inner conflict and breakdown.

But many are tied up inwardly and are walking conflicts who never get to institutions. They stay in normal relationships to make them abnormal by their inner conflicts. They project upon their surroundings their own inner conflicts. They cannot get along with themselves, and hence they cannot get along with others. They need deliverance just as badly as a man in the gutter. One is tied by his habits, the other by his attitudes.

Does the atonement of Jesus atone here? If not, it fails.

O Jesus, I thank Thee that Thou hast not passed by my central need—the need of deliverance from myself. Amen.

AFFIRMATION FOR THE DAY: *Delivered from myself, I'm now free to give myself to others.*

THE CROSS BREAKS US

We are meditating on the need for a central deliverance—the deliverance from the self. The self needs correction, of course. For you cannot wipe out the self. Self put out at the door comes back by the window in various disguises.

But what is the freeing power? It is the cross. The cross silently confronts this self with a demand—surrender! It does it powerfully and pervasively. For instance, here was a boy who had been adopted by a headmaster, who afterward became a bishop in India. The boy was increasingly wayward and rebellious and defiant. The headmaster was compelled to punish him one day after an especially flagrant act of disobedience. He took the rod and told the boy to stretch out his hand. The boy defiantly did so with bravado. The headmaster, instead of laying the rod on the boy's hand, laid it on his own hand and laid it on hard. The boy, seeing what was happening cried out with an inner pain, fell at the master's feet, and with streaming tears begged him to desist and to forgive him. He did so. From that moment the boy was changed. The tyranny of his self-interest was broken. He was forever attached to the headmaster in love. The center was shifted.

That same headmaster had to dismiss a boy from school. But on the day on which the dismissal was to take place he decided to fast all day. When the other teachers heard this, they asked to join him in the fasting. Then the older boys, hearing of what was happening, asked to join the teachers in fasting. When the guilty boy heard that practically the whole school was fasting because of his dismissal, he fell at the feet of the headmaster and begged to be forgiven and given another chance. All decided to give it to him. The boy was a completely different boy. The suffering of the group broke something inside him, and he was freed from himself.

The cross conquers the self without violating it. It frees the self from itself and then attaches that self-love to the One who hung on the cross. Deliverance has come.

O Jesus, the miracle of Thy deliverance! I am in the dust, and yet I'm raised to the highest heaven. Amen.

AFFIRMATION FOR THE DAY: *The cross melts me, molds me, and makes me.*

THE SELF-PROBLEM OR POSSIBILITY?

If the center of S-i-n is the "I," then the center of the deliverance from sin is the deliverance from the "I." Paul puts it: "I am crucified with Christ: nevertheless I live; yet not I, but Christ liveth in me: and the life which I now live in the flesh I live by the faith of the Son of God, who loved me, and gave himself for me" (Gal. 2:20). Here was an "I" crucified and yet alive. Here was the self fundamentally denied and yet fundamentally affirmed. "Who loved me, and gave himself for me"—to do what? Obviously to deliver me from the "I." Not primarily to save me from hell, or to get me to heaven, but to save me from the center of my trouble—myself—the "I." The business of redemption is not to get us into heaven, but to get heaven into us; not to get us out of hell, but to get hell out of us. And the center of hell in any life is the unsurrendered "I." Your self on your own hands is a problem and a pain; your self in the hands of God is a possibility and a power. As "dirt is matter out of place," so sin is the self out of place, off-center, making itself God.

And nothing can break down this idol except suffering love. A teen-age girl was told that if she stayed out beyond a certain time, she would have to eat bread and water at supper. She stayed out. At supper time she was given the bread and water, and then the father reached over and took the bread and water and gave the daughter his own meal. Something had happened to her—inside. The self-will was gently broken and the father-will gently substituted by her own choice. No threat of punishment, no fear of consequence could work that miracle. Only love, suffering love, could do that.

The pain of penitence takes the place of the pain of outward punishment, so that the outward punishment can be lifted from the soul without loss or degradation to the soul. It is an operation without anesthetics. A sharp pain of penitence goes through you, then you look up into that dear Face that bends over you, and you know that the operation is successful. You walk forth from that operating room free from a cancerous "I," and now free to live with an "I" that is Christ-centered and therefore contributive.

O Christ, I thank Thee that Thou art not healing lightly my central sickness. Thou art giving a deliverance indeed. Amen.

AFFIRMATION FOR THE DAY: *I am now free to be—to be the person God intends me to be.*

WATERING OUR SPARKS

We have been studying the necessity—the prime necessity—of having a transplantation from the weed-choked kingdom of self to the unencumbered soil of the Kingdom of God by conversion. Elsewhere I have defined conversion as "That change, gradual or sudden by which we pass from the Kingdom of self to the Kingdom of God by the grace and power of Christ."

That change may be gradual, or it may be sudden, or it may shade off between the two. A film showing the blooming of a flower, moving slowly, shows the swelling of the bloom and then a sudden burst into flower. It is gradual and sudden. The phenomenon doesn't matter; the fact does. If you can say in your heart of hearts: "I am no longer my own. I belong to Him," then you are in the Kingdom of God. Rejoice in that fact. Fix it by thanksgiving and by a sharing of it with others.

Many have had the fact of conversion in some form or other at sometime in their lives, but it has not grown. We don't sing about it; we sigh about it, for it is a bright spot in the past with intervening clouds and mists. We remember it but don't realize it. It isn't the working fact of our lives. We go through the motions of going to church—go through them through duty, but it is a dull performance; there is no sparkle in it. We pray, but our praying has no more significance than a Buddhist prayer wheel. We read the Bible, but it is a dead book. It does not speak. We fellowship with other Christians, but our fellowship is no Koinonia of the New Testament—the fellowship does not glow. It is an ash-covered coal with a feeble warmth within trying to fellowship in warm fellowship with other ash-covered coals. There are more ashes than glowing coal, and the meetings are non-expectant—perfunctory. This prayer prayed in a similar meeting would not be out of place: "O God, if any spark of divine grace has been kindled in this meeting, water that spark." Our sparks are watered.

O God, I thank Thee that Thou art stirring the cold embers of my heart. Stir it into flames. Amen.

AFFIRMATION FOR THE DAY: *I shall let the fire of God's love burn up all my cynical thoughts and moods and attitudes today.*

HALF-BAKED CHRISTIANS

We must look further at Christians who have come to a stalemate. Hosea describes Ephraim as "a cake unturned as it was baked" (Hos. 7:8, Moffatt). He is the type of the half-baked Christian. Portions of his life given to God, and portions held back—half-baked. The emotional side developed, the volitional undeveloped—half-baked. The receptive side baked, but the sharing side unbaked, so half-baked. The law side strong, but the love side weak—half-baked. "There is a paralysis of the nerve that leads from the brain to the hip pocket"— the purse isn't converted—half-baked. The conscious mind has been converted, but the subconscious mind has not been, so half-baked. Converted in actions but not converted in reactions—half-baked.

The half-Christians become the centers of problems to themselves and others. A half-Christianity is more of a problem than a power. Many people have just enough Christianity in them to set up an irritation—just enough to make them miserable. They don't belong wholly to the Kingdom, and they don't belong to the world; they are a halfway house trying to be a home. And no one can *rest* in half-wayness. He can only rest in full commitment, for that is what we are made for.

As a result of this half-baked condition decay sets in in Ephraim. "Foreigners eat away his strength" (v. 9.) We are made for the Kingdom—it is our native land. There we are at home. Coming into the Kingdom brings a sense of coming Home. There we are naturalized. But we allow alien ways of life to eat our strength. Love is natural and builds us up; we turn to resentments which are alien and which eat our strength. Self-giving is natural and strengthens the giver; we turn to alien selfishness which eats away our strength.

But the process is so slow that it is scarcely noticed—"unknown to him." Many a man decays so gradually that he cannot tell when he crossed the line from honesty to dishonesty, from purity to impurity, from being a Christian to being a pagan.

People seldom plan deliberately to go to hell; they slip into it inch at a time—"unknown to him."

Gracious Father, save me from the little decays that bring the big disasters, the little falls that bring the big ones. Amen.

AFFIRMATION FOR THE DAY: *No little things canceling the Big in my life today.*

WORSHIPING SECRET BAALS

We continue to look at the decay of Ephraim: "Gray hairs are here and there upon him, yet he knoweth not" (v. 9). When we cease to grow, decay sets in. Our friends can see the signs of decay, the appearance of gray hairs, but we don't see them. "He's slipping," they say in their hearts, but we go blithely on, unconscious of the decay.

This verse depicts graphically the steps down:

> Whenever Ephraim spoke, men were in awe;
> he was a prince in Israel.
> But then he worshipped Baal,
> and for his guilt he died.
> (Hos. 13:1, Moffatt)

Here is the picture of a man who, when he spoke, spoke with power straight out of the heart of reality. Men were in awe. For there is something awesome about truth and reality. They are so self-verifying. Men who deal with truth and reality become morally weighty and spiritually effective.

But then comes the subtle change: he inwardly bows the knee to some Baal—some secret idol in the heart. There is a subtle change from truth to a playing to the galleries; the herd becomes God. Or pride forms within the heart, and there is an inner bowing to the self as God. Or lust takes over and begins to be spelled Lust—it dominates. Or Mammon creeps in and wants to divide the affections with God.

A Hindu student was asked why he went to the Christian church and worshiped God, at the same time bowing before idol shrines, and he replied: "Examination time is just ahead, and I have to play safe." Many a Westerner would smile at the Hindu, but would do the same in his heart—God for eternity, Mammon for time; Truth for the ideal, lies and shady dealings for the real; for Sunday "God wills it," for the week days "Everybody does it." He represents Mr. Facing-both-ways.

Baal inwardly rules over death.

O Father, save me from the secret bowing of the knee to some hidden idol. Make me straight. Amen.

AFFIRMATION FOR THE DAY: *I have seen the face of Jesus. What are idols to me now?*

WE BECOME "JOINERS"

We turn now to see what Ephraim did when he saw that something had died within him:

> When Ephraim noticed his decay,
>
> Ephraim turned to Assyria.
> (Hos. 5:13, Moffatt)

When he felt his own inner power gone, he allied himself with outer power—to Assyria, the strongest outer power of that day.

We do that. When our inner spiritual security goes, we attach ourselves to this, that, and the other, to try to make up for our inner lack of security. We become joiners. We join one or more service clubs to make our prestige secure; one or more lodges to make our old age secure; a social club to make our leisure hours secure from boredom; a political party to make our political future secure; the church to make our eternal future secure!

But "Assyria" lets us down. Those who are going to the dust cannot save us from the dust. They drag us to their own doom. All the half-answers turn out to be no answers at all.

God is the Answer. Go straight to God and lay the whole thing before Him, tell Him frankly what has happened, ask Him for His solution, begin to listen to Him, and obey what you hear, and you'll soon find your feet upon the Way.

Pray the prayer: "O God, take me over and make me over." And He will do it, asking no questions except one, "Wouldst thou be made whole? Do you want to be well?" If so, then anything, yes, everything, can happen. If you open your life to the depths, then He will make you over at the depths. He will do as thorough a work as you will allow Him to do.

But don't slur things over trying to do a patched-up job instead of a renovation, a complete remaking. Don't sweep the center of the room and leave the corners untouched. A clean sweep!

Gracious Father, I've come to the crux—the parting of the ways. Help me to take Thy way—Thy way, only. Amen.

AFFIRMATION FOR THE DAY: *No hidden corners shall haunt the center of my life today.*

GOD DIGS AROUND US

When the owner planted a fig tree and came three years seeking fruit but found none, he said to the vinedresser: "Cut it down, why should it take up space?" But the vinedresser replied: "Leave it for this year, sir, till I dig around it and put in manure. Then it may bear fruit next year. If not, you can have it cut down" (Luke 13:6-9, Moffatt). Today we meditate upon: "I dig around it."

If, in our barrenness of soul, we feel proddings of conscience and unhappiness and upsetness of spirit, then that means God is digging around us. His diggings are not just to give a "dig" as punishment, but they are constructive diggings to make us fruitful.

Just as physical pain is nature putting up a red flag and saying, "There is something wrong here—attend to it," so spiritual pain is that same red flag going up. It is God saying, "There is danger of death here. Attend to it." God's prods are all redemptive, never just punitive.

When Jesus turned and looked at Peter, whose hot words of denial were still warm upon his lips, He did not look at Him to punish him; His look was redemptive. Peter felt this and "went out and wept bitterly." Then after Jesus' resurrection He asked Peter three times, "Lovest thou me more than these?" Peter had haughtily said that though all of these would deny Him, he would never do it. Now Jesus asked him *three times,* "Do you love me more than these?" It was a "dig." Three times Peter had denied Him, and now three times he compelled himself to say he loved Him—not "more than these," but he did love Him. It was a redemptive prod to correct his self-righteousness.

Once again Jesus used the "three times"—the sheet was let down "three times" as Peter was upon the housetop praying (Acts 10:16). Peter was racially arrogant in regard to Gentiles. The letting down the sheet three times was God's attempt to broaden his soul to take in Gentiles. It was a gentle reminder again of his three-times denial. The prod was a prod into the Kingdom.

Father, I know that you love me because you dig around me. Keep on, for I'd rather be dug than dead. Amen.

AFFIRMATION FOR THE DAY: *God will not need to give me digs— suggestions will do.*

THE STEPS DOWN—AND UP

We have been saying that the reception of grace is necessary to growth. This passage shows the steps down and then the steps up—through grace. "For we ourselves were once foolish, disobedient, led astray, slaves to various passions and pleasures, passing our days in malice and envy, hated by men and hating one another" (Tit. 3:3, R.S.V.).

Here we see the vivid description of a life lived apart from God. And it begins with a wrong idea: "foolish." A false notion begins all this train of consequences—the false notion that you are free, away from God. The most deadly of mistakes is the mistake of thinking that our way against God's way can ever lead to freedom. This is the lie of lies, the most deceptive of deceptions.

This false notion leads to the second step—"disobedient." The foolish idea becomes a foolish attitude, an attitude of defiance. This means the soul is on the defensive. An inner debate ensues, a conflict sets in; the civil war is on. What was in the mind now takes possession of the will, and a divided personality results.

The third step is inevitable—"led astray." The personality weakened by division is now open to suggestion from without—open to being led and "led astray" by others. For those who do not submit to God-control and do submit to mob-control, the herd becomes dominant. "Everybody does it" is the phrase that decides everything. Hunting for freedom from God, they end in bondage to men.

The fourth step is also inevitable—"slaves to various passions and pleasures." The seekers for freedom become "slaves" and slaves to the very things through which they hoped to find freedom—"passions and pleasures." These passions and pleasures curdle.

Then comes the next step: "passing our days in malice and envy." Frustrated with themselves, they pass on these frustrations to others—you hate others because you hate yourself. You envy others because you're jostling for attention you can't get. The days are not lived—"passing our days"—muddling through. Then the final stage: "hated" and "hating." You pass on your self-hate to others and get it in return.

O Father, give me sense not to be senseless. Save me from the foolish pride that becomes the pride of foolishness. Amen.

AFFIRMATION FOR THE DAY: *I shall squelch every foolish notion that knocks at my door today—no quarter given!*

27

THE RENEWING OF ALL OUR LATENT POWERS

We looked yesterday at the history of a wrong idea—a "foolish" notion, the steps down. We now look at the steps up. The steps up begin with steps down—God steps down to us. The "foolish" idea is now countered by the divine idea—the Word become flesh.

"But when the goodness and loving kindness of God our Savior appeared" (Tit. 3:4, R.S.V.). That word "but" is God putting a roadblock across our road to self-ruin. God intervenes in the Incarnation. We couldn't get back to Him, so He comes to us. The Incarnation is God's redemptive invasion of us. Over against all our badness He sets His "goodness," and over against our self-hate and other-hate He sets His "loving kindness." Grace intervenes.

And the result? "He saved us" (v. 5, R.S.V.)—saved us from ourselves primarily and from our sins and their consequences secondarily.

And the redemption is a redemption that can't be earned or bought, and of which we cannot be worthy. It is pure Grace: "not because of deeds done by us in righteousness, but in virtue of his own mercy" (v. 5, R.S.V.). All we can do to get it is to empty our hands of our own self-salvation and take the gift of God.

But the saving us is not merely saving us from our sins and their consequence; it is a saving of us as persons intrinsically: "by the washing of regeneration and renewal in the Holy Spirit." A new birth cancels the old and gives us a fresh start—the miracle of a birth from above. But it goes beyond that—the total natural powers are renewed—"a renewal in the Holy Spirit." The decay and destruction caused by sin and evil are arrested, and a renewing of all our latent powers is effected. A plus is added to all we have and are. And this is no meager giving: "which he poured out upon us richly through Jesus Christ our Savior (v. 6, R.S.V.). It is lavish, overwhelming. He puts you in the dust by the sheer weight of glory.

And then the capping of the whole: "so that we might be justified by his grace and become heirs in hope of eternal life" (v. 7, R.S.V.). Eternal life displaces this decaying life, and now growth—eternal growth—is possible. Intervening grace begins eternal growth.

O Christ, how can I thank Thee enough for this grace that lifts me from the deepest hell to the highest heaven? Amen.

AFFIRMATION FOR THE DAY: *I am drawing heavily upon grace; otherwise I'm bankrupt. Now I am rich, eternally rich.*

THE WORRIES OF THE WORLD

We have been observing the fact that we are made for growth. Then why do so many remain stunted and runted as Christians? Why are they half persons when they can be whole persons?

In the parable of the sower Jesus puts His finger on the reasons why growth was stunted: "But the worries of the world and the delight of being rich and all the other passions come in to choke the word" (Mark 4:19, Moffatt). Here the first choker of the word, enemy No. 1, is named as "the worries of the world." Is this the prime cause of stunted growth? I am persuaded He was right.

Note that He says "the worries of the world." Did he mean that if your life is planted "in the world," if you make this world the end-all and be-all of your existence, then you are bound to have a vague sense of anxiety, of worry? Why? Because the soul is made for the soil of eternity, and to be planted only in the narrow framework of time gives it a sense of choking, of having missed the end of its being, of living in a climate for which it is not made. An underlying sense of anxiety is bound to characterize one who is not living wholly in and for the Kingdom of God. For the Kingdom is our native land. And outside it you are outside yourself, hence the uneasiness.

Dr. Rollo May, in his able book *The Meaning of Anxiety,* says that the last two decades can be characterized as follows: the first as the age of covert anxiety and this one as the age of overt anxiety. The anxieties which were hidden have now come to the surface. Auden and Camus call this age "the age of overt anxiety." Willoughby goes so far as to say that "anxiety is the most prominent mental characteristic of occidental civilization."

Strange that with all our attempts to be secure, with all our endeavors at plugging up the holes of our earthly existence, with all our promises that the next gadget will bring the sought-for happiness— strange that the end of the whole thing is a feeling of insecurity, hence of anxiety. We feel naked and unprotected against an overshadowing catastrophy. What is this haunting specter that haunts our feasts and that makes even our mirth hollow and cackling and foreboding?

O God, our Father, Thou art teaching us the bitter lesson that if we are cut off from Thee, we are cut off from Life. Amen.

AFFIRMATION FOR THE DAY: *I am secure in God and in no other place and with no other thing.*

THE SEARCH FOR SECURITY

We were thinking yesterday on the reason that this age, with all its attempts at security, is ending in being the age of insecurity. Why?

The inspired writer says: "denotes the removal of what is shaken . . . , to leave only what stands unshaken" (Heb. 12:27, Moffatt). There come times in human history when an event brings to the surface hidden meanings and tendencies and when in that event we see the meaning of an age. For us that event was the falling of the atomic bomb. It partly created our insecurities and partly showed them. In any case it was the focal point.

I have stood three times in four years at the place in Hiroshima, Japan, where the first atomic bomb fell. When that explosion took place about 500 yards up in the air, a city lay in ruins, and 200,000 people were wiped out. A Japanese pastor pointed to a vacant spot and said: "This was where my house stood. In front of it my wife and child were standing. I came back to the city to begin life over again with nothing, absolutely nothing, but Christ." It all spelled unalloyed tragedy. But suppose he had come back to begin life over again with nothing, except nothing! He had Christ, and with Christ he could come back from anything, yes, anything. But suppose there had been no Christ with which to begin life over again. Then? Anxiety and nothing but anxiety. That has happened to our age. The atomic bomb has blown our seeming securities to bits and has left us—shall I say it? —questionably Christian. We were a mixed pagan Christian civilization, and this revealed it. In the flash of that bomb we saw ourselves—saw ourselves as we really are. And since then we have been afraid. Our defenses are down. Since then we have feverishly tried to set up the old defenses—the defenses of force. And we're still afraid. For these defenses don't defend, and we know it.

Nothing can defend us now until we get back Home. A sense of homelessness has taken hold of us. We made the wrong things our home. Since they were "things," they perished in the flash of that fire. God has allowed us to burn up the things we called home to reveal to us our real Home. Our Home is the Kingdom of God.

O Father, Thou art taking away this to give us That. Help us not to weep over this, but to grasp the That. Amen.

AFFIRMATION FOR THE DAY: *I am at home in God. Everything else is a stopping place.*

OUR SECURITIES ARE SHATTERED

We said yesterday that the flash of the atomic bomb exposed our civilization as questionably Christian and hence afraid. A newspaper columnist said that after the falling of the bomb he walked the streets of Washington for three days and never saw a smile on a single face. Why? Why weren't people elated that we now had the power of the atom on our side? The reason is that they knew instinctively that the bomb had fallen not merely upon Hiroshima; it had fallen on all our securities everywhere. Those securities were gone. The end of the quest for security was insecurity!

This grim picture has a bright spot. It is symbolized in this: A group of Japanese pastors and laymen and a group of foreign missionaries and laymen bowed, as in a football huddle, at the spot where the bomb fell and prayed that no Hiroshima should ever happen to anyone, anywhere, again. And they dedicated themselves anew to peace and to the methods of the Kingdom of God. In that little group was represented that vaster group in every nation unshaken by the falling of a bomb and undismayed by the ruin around them. They belonged to an unshakable Kingdom: "Wherefore we receiving a Kingdom which cannot be moved, let us have grace, whereby we may serve God acceptably with reverence and godly fear" (Heb. 12:28). And they knew that on the ruins of the old they could build a new Order on earth.

One of those pastors arose in his half-ruined church in Hiroshima at the close of an address on the possibility of using pain and suffering and said: "The fire of the flash of the bomb burned our city to ashes, but the Fire of the Spirit of God is burning in our hearts this morning, and this Fire is steadier and stronger than the fires of destruction. This Spirit of love and good will will build the City of God on earth. And it will not be shaken." He belonged to the unshakable Kingdom. And he was not afraid. Anxiety had been pushed out by the great Security. The future belongs to such.

Good God and Father, we thank Thee that we see Thy beckoning Kingdom, beckoning us because it is within us. Amen.

AFFIRMATION FOR THE DAY: *I am an unshaken soul, because I belong to an unshakable Kingdom.*

THREATENED BY SUPERPERSONAL FORCES

We have seen that we feel insecure because at the moment of the discovery of the atomic bomb we find that oceans which used to protect us are now mere ditches to be hopped over in a matter of hours, and boundaries between nations are not valid in the air, where planes roam at will. And there is no defense—no sure defense.

This is the over-all picture of our anxiety, but there are other contributory causes. We feel the threat of an alien way of life upon our civilization—atheistic Communism. As someone has put it: "The distinction is between a peripheral threat, *i.e.*, a threat which members of society can meet on the basis of the assumptions of their culture—and a threat on a deeper level—namely, a threat to the underlying assumptions, the charter of the culture itself." We could stand this if we were quite sure of our own culture. But into our own culture have penetrated alien elements that weaken it—pagan elements.

The psychologist Fromm expresses it in these words: "The individual is now threatened by powerful supra personal forces, capital and the market. His relation with his fellow men, with everyone a potential competitor, has become hostile and estranged; he is free—that is, alone, isolated, threatened from all sides." We have built, "Thou shalt love thyself," a pagan attitude, into our culture as its working principle, instead of "Thou shalt love thy neighbour as thyself," a Christian attitude. Hence we are uneasy, feeling we have missed the Way. We have said: "Every man for himself, and the devil take the hindmost" only to find the devil is not only taking the hindmost; he is taking us all—taking us all with fear.

We have just enough co-operation and good will and thought for others within our civilization to keep it going. But we are not certain for how long. For we are exhausting our moral and spiritual reserves. Feeling our moral and spiritual lack, we in America have tried to use the substitute method of buying our way into the hearts of men to gain what security they can give us, only to find that the thing we depended on most, money, hasn't the power to buy affection.

O Father, Thou art pushing us into the corner in order to talk to us. Help us to listen, for we've listened to alien voices. Amen.

AFFIRMATION FOR THE DAY: *Security is security only when it is guaranteed by God.*

FEAR THE RESULT OF INSECURITY

We have looked at the over-all climate of our civilization—a climate which is a climate of anxiety. And unless the individual has inner resources which make him immune to this invading climate, he will be a personal reflection of an uncertain civilization. He will be afraid.

Unfortunately the individual creates a lot of fears and anxieties of his own. There are only two fears born within us, so the psychologists say—the fear of loud noises and the fear of falling. The rest of our fears and anxieties are home-grown. They are ours.

They come out of a variety of causes and attitudes. We become self-centered, and we then become vaguely conscious that we are on the wrong center, off-center, and hence afraid. We hold resentments against people, and again we feel vaguely that this is an alien way to live—alien because it alienates us from others and from ourselves. We hate ourselves for hating. We hold guilt, unconfessed and unsurrendered, in our lives, and hence we are afraid. The first reaction of Adam when he disobeyed was, "I was afraid, . . . so I hid myself" (Gen. 3:10, Moffatt). Life goes underground when it isn't aboveboard. It knows that it no longer has cosmic backing and is therefore conscious of being naked, alone, and afraid.

But there is another basic fear—the fear of the soul that is cut off from its central Root, God. Many, when they look into their hearts, will know that they too are, as Auden puts it, "alive but alone, belonging—where? Unattached as tumbleweed." Hence afraid. When we don't belong to God, then we do belong to fear.

Here is an illustration of belonging to an illicit love instead of belonging to God: "I loved my employer, a married man. He had an affair with another woman. I told his wife. She divorced him, and he married the other woman. It is she against whom I hold resentments. But I'm so tired of hating someone, so tired of being a sinner." She attached herself to the wrong center.

Our Father God, our fears come in when Thou dost go out. I take Thee in, and fears go out. Amen.

AFFIRMATION FOR THE DAY: *There is no fear in love. I am rooted in love; therefore there is no fear in me.*

THE FEAR OF RESPONSIBILITY

We separate fears and anxieties. "Fear has a specific object, whereas anxiety is a vague and unspecified apprehension."

We come now to what Rank calls "the life fear" and "the death fear."

There are two forms of fear throughout our career: life fear and death fear. The one is the fear of having to live as an isolated individual. Whereas the life fear is anxiety at going forward, becoming an individual, the death fear is anxiety at going backward, of losing individuality. . . . Between these two fear possibilities, these poles of fear, the individual is thrown back and forth all his life.

The first fear, the fear of life, is vividly illustrated by a boy's answer in an examination to the question of the explanation for twins: "I suppose the reason for twins is that little children don't like to come into this world alone." But the individual not only fears to face birth alone; he fears to face life alone. For life brings responsibility, and many are afraid of responsibility.

It is at this place that many neuroses appear. The fear of responsibility makes many people retreat into illness. It is a refuge out of responsibility. Freud found the cause of a neurosis in the past—in childhood. Jung found it in the present. He says: "I no longer find the cause of neurosis in the past, but in the present. I ask, What is the necessary task which the patient will not accomplish?" This backing out of the responsibilities of life through fear of life and its responsibilities is at the root of many of our problems.

A woman was about to have an operation for cancer. A final examination was made, and she was told that a mistake had been made, that there was no cancer and no operation would take place. She was more upset by this announcement than by her illness. She refused to leave the hospital. "I cannot bear to think of facing life again." She was suffering from a fear of life and its consequences, so she welcomed illness as a way out.

O Christ, I am grateful that Thou hast come to give us life and to give it abundantly so we need no longer fear life. Amen.

AFFIRMATION FOR THE DAY: *What can life do to me? I am possessed by Life!*

THE DEATH FEAR

Many go through life with the single aim to avert death. And yet how completely futile the attempt is! It is bound to fail. "As certain as death and taxes" is pretty certain.

There are three reasons for this attempt to avert death. (1) We are afraid of the unknown. (2) We have not lived our lives the way they should have been lived, so we hesitate to go where "We shall know as we are known." (3) We are afraid that death is equivalent to extinction. The urge to live is strong within us. Some of these are contradictory, but then life is often a contradiction.

The maid of the lady next door shuts herself up in a closet when a thunderstorm is on—in bondage to the fear of death. And yet children are not naturally afraid of a thunderstorm. A mother was concerned about her little boy alone in his room during a severe thunderstorm. She thought she would find him terror-stricken. Instead she found him at the window dancing in glee, and when a particularly hard clap of thunder came, he yelled, "Do it again, God." Then there was another mother who, thinking her little girl would be frightened during a thunderstorm, went into her room and got in bed with her and slept there all night to make her feel safe. In the morning the little girl said, "All right, Mother, whenever you're frightened again, you can come and get into my bed."

Many go through life spoiling it because of a fear of death. It overshadows all they do. This verse expresses it: "And release from thraldom those who lay under a life-long fear of death" (Heb. 2:15, Moffatt). Look at the terror in those words: "thraldom . . . lay under . . . life-long fear of death."

Is this necessary? Are we bound to be tossed from one horn of the dilemma to the other, namely, between the life fear and the death fear? Can there be a release from both fears?

It is to the glorious possibility of freedom from both fears that we now turn. The word "release" in the above sentence points the way to an open door.

O God, my Father, I thank Thee that I need not be in thralldom. I can be free, gloriously free, and free now. Amen.

AFFIRMATION FOR THE DAY: *No fear can touch me, for God dwells in me and encircles me.*

REDUCING AND DISGUISING FEAR

We turn this week to the remedy for fears within and without. First, we must look at some of the wrong methods of trying to get rid of fears.

Various methods are used: (1) Diverting oneself from the thing one is afraid of. Symonds says: "It would surprise most persons to realize how much of their behavior is motivated by a desire to escape anxiety by either reducing it, or disguising it in one way or another." "Reducing it, or disguising it"—when we can't reduce it, we disguise it.

We try to reduce it by diverting ourselves from it. A great many of our so-called "diversions" are simply methods of running away from fear. The fierce running from place to place is an endeavor to forget, to run away from one's fears. We step on the gas to go faster than the fears that are running their useless motors within us.

This civilization is drinking more and more in order to forget. I passed a place with a sign on it, "Paradise Enjoyment," but it was a gambling and drinking joint. A paradise of forgetfulness! But it was "a fool's paradise"—a paradise of rude awakenings. People get drunk in varying degrees to forget, to run away from their fears. The effect of alcohol is not that of a stimulant; it is a depressant. It deadens certain portions of the brain that serve as a brake on certain actions and emotions—it frees one from inhibitions. It gives a false sense of freedom. But it is only a freedom from inhibitions set up to save us. So we are free from salvation, free to go to the devil in general. The payoff comes from the wearoff. The next morning the fears are back, multiplied. All taking of narcotics is an attempt to escape, a failure of nerve.

I once listened to a broadcast of a very important baseball game, sponsored by a certain brand of beer. If the players had taken one glass of beer, their batting would have been "off" 10 per cent; two, 20 per cent; and three, out of the game, unfit to play. The beer feeds on the fear to live. It is a dead-end remedy.

O Father, I thank Thee that I do not have to turn to false remedies for fear. Thou art my answer. Amen.

AFFIRMATION FOR THE DAY: *No crutches for me today. I'm not a lame duck. I'm a Christian.*

FALSE METHODS OF GETTING RID OF FEAR

Akin to the method of using alcohol as a way out is the method of using the normal function of laughter. Laughter is legitimate because it is God-given. But there is a difference between using laughter as the expression of inner gaiety that is real and spontaneous and using laughter as a defense. "She is laughing it off" means she is using laughter as a defense, to hide her fears. She hides them; she does not solve them. The laughter is hollow, for it isn't real laughter. It is a blind.

Then there are those who turn to what the psychologists term "compulsive sex activity." It has the same effect as alcohol—it tends to make one forget for a time. It too leaves the fear still there, but guilt is added to it, and hence the fear augmented.

Another method of diversion is overeating. I have seen a lady who is obviously overweight eating potato chips before lunch and chocolates after. She was frustrated and fearful and obviously trying to divert herself from fear that was gnawing like a rat in the depth of her consciousness.

Still another method of meeting fear is "to shrink the area of awareness and activity, thus obviating the conflict which causes the anxiety." The fearful person closes up—becomes a "shut-in" even when walking about in the world, for the closing up is an attempt to keep life from hurting him.

Another method, the opposite of the above methods, is to try to get rid of fear by fighting it. But the method fails, for it is a law of the mind that "whatever gets your attention gets you," and if your fears get your attention, even though it be a fighting attention, they will get you. If you try hard to avoid a stone in the road while riding a bicycle, you will probably hit it. The stone gets your attention, so it gets you. To fight anxiety, as someone has said, is often "like fighting something in the dark when you don't know what it is." True, there are times when you have to fight fears, but it is "the good fight of faith"—faith in Someone beyond yourself.

O God, help me not to take a road with a dead end in trying to get rid of my fears. Put my feet upon the Way. Amen.

AFFIRMATION FOR THE DAY: *Fear has no part in me, for God has all of me.*

MORE FALSE METHODS OF GETTING RID OF FEAR

To urge people to fight fears is, as someone says, "like calling to a drowning man to swim, when they don't know that under the water his hands and his feet are tied." Often there are subconscious fears that tie up the inner life and the exhortation to fight them is futile. The remedy must go deeper.

Another futile method is one suggested by Rollo May: "to be anxious about anxiety." He cites the case of a woman of whom it may be said that her only protection against anxiety was to be anxious, *i.e.*, to live continually "on her toes" and in a state of constant preparedness. This is obviously self-defeating, for to try to cure anxiety by more anxiety is like pouring oil on fire to put it out.

Another method which is bound to end in futility is the method of using anxiety as a defense against anxiety: "See how anxious I am. Do not make me more anxious." A very disrupted person full of fears said to me: "You are wrong in your psychological approach to me. A neurotic person should never be contradicted or opposed." He was obviously using his anxiety to keep me from making him more anxious. He wanted a palliative rather than a cure. He tried to steer me away from the sore spot.

We have looked at methods of evading fears. A method akin to these is to try to disguise them. A man may be full of fears and at the same time be acting with bravado and apparent bravery. I know of a man who was a "he-man" type on the outside but an "it-man" type on the inside. Fears had him. He was disguising his fears by bravado. Many a person who feels inferior on the inside swaggers and blusters and bosses on the outside in order to cover up an inferiority complex. On the other hand many people attempt to cover up a superiority complex by an overhumility on the outside.

Then there is the method of trying to exorcise fears by slogans— pretty, pat slogans that salve the boil, but do not cure it. Salvation by slogans is a modern attempt at evasion. For it leaves the causes of fear untouched.

Father, Thou art closing doors to open the Door. When we see the Door, help us to walk boldly through it into release. Amen.

AFFIRMATION FOR THE DAY: *No subterfuges as refuges—I've found my Refuge.*

THE STEPS OUT OF FEAR

Let us look now at the steps out of fear:

First, *if you have a fear, don't be afraid to admit that you have it.* To try to conceal it is but to reveal it in hurtful ways. Reveal it in a sound way, and then you'll not reveal it in unsound ways. For example, here was a girl the pitch of whose voice revealed that she was deaf and in need of a hearing aid. She was alarmed when I suggested that she get a hearing aid. "How did you know I needed it?" She was obviously trying to conceal her anxiety about confessing the need, and it was disrupting her. She was a very upset person. And she need not have been.

If you conceal a fear, it will be driven into the subconscious, and there it will work havoc. Bring it up and out and look at it.

Second, *Give up all justification for your fears and anxieties.* "I thought it was my Christian duty to worry," said a very harassed woman. She baptized her worries with a Christian baptism. But they still remained what they were—pagan fears.

Here was a pastor's wife who was very tense and anxious about her husband's sermons. She sat on Sunday morning in an agony of anxiety that he say the right thing. She went to bed all Sunday afternoon, worn out. She has had eight operations, all of them the result of her tensions and fears. Her husband, knowing of his wife's anxiety while he was preaching, became self-conscious and tied up by her very method of trying to help him.

The Christian faith is set to deliver you from fears, not to justify them.

A very intelligent and cultured woman felt she couldn't go through a certain door into a public dining room, for the last time she had gone through that door it was with her mother, who in the meantime had died. She felt she was loyal to her mother by exhibiting that fear. I marched her through the door to explode that false loyalty.

Fears and anxieties are disruptive; therefore they cannot be right. God wills wholeness.

O Christ, Thou art trying to save us from our fears. Help us not to justify them, and thus cut ourselves off from Thy redemption. Amen.

AFFIRMATION FOR THE DAY: *I am afraid of no doors. I can go anywhere with God.*

"CEASE BEING A FOOL"

We now take the next step in release from our fears:

Third, *Fix it in your mind that to be worried and tense and anxious and afraid is a fool's business. So cease being a fool.*

A highly intelligent woman was afraid of having a malignancy. She suffered from constant headaches as a result. She calmly made up her mind that to worry herself sick in this fashion was a fool's business. She would quit it. And she did. Her headaches dropped away. She might have worried herself into a cancer as one woman probably did. She was afraid of it and got what she was afraid of. "The thing which I greatly feared came upon me," said the sacred writer.

An illustration of this was a woman who was tense and anxious about everything—chronically worried. When an operation took place, she died when she should have got well, the doctor said. She blocked the healing processes of nature by her tense fears and anxieties. But we block the healing power of nature not only in an operation crisis; we do it all the time when we are worried and anxious. "I could literally feel the warmth go into the lower portion of my body when I surrendered my tense anxiety, and I was well," said a woman to me. Her tense anxiety blocked off the circulation from the lower portion of her body and made her an invalid. She was not only "tied up" spiritually; she was "tied up" physically.

Schoolteachers should have common sense as well as sense. Some do not. Here was a schoolteacher, very devoted and intelligent, who confessed to me: "I have taught school for forty-five years. And yet I always had nervous indigestion for a week before school began. I was afraid of my children." And the children were probably afraid of her! And neither one had anything to fear. There was nothing to fear except the fear.

Am I severe in urging you not to be fools? No, I'm only echoing our own Master, who said, "O foolish men, with hearts so slow to believe" (Luke 24:25, Moffatt). Faith is sanity; fears are insanity.

O Father, save us from the foolishness of fear, and introduce us to the wisdom of faith. In Jesus' name. Amen.

AFFIRMATION FOR THE DAY: *Faith, not fear, shall characterize all my thinking and acting today.*

SURRENDERING OUR FEARS

We are taking the steps out of fear:

Fourth, *Since fears and anxieties are foolish, surrender them into the hands of God.* This isn't as easy as it sounds, for it probably means the giving up of a whole life strategy. You have been depending on your fears and anxieties, and now you renounce them as a way to live. This means reversal—a life reversal. You will be tempted to compromise—half give them up and half keep them in your hands. This means a halfwayness which will mean a whole failure.

If you surrender your fears and anxieties into the hands of God, then He has them, not you. This shifts the basis—you are not struggling to overcome them; you and God are working it out together. Your eyes are now on God and not on yourself and your fears. To look at God creates faith; to look at yourself and your fears creates more fear—the fear of fear.

Here is a testimony to what surrender does:

Only the grace of God has brought me here [Camp Sierra]. I was afraid of the heat of the Valley. Having been brought up on the plains of Illinois, I was afraid of a two-foot ditch and said that I would never come up that awful mountain road. But after a year of illness brought on by fears, worries, resentments, and self-centeredness, I was in a desperate state. . . . The goodness of being in God's hands and the faith *of* (not merely in) the Son of God and prayer have brought release and the knowledge of the Holy Spirit taking over the subconscious has become a blessed fact. I'm free and well.

And she was!

So this surrendering of fears and anxieties is no mere make-believe, a playing of tricks in the mind. It is a real transaction. He takes them over and makes you over with the fears left out. Blessed freedom!

O Father, when into Thy hands we commend our spirits and their fears, then Thou dost dissolve our fears in Thy quiet. Amen.

AFFIRMATION FOR THE DAY: *I need no mental tricks to keep away my fears. I am a man of God.*

DO THE THING YOU ARE AFRAID OF

We continue the steps out of our fears and anxieties:

Fifth, *Now that your fears are in the hands of God, you can now go out and do the thing you are afraid of.* A woman was afraid to drive. She got her children to drive for her. "But I decided that God and I would try it here (Ashram), so I did the thing I feared, and the fear is gone."

A young man told of being afraid of alleyways. So he deliberately went into every alley he could find. He is now free of alleyway fear.

I was staying in a home where a little girl and I had lovely times together. "Aren't you afraid of him?" asked some of her school-mates. "Oh, no, I'm not afraid of him. We have pillow fights!" That's it, walk up to the thing you are afraid of and have a pillow fight with it. Then laugh! The fear will vanish.

The new technique of teaching swimming is to get the learner to swim with his face under the water. This overcomes the initial fear of getting the head under the water.

If you are afraid of the boss, walk up to him and tell him you have been afraid of him, but now you are not. Then laugh. He will too!

If you are afraid of great heights, go up in a tall building and look off it. And walk away free.

A student nurse was put into an ice pack to let her see how it feels for a patient to be in one. She became hysterical and had to be taken out. She was suffering from claustrophobia, a fear of closed places. The obvious thing for her to do was deliberately to go into a closet and shut the door on herself. She had probably been shut up as a child, and it had left a buried fear. Now she could let out that fear by closing herself up. When she found that nothing happened, then the spell of that fear was broken.

A woman had a fear of dropping a cup at a tea party. At a tea party I took the cup from her hand and let it drop before all. She went away laughing. She was free. If you have been afraid to write that letter of confession, then write it. And write it now.

O God, I thank Thee that I need not be tormented with any fear, of any kind. I accept my freedom. Amen.

AFFIRMATION FOR THE DAY: *Freed from fear, I shall dispel the fears of others today.*

"SO WHAT?"

We must continue into this week the steps into freedom from fear and anxiety: Sixth, *Now laugh at fears if they put up their heads again and ask to come back.* Often there is a real release from fear and then a temporary relapse. Fears intrude again. Laugh them out. I mean just that. A woman who was afraid her child would cry in a meeting, and hence never took him to a meeting, said: "You have taught me to say, 'So what?' I've been deathly afraid of my child crying in a meeting. Now I've learned to say, 'So what?' And laugh." That laugh was releasing. It is silly to tie oneself up in knots and spoil one's life over fears imaginary or real.

About 90 per cent of our fears are imaginary; about 10 per cent are real. We can deal with the real if we laugh out the imaginary ones. And then we can deal with the 10 per cent.

Fifty fat people talked and laughed themselves out of 1,200 pounds of surplus flesh by a group therapy. For four months once a week this group of overweight people talked to one another about the reasons at the root of their personal difficulties which drove them to seek solace in food, just as an alcoholic seeks solace in drink. They laughed at themselves and at one another and soon found their fears were gone. And with them a lot of surplus baggage.

A woman sat on a mountainside in an out-of-door chapel and looked across the valley to an opposite mountain down which came great pipes from a lake above. Why should they spoil the mountain beauty? Her eyes concentrated on those pipes and spoiled the enjoyment of the lovely mountains around. Then one day she broke into smiles and then into laughter. Those pipes did not spoil beauty; they made beauty. They carried the water that turned the huge turbines that gave light and power to a large section of the country. She was worrying over nothing. Her laughter turned worry into worship. She could thank God for pipes. Her viewpoint was changed.

Father, teach me to see in everything some good, so that my worrying point becomes a worshiping point. Amen.

AFFIRMATION FOR THE DAY: *Not worry, but worship, shall possess the shrine of my heart today.*

PERFECT LOVE CASTETH OUT FEAR

Now the next step in getting rid of fears and anxieties:

Seventh, *Keep repeating to yourself this verse: "There is no fear in love; but perfect love casteth out fear."*

This verse is important—very important, for if there is no fear in love, then the obvious thing for me to do is to love, to love everybody and everything. Fear can come only where love is not. Where love is, fear is not. Fear turns the doors inward, narrows the soul and its contacts, and thus feeds on itself. Love turns the doors outward, broadens the soul and its contacts, and thus feeds on itself. The more loving you become, the more love you get back.

Albert Schweitzer has taken for his life attitude the philosophy "reverence for life," in other words an attitude of love for every living thing. At the hotel in Estes Park, Colorado, a large St. Bernard dog was the object of attention from visitors. He spurned their attentions by silent disregard. But when Schweitzer came, the dog of its own accord made its way through the crowd and deliberately put up its paw to him. The dog then came to the dining hall and lay down by Schweitzer's table. Love lets down the barriers of fear between persons and persons and between persons and animals. There is no fear in love.

The story is told of Helen Keller's wanting to see what a lion is like. She is totally blind and could not "see" unless she felt. So the keeper gave reluctant leave to enter the lion's den but made precautions in case of an emergency. No precaution was needed. She began lovingly to pass her hands over the lion, and the lion allowed her. For he felt the touch was the touch of love and faith. He responded in love and faith. There is no fear in love.

Everybody was afraid of the acid tongue of a certain woman. At a tea party a woman who could have been the object of her attack sat beside her and began to give out love, the only thing in her heart. The barb thrower melted, wrote her a letter afterward, and sent her love and said she wanted to see her again.

O Christ, Thou didst conquer our hearts by love. Help me this day to conquer everyone and everything by love. Amen.

AFFIRMATION FOR THE DAY: *My love shall melt all fears within me and around me today.*

"LIFE BY THE INCH IS A CINCH"

We continue our steps out of fear and anxiety:

Eighth, *Meet the fears and anxieties of life one day at a time.*
Jesus is the author of this suggested attitude:

> So never be troubled about tomorrow;
> to-morrow will take care of itself.
> The day's own trouble is enough for the day.
>   (Matt. 6:34, Moffatt)

It is good that God has so arranged that life comes to us in manageable portions—one day at a time. Suppose all the future were dumped into our lap at one time. We would be overwhelmed. But the wise God broke life up into portions so small that anyone can manage it if he takes it as it is given—one day at a time. So shut off yesterday and do not admit tomorrow—deal with today, today. The worries of yesterday plus the worries of tomorrow, piled into today break the stoutest spirit. But divide your worries and conquer them.

> Life by the yard is hard.
> Life by the inch is a cinch.

But, you say, what can I do about the anxieties of yesterday and tomorrow? Well, if God has you, then He has your yesterdays and your tomorrows. He has your yesterdays and forgives all that has been amiss in them; He has your tomorrows and will provide grace and power to meet them. But only *as they come.* He will not provide for what is not yet here. His grace is like manna—when kept over for the next day, it spoiled. It had to be eaten day by day.

Here is the verse that offers the open door: "You can rest the weight of all your anxieties upon Him, for you are always in His care" (I Pet. 5:7, Phillips). Note: "the weight of all your anxieties upon Him"—but He takes them one day at a time.

O God, I thank Thee that I can rest the full weight of all my anxieties upon Thee. Thou art "daily" bearing my burden. Amen.

AFFIRMATION FOR THE DAY: *The full weight of my anxieties shall rest upon Him, not upon me, today.*

THE HOLY SPIRIT—SOURCE OF PEACE AND POWER

We come now to the last step in overcoming fears and anxieties:

Ninth, *Accept the Holy Spirit within you as the source of your peace and power.* God, the Holy Spirit, moves in and takes over where fears and anxieties have reigned. He is there—in control.

In a hotel room was this sign on the door: "Rest assured. Bolt your door." But suppose you can't bolt your doors against fears—they are within—then what? You cannot "rest assured" unless the rest is within. It can be.

Here is a testimony:

I had always been a nervous individual; my doctor once told me I was about the most nervous individual he had ever known. Anyway I couldn't seem to locate the source of my difficulty, but under the pressure of responsibility my blood pressure went skyrocketing, and I became dizzy and ill. The doctor gave me pills and suggested that something might be worrying me, but I insisted that all was well with my emotions and thoughts. . . . One day I wanted something from upstairs, so I went up to get it, but I found my heart objected, and I was so ill I didn't try that again. Then I got hold of *Abundant Living.* I knew I had a very active subconscious mind. The readings on divided loyalties gave me the key to my inner conflict. Through long night hours I was battling within myself over the spiritual and financial problems that were mine, so that on rising I was dreadfully dizzy. To quote you, My soul instead of being poised was pursued. As I read the steps in receiving the Holy Spirit, I saw I had enough light to raise an intelligent petition to God for deliverance from my fears. . . . I arose and lay back on the davenport. For a brief moment my faith was tested, for nothing seemed changed, but I felt no bitterness, just a surrendered feeling that I had offered all and wouldn't fear, when—wonder of wonders—it happened! I felt a Touch gradually move all the way down my spine, and a tension was released that has never returned. In its place came the complete joy of the indwelling Spirit, giving me a thankful testimony to family, friends, and neighbors. My fears vanished until my responsibilities seemed very small indeed.

She didn't fight her fears; she accepted the gift of freedom.

O gracious Holy Spirit, I open the depths of my being to Thee. I know that where the Spirit of the Lord is, there is freedom. Amen.

AFFIRMATION FOR THE DAY: *The Spirit within is adequate for anything and everything around me today.*

"TENIGUE"

We have been studying release from fears and anxieties; we now turn to something akin to those two—tensions.

There are many who are not full of fears or anxieties but are tense. They have not learned the art of relaxed receptivity. They become exhausted and tired, for they do not know how to receive. Even when they are sitting without activity, they keep their motors running. And even at night while they are asleep, their subconscious minds are working overtime, in fact on a twenty-four-hour shift.

Of course some tenseness may be good, just as some fears and anxieties may be good. If they are harnessed to construction and achievement, they contribute. It is where fears and anxieties and tensions become useless, when they are attached to nothing constructive, that they become a liability and worse. Worry is like a rocking chair—it will give you something to do but won't get you anywhere. Worse, it will wear you out getting nowhere. So tensions, not harnessed to the meeting of an emergency, but passing into a chronic state, can leave one depleted and exhausted.

There is a new disease—"tenigue," made up of parts of tension and fatigue. There are millions of casualties from it! Asked what is the remedy of it, the head of an auto association said: "Coffee. I stop and take coffee every one hundred miles or so." Are you tense? If so, coffee—more stimulant! It's a vicious circle. All pick-me-ups are eventually drop-me-downs.

At an altar of prayer two men knelt beside a penitent and whispered opposite advice. One said, "Hold on," and the other said, "Let go." These two bits of advice depict two types of religion. One says, "Grit your teeth, fight, whip your will, hold on." The other says: "Surrender your will, accept the Gift of God, let go and let God." They issue in two types of persons—one strained, the other confident.

O Father, I am grateful that I need not live strained and anxious and tense. I can be free in Thee. Amen.

AFFIRMATION FOR THE DAY: *I shall not be strained today, because I am restrained by the Spirit within.*

"A GOOD PROVOCATION"

If the Christian faith teaches relaxation and receptivity as its strategy to meet life, then where is the place for ambition, for the desire to excel? Is it out?

No, there is a place for ambition: "The Lord make you increase and excel in love . . . , so as to strengthen your hearts and make them blameless in holiness" (I Thess. 3:12-13, Moffatt), "but you are to excel in it still further" (4:1), "brotherly love. . . . to excel in this more and more" (4:9, 10). This is the way to excel—in loving. To excel in appearance, in dress, in intellect, all produce reactions of envy and jealousy; but to excel in love creates reactions of good will, and it does something for you—it "strengthens your heart" and makes you "blameless in holiness." It is constructive all the way round. This fulfills the Scripture: "Let us consider one another to provoke unto love and to good works." This is a good provocation. But where there is a selfish ambition to excel, then it provokes to jealousy and resentments.

Where ambition is harnessed to the collective good in a competition as to who can give the most to that collective good, then the ambition is right, for it is directed toward right ends. "Whosoever will be chief among you, let him be your servant"—here is a desire to be great harnessed to the good of all by becoming the servant of all. If you stoop low, you can go high. This is the open door to a a strenuous, ambitious life without strain and tension, for you yourself are inwardly relaxed, for you are not fighting with yourself over your goals, and you are not jostling others, except toward love and good works. You are relaxed amid your strenuousness. You have what is described as "a moving equilibrium."

"Aim at peace with all, at that consecration without which no one will ever see the Lord." (Heb. 12:14, Moffatt.) When you are wholly given to God ("consecration"), then you are wholly at peace with yourself and others.

O God, take out of me all strains set up by my wrong ways of life. Thy way is my peace and my power. Amen.

AFFIRMATION FOR THE DAY: *Today my motto: "A minimum of strain with a maximum of result."*

CAUSES OF TENSIONS

Why are we tense? The answer is that we are trying to live life against itself. We are not sure God is back of us, so we have to back ourselves up, to work harder to make up.

For instance, a girl said: "I want this man, and if I can't get him, I won't be happy." She ended in a mental hospital. If she had said, "I want this man if it is the best thing for me. If I can't get him I'll use the disappointment for higher purposes," then she would be a useful, radiant member of society and more eligible for a bid!

Sometimes we set up tensions because of our children's choices. Here was a mother, proud of her ancestry, who set up a tension within herself because her son, her only son and darling, had married a girl who was not of the mother's "station" in life. But the girl, of humble but very decent parentage, had everything—education, looks, ability, stability, and devotion to her husband. The mother should have rejoiced.

Sometimes a tension is set up because of a false sense of duty. A girl was on the verge of a nervous breakdown because she blamed herself for the death of her mother. She had to decide between giving up her job and thus being able personally to attend to her mother or putting her in a hospital. She took the latter course and rightly, for otherwise there was no way to finance the situation. But when her mother died, she blamed herself for her death, for if she had attended to her, she would have lived—a false assumption, for the mother was seventy-six! When the daughter surrendered her false blame to God, she was completely changed and was radiant.

Even where the scales are more evenly balanced between right and wrong, one may have a tension set up until the matter is settled one way or the other. A young missionary, devoted and able, couldn't decide between her missionary career and going back home to marry. She was on the verge of a break because of the tension. The doctor decided it by sending her home—and rightly so. She had to get off the horns of that dilemma. It made her tense.

Gracious Father, help me to decide things in the crisis in Thy way, since I've been deciding them in the commonplace in Thy way. Amen.

AFFIRMATION FOR THE DAY: *I can meet the crisis with calmness, for I meet day-by-day happenings with Christ.*

"SLOW ME DOWN, LORD"

Sometimes tensions are caused by getting hold of a wrong verse of Scripture and centering one's life around it. A bishop told me that every time he stands up to preach, a verse comes before him: "Lest . . . , when I have preached to others, I myself should be a castaway." He said he lives in a tenseness, verging on terror, over that verse. I was grateful I could tell him I am not afraid of my life verse, that every time I stand up to speak, I remind God of my verse—a verse He has given me: "Ye have not chosen me, but I have chosen you, and ordained you, that ye should go and bring forth fruit, and that your fruit should remain: that whatsoever ye shall ask of the Father in my name, he may give it you" (John 15:16). His verse was a marginal reminder of a danger, but not intended to become the focus of attention. Paul, who uttered it, did not make it the focus of his attention—that attention was focused on grace, not on an overhanging club. The bishop, with all his wisdom, was here psychologically unwise. His verse left him with a sense of a tension, mine with a sense of triumph.

Sometimes we get tense just because we have allowed the modern tempo of jumping from thing to thing to get into us. We think we are not doing anything unless we are doing things in a hurry. The little girl expressed her nervousness to her mother: "I feel in a hurry all over." Hindus worship the great god Hari—pronounced, Hurry! America does too! Many find this prayer of a Negro suits them:

> Slow me down, Lord,
> I'm going too fast.
> I can't see my brother
> When He's walking past.
> I miss a lot of good things day by day,
> When it comes my way.
> Slow me down, Lord,
> I'm going too fast.

Many need to pray that prayer, for we are going too fast.

Father, slow me down. The fevers of the world cannot supply my fervors. They must come from Thee. Amen.

AFFIRMATION FOR THE DAY: *"Around my incompleteness His completeness, around my restlessness His rest."*

"WITH THE LEISURED HEART"

What are the steps out of tensions?

First, *Fix it in your mind that you get most done when you do your work with a quiet heart.* The man who works with a tension within produces tensions without, and tensions sooner or later produce tangles, and tangles take time to unravel.

The Man who accomplished most on this planet of ours was never in a hurry, never ran, never pushed people around, was never fussily busy. He moved from task to task with the leisured heart. He used even His interruptions and made them into interpretations. He comported himself amid his duties as one on a holiday. The whole thing spells out Calm, but, oh, what a tornado lay at the heart of all His doings! It has stirred the world.

Second, *You gain followers as you learn to follow.* You don't gain followers by bellowing for people to follow you. You gain them by the poise you gain by following—by following something beyond yourself—God. Then you love people and thus cease trying to manipulate them.

They tell us that a piece of steel is magnetized by setting all its molecules in harmony with each other. As long as the molecules are at cross purposes, there is no magnetism. When they come together and pull together, then they really pull. You are an unmagnetized person if you have tensions within—conflicts that cancel power. The person who is harmonized within is not wasting his time and substance on an inner civil war. All his powers are set free from self-preoccupation to wage an effective foreign war on outer foes. He is God's free man—free to give!

Michelangelo said: "I have no friend and I do not want any. Whoever follows others will never go forward and whoever does not know how to create by his own abilities will never profit from the work of other men."

He followed nothing beyond himself and thus succeeded in projecting into his creations his own agitations. We can safely and successfully draw people only as we are drawn to Another.

O Christ, men followed Thee, because Thou didst follow a will not Thine own. Help me to do just that. Amen.

AFFIRMATION FOR THE DAY: *All the molecules of my being set around His will. I'm magnetized in Him.*

SURRENDERING OUR TENSIONS

The next step into release from tensions is:

Third, *Surrender the point of tension to God and let Him handle it for you.*

Here was a teacher whose tension point was a sense of inferiority. She tells her story:

You will rejoice to hear of the wonderful healing I have experienced as a result of attending the Ashram. I have suffered from a severe case of inferiority, even feeling timid before some of my own pupils. I have now found release. Pupils and teachers alike tell me that I am so changed that I am an entirely different person. The only way I can describe it is that I feel like an egg just released from its pent-up condition in the shell and now resting relaxed and free in an open dish.

When God took over her tension point, her inferiority, she was no longer inferior. With His reinforcement she was capable and adequate.

A very intelligent and able playwright tells of her release:

I'd always been a poor sleeper. The doctor said it was because I was afraid I would miss something. When you spoke of the Holy Spirit and the subconscious, I was thrilled. That night I simply said I would trust the subconscious to the Holy Spirit. I overslept! For the first time in years! It's amazing.

The point of tension was that she was unwilling to surrender herself and the world to God—she had to stay awake to see if everything was running right! She abdicated as cosmic night watchman and let God look after His world—and her. A young man in one of our Ashrams said, "I came up here feeling I had to carry out the functions of general manager of the universe. I've resigned. I'm relieved and relaxed. I'm free."

Someone has said that "fear is faith in the thing we don't want to happen." This produces a tension over that thing. Then surrender that false faith in the wrong thing and fasten that faith on God, your Father.

O Father, show me my tension points and help me to surrender them unreservedly and do it now. Amen.

AFFIRMATION FOR THE DAY: *No tension points because He has all my points.*

"RELAXED RECEPTIVITY"

Now that you have surrendered your tension point, take the next step:

Fourth, *Learn to live by relaxed receptivity.* Jesus said, "Consider the lilies how they grow." We usually quote the first part, "Consider the lilies," and leave the part "how they grow" unemphasized. But the emphasis is on that last part. He is teaching men how to grow. And he points to a plant. How does it grow? By getting tense and anxious and striving to grow? Jesus rejected this: "And which of you by taking thought can add one cubit unto his stature?" You can't grow by being anxious and tense about growing. The plant grows by receptivity to earth and air and sun. It learns how to *take,* to *receive.* It keeps the channels of receptivity open, and the earth and the sun do the rest. This is the secret Jesus is teaching us through the lilies—"how they grow." When we learn that, we have learned the most important lesson life has to teach us. Without it life is a fight—a fight from your own center, with your own resources, and the end is tense exhaustion. With it you fight the good fight of faith from God as the center, with His resources, and the end is triumphant exhilaration. You have enough and to spare for the next encounter. You are more than a conqueror; you are a conqueror who has conquered his own exhaustion.

At a well-known national shrine in India someone said to a visitor: "This is not a place of pilgrimage, but of striving." "A place of striving"—that represented the spirit of the place, for it was characterized by a severe self-discipline. Salvation was to be attained by one's own disciplined efforts. It was an attainment. I whispered to my grateful heart: "I'm glad salvation isn't an attainment, but an obtainment—the Gift of God." Instead of "a place of striving," I perferred "a place of surrender and receptivity and overflowing."

This is the order: First, surrender, becoming God-centered instead of self-centered. Second, receptivity, taking the gift of God and living by grace, instead of taking our own resources and living by groans. Third, overflowing, because we are linked to infinite resources. All you have to do is take in and give out.

O God, my Father, how can I thank Thee enough that I have found the secret of receptivity? Help me to use it. Amen.

AFFIRMATION FOR THE DAY: *I know how to receive. Therefore I shall never be empty.*

53

"BE PASSIVE AND RECEPTIVE"

We discussed yesterday "a place of striving." Such a place produces a strained piety, and where there is strain, there is drain—strained souls become drained souls. In our Ashrams we prefer this outlook: "Let this be a place of renunciation, or receptivity, of rejoicing"—and in that order. First, renunciation—you must learn how to let go at the center, yourself, and then with empty hands you can take the whole Gift—God. Second, receptivity—you must not only give, you must learn to take. The story goes that someone, seeing a number of packages around the gate of heaven, asked the attendant what they were and why they were there and received the reply: "These are blessings asked for my people, but they never came to get them." The invitation to receive is just as definite as the command to renounce. And when you begin to learn the art and attitude of receiving, you come automatically to the next step: rejoicing. This becomes the natural result, for a grateful heart cannot feel and think of Grace without rejoicing. The "striving" attitude does not sing, for it is never certain it has arrived. It is always questing and with question marks. A radiant soul who has learned the secret writes: "This year more than any other my heart is full to overflowing and I could not stop it if I wanted to." Another puts it this way: "I am still as happy as can be in spite of getting up every morning at six o'clock. I haven't taken a pill since I came home; neither have I felt tired. It is wonderful. What a fool I've been all these years."

Here is a contrast of two kinds of outlooks:

You crave for something and don't get it, you are jealous and envious of what others have got and you don't possess it yourselves. Consequently in your exasperated frustration you struggle and fight with one another. . . . Do you imagine that this spirit of passionate jealousy is the Spirit He has caused to live in us? No, He gives grace potent enough to meet this and every other evil spirit, if we are humble enough to receive it. (James 4:1-5, Phillips.)

"Humble enough to receive it"! That's it. That takes out the tensions.

O Spirit Divine, dwell within me fully and wholly, and then all the inner clashes will cease, and I shall be at peace. Amen.

AFFIRMATION FOR THE DAY: *I shall be humble enough to receive, grateful enough to pass on.*

"THIS SERENE ASSURANCE"

We pause a little longer on the attitude of receptivity. When we are planted in Christ by surrender, then is fulfilled this verse: "Grow out of him as a plant grows out of the soil it is planted in, becoming more and more sure of your 'ground' and your lives will overflow with joy and thankfulness" (Col. 2:6, Phillips). When we are rooted in Christ and see our effortless growth, we are more and more sure of our "ground." We know that we are made for *this*—it is our native "ground"; we and the soil are made for each other, there is a deep affinity. Out of this self-verifying assurance that this is our "ground" we begin to overflow with joy and thanksgiving. Not a joy and thanksgiving over this event or that event, but over the fact that our lives are planted in that which can sustain us now and forever. It is a life joy, not an event joy.

Another verse points to receptivity and consequent unshakable assurance: "Therefore let us render thanks that we receive a Realm (Kingdom) unshaken" (Heb. 12:28, Moffatt). Note: "receive a Kingdom"—we don't build it, strive for it; we receive it as a gift. And then we are sure of our "ground"—it is unshaken and unshakable. This takes out the tensions, for we are sure this is "It."

This kind of assurance, being so sure of itself, has the quality of serenity in it: "So, beloved, as you are expecting this, be eager to be found by him unspotted and unblemished in serene assurance" (II Pet. 3:14, Moffatt). This "serene assurance" comes only through grace, and grace only through receptivity. "A place of striving" is not and cannot be a place of serene assurance. For you are never certain when you strive, for *you* strive, from your own center, with your own resources. Life doesn't approve of that.

This serene assurance can characterize a very busy and outwardly burdened life. Here is what Dr. William Osler says: "I begin each day with Christ and His prayer. At night as I lay off my clothes, I undress my soul too, and lay aside its sin. In the presence of God I lie down to rest to waken a free man with a new life."

O Father, I thank Thee that in Thy calm our fevers are dissolved, and we are at peace with Thee and ourselves. Amen.

AFFIRMATION FOR THE DAY: *In serene assurance I shall face everything today, for I'm adequate in God.*

IS HIS REST THE REST?

We come to the last step out of tensions:

There can be no freedom from tensions unless we realize that that to which we have committed ourselves is ultimate. Fifth, *Get hold of the fact that this is "The Rest."*

These verses point in that direction: "Well, then, as the promise of entrance into his Rest is still left to us, let us be afraid of anyone being judged to have missed it. . . . For we do enter the Rest by our faith" (Heb. 4:1, 3, Moffatt). Here "His Rest" is "*the* Rest." Is this true?

When we surrender wholly to God and by faith enter into "His Rest," do we have the inner assurance that this is "*the* Rest"? Yes! It is the Rest of adjustment to reality, of feeling that this is the ultimate way to live, that we have cosmic approval for this way of life, and that the sum total of reality is behind us and is approving of us and is furthering us. Anything short of this leaves a feeling of tension—"Is this It?"

But when you enter "His Rest," then you are adjusted to God, to yourself, to everything good—to reality itself. You are adjusted to everything except evil. You are out of harmony only with disharmony. And evil is just that. You are in harmony with Harmony, you realize Reality.

And everything within you cries out and says this is "the Rest." Everything else is a rest, a temporary expediency, a makeshift. But when you settle down here, something "clicks" within you—it is the click of complete adjustment to complete Reality. You then enter into the same kind of Rest that God has. He sees the beginning and the end and is not disturbed by anything between, for He sees how it will all come out. It will come out to Victory. We share this invincible certainty. We rest in "the Rest."

"Spiritual stability depends on the grace of God, and not on rules of diet" (Heb. 13:9, Phillips). It depends on what God does for us and not on what we do for Him.

O God, my Father, I thank Thee that through the door of faith I can now enter into Thy Rest—the Rest. Amen.

AFFIRMATION FOR THE DAY: *I am rested in His Rest—all my restlessness dissolved.*

RESENTMENTS AND RELEASE INCOMPATIBLES

We pass from our tensions to another cause of stunted growth, namely, resentments. We have been noting that only an acceptance of and a living in grace can save us from tensions.

There is another result of missing the grace of God. "See to it that no one misses the grace of God, that no root of bitterness grows up to be a trouble by contaminating all the rest of you." (Heb. 12:15, Moffatt.) When we cease to grow in the grace of God, then roots of bitterness, resentments, begin to grow in us. Of all the things that choke and poison spiritual growth, resentments, justified or unjustified, are probably the most devastatingly effective.

Resentments and release are incompatibles. If you hold resentments, you let go release, and if you take release, you have to let go resentments. A resentful heart is a restricted heart.

A doctor says:

A client of mine literally became a prisoner as a result of fears and resentments. He was full of resentments toward his wife and in-laws. These were accumulated over a period of fifteen years. He would talk for hours about incidents which happened years before. He couldn't go out of his house—he was a prisoner. Then he had to go out to have an operation on his thyroid brought about by his resentments.

The resentments upset not only his soul but his body as well. His glands could not function properly, for they were upset by hate. They were made for good will and would function properly only under good will. Ill will upset them.

A woman said to me:

Several years ago I got fed up with myself. I was restless and resentful and unhappy. I took eight months' leave of absence to think it over. As the time drew near to go back, it seemed I couldn't go back. The inner tension was so great I developed shingles. I had sense enough to know that I had brought it on by my own rebellion, and so I surrendered the problem to God. The shingles lasted for three weeks, but the doctor told me the normal course was six months or a year.

O God, I am made for love and cannot assimilate hate. Help me to give up my hates before they get me down. Amen.

AFFIRMATION FOR THE DAY: *My heart is too glad and gay in God to harbor any resentment.*

RESENTMENTS ARE POISON

A schoolteacher was resentful that her brother had stolen her share of the inheritance. She became a complete cripple, bent double with arthritis. She probably felt she was justified in her resentments, and yet, justified or unjustified, they left her a cripple.

I am not saying that all illnesses are the result of wrong emotions. We will discuss that later. But there is no doubt that many of them are.

Here was a young wife who was so upset over her husband's saying that he was leaving this particular religious gathering that she became ill and could not eat her lunch. I saw the man and got him to consent to stay, and she ate her lunch without any signs of upset.

These three men met the same thing in a different way with different results—they were all flunked by professors in college. One of them for years, whenever he would meet anyone, would talk about a college professor who had mixed up his grades with a man of the same name. This grudge blotted out all his college memories. Another man was kicked out of an Ohio college, then became a trustee of it and gave much of his money to it, for he felt his being kicked out was the thing that awakened him. A third man held a bitter grudge against a professor who had failed him in Greek. It was a lifelong grudge and poisoned his life—uselessly.

A man thought he had an allergy to his mother-in-law's fur coat. He had an attack of asthma every time he got near it. Then he had an attack when he came near her when she was wearing another coat, not fur. Then he found he had an attack while talking to her over the telephone. It was not an allergy, but a resentment, that brought on the asthma.

This works in East and West. An Indian mother-in-law did not like her daughter-in-law. It was a mixed marriage between two castes. The mother-in-law went to bed and stayed there four years, an invalid—a sad case of self-crippling.

Human nature is the same around the world. It is made for good will and thrives under it; under ill will it withers.

Father God, Thou art teaching us the hard way that we are made for love. Help us to learn quickly. Amen.

AFFIRMATION FOR THE DAY: *No hurt egotism shall spoil my happiness and usefulness today.*

"I CAN'T AFFORD TO BE BITTER"

Before we go on to the steps out of resentments, we must look back a little longer at the results of resentments so that we may be the more inclined to take those steps.

A very intelligent professor in a great university had suffered much because of losing her husband to another woman, but she said very simply: "I can't afford to be bitter, for, if I am, it gives me arthritis."

Here was another woman not so intelligent nor so wise. She became irritable and resentful and unreasonable. She accused her husband of drinking and of being unfaithful. She sent the children out to work whenever and wherever possible. She quarreled with the children and they with each other. She thought any form of recreation was wrong. She was frequently ill with arthritis and pains in her abdomen, and she had her teeth taken out. She had no ulcers, but she was poisoning herself and the whole family by her ulcerated spirit.

Another illustration from the other side of the world, India. A young man was brought up in a strict family where the parents wanted him to be a minister. He revolted against this desire and he tried to join the army, but he was rejected. He is now afraid of everything—to go near a well, or a bus. He is so resentful against his father that he breaks into a sweat every time he sees him. He has had a brain operation, but his trouble is not physical but mental and spiritual. Resentments are getting in their deadly work.

Some see the ravages of the termite and head it off. A man built up a lumber business, but his partner maneuvered things so that he lost thousands of dollars. When the man realized what had happened, he said: "I was so angry that if I had had a gun, I would have shot him on the spot." He developed such an acute attack of arthritis that he was unable for a time to feed himself. After seeing the futility of his attitude, he gave it up, was able to overcome his physical handicap, and is now a generous, happy man.

This plague of resentment struck a missionary. He hated his mother, and he felt he was justified. It caused a nervous breakdown, and he was sent home. His career was ruined.

Father, forgive us that we nourish in our bosoms these cobras of hate. Help us to get rid of them. Amen.

AFFIRMATION FOR THE DAY: *I'm exterminating the termites of resentments with the breath of prayer today.*

"RESENTMENTS SOUND THE DEATH KNELL"

The wife of a professor of psychology said: "If I have another baby, I'm going to bed and stay there." She did have another baby, and she did go to bed and stayed there for ten years and was waited on by the family as an invalid. Then she divorced her husband, got up from her bed, got a job, and went to work. Resentments made her an invalid for ten years.

A handsome man with a well-trimmed beard sat in all my evangelistic meetings in one of the countries of the world. He was handsome but frustrated and useless. He went overseas and obtained an M.Sc. in Engineering and came back expecting to get a big government job. Instead he was offered a job which he thought was too small for him, and he refused it and has done nothing ever since, allowing his mother to support him while he chews on his resentments.

Some of these resentments may be buried deep down beneath an outer show of good will. A schoolteacher writes: "Yes, I can see now, I did not give myself to anyone. I resented the Head's criticism of public schools. I resented (inside) while I seemingly liked everyone and everything. In January I had a violent attack of rheumatoid arthritis." The outer likes could not atone for the buried dislikes. They got in their blows and laid her up.

Sometimes the resentments are not against people but against the thing one is compelled to do, one's job. A man's stomach literally tied itself in knots because he was inwardly angry against his business. He had X rays, all kinds of treatment, but nothing helped. He then read *Abundant Living*, and as he let go his resentments, he says, "I felt a warmth go through my diaphragm." The resentments had stopped the flow of blood through his system impeding digestion, and when he let them go, he literally felt the warmth of the released blood flowing through his system. This reading of the book gave him a shot in the arm, made him feel better, but he had complete release when he surrendered not only his resentments but himself. Then he walked out a free man.

God, our Father, we pray that no inner grudges shall spoil our lives and those of others around us. In Jesus' name. Amen.

AFFIRMATION FOR THE DAY: *I belong to grace. How can such a one hold a resentment?*

60

STEPS OUT OF RESENTMENTS

We must be eager now to take the steps out of resentments into release:

First, *Don't get hung up on the attempt to justify the resentment by calling it "righteous indignation."* There is such a thing as righteous indignation. Jesus had it when he "looked around about on them with anger, being grieved for the hardness of their hearts" (Mark 3:5). This was anger at what was happening to someone else and not personal pique at something that was happening to Him. It had grief in it—"being grieved"—at what was happening to another. When our anger has a grief in it at what is happening to someone else, and not a gripe in it at what is happening to us, then the anger is right and righteous.

Second, *Even if the anger is righteous, don't keep it too long within the heart.* It will fester. Paul says: "Be ye angry and sin not. Let not the sun go down upon your wrath" (Eph. 4:26). Here was an anger that could be held without sin. But if you are to be angry and sin not, then you must be angry only at sin. However, even this kind of anger must not be kept overnight—"Let not the sun go down upon your wrath." For even a righteous indignation can eat away the love side of your life and leave you righteously cantankerous, an unlovely person.

Third, *Remember that whatever you give out comes back:* "With what measure ye mete, it shall be measured to you again." You cannot give out ill will without getting it back to yourself again. The hater is hated, the resentful resented, the lover loved—automatically.

The story goes of a Hindu god who enchanted an arrow, which flew around killing people. But after it had finished killing people and had no one else to kill, it came back to the god and got after him. So the god spent his days flying before the arrow he had sent out against others. Even the "gods" are not exempt from this law of sowing and reaping!

No one can afford a grudge. It charges too much toll. You chew your own tongue when you chew on a resentment.

O loving God, make me loving. Take from my heart all unkind, ungenerous, unloving thoughts. Amen.

AFFIRMATION FOR THE DAY: *My loving thoughts will push out all unloving thoughts today.*

THE HIGHEST STATEMENT OF MORALITY

We continue the steps out of resentments.

Third, *Forgive others as Christ forgives you.* As you stand in need of forgiveness, so give it to others. For if you refuse it to others, this blocks the forgiveness toward you. God cannot forgive the unforgiving. His hands are tied. So if we refuse forgiveness, we break down the bridge over which we must pass—the bridge of forgiveness.

The highest statement of morality ever given on this planet of ours is this one: "Treat one another with the same spirit as you experience in Christ Jesus" (Phil. 2:5, Moffatt). This transcends all Ten Commandments and goes beyond all moral codes—Treat each other the way Christ treats you! He forgives and forgives freely, and He forgets and forgets wholly, and He buries and buries completely.

The one thing Jesus turns back upon and comments upon in the Lord's Prayer is this: "For if you forgive not men their trespasses, neither will your Father forgive your trespasses" (Matt. 6:15). Some children in Belgium were behind the lines in a church during the last war, praying the Lord's Prayer. When they got to the phrase "Forgive us our trespasses," they paused before the rest of the sentence. Could they forgive those who had ruined their country? In that pause a voice behind said: "As we forgive those who trespass against us." They turned and saw it was the King of Belgium, who had lost everything—except his soul.

A girl in college hated a man who had killed her own mother in her kitchen. She went into a chapel and for two hours prayed. She emerged forgiven and forgiving. She went to the prison and poured out her love to prisoners. Concerning the boy who killed her mother she said: "He's sick. He should be in a hospital instead of in a prison." This girl gave her life for prisoners. She herself was free, and she helped free others.

A woman writes: "When I first opened the book—believe it or not —it was at the place of resentments. I was held enthralled until suddenly I happened to look up and—what do you think? I had none. They were gone." Simple? But very effective and releasing.

O forgiving God, help me to forgive as freely and fully as Thou dost forgive. I do, for Jesus' sake. Amen.

AFFIRMATION FOR THE DAY: *I shall take forgiveness with one hand and give it with the other.*

WORKING OUT TECHNIQUES

Fourth, *Work out techniques for keeping resentments out of your heart and out of your relationships.* (1) A woman writes: "Oh, I don't know what I would do without my garden. You can bury so many things with a trowel. And the things you bury become fertilizer for the flowers." Then take your trowel and go out and bury your resentments in your garden.

(2) Some write down their resentments on a piece of paper and then burn the paper.

(3) A couple who both had tempers had an agreement that when either one was angry, he or she would go out for a walk.

(4) Nip resentments in the bud. Pray them out by a quick prayer for release. One man wrote: "About budding resentments—I have gotten rid of twelve."

(5) Let group prayer be made for the resentful. "The workers of the library have been praying that our librarian's disposition might change. To the surprise of all he apologized to us all last week and said he was going to turn over a new leaf. He has been lovely to us ever since. It almost seems unbelievable."

(6) Open your heart each day to the invading spirit of love. A man writes: "Resentments come as a result of resisting the wooing of grace." Grace is always ready to invade and pervade you. Let it in.

(7) Melt people; don't maul them. It is easier to melt a block of ice than to break it up by smiting it with a hammer.

(8) If a little bit of love isn't effective, increase the dose. The remedy for the ineffectiveness of a little love is more love. The Chinese have a saying: "Don't try to put out the fire of a load of hay with a cup of water." Increase the dose!

(9) When you think of someone against whom you are tempted to be resentful, breathe a prayer for him and send your love to him.

(10) The victory is in your being loving, even if the other person does not receive it. You are more loving for having loved—that is the victory. Rejoice in it.

O Christ, Thou didst love enemies even while on a cross. Help me to catch Thy spirit and do the same. Amen.

AFFIRMATION FOR THE DAY: *Love is the victory. If I see no results, love is itself the victory.*

63

LOOKING AT GREEN-EYED JEALOUSY

We have all seen logs caught on a rock in midstream and held up there, never reaching their intended destination. Many are hung up on the rock of jealousy, and life flows past them. Jealousy is akin to resentments, so we must discuss it next as a hindrance to growth.

In an interesting passage Paul says: "Let us live decorously as in the open light of day—no revelry or bouts of drinking, no debauchery or sensuality, no quarreling or jealousy" (Rom. 13:13, Moffatt). Here he puts jealousy in the same category with drunkenness and debauchery. These latter two are the sins of the flesh; jealousy is a sin of the spirit. The younger brother in the parable of the prodigal son sinned in the flesh—in debauchery and drunkenness; the elder brother sinned in the spirit—in jealousy. And when the curtain went down on the drama, the man who sinned in his flesh was on the inside of the Father's house, and the man who sinned in his spirit—in jealousy—was on the outside. Jealousy can close the doors of the Kingdom of God and its resources and shut one off from development.

Children exhibit jealousy often, and it upsets a household. A little boy in the family developed deafness when the new baby came. The doctors could find nothing wrong with his ears. Then the mother began to pay more attention to him, and he began to hear again. He developed deafness to gain attention. He was jealous of the attention given to the new baby. A little girl looked at a picture of a lovely lakeside and commented: "It looks like a horrible place." Her little sister had gone to this place, and she was jealous because she didn't go; hence she had to be derogatory.

That's the trouble with jealousy—it distorts everything, throws everything out of focus. A jealous husband or wife can make life miserable for himself and others by reading meanings into actions. The result is a spreading misery. It is as dangerous as a spreading cancer. "I'm on the road to recovery from a cancer—a mental cancer," said a woman who called her jealousy by its right name. Her husband responded—it helped him to get rid of things: "It's been like emptying out a garbage can. I'm happy and free."

O Father, this jealousy that eats like a cancer at my relationships, I surrender to Thee, now and forever. Amen.

AFFIRMATION FOR THE DAY: *I shall pour out special love and prayer for those of whom I'm envious.*

JEALOUSY CAN INVADE THE BEST

I watched two jay birds pecking at each other over the possession of an elderberry on the ground. Just above them was a bush full of elderberries, and they could have had all they wanted. But each wanted the particular berry that the other wanted. Silly? Yes, but no more silly than two persons pecking at each other over the possession of attention which each could get if he would forget himself in the service of others.

Suppose the eye should become jealous of the hand, and they began to fight each other instead of co-operating in the service of the whole body. That would be no more fatal to the body than two members of a household or a community at cross purposes because of jealousy.

Jealousy can invade the bosoms of the best. Alexander Whyte ruled in his great Scottish church like a king. Hugh Black was a junior colleague. "In the morning," as someone has said, "Whyte blackballed the saints, and in the evening Black whitewashed the sinners." Then Black forged ahead with bigger crowds. Whyte became jealous. His friends could not believe it. But Whyte replied, "Ah, you don't know the black depths of the human heart."

Human life is so arranged that all our attitudes and acts toward others register themselves in us. You cannot throw a barb at another without that barb coming back and sticking in your own soul. The story goes of a man who got a new boomerang and then spent the balance of his days trying to throw the old one away—it came back each time. Jealousies come back to plague us. A woman who became jealous of another woman, who was her mental and spiritual superior, kept throwing barbs at the other in private and in public and succeeded only in making her own soul a pincushion carrying around the returned barbs. She was vastly unhappy and frustrated.

When a woman gave up her jealousy of another, a shadow passed from her face, and there was a sunrise.

O Father, take the shadows cast by jealousy from my face and from my heart and make me free. Amen.

AFFIRMATIONN FOR THE DAY: *No barbs, only blessings for everybody in every situation today.*

STEPS OUT OF JEALOUSY

A young man said to me: "I'm a quiet chap, and I'm in love with a girl, but I'm jealous. I get jealous when I see her having a good time with a crowd. She gave me up because of this jealousy and says she won't take me back unless I get over my jealousy. How can I?" It's a good question, so we turn to see the steps out of jealousy into freedom.

First, *Fix it in your mind that jealousy is self-defeating.* Nothing whatever is to be gained by it except one's own increasing frustration. If you want to gain the love of another by the method of jealousy, it only makes you less lovable. It is difficult to love a jealous person. It is bad strategy.

Second, *By a deliberate act surrender that jealousy into the hands of God.* You can't handle it, but you can consent for Him to handle it. Give it to Him. From this moment on, He has it, and you are now to look at Him and obey.

Third, *Consider whether you should confess your jealousy to the person of whom you are jealous.* In talking over the matter you may discover that the other will offer suggestions that will lift the whole matter to a higher plane. And the jealousy will drop away.

Fourth, *Think and say everything good you can about the person of whom you are jealous.* This will dissolve the jealousy by good will.

Fifth, *Not only think and say all the things you can about that person, but also do things that will further him.* Look for chances of boosting him—not in cant, but in sincerity. In doing so, you yourself will go up in your own eyes and in the eyes of others. And you will go up in fact.

Sixth, *Fulfill this verse: "So let us concentrate on the things that make for harmony, and on the growth of one another's character"* (Rom. 14:19, Phillips). You are a Christian, and you can be a Christian only as you try to Christianize others.

Seventh, *Whenever you think of that person, think of him in prayer.* Send out waves of prayer to him. They will come back and wash your own soul clean of all jealousy and envy.

O Christ, give me the loving attitude toward all and especially toward those of whom I am jealous. Amen.

AFFIRMATION FOR THE DAY: *Envy and jealousy can have no part in me, for Jesus has all of me.*

THE CENTER OF OUR PROBLEM—
THE UNSURRENDERED EGO

The things we have been studying as blocks to growth are all pushing us nearer and nearer to the center of our problems—the unsurrendered ego. We now turn to it. For all else is fruit; this is root.

I say "unsurrendered ego," not the ego. I am sure that the ego is God-created and as such is God-approved and is to be developed. It is not to be canceled or suppressed; it is to be expressed in God's ways. When the ego has found its place, it has found its place of growth and consequent happiness.

Then just what is its place? Its place is not on the throne of the universe. When Swinburne, replacing God, said, "Glory to Man in the highest," he made man ridiculous, for events since have laughed at the statement. Man has shown an infinite capacity to trip over himself and to sprawl in the dust of humiliation when he makes himself a little tin god.

An Anglican bishop was trying to impress on his servant who had done wrong that there was One to whom he was accountable: "Do you know that there is Someone before whom even I am a worm of the dust?" And the servant replied: "Yes, the Missus."

This has its counterpart in a pompous man who announced a certain meeting and ended by saying: "I myself will be there." He would be there in person! The audience smiled—inwardly.

Daughters can be devastating in their criticism of their daddies. The daughter of a prominent religious leader said to her father: "Did anyone ever tell you that you are wonderful?" And when the father replied, "No, I don't think so," she said: "Then where did you get the idea?" Daughters can mow down the budding gods.

And we do it with one another when one begins to try to be always in the public gaze. Of one Presbyterian preacher it was said that he was thinking of becoming a Baptist, but he couldn't bring himself to undergo immersion, for it would mean a disappearance from the public gaze for awhile!

O Father God, I know that when I strut, I stumble; when I surrender, I succeed. Help me. Amen.

AFFIRMATION FOR THE DAY: *No ego-antics, only ego-consecration shall characterize me today.*

"COME . . . TAKE . . . LEARN"

In reading books on counseling I have been amazed at the way this question of self-surrender to God is side-stepped and bypassed. Advice is given about every question, but this central question is skirted. And this by Christian leaders. They seem to hesitate to confront the persons counseled with the supreme need of getting themselves off their own hands into the hands of God—by self-surrender. They name their method "nondirective counseling." They do not direct the counselee; they allow him to do it himself. Suppose Jesus had used this nondirective method. Suppose in the Sermon on the Mount he had gathered afflicted humanity about Himself and had said to them: "Now talk about yourself. I'll throw in a question now and then." No. He directed men, for He knew the direction and they didn't. He directed them through presenting truth which was self-verifying, and for which they were made.

At the very center of that truth was the law of self-surrender—you save your life by losing it. This He repeated five times for emphasis. He was lifting up out of reality a law as inescapable in the moral and spiritual realm as the law of gravitation is inescapable in the realm of the physical.

So Jesus said: "Come . . . take . . . learn" (Matt. 11:28, 29, Moffatt). Note the order: the first thing is our relationship to Him—"Come to me." Settle that, and you settle everything. But you don't "come" by just coming; you "come" by taking His yoke—"Take my yoke," surrender to my sway. Then you learn—"Learn of me," for He can teach only those under His yoke, surrendered to Him. Religious education, for the most part, with some exceptions, reverses this process and says, "Learn. . . . Take. . . . Come." Often the process doesn't get as far as "take" or "come"; it stops at the "learn." Insofar as it does so, it ends at sterile knowledge.

No, Jesus insisted that we surrender the self—the center of our problems. If we don't surrender that, the center, we have no right to ask Him to solve our marginal problems as they come day by day.

O Jesus, Thy finger has gone unerringly to our problem—the problem of self-surrender. Help me to let that go; then all goes. Amen.

AFFIRMATION FOR THE DAY: *My self in God's hands is a possibility and a power. It shall be there.*

"AM I NOT A FOOL?"

We are considering self-surrender as the center of our spiritual problems. This is *it*. But we often shy off from it and take a bypath, instead of the Way.

In the book *Mask of Mercy* by Robert Frost, when Jessie and Jonah are talking, Jonah brings the subject around to Jessie's life. "Let's change the subject, it makes me nervous," she says. And Jonah replies: "That's all the great questions ever make you."

It makes us nervous to get close to the center of our problems—self-surrender. We shy away from it and promise to do anything, anything except that. And the results are not the heaven of self-possession, but the hell of self-losing. A barrenness sets in. This is how one who has tried it describes it: "Two verses describe my condition: 'Ever learning, and never able to come to the knowledge of the truth' and 'Having a form of godliness, but denying the power thereof' (II Tim. 3:7, 5). I hate this dominance of myself that has made my life a hell." The dominion of Christ makes life a heaven, and the dominion of self makes life a hell. That's all there is to it. Everything else is commentary. And there are no exceptions—none.

In an Ashram in Burma a police officer put the matter in these vivid words. "I am a fool. I see that if I die, I will live again. But I pull back. Am I not a fool?" And all life echoes back: "Yes!"

The white corpuscles are the sentinels of the blood looking for infection. But when they cease their function and think only in terms of multiplying themselves, then leukemia sets in. The white corpuscles are not doing their job, so infections take over, and the person dies.

We spoil ourselves, afraid God will spoil us if we surrender to Him. The strangest thing on this planet is our fear of surrendering to the one safe place in the universe—God. We hug our present delusions, knowing deep down that they are delusions; but they are present, and we hug them for fear of the unknown. But that unknown is love.

The earth when it runs away from the sun simply runs into the dark. When we run away from God, refuse to surrender ourselves, then we get one thing—the dark.

O Father, I cannot run away from Thee without running away from myself. I surrender. In Jesus' name. Amen.

AFFIRMATION FOR THE DAY: *My self on my own hands is a problem. In God's hands—a possibility.*

A SELF YOU CAN'T LIVE WITH

We are looking at the central problem, the problem of self-surrender. It is not a problem really; it is a possibility.

Here is one who turned the problem to a possibility: "I've been choked with pride and selfishness. But I'm loosed. I even laughed this morning when the soap slipped out of my fingers and fell into the dirt." Another woman puts it this way: "It's wonderful to get yourself off your own hands and into the hands of God. It's so comfortable." It is just that. When you are not surrendered to God, you are alone; nothing backs you except yourself.

If we center ourselves on ourselves, we won't like ourselves. The penalty is to live with a self you can't live with. This passage expresses it: "Destruction and misery are in their ways" (Rom. 3:16, Phillips)—not as a result of their ways, but inherently *"in* their ways." So the penalty for an unsurrendered self is a self that you surrender to.

If instead of God you choose yourself, you lose yourself. Life is made that way, and there is no use kicking against the goad, as Paul did and hurt himself. But when you become dependent on God, you become independent of others—and of your self. Strangely enough, independent of your own self. Your self is freed from itself only as it surrenders to Another. This cannot be explained. It must be experienced.

Amazing authority and power come to the self-surrendered. This passage tells of it: "The conqueror I will allow to sit beside me on my throne, as I myself have conquered and sat down beside my Father on his throne" (Rev. 3:21, Moffatt). Here is the amazing possibility of sharing the authority and power of Christ—of sitting beside Him on His throne. But the secret is in the second portion: "as I myself have conquered." And how did He conquer? "He emptied himself." The self-emptying became a fullness that "fills the universe entirely" (Eph. 1:23, Moffatt). Giving all, He received all—even a throne. And we share that throne; we rule without wanting to rule. We naturally go to the place of authority. It is inherent.

O Christ, Thou didst walk through a cross of self-losing to the throne of the universe. I follow. Amen.

AFFIRMATION FOR THE DAY: *I shall share God's authority, for God has my all.*

STEPS OUT OF SELF-CENTEREDNESS

We come now to the important matter of steps out of self-centered-ness into God-centeredness. These steps are important, for they may put your feet upon the Way. If you miss step here, you may wander in bypaths of confusion and defeat all your days.

First, *Fix it in your mind not as an idea, but as a maxim, that if you are self-centered, then you are off-center, and nothing will come out right.* You are not the center of the universe, never intended to be and never can be. If you try to be, you will try the impossible, and you will come out a frustrated and unhappy person, inevitably. I have never in these years seen one single happy, adjusted person who is self-centered.

If you start with a basically false premise like two and two make five and put this in your mathematical calculations, then none of your sums will come out right. If you start in geometry with the false axiom that things equal to the same thing are not equal to each other, then none of your geometrical calculations will come out to reality. Just so, a person who, either consciously or subconsciously, starts out to make the universe revolve around him, will live in a false universe that will tumble about his head in awful confusion. God is the Center of this universe. And the only attitude to take is self-sur-render to the Center. And when you do this, your life sums begin to add up to sense. "Seek ye first the kingdom of God, . . . and all these things," including yourself, "shall be added unto you." Seek something else first, for instance yourself, and all these things, including your-self, will be subtracted from you. This is as axiomatic as two and two make four. And there are no exceptions. You will not be an exception. Nail that down in your mind.

This axiom gives a firm basis for self-surrender and lifts it out of romantic adventure. It is just common sense. If you belong to the One to whom the universe belongs, then you belong to the right One.

On the other hand, to belong to yourself means that you trip over yourself at every turn, get tangled up with yourself, and become in-creasingly fed up with yourself. You are a problem instead of a person.

O God, my Father, I come to Thee to let go the one thing I have—myself. Take me over and make me over. Amen.

AFFIRMATION FOR THE DAY: *Belonging to God, I belong to nothing else. I am afraid of nothing.*

A FUNDAMENTAL CHANGE OF OWNERSHIP

Second, *Fix it in your mind also that self-surrender means more than denying yourself this thing, that thing, and leaving the self intact; it is a fundamental change of ownership.* Self-denial usually has been watered down until it means little more than doing without luxuries. When Jesus used the phrase "let him deny himself," it literally meant, "utterly reject himself," or "lose sight of himself." The phrase "utterly reject himself" doesn't mean you won't have a self—you will have a self and a better self than ever; but it does mean that you have a self that doesn't belong to itself any longer. Ownership has been changed. And this is no mere make-believe, a bantering of words. Something vital and eternal has taken place. You belong to Another. He decides your life plans; He directs the details; He is the source of your power, for He is the center of your affections and loyalty. This is a change as real as if a planet wandering through space without goal suddenly became attached to a star and henceforth revolved round that star.

Say within your mind these decisive words: "I belong to One and to One alone. It is settled—and settled forever."

Third, *Don't try to fix up a compromise.* It will be unsatisfactory and will let you down. A businessman said to me, "My self says to me twenty times a day: I'll do this, I'll do that, I'll give up this, and I'll give up that, but please let me stay at the center." And then he added: "I'm trying to live the Christian life, but I'm having a hard time at it." No wonder. In prayer he surrendered his self completely, and then he began to have an easy time being a Christian. "Thank you for giving my husband back to me," said his wife. But I didn't give her husband back; he gave himself to God, and then God gave him back to himself, to his family, and to the world.

A king of France gave the whole of a province to the Virgin Mary but reserved to himself the right to collecting the revenues. We thus give to God—with strings attached! But those strings become cart ropes that tie us in knots. Half-giving results in half-living. And half-living results in whole-dying.

O Father, no half-giving with Thee. Thou dost give all, and Thou dost demand my all. I give it. Amen.

AFFIRMATION FOR THE DAY: *The surrendered heart shall be the serene heart within me today.*

THE TAIL WILL WAG!

Compromises with God kick back and become compromises with ourselves, which in turn issue in compromised selves. We cancel ourselves out. In the elections in India the different parties—about ten of them—had different ballot boxes in the voting booths with a symbol on the outside so the illiterate could vote for the candidate he desired without having to read his name. One man wanted to play safe—he would vote for everybody; so he tore up his ballot into ten pieces and dropped a piece in each of the ten boxes. He voted for everybody—and nobody! He belonged to everybody—and to nothing!

Commit yourself. A committed self is a converted self, and a converted self is a consecrated self, and a consecrated self is a contagious self. It goes places, and it helps others to go places. "One man wholly given to God influences the countryside for ten miles around"—and beyond.

But if we try to compromise, the compromised thing will upset all our consecrations. A man was demonstrating before a group how his dog could play dead. It was a marvelous exhibition of the dog's ability to look like a completely dead dog—his eyes were closed, his jaws open and relaxed, his legs stretched out. He looked completely dead, except that the very tip of his tail was wagging. That gave away the whole show! And thus it is with us. If we do not really die, if we keep back part of the price, then the self still there alive and intact will show itself by manifestations of anger, of self-pity, of self-assertion—the tail will wag! There is nothing covered that shall not be revealed.

Up until Pentecost the disciples had not really surrendered themselves—they had given up everything except themselves. So they disputed on the way about who was greatest. Jesus knew "the dispute that occupied their minds." What a subject to occupy their minds—the minds of the people who were to save the world! The tails of their unsurrendered selves were wagging!

The little allusions, the mannerisms, the bids for attention, will reveal the unsurrendered depths.

Father, give me the fully consenting heart—the heart that says "yes" to Thee and says it from the depths. Amen.

AFFIRMATION FOR THE DAY: *A half-given self is a wholly divided self. None of that for me.*

ONCE-AND-FOR-ALL AND UNFOLDING

We are taking the steps out of self-centeredness.

Fourth, *Not only give all, but give the all for all time—make it once-and-for-all.* There are those who would insist on the daily self-surrender. There is a truth in the necessity of a daily surrendering of the self. But the daily surrendering of the self has no meaning if at the basis of it there is not a once-for-all giving. Suppose a husband or a wife should say to the other: "Dear, let's get married over again today." The other would be shocked. The basis would be shaky. No, a real marriage is a once-for-all business. It is a mutual self-surrender with no reservations. Then and then only is it a real marriage.

But around that central once-and-for-all giving there can be daily self-surrenders. For the "all" which you give is an unfolding all; you see new areas where this thing, that thing, or the other thing comes under the initial giving. So it is absolute and yet unfolding. It is complete and yet never complete. It takes a very short time to be married—a few minutes and it is over. But it takes a long time, a lifetime, and perhaps an eternity to be perfectly married, for there are daily adjustments to be made, a daily fitting in at deeper and deeper depths and in wider and wider areas.

But those who advocate the daily surrender without an absolute surrender underlying it and giving basis to it are providing in thought for a disloyal center to be atoned for by a lot of daily giving. No, we must not only give; we must give up.

Jesus said to the tempter: "Begone, Satan! it is written, you must worship the Lord your God, and serve him alone" (Matt. 4:10, Moffatt). Then, "at this the devil left him." The word "alone" was decisive. The devil left when Jesus used that word—no toe hold in Him! But later in Gethsemane Jesus had to relate that once-and-for-all giving to a specific issue: "Father, if it be possible, let this cup pass from me: nevertheless not as I will, but as thou wilt." On that specific issue he surrendered His will, a will that was perfectly surrendered to the Father. It was absolute and yet continuous.

O Jesus, teach me Thy secret of the "alone" and yet the continuous, for I need that lesson. Amen.

AFFIRMATION FOR THE DAY: *In my "all" are many little "alls." I'll let God have them as they unfold.*

THE GENEROUS EYE

We come now to an important step in release from self-tyranny.

Fifth, *Not only completely surrender to Christ, but also commit yourself to tasks and interests outside yourself.* This committal of yourself to interests and tasks outside yourself will keep you committed to Christ and will help keep you from self-attention and hence self-centeredness. Your self-surrender is not in a vacuum. It is a self-surrender in order to a self-committal to other-than-self interests.

I have been in princes' palaces in India where the rooms were surrounded by mirrors. Whichever way you looked, you could see yourself, for even the ceiling and the floor were mirrors. So there was no escaping yourself whichever way you gazed—around, or up, or down. You were imprisoned with yourself.

Then there are the rooms where you are surrounded by windows instead of mirrors—you look out at the world and others instead of at yourself. Life for you now must be a room with windows instead of mirrors. You are going to be a God-centered and other-centered person.

There are several verses which have become life-verses to me. A recently acquired one is this one:

> If your Eye is generous,
>   the whole of your body will be illumined,
> but if your Eye is selfish,
>   the whole of your body will be darkened.
>   (Matt. 6:22-23, Moffatt)

That first part has gripped me: "If your Eye"—your outlook on life, your way of looking at yourself and others, your viewpoint—"is generous," your whole personality is illumined. And because you are lovingly interested in others, then others are lovingly interested in you. The generous Eye produces the generous "I." Your outlook becomes you—your "Eye" determines the whole body.

So to break the tyranny of self-interest after the surrender of the self, there must be a very definite commital of yourself to tasks outside your self. This will keep the self in its place—subordinate.

O Living Christ, attach my heart to Thy attachments. Help me to be interested in Thy interests. Amen.

AFFIRMATION FOR THE DAY: *I shall look with the generous Eye on all things and all persons I see today.*

75

DISCIPLINED AROUND A NEW CENTER

Now that the self is surrendered and you have committed yourself to interests outside yourself, you are ready for the next step:

Sixth, *Lay on yourself a real self-discipline.* Self-discipline can now come in. Had we put it first, it would have been the wrong order; it would have been an attempt at disciplining an unsurrendered self. This cannot be done. It all results in a sitting on the lid and holding down that which cannot be held down successfully. The attempt simply ends in a conflict between you and yourself, and such a conflict is self-defeating, for in it you have to give yourself more attention than ever—the very thing you wanted to avoid.

But now that God has you, you can discipline yourself around this new center. Even after it is surrendered to God, the self will try to come back as dominant. For the self is not like a habit—you cannot wipe it out as you do a habit. It is a part of you—a part of you that cannot be wiped out, for it is one of the basic urges. It is a basic urge that is legitimate in its place, which is subordinate. But it will tend to come back to dominance and get out of place. Therefore we must discipline the self. How?

(1) By adopting a set of life habits in which the self takes a subordinate place. Make a framework of habits in which God is first, others second, and you third. Even when the suggestion about being third is made, the self will utter a silent protest. Is it to be left at the tail end of things? No, for by a strange law the self being "lost" will tend to be found. You will have a self you can live with and a self that others can live with. You're "found."

(2) Within this general framework of disciplining yourself to third place, work out specific disciplines to keep the self there. "In honour preferring one another"—pass on the honors to others. If you get compliments, give more to others. Take the tasks no one else wants. Where there is a menial job, make it yours. If there is blame, take it on yourself, if you can honestly do so. Tie the self with self-losing attitudes.

O Father, help me to be a disciplined self, disciplined by Thy love and power, not by my strained trying. Amen.

AFFIRMATION FOR THE DAY: *My soul now disciplined can dance along life's way.*

EVERYTHING FOR THE LOVE OF GOD

We come to the last step in dealing with the self. Seventh, *Do everything you do for the love of God.* You have been doing everything for the love of self; now do everything for the love of God. This changed motive will glorify everything. The menial task now becomes the meaningful task, for it is done for the love of God.

On an evangelistic tour of Japan, going to seventy-two cities in three months, speaking from two to five times a day, with many meetings lasting over two and a half hours, changing beds every night and meeting new people and situations every day, I asked myself: "Why do you do this at your age? Why aren't you slowing down instead of accelerating?" And the answer came back, "I love to do it. It's fun. It's fun to do everything for the love of God. Life then becomes a play spell. I do it because I can't help it. No credit."

A wealthy man watched a missionary nurse attending to lepers in China. He said to her, "I wouldn't do that for a million." And the nurse quietly replied: "Neither would I. But I do it gladly for the love of God."

This is the deepest discipline of self I know—do everything you do for the love of God. Then you are not struggling to keep the self under; you are expressing the self on another level with another motive. Then the self partakes of the glorifying of the task; the self itself is also glorified.

Paul says: "The love of Christ constraineth us"—narrows us, holds us in check, keeps us in bounds. This then is not a negative holding down of the self, but a positive expression of the self. It is a Yes, not a No. It does not end in strained effort, but in constrained overflow. You are disciplined by the mightiest and the gentlest force in the universe—the love of Christ. When the natives of Africa, puzzled by Dr. Albert Schweitzer's coming among them to serve their sick and wounded, asked him why he came, he answered very simply, "Jesus sent me." That phrase "Jesus sent me" has been the source of the world's greatest service and has been the secret of the world's greatest servants.

O Christ, Thy love goes to my depths and holds me and frees me in the holding. I thank Thee. Amen.

AFFIRMATION FOR THE DAY: *The love of Christ will constrain me and train me in everything.*

OUR REACTIONS

We are looking at the things that choke or cancel out our growth. We must look at something akin to the unsurrendered self. The test of whether the self is surrendered or unsurrendered is our reactions to what happens to us.

If the self is surrendered, we react on the whole with love, but when the self is unsurrendered, then we react in resentment, anger, self-pity, or retreatism. It is a simple but profound test. So the reactions are a revelation.

What we do to life around us is important—our actions count. We become what we do. But what life does to us is just as important, for we become our reactions. We become what we react. Our reactions not only reveal us; they make us.

There are many who are converted and correct in their actions, but they are not converted in their reactions. They don't lie, nor steal, nor commit adultery, nor get drunk. They are correct in their actions. But they react badly to what happens to them—they react into resentments or self-pity. Wrong actions can and do spoil us, but wrong reactions just as definitely and devastatingly spoil us. And sometimes more so. For you can make a case to justify the wrong reaction: "Look what they did to me"; "Why should this sorrow happen to me?" "I didn't do anything to deserve this." But whether justified or unjustified, wrong reactions will leave us devastated.

Here are two people who have the same thing happen to them: One lady loses her son, a medical student. She puts her spacious home at the disposal of medical students, makes them welcome, does everything she can for them, and does all this in the name of and for the sake of her son. She turns the loss of her son into gain for other people's sons. She is adjusted and happy. But another woman loses her son, goes into excessive, unhealthy grief, shuts herself away from life, and nurses her grief. It leaves her just as devastated a personality as going out and breaking all the moral codes would do.

O Jesus, Thou who didst react in love to every person and every happening, help me to do the same. Amen.

AFFIRMATION FOR THE DAY: *My aim in life: all my actions and all my reactions Christian!*

REACTING BADLY TO WHAT HAPPENS TO US

Take these statements from one of our Ashrams on "The Morning of the Open Heart" where we tell our needs: (1) "My witness is marred by irritability in the home and in the school." (2) "I get so upset. I need to find the answer. I need to plug into God's power." (3) "I came here for fellowship. My wife died fourteen months ago. I'm lonely." (4) "I'm self-centered, thinking of what others think of me." (5) "There is a bitterness in my heart. My daughter married a Roman Catholic."

Sometimes we react to the wrong thing and leave the central problem untouched—we react to the results of our sins and not to the sins. An Assyrian war lord who lived before Christ, wailed:

The rules for making offerings to the dead and libations to the ghosts of the kings my ancestors, which had not been practised, I reintroduced. I did well unto God and man, to dead and living. Why have sickness, ill-health, misery and misfortune befallen me? I cannot get away with the strife in my country and dissensions in my family. Disturbing scandals oppress me always. Misery of mind and of the flesh bow me down; with cries of woe I bring my days to an end. . . . How long, O God, wilt thou deal thus with me? Even as one who hath not feared god and goddess am I reckoned.

Toynbee the historian comments:

This confession is moving in its sincerity, and even pathetic in its bewilderment, but above all it is illuminating in its blindness. When this mood overtook him, did the last of the Assyrian war-lords never find himself silently reciting that terrible catalogue of cities sacked and peoples wiped out by Assyrian arms?"

The answer is No. For he was reacting to the wrong thing—to the results of his sins and not to his sins.

We often do that. Instead of reacting in repentance and reformation to our sins, we moan and bewail the results of our sins and feel self-pity. This road leads us to a dead end—we are frustrated.

O God, our Father, help me to react in repentance to my sins and not react in self-pity for the results of my sins. Amen.

AFFIRMATION FOR THE DAY: *If my reactions are to be Christian, my repentance must be Christian!*

PHYSICAL RESULTS OF WRONG REACTIONS

We have seen how some react to the results of their sins and not to the sins themselves. This is devastating. But devastation can set in also if we react badly, not to evil, but to such things as limited ability. A man was frustrated all his life about not being able to see the results that Moody the evangelist had. But one day the conflict was resolved when he came to the conclusion that God got hold of a bigger man when He got hold of Moody. That simple adjustment to a fact removed his frustration. A woman was adjusted when she ceased comparing her life and its results with another. She decided she was called to do her work, with her ability, and not some other woman's work. Your limited ability may be an asset in that it makes you draw more heavily on God.

We have looked at the spiritual results. We must now look at the physical results of wrong reactions. Dr. Alvarez, the great stomach specialist at the Mayo Clinic, quotes a patient:

All my trouble must be psychic in origin, because my first attack came twenty-five years ago when my girl refused to marry me; the second came later when she changed her mind and I had the excitement of a big wedding; the third came, when in the crash of 1907 I got caught with all my money tied up in a copper mine; the fourth came in 1918 with the strain of my participation in the Argonne drive; the fifth came in 1929 when I lost all my savings.

Dr. Karen Horney tells of a man who felt well when he went to a musical comedy with his wife and some friends. During the show his head began to ache and he blamed it on the show, which was not as good as "the one he would have preferred." Then he realized that he resented being overruled in the choice of plays—hence the headache.

Reactions react upon the total person and especially the body. We upset or set up our organs by our reactions.

Father, Thou art hemming us in. We cannot react against Thee without reacting against ourselves. Amen.

AFFIRMATION FOR THE DAY: *My reactions determine me, so I shall determine them.*

"HE MAKES ME SICK"

Dr. James Dale Van Buskirk tells of a patient, a widowed mother of a grown daughter, who had migraine headaches almost every time she unsuccessfully attempted to dominate her daughter.

Dr. William Sadler says:

Psychoneurotic pain is not imaginary; it is as real and as distressing to the patient as "organic" pain, and the accompanying fear and anxiety make it worse. Since emotional maladjustment is the basis of such fear and anxiety as well as the symptom itself, these reactions are more intense than those based on bonafide organic difficulty.

We say of people: "That man is a headache." He is, because we react in resentment against him. Again we say: "She's a pain in the neck." She is, because the resentments toward her tie up the nerves in the neck, and we get a pain. We say to one another, "You'll make yourself sick over this matter," and we do. Our reaction makes us sick—literally. When Woodrow Wilson said to Lloyd George in a crisis, "You make me sick," he probably did. Such expressions as "pale with horror"; "stiff with fear"; "so angry I couldn't see"; "my knees quaked with fear"; "goose flesh rose up all over me"; "speechless with dismay"—all these expressions embody the experience of the race and register the physical results of our reactions to what happens around us.

Add to these physical results the personality results, and we can see how decisive are our reactions, one way or the other.

The effect of conflict can be seen in this: A mail driver became engaged to a fine young widow. The date was set for the marriage. Just before the ceremony, he became ill; the ceremony was postponed. Another date was set, but just before the day, he ran his truck into the abutment of a bridge and was killed. The widow called up his home folks in another city to condole with them. She found he had a wife and family. His illness and the accident were purposeful—to get him out of an inner dilemma.

O God, we thank Thee that our actions and our reactions are driving us to Thee. We cannot get along with ourselves unless we get along with Thee. Amen.

AFFIRMATION FOR THE DAY: *Since my body and my soul will register my reactions, I shall decide what I register.*

STEPS TO CHRISTIAN REACTIONS

We come now to the steps we are to take to develop Christian reactions to what happens to us.

First, *Settle in your thinking the matter, To whom do you belong?* If you belong to yourself, you'll be touchy when that self is touched. You will react in resentments when someone crosses the self. You will live on the defensive. And he who lives on the defensive lives by fear. If you belong to the herd, you will be very sensitive to what the herd does or does not do. You will always be "in hot water" with the herd—nervous, going up and down with the approval or disapproval of the herd.

But if you belong to Christ, you will react with His reactions.

Second, *Study how Jesus reacted to what happened to Him.* Take the central tragedy that befell Him—the Cross. When He made the announcement to His disciples that He was going to the cross, there were four reactions: (1) Peter reacted in fussy, self-assertive assumption of authority. "Peter took him and began to reprove him for it; 'God forbid, Lord,' he said. 'This must not be!'" (Matt. 16:22, Moffatt). The authority which Jesus had just given Peter went to his head, and he began to be managerial and officious.

(2) The mother of James and John reacted in an ambitious attempt to get something out of the tragedy for her sons. She tried to get places at Jesus' right and left hand for them. We often react in ambition, trying to gather out of happenings, however tragic, something for ourselves.

(3) The ten reacted in anger: "When the ten heard of this, they were angry at the two brothers" (v. 24, Moffatt). We often react in anger at other people's reactions.

(4) There was the reaction of Jesus to this tragedy—He decided to use the catastrophe: The Son of man had come, He said, "to give his life as a ransom for many" (v. 28). He made the tragedy redemptive. He rescued victory out of defeat.

O Christ, Thou didst turn Thyself from a victim to a victor by Thy reaction. Help me to do the same. Amen.

AFFIRMATION FOR THE DAY: *All my disasters shall be doors, for I shall meet them as Jesus did.*

IMPERVIOUS TO PRAISE OR BLAME

We saw yesterday that Jesus reacted constructively to what happened to Him. He took the worst thing that could happen to Him. namely, His death, and turned it into the best thing that could happen to the world, namely, its redemption. We must learn the secret of reacting constructively.

Third, *Discipline yourself to a certain imperviousness to both praise and blame.* Someone has said, "But the man who maneuvers for compliments and praise, putting his back in a position to be easily patted, is thereby rendering himself vulnerable." If he gets praise, he is falsely up; and if he doesn't get it, he is falsely down. Determine beforehand to lay at the feet of Jesus both praise and blame—the praise to belong to Him, and the blame to belong to both of us for correction, if true, and to both of us to use it, if untrue.

Fourth, *Often you can take sides with your critics against yourself and be more severe than they have been.* A good motto is: "Severe with self; gentle with others; and loving with everybody." The only real way to correct others is to correct yourself. Then others, seeing the correction in you, are corrected by that correction. A slum worker tried in vain to get the slum children to wash their faces. No result. Then she brought a clean child into their midst, and they began to go off and get their faces washed.

Francis of Assisi used the method of self-criticism. In his *Little Flowers* he says he is able to bear the attacks of harsh opponents who say terrible things by reminding himself, "humbly and charitably," that the critic knows him truly. Crucify yourself; then you can't be crucified by others—it's already done!

When a minister publicly made an attack on Emerson, while he was in the audience, someone of the Middlebury faculty attempted to apologize to Emerson, but Emerson said genially: "I thought your minister was a very conscientious, plain-spoken gentleman." There it was buried, as far as Emerson was concerned. He reacted as a Christian should. The reaction was the release.

O Christ, teach me the secret of spontaneous right reactions. Help me naturally to show Thy spirit. Amen.

AFFIRMATION FOR THE DAY: *Praise and blame shall find me unswerving toward my central goal.*

GIVE OUT LOVE TO EVERYBODY

We come to another step in our reactions. Fifth, *Keep on growing so that anything derogatory that is said about you will belong to the man who was and not to the man who is.* Dr. Elton Trueblood quotes a contemporary college president who, when asked how he could keep his composure in the face of continual shots fired at him from students, from professors, from alumni, and from the general public, replied, with a broad and generous smile: "Oh, I just keep moving and let the shots drop behind me."

Sixth, *Make it a life attitude to give out love to everybody—good, bad, or indifferent—whether they be friend or foe.* This is always safe. "Love never fails," for the giving out of love is the victory. If the person concerned accepts it, then you have won; if he does not accept it, you have also won, for you are the more loving.

Seventh, *In everything that happens look for the growing point.* Every disturbance can disturb you upward.

Here is what a minister, stricken with polio, said after having seen the possibility of not merely bearing this disability but of *using* it: "When I found my leg muscles atrophied with paralysis it occurred to me that this was an opportunity to explore the possibilities of Christian faith in personal experience. But how could I *use* polio?" And then, lying in bed, he came to the following conclusions:

1. I would keep alert for ways in which the polio experience could be used. 2. Few people live over eighty years. Even this is such a short span that time itself limits the occupations one can pursue, the experiences he can have, and the good he can do. 3. Paralysis arbitrarily limits me. Nevertheless, if I had to spend the rest of my life in bed, there are still so many possibilities open to me that I would not have time to explore them all, even if I did live eighty years. 4. Why give any thought, then, to those things that were beyond the limits of my physical powers? 5. I would replace such negative thoughts by devising ways to do things that are within my scope.

He reacted constructively to polio and made polio into power.

O Jesus, Thou who didst take all that came and didst make it into something else, help me to do the same. Amen.

AFFIRMATION FOR THE DAY: *Everything that comes today shall be grist for my Kingdom mill.*

THE HERD HINDERS GROWTH

We come now to study another factor which keeps us from being growing persons—the herd.

I once flew down the center of Africa, and again and again I could see herds of wildebeest feeding. Invariably there would be four sentinels standing at the four corners of a square facing away from the herd, impassively watching for the approach of an enemy. They stood there, eating nothing, on guard.

The herd protects us, gives us a sense of a common life and a sense of security. We belong. Without the sense of belonging we are ill at ease and frustrated. The rogue elephant is the elephant which has been put out of the herd by the other male elephants; he turns destructive, tearing up gardens and huts and creating havoc in general. He is out of the herd, hence beside himself. We too are social beings and cannot live a full life apart from society.

Here is what a brilliant German doctor once wrote me: "Any how I am at the point where I can get along with anybody except people." And then she added: "For myself. It is strange watching my self deteriorate more and more. I can't help it. Send me a good word." But a good word from me would have done little. She was bottled up within herself, cut off from the herd.

Dr. Overstreet says that the human personality has four needs: (1) the need to belong; (2) the need for independence; (3) the need for reasonable security; (4) the need for personal significance. The first need is the need to belong. But this need to belong must be compatible with and must further and sustain the other three. We must belong to something that gives us independence, that gives reasonable security, and that gives us personal significance. If we belong to the herd, does it give us these three things? Obviously it does not. It makes us subservient, makes us go up and down with the fortunes of the herd.

Here, then, is the dilemma: We must be members of society, and yet if we belong to it, we are stunted.

O God, our Father, teach us the way out of this dilemma. Give us Thy answer. In Jesus' name. Amen.

AFFIRMATION FOR THE DAY: *It is inevitable that my life be lived in the herd, but my springs shall be Elsewhere.*

85

LOVING SOMETHING MORE THAN THE HERD

We saw yesterday the dilemma: If we belong to the herd, we are stunted; and if we are not members of the herd, we are frustrated. What is the way out?

The way out with the herd is the way out for the individual. The herd must be deliberately and decisively surrendered to God. You no longer belong to it; you belong to God. The tyranny of the herd is broken—you are emancipated from it by a higher loyalty. But now that the power of the herd over you is broken, you can be a member of the herd, an emancipated member. Inwardly you are free, free to be a member of the herd, because you do not *belong* to it. You are *in* it, but not *of* it.

You can be loyal to the herd as long as loyalty to the herd is consistent with loyalty to God, your supreme loyalty. When it is not consistent, you break with the herd—break with it on one level, hoping that you will thereby meet it on a higher level. The break is not for the sake of a break, but for the sake of meeting on a higher level. You hope that by your break you will call attention to the evil with which you are compelled to break, and that the herd thereby will renounce it and meet you on a higher level. If it doesn't, then you are on a higher level, awaiting the step-up of the herd. The break is not for the sake of a break, but for the sake of a higher fellowship. This makes a clean break instead of an infected one—infected with cantankerousness, or resentments, or self-pity.

You can now love the herd since you love something more than the herd. The herd is no longer God. You are no longer afraid of it. Now you can love it with a love that is not corroded with fear.

The supreme example of identification with the herd and yet with an inner isolation from the herd is Jesus. He identified Himself with men so deeply that their sorrows became His sorrows, their sins His sins, at a cross. And yet He did not belong to the herd; He belonged to the Father. With that supreme allegiance intact He could go into the herd emancipated.

O Father, since I belong supremely to Thee now, send my emancipated soul deeply into the herd to lift it. Amen.

AFFIRMATION FOR THE DAY: *The herd shall feel my life, but it shall not determine my life.*

"THE CONTAGION OF THE WORLD'S SLOW STAIN"

We come now to see how when we have wrong relations with the herd, it keeps us from growing.

When the herd becomes God and determines our conduct, then all human relations are thrown into confusion. Take the case of Herod. He made a foolish oath to give the daughter of Herodias anything she asked. When she asked for the head of John the Baptist, Herod was sad, "but for the sake of his oaths and his guests he did not care to disappoint her" (Mark 6:26, Moffatt). He made a foolish oath because of the herd—the guests, and having put his feet into that fly paper, he did not know how to get out, and so he ordered the head of John to be brought, because he couldn't reverse himself before the herd. Not the fear of God but the fear of men determined his conduct and left him a miserable murderer of the one man he respected most. He killed his conscience when he killed John the Baptist, for John was his conscience. The herd snuffed out the last flickering ray of light within Herod. Many thus succumb to the herd. Often the statement applies: "Beware of the contagion of the world's slow stain." The herd standards invade us, and we take them over, and our Christianity is slowly stained out of us.

Take the religious leaders of the days of Jesus. They might have been the agents of the coming of the New Order, the Kingdom of God. But in the crisis their minds were filled with what men thought of them: "Besides, all they do is done to catch the notice of men" (Matt. 23:5, Moffatt). They looked around, not up, and hence when the Kingdom of God was offered to them, they missed its meaning and are marked down as the most pathetic figures in history. They were angling for the notice of men and missed the signs of the coming Kingdom.

Sometimes the herd appeal is so strong that we blindly follow it—to our doom. "Everybody does it" is the last gurgle you can hear as men and women are submerged into the herd.

Father, give me the moral courage to be inwardly and outwardly different. Help me to be myself—in Thee. Amen.

AFFIRMATION FOR THE DAY: *To resist the herd when necessary, to raise it always.*

"ALIBI PARKING LOT"

We continue to look at the effects of our following the herd blindly.

Often men escape into the herd as men escape into alcohol. They refuse to make moral choices of their own—they escape into anonymity. They simply echo the herd. The herd becomes God. They are herd-centered and herd-directed and herd-submerged. Their personality is canceled. In this way they escape criticism—the criticism of standing for something and therefore of being something. But the price is heavy. They become an echo instead of a voice.

"The way to escape criticism is to say nothing, think nothing, and be nothing." And the best way to this escape seems to be to take the anesthetic of merging yourself into the herd. Then you move into the kind of state depicted by the sign on a parking lot: "Alibi Parking Lot." Many are parked there. The herd is the alibi. The standards, the customs, and the mentality of the herd are taken over, and they become the alibi for not being morally independent and free. Here was a young singer who felt that unless she drank liquor with the herd, she would be "out." So she suppressed her conscience and her training and parked in "Alibi Parking Lot." She is spiritually only the half-person of what she was. She felt that she could win the herd by doing what the herd does. This is a mistake. If you are to win the herd, you must win the herd to something. To win it to something you must have something and be something different, or else there is nothing to win the herd to.

I have just been in a place where I asked the usual question: "What is the special characteristic of this place?" I got back this illuminating reply: "The people of this place never commit themselves publicly to anything. They perpetually look at one another waiting for a cue—a straw to show which way the wind blows." And then I asked, "What are the special products of this place?" And then the illuminating reply: "We have no special products." Many of us are like those men. We don't vote; we veto—we veto our very selves. We stand for nothing, so we mean nothing, are nothing.

O God our Father, help me to be Thine primarily and then fit in all my lesser loyalties to that central loyalty. Amen.

AFFIRMATION FOR THE DAY: *I shall vote with my life, even if I have to vote alone.*

"EVERYBODY DOES IT"

As I was about to go across a street, a woman pulled me by the arm and said, "Look at the red light." I replied rather weakly: "But look at the people going across," and her reply was: "Don't look at them. Look up at the light and follow it." Good advice. For she put the whole thing in a nutshell. Are you getting your walking signals in life from God, or from the herd? Are you breaking His laws to keep step with them?

Here was a woman whose home was about to go on the rocks. And it was over a very tiny thing—her husband disliked red fingernails. I urged her to let the red fingernails go and keep a warm relationship with her husband. But she looked at me in dismay and said: "How can I? Everybody does it." That settled it—"Everybody does it"—husband or no husband, home or no home, she must keep step with "Everybody"—whoever that is!

There is an interesting account of how the Pharisees joined with the Herodians "to trap him in talk." They said, "Teacher, we know that you are sincere and that you teach the Way of God honestly and fearlessly; you do not court human favour. Tell us, then, what do you think about this: is it right to pay taxes to Caesar or not?" (Matt. 22:15-17, Moffatt). They wanted to catch Him on the horns of a dilemma: If He said "No," He was in trouble with the government; if He said "Yes," he was in trouble with the people. But Jesus was caught on neither horn, and he passed straight through the dilemma, and the result of this maneuvering on the part of His enemies was to leave this statement for the ages to see: "You do not court human favor." He sought God's favor first, last, and always, and as a result He has gained human favor as no one on this planet has gained it. We are at His feet. They sought human favor first, last, and always and lost it—the ages being witness. And with it they lost themselves. The god they worshiped—the herd—let them down. It always does.

O Father God, I thank Thee that the grip of the herd is broken when we surrender to Thee. Amen.

AFFIRMATION FOR THE DAY: *Emancipated from the herd, now I shall be able to emancipate the herd.*

STEPS IN GAINING FROM THE HERD

What we have been saying about the herd needs the other side to make a fair picture. If the herd often stunts us, to live without it will also stunt us. James K. Polk in his first year in the University of North Carolina would have little to do with the other students. He would not join a literary society, would not eat at the "commons," walked six miles to get his meals, was unsocial, and was considered "queer." The next year he reversed his attitudes, became a member of Dialectic Society, and was elected head of it twice. Had he continued his first-year attitude, he would never have become President of the United States.

You can't live under the herd, and you cannot live apart from the herd. What is to be done? The steps in gaining freedom from the herd and within the herd are these:

First, *Do with the herd what you do with yourself if you are to be free—namely, surrender it to God.* Just as there are self-centered people, so there are herd-centered people. And just as self-centered people get release from themselves by the surrender of themselves to God, so herd-centered people can get release from the herd by the surrender of it to God. God is God, not the herd.

Second, *Now that the herd is subordinate and God is primary, you are free to go into the herd because you have an inner check—your primary loyalty to God.* You can go with the herd as long as this primary loyalty is not violated. When it is, then you break with the herd. Then the herd will respect that loyalty, for they know that they cannot keep you if that loyalty is violated. It is a check on them. You come to a working agreement with the herd. You are adjusted.

"Once you become truly dependent upon Him, you become automatically independent of others."

If you seek first the Kingdom of God, then all these things, including the herd—and yourself—will be added to you.

O Christ, Thou wert above, aloof, and alone and yet how deeply in. Help me to Thy attitudes. Amen.

AFFIRMATION FOR THE DAY: *Nothing above the Kingdom, nothing against the Kingdom, everything for the Kingdom.*

YOU CAN LOVE THE HERD—PROVIDED!

Now that you are adjusted to the herd—it is in its place, subordinate—you can appreciate the herd and love it.

Third, *The herd can help you to grow. Look on it as the agent of redemption to you.* The herd can give you release from self-preoccupation—a very important release. The herd can give you avenues of outgoingness. This passage gives us that insight: "Let us consider how to stir up one another to love and good deeds, not ceasing to meet together, as is the habit of some, but admonishing one another" (Heb. 10:24-25, Moffatt). Note: "how to stir up one another to love and good works"—often we stir up jealousy and resentments in one another. But the group can stir up the best in you and not the worst.

Fourth, *Expect much from the herd, but don't expect too much.* Otherwise you will be disappointed and disillusioned. Many people go from group to group, thinking each time that they have found the perfect group. Then the "idol" is found to have feet of clay. And disillusionment sets in. Then you become a homeless soul wandering again in search of a perfect group. You won't find it. For if it were perfect before you got into it, it would not be perfect after.

Accept the group with all its imperfections. And then give yourself to making it better. In the effort to make it better, without disillusionment and without cynicism, you yourself will be better. For your endeavors become you.

Fifth, *Don't go to the herd to see what you can get out of it but what you can give to it.* If you go to the herd only to get something out of it, you'll get little. But if you go to it in order to contribute to the group and through it to others, then you'll get much—as a by-product. You'll lose yourself and find yourself again. You will grow with the growth of the group. But even if the group doesn't respond to your efforts, you are the better for having given them. In any case you win.

To sum up: The herd can be a tyranny, or it can be an opportunity, according to where you put it. If you belong to it, you're sunk; if it belongs to you, because you belong to God, then you're saved and free.

O Christ, teach me that secret of being like and yet unlike, of being a part and yet apart. Amen.

AFFIRMATION FOR THE DAY: *Society shall be not a force for my suppression; but my field of operation.*

HARDENING OF PRESENT ATTITUDES

We have been looking at the various specific things that hinder growth. Before we pass on to the growth in specific phases of our lives, we must look at something that stops growth more than any other thing—*simple hardening of present attitudes and attainments.* The hardening of the *is* prevents the *to-be.* The present is often the enemy of the future, for it often keeps the future from being anything but the present. The present becomes like domineering parents who won't let their children grow up in their own ways, but keep jamming them back into yesterday.

A few days ago I was being shown a breath-taking garden of dahlias, some of them twelve to sixteen inches across. The man who showed me his flowers, and who loved them, stopped and plucked a gorgeous dahlia, and when I looked surprised, he said: "This bloom is past its prime. If I don't pluck it, the plant will think its work is done and cease blooming. But if I pluck this, it will go to work again and start producing more blooms."

Many of us are progressively damned, not by what we do, but because we are content with what we have done. We call it a day and sink into the *is* and refuse the call of the *to-be.* A milkman put a note on each of his customers' bottles: "This milk is not from contented cows. Our cows are striving to be better and better every day." If we are contented cows, then we're just cows—contented moral cows in our plump comfortableness!

We often speak of hardening of the arteries as one of the greatest dangers in advancing years, but Dr. Douglas Speere speaks of a greater danger: "the hardening of the categories." We harden our viewpoint, refuse to look at anything beyond that viewpoint; we groove our thinking and acting, and the grooves get deeper and deeper until they become graves that bury us.

As someone put it, "You don't grow old; you get old by not growing." Some people are dead at forty although their funerals are postponed until they are sixty. Dead personalities.

O Father, Thou who art the ceaseless Creator, make me a ceaseless creator. Break my molds and give me new ones. Amen.

AFFIRMATION FOR THE DAY: *No good shall keep me from the better, no better keep me from the best.*

"GREAT IDEAS MAKE ME SLEEPY"

Grandma Moses took up painting after eighty, and at eighty-eight she says: "Anyone can paint who wants to. All you have to do is get the brush and paint and start in." She is still growing. It is grow up or go down.

But for many life has settled into ruts—mental, physical, spiritual ruts. And "a rut is a grave with both ends knocked out." In Canada was a sign on a dirt road: "Choose your rut, you'll be in it for the next twenty miles." When New Year's Day comes, many could say to themselves: "I'm choosing my ruts, for I'll be in them for the whole of the year." Life for them has no adventures, hence no surprises. It is dull, lusterless, and will soon be an ash.

Many are like the man in H. G. Wells's *Croquet Players,* who exclaimed in irritation: "I am willing to fall in with anything that promises any good. But if I am to *think,* it is too much." An African chief said: "Great ideas make me sleepy."

One of the kings of France in a crisis sat and listened while a representative of the people presented their case. His well-fed majesty promptly went to sleep. His mind was asleep, so his body followed suit. That sleep cost him his life. Our mental sleep costs us our future, for an alert present means an alert future.

A professor lost his wife, upon whom he was greatly dependent. It shook him. He began to go to pieces. Then he remarried and was his own vivacious, sparkling self again. Commenting on it, he said this significant sentence: "I got tired of looking over my shoulders to the past." When men look back, they are back. They sigh over the past, and their souls sigh over them. They belong to "the cult of the Backward Look." The founder of the cult was Lot's wife. She looked back and became a pillar of salt. And tasteless salt at that. Jesus speaks of "salt become insipid" (Matt. 5:13, Moffatt). And then he adds: "After that it is fit for nothing." Lives out of which the taste has gone—insipid, uninspiring, noncreative—this description would fit a large part of the church members today.

O Christ, give me the taste of growth, the feeling of going forward, the sense of opening vistas and great adventures. Amen.

AFFIRMATION FOR THE DAY: *Life shall have taste in it, for I shall put the taste of living interest into it.*

"NARY A DROP IN OR OUT"

Mrs. Overstreet tells of being met at the station by a welcoming committee in a town where she was to speak. In describing the people of the town they said: "Perhaps you'd like to know something about us. We don't drink, we don't smoke, we don't dance, we don't swear, but we have no significant virtues." We have no significant virtues! Only virtues out of which the *vir*—strength—has gone. They had goodness which was good for nothing. It was negative—"We don't."

A man stood up in a meeting and said: "Twenty years ago my cup was filled, and since that time nary a drop has gone into it and nary a drop has come out of it." Another, hearing, said: "Then by this time there must be wiggle-tails in it." And there were! If we are not being refilled constantly, then there are bound to be wiggle-tails in our souls. We breed larvae which breed mosquitoes which breed malaria. We spread something if we spread nothing—the negative nothing passes into the positive something and that something harmful.

Coleridge gives a biting description of many who have "bed-ridden truths which lie asleep in the dormitory of their minds." Many of us hold truths, but they are "bed-ridden truths"—they don't walk and dance and go in procession with banners waving. They are asleep when the world is awake, bedfast when the world is on the march.

Dr. Halford Luccock in *Marching off the Map* quotes Gibbons' indictment of the monks of Constantinople, the sterile pedants of the tenth century: "They held in their lifeless hands the riches of their fathers, without inheriting the spirit which had created that sacred patrimony. They read; they praised; they compiled; but their languid souls seemed alike incapable of action and thought." If Jesus were here today, he would probably say, "Beware of the leaven of the monks of Constantinople." And He would look straight into our eyes and read there the same sterility. Amid the bustle of this age there is the same dead center.

O Father, wake us up lest we sleep the sleep of death. Stab us broad awake with Thy Spirit. Amen.

AFFIRMATION FOR THE DAY: *All my truths alive and in operation today, no bed-ridden truths!*

"HE CLEANS OUT THE GUTTERS OF MY MIND"

Here is an English lady, intelligent and gracious, who said rather pathetically: "I'd like to leave India and go back to England, but I can't. I have a dog and a horse I can't leave." Her whole life bound to a dog and a horse! Her interest centered around a small interest, her whole life grew small with the smallness of that interest.

It was said of George Appley that when friends and relatives gathered around his bed to catch his last words, they heard a solemn whisper: "Do not disturb the rose bushes." He lived in a world of rose bushes, which was good, but not good enough. He was caught by interests too small for a child of eternity.

If our interests become small, our outlook becomes small too, and the very smallness clogs us. In a cave where there were many gorgeous stalactites and stalagmites, the guide told us that the stalactites stop growing when the tiny hole in the center, through which the liquid is poured, is stopped up. When the channel is clogged, growth stops. Many are spiritual stalactites with channels clogged.

We need perpetually to get rid of the things that clog mind and spirit. Someone asked a working woman why she went to hear a preacher who was noted for his thoughtful sermons and got this surprising reply: "He cleans out the gutters of my mind." We need to have the gutters of our minds and spirits perpetually cleansed.

We need to have old, lingering griefs cleaned away. A woman kept the body of her son killed in the World War in her home in a hermetically sealed coffin for four years. "I can't think of him being placed in the cold earth. I want him beside me." She didn't know it, but she was slowly committing suicide as a personality in brooding over a dead past.

A prominent pastor, widely known, lost his wife, and instead of taking the tragedy in his stride as a Christian should, he went to pieces under it, lost his faith, and ended in a sanitarium. He too was trying to hold a dead past instead of using that tragedy to make present tasks more beautiful.

O God, we come to Thee for cleansing of our minds and spirits from dead forms and festering griefs. Amen.

AFFIRMATION FOR THE DAY: *No choked springs; all my springs free and flowing.*

"THE WICKED WALK IN CIRCLES"

One of the chief emphases in the New Testament is *hope*. It is not something extraneous, stuck in to back up the flagging spirits of men. It is something that expresses the very nature of the Christian faith. For the Christian faith believes in progress—an eternal progress.

The non-Christian faiths never have believed in progress. It is interesting that the chakra, or circle, was developed in Greece, India, and China about the same time, as representing the belief that life is a circle, turning around on itself endlessly. In such a scheme hope could have no place, for life perpetually turned back on itself, coming back to where it had been. In fact, hope was looked on as an evil.

Then comes the Christian faith with its belief in progress for the individual and for society. This brought to birth a new thing—hope. "We are saved by hope." "Prove equally keen upon realizing your full hope to the very end, so that, instead of being slack, you may imitate those who inherit the promises by their stedfast faith." (Heb. 6:11-12, Moffatt.) "May the God of your hope so fill you with all joy and peace in your faith, that you may be overflowing with hope, by the power of the holy Spirit!" (Rom. 15:13, Moffatt.)

According to Dr. John Baillie the wise man among the ancient non-Christians was "the man who is as much without hope as he is without fear, the man who is altogether indifferent to what the future may bring." He saw no future, hence was not interested in it at all. Paul reminds the Gentile Christians that at one time they were "without hope."

Then came the mighty stimulus of a faith that believed in and produced progress—progress in the total man, for the total humanity. Hope was born. Whenever real Christianity is operative, there hope is born and there hope flourishes.

Augustine translates Psalm 12:8: "The wicked walk in circles." They do. They get nowhere. But a great many Christians "walk in circles"—they too do not get anywhere.

O Father, shake me out of my circles. Let me have a deathless hope of an infinite plan, infinitely unfolding. Amen.

AFFIRMATION FOR THE DAY: *No going in circles for me. I take the Open Road, always.*

STEPS FOR BREAKING THE STALEMATE

We come to face now the problem of how to break up this stalemate in our lives and begin growing again.

First, *Make up your mind that though the body is doomed to decay, the mind and spirit are not a part of that decay unless we allow them to be.* If you have bound the two together and expect them to decay together, then break that fatal alliance and declare the independence of mind and spirit. They are capable of an infinite growth. Clear up to the end of an earthly existence they can be alert and growing. Expect it and plan for it.

Second, *Do as someone suggested: "Take out your brain and jump on it," if it has become hardened and unresponsive.* This may be the equivalent of "shock treatment"—personally administered. It will jolt your thinking and attitudes out of the old ruts and start them into new and constructive channels. A doctor said to a minister: "You've got to get a new faith or undergo shock treatment." The new faith is shock treatment. It jolts life out of the old into the new.

Third, *Don't look back over your shoulder at past achievements. Look forward to future accomplishments.* A woman of thirty-five was told by her dentist that there were twenty-six cavities in her teeth, but that her teeth could be saved; this was her last chance, and it would cost $175. She said she would consult her mother. She came back and said: "My mother says that now that I have caught my man, it isn't necessary to go to that expenditure." She had caught her man, but something else had caught her—decay. And she surrendered to that decay. And the real surrender was mental.

A sign on the roadside said in reference to the coming of Christ: "Millions now living will never die." Someone wrote under it: "Millions now living are already dead." Don't surrender to death; surrender to Life.

Jesus said, "No man, having put his hand to the plough, and looking back, is fit for [or can fit into] the Kingdom of God." He cannot fit into the Kingdom, for the Kingdom is ongoing, outreaching, creative, redemptive. Only those who live by a Yes can belong to it.

O Jesus, I thank Thee that belonging to Thee, I belong to Life, and Life belongs to me. I'm grateful. Amen.

AFFIRMATION FOR THE DAY: *I belong not to the Men of the Backward Look, but to the Men of the Forward Look.*

DO SOMETHING EACH DAY YOU'VE NEVER DONE BEFORE

We continue the steps to break up old molds and patterns of thought and action.

Fourth, *Do something new each day—something you have never done.* An able doctor lecturing to us in the Sat Tal Ashram said:

> Break up the old patterns of thought and action by doing something you don't usually do. If you've walked on a pavement, now walk through a plowed field; if you have regular meals, do without one to show you can; if you get a full night's sleep every night, have one in which you don't sleep, to prove you can do without a night's sleep. Break up the routine, for the routine may become a rut.

Speak to someone you've never spoken to; visit someone you've never visited, especially people of another class or color or religion. You'll find they are people just like you.

Fifth, *Keep a mental and spiritual wastebasket near so you can throw into it outworn categories, outworn habits, and outworn thoughts.* Someone asked a successful college president what was the outstanding necessity for a college president, and he replied, "A wastebasket." Throw away the bad to get the good, throw away the good to get the better, and throw away the better to get the best, and throw away your best to get His best.

A man who was the head of a very important school pointed to an incinerator and said: "Without that this school could not go on." Out of the ashes of the old refuse and filth arise cleanliness and health. Life depends as much upon elimination as upon assimilation. A woman in Chicago piled up antiques in her huge house until she had only one tiny room left to live in. Many of her prize museum specimens had never been taken out of their boxes. She was smothered by the past—the past crowded her out of the present.

A Negro minister came out of a meeting and said to me afterward, "When I came away from your address, I felt like throwing away something. I reached into my pocket, felt a cigar, and threw it away." Whatever is a symbol of the old and outworn, throw it away.

O God, I empty my hands of old habits and attitudes, and I now take the Gift—the Gift of Thyself. Amen.

AFFIRMATION FOR THE DAY: *My wastebasket near today, into which will go all dead issues and forms.*

"BY ALL THE STIMULUS OF CHRIST"

We have been studying the things that hinder growth—things that tie us up. We now turn to the more positive side to look at the things that stimulate growth. We say things that stimulate, but the first thing we look at is not a thing, but a Person. The most absolutely stimulating fact that has ever had an impact upon the mind, the body, the soul, of the human race is Jesus of Nazareth. No other stimulus can be compared to Him. Other forces are faint echoes; He is a firsthand stimulus direct out of the heart of Reality.

Paul felt this and wrote: "By all the stimulus of Christ" (Phil. 2:1, Moffatt). We call him Saviour, and He is—gloriously a Saviour! But while He is a Saviour, He is just as much, and perhaps more, a Stimulator. He saves from the bad and the half-bad, and then He stimulates all the good, innate and introduced, and makes it grow and develop; and He will do so forever. The most wonderful thing about the Christian life is this: You are subjected to the most absolutely stimulating moral and spiritual and intellectual and physical force in the universe, namely, the spirit of Christ. And it stimulates in the right direction, with the right motives. It is not only stimulus; it is right stimulus. And it is a stimulus which we can accept in its entirety—"by *all* the stimulus of Christ." This is a stimulus of which you can't get too much! For it stimulates you to develop and to restrain. It keeps you from going into all sorts of sidetracks, for it is infinite Sanctity and infinite Sanity. It makes you burst your bonds and then helps you to keep your balance. It is the stimulus of Life.

The stimulus of Christ is the stimulus of an aggression. It is aggressive like the sun—"it coaxes a June out of a winter." It coaxes the bird out of the shell. It coaxes the song out of the saddened heart, and life out of the dead spirit. It is Life stimulating life and making it into its own image.

Aaron's rod that budded is nothing compared to the "sticks" that put out new buds of hope and achievement under the life-giving stimulus of Jesus.

O Christ, Thy hand touched the dead. Thy voice penetrated to them, and they arose. Do it again—to me.

AFFIRMATION FOR THE DAY: *All my being shall be exposed to all the stimulus of Christ.*

RUN-DOWN SOULS

We are meditating on the stimulus of Christ. Life has a tendency to run down, to get jaded and ragged at the edges, tired. Since many do not know of the stimulus of Christ, they turn to stimulants—something to pick them up, to tide them over.

This is an age of run-down lives trying to live on hand-to-mouth expedients. They know nothing of the exhilaration of Christ, so they turn to liquor, to drugs, to anything, for relief. But all such pick-me-ups are let-me-downs. The inevitable hang-over, the dark brown taste, the headache. Then more stimulants to pull you out of the results of the last ones and so on down the vicious corkscrew tail spin.

We are told that five million people in our country depend on sleeping tablets to put them to sleep. If they knew of the stimulus of Christ, they would also know of the sedative of Christ when nightfall comes. He stimulates all our powers and makes them work harmoniously and effectively, and then at nightfall we fall to sleep like babes, for we are natural and unstrained and full of peace. We are through with crutches; we can stand on our own two feet. We are not propped-up things; we are persons. We are stimulated from within.

Here is a sample of the run-down life, a statement from a Ph.D.: "I'm tired of reading philosophy. I'm tired of reading newspapers and magazines. I'm bored at home, I'm bored outside. I'm tired of my work. I am tired." That man needs a stimulant, but a stimulant of a different kind. He needs something at the center of his being, re-creating him there—an impact of Life upon life. Then his boredom with himself and his work would drop away, and he would know the zest of being alive to his fingertips.

In Japan I found a society called Roze with a button with O and a line drawn through it. When I asked the meaning of it, I was told that the word is Zero cut in two and reversed, so that what was zero becomes Roze. The purpose of this society was to do away with zeroism—negativism—and make life positive and masterful.

Jesus does that—He cancels out our zeroism. He makes life from the faded into the rosy. He is Life.

O Jesus, Thy impact and lo, all our sunsets turn to sunrises, all our winters into springs. Amen.

AFFIRMATION FOR THE DAY: *My quest for zest shall begin with the Best.*

"FAITH AND LOVE THAT JESUS CHRIST INSPIRES"

The simple fact is that life without Christ is insipid, full of boredom. The wages of sin is boredom. The vast endeavor of people is to put taste back into the salt of life that has lost its savor. Jesus said: "If the salt have lost his savour, wherewith shall it be salted?" And the vast entertainment and amusement world is an attempt—a futile attempt—to answer that question.

For life can get taste back only when it has total meaning, total value, total relevance, and total goal. But this cannot be had apart from Christ. No shot in the arm will do it, no temporary dodging of issues, no subterfuges will do it. For just as you cannot tell the subconscious mind a lie and get away with it, so you cannot tell life a lie and get away with it. Life will not accept the lie. It will sit and mope in its corner of the universe. It refuses to sing unless there is something to sing about. You simply cannot play tricks on life.

Jesus steps into all this disillusionment and boredom and stimulates everything He touches, and He touches everything. This passage depicts his impact: "Faith and love that Christ Jesus inspires" (I Tim. 1:14, Moffatt). Now, interestingly enough, psychology is more and more emphasizing these two things, faith and love, as centrally necessary to mental health. If you do not have faith, you become cynical; and if you do not have love, you become self-centered; and if you are cynical and self-centered, you are on the road to inner disruption. Only those who have faith in others and faith in themselves have the basis for mental and spiritual and hence physical soundness. And only those who have love—genuine, outgoing love for others—are themselves healthy personalities.

But you cannot have faith in and love for others unless they are rooted in faith in and love for some center other than a human center—God. So Jesus, by producing faith in and love for God, by making God worthy of faith and lovable, stimulates in men the two things essential to mental and spiritual and hence physical health. The impact of Jesus upon human nature has stimulated more growth than any other single influence.

O Jesus, I feel the tingle of Thy Spirit upon my spirit inspiring it to love and faith. I thank Thee. Amen.

AFFIRMATION FOR THE DAY: *Love and faith shall be the climate of my life today—and always.*

LIFE TIPPED FORWARD

We are studying how Christ puts zest and taste and worth-whileness into life with His impact upon our inner spirits. He is like the first rainfall of the monsoon in India—the dry, dusty ground, so barren and hard, the very next day has a green film of vegetation over it. The moisture touches the apparently dead soil, and lo, it is alive. So Jesus touches our parched and barren lives, and lo, they sprout with life and vitality and hope.

A workman in a factory told of how before Christ came, he always wore out his shoes at the heels, but after Christ came, he wore them out at the toes! Guilt, frustrations, fears, inferiorities, hopelessness, had tipped life back—made him rock back on his heels on the defensive. But Christ, by cleansing the guilt, frustrations, fears, inferiorities, and hopelessness, tipped life forward.

This passage expresses it: "We too might live and move in the new sphere of Life" (Rom. 6:4, Moffatt). Jesus brings a new sphere of Life where everything lives and lives abundantly. Outside of Him we live in the old sphere of Death; everything we touch withers, dies. All the colors of evil are fading colors; all the colors of Christ are fast colors—nothing can wash them out; they get brighter with every washing. But evil is drab and uninteresting and has a sting and disappointment at its heart. This is written in Hollywood. Two days ago a distracted middle-aged woman told her story: "I was brought up as a Quaker, but I wanted to see the other side of life. I did. But my home was broken up, and now I'm totally distracted." She was. Then the prayer and the surrender of herself and her problem, the acceptance of the saving power of Christ. Then the smile spread across her tear-stained face. Hope and an open door had come.

No wonder He is called "Christ Jesus our Hope" (I Tim. 1:1, Moffatt). He capitalizes the word and makes hope into Hope. Or, as this passage puts it, "Born anew to a life of hope" (I Pet. 1:3, Moffatt). Hope isn't a momentary mood. You have a life of hope, yes, of Hope.

O Christ, Thou dost make my drabness into delight, my grief into glory, my life into Life. I thank Thee. Amen.

AFFIRMATION FOR THE DAY: *I am going to love love out of the loveless and hope hope out of the hopeless.*

102

THE WHOLE PERSON STIMULATED

Jesus stimulates laughter even at the unexpected. A woman said in one of our Ashrams: "My daughter married a Roman Catholic. I was resentful. I was given a coat to mend, and I did a good job. Then another, and it was "Father" so and so's. I was boiling inside. Now I can laugh at it." That is the remedy.

Here is a passage which tells of the total impact, with the total awakening, bringing total meaning: "Let the inspiration of Christ dwell in your midst with all its wealth of wisdom" (Col. 3:16, Moffatt). Here is the awakening of the mind, giving it a wealth of wisdom. Then: "Teach and train one another, with the music of psalms, with hymns and songs of the spiritual life" (v. 16). Here is the awakening of the emotions, giving vent in rapturous song. Christians sing—they have to or burst! Then: "Indeed, whatever you say or do, let everything be done in dependence on the Lord Jesus" (v. 17). Here is the awakening and stimulation of the will.

Here the whole person—mind, emotion, and will—was stimulated and trained. Some train the mind to the neglect of the emotion and the will—this makes the intellectualist in religion. Some train the emotion and neglect the mind and the will—this makes the emotionalist in religion. Some train the will and neglect the mind and the emotion—his makes the moralist and the legalist in religion, hard, and not very lovable. The impact of Jesus inspires the total person and makes him grow in his total being—mind, emotion, and will—hence a balanced person.

This passage gives the stimulation and enrichment that comes to the total person with the coming of Christ in our lives: "Who in Christ has blessed us with every spiritual blessing within the heavenly sphere" (Eph. 1:3, Moffatt). You don't need to go beyond or outside Christ to get any blessing in earth or in heaven. Everything is in Him.

And now this one: "By his power to fulfil every good resolve and every effort of faith" (II Thess. 1:11, Moffatt). Our good resolve and efforts of faith are stimulated and fulfilled. He is the genesis of the desire and the fulfillment of it. He creates and He consummates.

O Christ, I thank Thee that Thy Life upon my life makes me live— live to my fingertips. Amen.

AFFIRMATION FOR THE DAY: *I'm alive, and I'm going to be life-giving to all I touch today.*

CONVERTING OUR SKILLS

We continue to look at the fact of Jesus the Stimulator.

He stimulates all our skills by turning them into new directions and using them for higher ends. He said to fishermen: "Come, follow me, and I will make you fish for men" (Matt. 4:19, Moffatt). Here He was taking hold of the old skills—their abilities as fishermen—and turning those skills into new and higher uses—the fishing for men. Their skills weren't wiped out; they were simply turned toward higher ends—converted.

If you have been a clever rascal, you can become a clever Christian—your cleverness converted and Christianized. If you have been a dominating person, your executive ability can be redeemed and turned toward Kingdom ends. If you have been pugnacious, then your fighting spirit can be redeemed and harnessed to fighting for great causes. If your sex urges have been strong, then they too can be turned into creative activity on another level, creating new hopes, new lives, new movements. If you are skilled as a salesman, your skill in sellng can be turned into salesmanship for Christ, knowing how to present Him in the best possible way. If you are a musician, all your musical ability can be intensified and made more beautiful by being used now not for personal applause, but for the glory of God.

If you have literary ability, you can offer it to His service, to be used not to show your cleverness, but to show His beauty and power. If you have charm, that charm can be a dedicated charm, calling attention, like the moon, to the fact that all your charm is reflected from a Face. If you have a strong maternal or paternal instinct, you can dedicate it to mothering or fathering the helpless, the weak, the orphaned. If you are a thinker, let Him have your brain processes to help you think out the meaning of the Kingdom to total living. If you are a good housekeeper, then make an attractive home, for we need such homes. If you are a teacher, don't teach subjects; teach young people how to live. If you are a good conversationalist, then bring people through that ability to see the One worth seeing—the Son of God. He uses everything; nothing is lost.

O Christ, Thou art the great heightener, heightening all our skills for higher purposes. I thank Thee. Amen.

AFFIRMATION FOR THE DAY: *All my skills made more skillful under His touch.*

THE NOBODIES BECOME THE SOMEBODIES

We continue our emphasis on Christ the Stimulator.

He not only uses our great powers; He stimulates our little ones and puts them to great uses. The light in a lighthouse is feeble in itself, but it's the lens that magnifies it and makes it go far out to sea to guide confused mariners. Jesus is that lens that magnifies our otherwise feeble rays and makes them into a lifeguiding and life-saving agency. Jesus said to people who crowded about Him with feeble torches: "You are the light of the world." It was absurd. But that absurdity became accomplishment. They did become the light of the world. And we are still guiding our lives by the light they lifted up.

He said: "You are the salt of the earth," and He said that to tasteless, insipid human beings. But they did put taste and meaning into life for the multitudes whose lives had turned drab and full of boredom.

The Man who never used the word "hope" has put Hope into the lives of millions of hopeless beings. The Man who "descended into hell" has lifted more people out of the hell of meaningless and disrupted living than all the philosophers and moralists combined.

I love Jesus because, for one thing, He shed a shaft of light upon the disinherited peoples of the earth. "You come and walk through the compound of my humble cottage, and it will be purified of all its impurities and inferiorities," said a sweeper, the lowest of the low, to me after he had become a Christian by baptism. I knew his faith was misplaced; I couldn't do that. But I knew Jesus could do and did just that. He walks through our minds and spirits and homes, and lo, life is purified of its impurities and inferiorities. Legend says that where Jesus walked, flowers sprang up in His footprints. That is legend, but the moral and spiritual equivalent of that does happen. Barrenness breaks into bloom; dead sticks, like Aaron's rod, begin to bud. The nobodies become the somebodies; the ordinary become the extraordinary—life begins to live. Dead harps feel the sweep of a Hand and sleeping music is awakened.

O Christ, Thou art the same who said to sleeping Lazarus, "Come forth," and today at Thy voice we do come forth. Amen.

AFFIRMATION FOR THE DAY: *I am the subject of an eternal Stimulus.*
Let it stimulate now and forever.

GROWTH IN THE POSITIVE

After having studied Jesus as Stimulator, we now turn to growth in the positive as a natural sequence. Many are not growing as spiritual beings because they are negative in their attitudes. And you can't grow on a No; you must grow on a Yes.

We have seen that you do have to be negative to certain things in order to be positive to others. "Shut your mind," said Paul (I Tim. 4:7, Moffatt)—shut it to some things which are noncontributing, in order to open it to the creative and contributing. There is a place for the negative. Gayelord Hauser says: "Examination of men and women over one hundred years of age at some of our famous clinics revealed that they had four outstanding qualities: (1) Strong digestive juices. (2) A slow rhythmic heart beat. (3) Good elimination. (4) Happy dispositions." Note that physically and spiritually life depends upon "elimination." Someone asked a college president what was the first qualification of a college president, and he answered: "The capacity to inflict pain." If he wasn't able to deny students this, that, and the other, he couldn't open the gates of opportunity to students for the really great things.

I repeat what I have said before: Life depends almost as much on elimination as upon assimilation.

But having said so much, I must now insist that the negative is only a means to an end—the positive. We let go to take; we eliminate to assimilate.

The Christian is the most affirmative person on our planet. He believes in life, so much so that he has to spell it Life. Someone has defined Christianity as "life at its best." It is. It is life at His best, and this Life is so wonderful in quality and duration that it has to be called Eternal Life. All the powers, all the faculties, all the relationships are affirmed unto eternity, and beyond. Cynical, negative attitudes are as alien to the Christian as a thorn is to the flesh.

At the Ashram the one waiting on the table asked someone if he wanted some tea, and he replied, "Yes," but his cup remained turned down. That's the negative Christian—he has his cup turned down!

O God, Thou art waiting to pour everything into our lives, and we have turned them down. Forgive us. Amen.

AFFIRMATION FOR THE DAY: *My cup turned up today for everything God has to give me—everything.*

SPOILING SUNNY JUNE!

It was a beautiful day in June, rains wonderful, crops fine, and a friend of mine remarked to a rich farmer what a wonderful day it was. The farmer replied: "Yes, but if we have three weeks of sunshiny weather and then it should rain heavily, and if an early frost should come, then this country is in for a hard time." He spoiled sunny June by looking at and borrowing frosty September!

Here is a friend whose mother kept saying for fifteen years that she was going to have a cancer. She did have one! She thought and worried herself into a cancerous condition. An operation was necessary. A mental operation fifteen years before would probably have prevented it.

Buddhism is based on pure pessimism about life: Life and suffering are one. But man, while apparently following that pure pessimism, will find ways to get around it. For instance, the Burmese are a life-loving people, so they salute Buddha and follow fun and gaiety; the Chinese, also life-loving, have converted Buddha into a "Laughing Buddha"; the Japanese get the Buddhist priests to bury them, but the Shinto priests to marry them. In order to live, these have all compartmentalized their pessimism, incased it, and lived by something else. In Christianity you don't have to do that, for Christianity is pessimism turned into optimism—the cross turned into an Easter morning. It begins with pure pessimism and comes out pure optimism. But it is an optimism based on the worst faced and conquered at a cross and issuing in an Easter morning.

Around our lake at Sat Tal, India, is a bird which is the champion pessimist. He goes around all day saying in a shrill voice: "Pity-to-do-it, Pity-to-do-it," and at night, they say, he sleeps on his back with his long legs in the air to keep the sky from falling! This perhaps is a slander on the bird, but I've seen some "birds" like that—during the day they spread pessimism and doubt and fear, and at night they do not know how to relax in sleep; they are afraid the sky will fall!

O Christ, Thou dost turn our dead leaves into leaves for the healing of the nations, for Thou art Health and Life. Amen.

AFFIRMATION FOR THE DAY: *I am an affirmative person with an affirmative outlook and an affirmative purpose.*

TUESDAY—Week 16 *II Cor. 4:7-13*

"THE SQUEAK IN THE PULPIT"

Since life is an ongoing concern if it continues as life, then we must be ongoing, which means that we must be positive if we are to live.

Melvin Evans, a management engineer, presents four things which are essential to growth and achievement: (1) development of character; (2) development of positive attitudes; (3) acquisition of knowledge; (4) direction of energy. These four equal growth and achievement. All four of these are positive although only the second is mentioned as such.

So the positive attitude must not be imported into one little portion of life; it must be the life attitude. A man said very simply at the close of a meeting: "I have been negative." He was right—the "I," the person, had been negative.

Very often the person can be negative in asserting the positive. In a service club that specialized in the positive I overheard one man saying to another: "John, don't be negative. If you are negative, I'll hit you over the head to drive it out of you!" He was negative in trying to get rid of negativism!

Many are afraid of being positive, for they are afraid of criticism. They retreat into the negative to escape reactions. The escape into the innocuous to escape opposition is as deadly to character, though less obvious, as escape into drink. The negative in attitude soon become the negative in essence. Someone has defined a great deal of preaching as "a mild-mannered attempt by a mild-mannered parson to get mild-mannered people to become more mild-mannered."

It doesn't get anywhere, for it doesn't aim at anything except to escape criticism! In the minutes of an old church in New England there was this entry: "A committee was appointed to examine the squeak in the pulpit." There are a lot of ministers who could answer that description—"a squeak in the pulpit." The real man of God is not a "squeak," but a Voice. He sounds out eternal verities in a positive way and produces positive results. He is positive.

O God, create in me the positive. Thou art creative. Make me creative too. In Jesus' name. Amen.

AFFIRMATION FOR THE DAY: *I shall negate my negatives and posit my positives.*

108

LIFE TRULY LIVED IS A RISKY BUSINESS

A dentist who was successful as a dentist—he filled cavities with positive remedies—was a failure as a moral being, for he said of himself: "I am a man who thinks all around a subject, but I never make up my mind and act." Everything for him was "sicklied o'er by the pale cast of thought." The thought never took legs and began to walk; it remained a thought. Many are so afraid of making a mistake that they don't make anything else! They have so much tact that they have no contact.

"Any life, truly lived, is a risky business, and if one puts up too many fences against the risks, one ends in shutting out life itself." Many are prisoners of their own fears of making mistakes. There are many who are afraid to speak to others about Christ, for they are afraid of making mistakes. But the biggest mistake is not to do it. If a man doesn't make mistakes, he doesn't make anything else. The biggest mistake is the fear of making mistakes. It leaves one negative, and that is a mistake.

There are some who build their whole lives around negatives. Note: "Now the Pharisees gathered to meet him, with some scribes who had come from Jerusalem. They noticed that some of his disciples ate their food with 'common' (that is, unwashed) hands" (Mark 7:1-2, Moffatt). They came all the way from Jerusalem to meet Him, and their life attitudes were so negative and faultfinding that all they saw was unwashed hands. They couldn't see the greatest movement of redemption that had ever touched our planet—a movement that was cleansing the minds and souls and bodies of men. All they saw was a ritualistic infringement. Their eyes were open wide to the little and marginal, and blind to the big. So history forgets them, the negative—forgets them except as a background for this impact of the positive Christ. They left a criticism; He left a conversion. They picked flaws; He picked followers.

There is only one way to live—the positive way. There is only one way to die—the negative way.

O Christ, I thank Thee for Thy awakening, stimulating impact upon my spirit. Thou dost produce life at every touch. Amen.

AFFIRMATION FOR THE DAY: *I am not afraid to make mistakes, for I'm out to make something bigger than the "Is."*

"BETTER AT HATING THAN LOVING"

We saw yesterday that when you denounce, you do not announce. Here is a picture of a church that was better at hating than at loving: "I know that you cannot bear wicked men, and that you have tested those who style themselves apostles . . . and detected them to be liars" (Rev. 2:2-4, Moffatt). They were good at hating, but poor at loving: "You have given up loving one another as you did at first" (v. 4). They were negative, hence in the process of decay.

I was admiring the garden in a missionary compound in Japan. It was a thing of art and beauty. "How did you get such a garden?" I asked. And the reply: "Well, we called a gardener and showed him our barren yard, and we said to him: 'Do you think you can make anything out of this?' He thought a moment and then slowly replied: 'Yes, I think I can.' And this thing of beauty came out of it." He was positive, hence creative.

No wonder Paul says: "In all that you do, avoid grumbling and disputing" (Phil. 2:14, Moffatt)—grumbling within yourself and disputing with others. This simple rule would help us to grow tremendously. Add to this rule of avoiding, this one that is positive: "I believed and so I spoke" (II Cor. 4:13, Moffatt). If we would refuse to speak unless we can speak a believing word, how positive we would become! Many of us can say, "I doubted and so I spoke," and we have a negative effect instead of a positive one. Believe your beliefs and doubt your doubts, and don't speak unless you are voicing belief. Seal your lips to doubt, and unseal them to faith!

A very able man, brilliant and learned, at the end of a series of addresses said: "Well, I hope I pricked some bubbles." His great abilities were dedicated to the pricking of bubbles. And when this was accomplished, what was left? A wet spot! And that was all. Nothing constructive. Result? He became what he produced—a damp squid.

The pay-off of being negative in your attitudes is that you become negative, for you become what you habitually give out. Determine, then, that all your negatives shall be in the service of the positives— the end is a Yes, and not a No. Then you yourself will be a Yes.

O God, help me to make everything in my life to come out at the place of the positive, the creative. In Jesus' name. Amen.

AFFIRMATION FOR THE DAY: *Anywhere, if forward; anything, if worth while.*

DON'T ENGRAVE YOUR HATES

Nothing is ever corrected by negativism. A prison expert tells us that no prisoner is ever corrected by solitary confinement. He is only hardened in his attitudes. Prisoners in a New Jersey prison have a clinic of correction in which they help solve one another's problems by group thought—a group therapy. There is the positive approach.

Here is a mother, a Chinese woman upon whose face was written misery and despair. Her three sons were unfilial, and her daughters-in-law were also unfilial. A missionary asked her if she would join the Hour-a-Day Club, a club in which an hour a day was spent in reading the Bible and praying. Three years later she was a changed woman—"the most illumined face I ever saw; every hard line gone from her face." She herself said: "I used to have a bad temper, but now as I read the Bible, my angry heart all vanishes away."

Sometimes we augment our negativism in decisive action that fixes it. In New Hampshire is a tombstone about a hundred years old, with twenty lines engraved, giving the account of a church quarrel, telling how the deacons of the church tried to take away a certain woman's character and reputation. Engraving it on a tombstone settled nothing. It was a negative remedy. Fortunately kindly time is gradually erasing it. In another fifty years it will be totally obliterated! Don't engrave your negative reactions into fixed attitudes. Don't write them down, but if you do, then write them in "washable blue."

Don't try any negative method as the way out. It simply won't work. Life is positive, and the remedy for life's ills must be positive. Here is a testimony from our Ashram in India: "I went back from here and found my colleagues were dishonest and quarrelsome. I had a nervous breakdown to escape. I went to a theological college to study and thus to escape. Here at the Ashram I found Christ." He escaped into the Yes, no longer into the No. Christ is a central life Yes. Then having accepted Him as a way of life, find a positive in every single situation you face. There is something to which you can respond positively in every situation. Find it.

O Christ, Thou who didst see something good in every person and situation, help me to do the same. Amen.

AFFIRMATION FOR THE DAY: *I will speak the good, I will see the good—and produce it out of the seeing.*

GNAWING ON BONES

We continue our meditations on growth in the positive.

An example of a negative reaction is this one: A woman who was determined I did not believe in the Virgin Birth heard me say in public that I did. This was her comment: "Yes, he said he believed in the Virgin Birth, but he didn't say Jesus was born of the Virgin Mary." Some people are troubled if you take away the bones on which they habitually chew for spiritual sustenance.

Here is a good "Credo of Love" by Raymond Francis Forgarty:

When I am told of discord in another's life,
I counter-point it with the harmony of life.
When I am assailed by the arrows of fear and doubt,
I will put on the armour of faith.
When my tongue is tempted to carry a malicious tale,
I will occupy it with a prayer.
When hateful thoughts take residence in my mind,
I will remember that the pernicious termite of hate undermines my own
    house, not my neighbour's.
When in anger I would beset another,
I will realize my weapon is a boomerang that pierces my heart.
When I pray for forgiveness for my sins of commission,
I will recall those of omission as well.
When, I may, in some measure live this creed
I pray God it may be with humility as an agent of His love.

This presents a positive attitude against every negative one. The negative attitude, if dominant, cancels the positive. I once saw a sailboat in the backwaters of Travancore, India, with a sail that had so many holes in it that the hole space was almost as much as the sail space. The ship crept along instead of bounding along. Many of us have so many negative places in our lives that the winds of God are wasted on us. Their impact is dissipated, and they don't drive us. But when we are wholly positive, we get the full benefit of the positive impact of God on us. When we are negative, we negate God—cancel Him out.

O Father, God, draw together with the cords of Thy love my negative spots, and help me to receive the full impact of Thy wind. Amen.

AFFIRMATION FOR THE DAY: *I'm plugging up all my negative places so I'll receive and hold God's fullness.*

STEPS INTO THE POSITIVE

Before we leave our meditations on growth out of the negative into the positive, we must take some definite steps.

First, *Go over your life prayerfully, and with a fine-tooth comb, to see if there are places in your life where you are still negative.* Those places will not be easy to find, for we all have our blind spots. We build up defenses around those blind spots, defenses of rationalization. It's hard to get past the defenses we ourselves have built up. But with the new positive attitudes we have taken we can do it. Push past these defenses and root out the negativism. Fling them away, decisively and forever.

While this is being written, a friend tells me of a young man who has everything—intelligence, preparation, real devotion—but he is never chosen for leadership, always for a marginal job. Why? Well, there is a strain of negativism that comes out in a crisis—a word, an act, an attitude. By this negativism he cancels out everything else. He leaves the group uncertain of him. The negativism negates him. He, too, is bewildered as to why he is unacceptable. It is his blind spot.

Find that spot in yourself. Ask God and man and yourself to find it.

Second, *When you find a negativism in your life, don't fight it; replace it with the positive.* If you just fight it, you are simply putting a negative against a negative. The only way to overcome evil is with good, hate by love, a negative by a positive. For instance, when you have been responding negatively to any new proposal, pause before you react and see if there isn't something in the proposal to which you can respond positively. If you have been responding negatively to assuming responsibility, deliberately take responsibility to break the habit of negativism. If you dislike certain foods, eat them whether you like them or not. If you dislike certain persons, go up to them and meet them and be decent to them. If there is a distasteful task you have been shying away from, walk up to that task and perform it. You will find you have been shying away from a bugaboo.

O Father, Thou art teaching me how to be positive and outgoing. Help me to respond. Amen.

AFFIRMATION FOR THE DAY: *I'm going to do the thing I don't like to do today, just for the fun of doing it.*

WINNING A POSITIVE OUT OF EVERY NEGATIVE

We are continuing the steps out of the negative into the positive.

Third, *Find the positive in every negative situation.* I know of an executive who, when he finds a discussion getting tangled up with negatives, keeps looking for something positive to stress so that the end of the discussion will be on a positive note, with a positive plan.

Jesus did that. The Pharisees criticized Him, complaining that He ate with publicans and sinners, implying that He was thereby like them in character. That was negative, very negative. Did Jesus meet a negative with a negative? No, instead He gave the three parables of the lost sheep, the lost coin, and the lost son—a positive presentation of the seeking love of God. He came out on the positive side of that negative situation.

He always did that. At the Cross He won a positive out of a negative. The Cross was sin, and He turned it into the redemption from sin; the Cross was hate, and He turned it into a revelation of love; the Cross was man at his worst, and Jesus through it showed God at His redemptive best. This made Jesus the great Affirmation. "The divine 'yes' has at last sounded in him" (II Cor. 1:19, Moffatt).

Paul knew this rescuing of the positive out of the negative.

We are handicapped on all sides but we are never frustrated; we are puzzled but never in despair. We are persecuted but we never have to stand it alone; we may be knocked down but we are never knocked out! . . . We may also know the power of the life of Jesus in these bodies of ours. We are always facing death, but this means that you know more and more of life (II Cor. 4:8-12, Phillips).

And this passage shows the amazingly positive attitude of Paul: "Wherever I go, thank God, he makes my life a constant pageant of triumph" (II Cor. 2:14, Moffatt). Most of us would have said that his life was a constant pageant of trouble. It was, but Paul made the trouble into a triumph, the negative into a positive. He rescued out of the heart of every death situation a life contribution.

O Father, I thank Thee that I too can come out on the affirmative side of everything. Help me. Amen.

AFFIRMATION FOR THE DAY: *I affirm what God affirms and negate only what God negates.*

CATCHING THEM AT HIGH TIDE

This rescuing a positive out of a negative was seen in the account of Jesus' calling His principal disciples, Peter, James, and John, partners in the fishing business. They had toiled all night and had caught nothing. Jesus might have said to Himself, "This is the time to get these men—they're discouraged about their fishing business. I'll capitalize on their disillusionments and get them to follow Me when they don't know which way to turn." No, he got them to try again, filled their boats so full with fish they began to sink, and then at that high tide of occupational prosperity He said: "Follow me, and I will make you fishers of men." They immediately left their fishing boats and followed Him—followed Him at their most prosperous moment. That set a pattern—this new faith was not merely for the down-and-out, the disillusioned, and the discouraged, the negative. It was for the positive, the successful, the prosperous, as well. All life needed Him. The best was not good enough.

Moreover, it set a pattern for their fishing for men. If He had said to them after their night of fruitless toil, "Follow me, and I will make you fishers of men," they would have said to themselves, "Well, I suppose we will be about as successful in this fishing-for-men business as we were last night. We won't get anything." But He talked to them about fishing for men when they were looking not at empty boats, but at boats brimming with fish. That set a pattern of positive and overflowing achievement in His name. And it happened. Their faith and confidence were so triumphant that their boats launched on the sea of this new faith very soon were almost swamped with three thousand converts in a day! These were not negative, nay-saying individuals giving themselves to a negative, nay-saying faith. They were positive men, following a positive Christ, achieving positive results, and all framed in a positive outlook. The Christian faith was a Yes, not a No. And people, tired of cynicism and defeatism and negativism and tired of faiths that had lost their nerve and had taught their followers to escape, turned to this new faith, for it had faith and nerve and adequacy at its heart.

O Christ, I do thank Thee that in Thee I'm caught up with the victorious, the transforming, the Eternal Yes. Amen.

AFFIRMATION FOR THE DAY: *The Eternal Yes shall be operative in all my actions and attitudes today.*

"NOT HEEDING THE WORD SPOKEN"

A president of a synagogue fell at the feet of Jesus and implored Jesus to come and save his dying daughter. Jesus went. On the way He was interrupted by a woman touching the border of His garment. In the delay the daughter died, and word was brought that they should not trouble the Master any further, for the child was dead. "But Jesus, not heeding the word spoken said to the father of the child, Fear not, only believe." "Jesus, not heeding the word spoken." But the word spoken was a fact—the child was dead. Was He unrealistic in not heeding a fact?

No, for He was listening to a higher set of facts. The lower set of facts said, "The child is dead," but the higher set of facts said, "The child will live." And Jesus listened to that higher set of facts— the Kingdom of God facts. He was realistic there. Some call themselves realistic when they are realistic to the lower facts—things as they are: death, hopelessness, pessimism, negation. But this isn't realism; it is lower realism. Jesus was realistic on a higher level— life, hope, faith, the positive. The lower set of facts is not the last word; the higher set has the last word.

When Jesus said, "Why make a noise and wail? The child is not dead but asleep," the account says: "They laughed at him. However . . ." (Mark 5:39-40, Moffatt). After our incredulous laughter there is always His "however." He always has the last word, and the last word is faith. And this faith produces a fact—the child lived. The last word was not with death but with life. His realism was realistic.

Here is a strange emphasis for a translator to give. Moffatt translates "the Kingdom of God" as "the Realm of God" throughout his translation. But in Colossians 1:13 he translates the passage thus: "rescuing us from the power of the Darkness and transferring us to the realm of his beloved Son!" The "Darkness" is capitalized, but the "realm" is in a small "r"! Isn't that about the way we look at things? Darkness—the negative—is "Darkness" to us, and the Realm —the positive—is "realm" to us. We live under the capitalized negative and the reduced positive.

O Christ, help me to be negative to all negatives and positive to all positives. Help me to be a positive, creative person. Amen.

AFFIRMATION FOR THE DAY: *My Kingdom of Light is stronger than the kingdom of darkness. I shall illustrate.*

A POSITIVE VOCABULARY

We come now to the next step in growing in the positive. Fourth, *Go over your vocabulary and weed out all negative, weak, paralysis-spreading words.*

Very often after we have changed our inner attitudes from negative to positive, a lot of negativism still remains embalmed in our vocabulary, leftovers from our old way of life. If we continue to use them, they will keep alive our negativism by their repetition. So weed them out and replace them with positive, alive, yea-saying words. If you've been saying, "Can't do," say, "Can do"; if you have been saying, "No time," say, "I'll find time"; if you've been saying, "I am not feeling well," say, "I'm feeling well in God"; if you've been emphasizing, "I'm feeling tired," say, "I'm rested in God'; and if you've been dodging responsibility with a "No," accept responsibility with a "Yes"; if you've been saying, "I don't like," begin to say, "I like"; if you've been responding negatively to each new proposal by saying an abrupt "No," begin to say, "I'll see what I can do." If you've looked for the ugly, look for the beautiful; if you've expected people to let you down and have become distrustful, now begin to trust people and expect the best from them. You will tend to create the thing you expect. If you've been looking at the hole in the doughnut, look at the doughnut. If you've been doubting your own ability, keep saying to yourself: "In Him who strengthens me I am able for anything." And you will be!

A student came up at the close of a meeting and said: "Thanks for suggesting that we say 'Yes' twenty-five times to ourselves. I'm starting straight off." That's it, start straight off to be positive. Don't be procrastinating and negative in starting to be positive.

Have a funeral service and bury your old dead words and attitudes and put a "No-Resurrection" sign over them. At first you'll miss these companions of the years. They have provided you with a refuge—a false refuge, it is true, but nevertheless a refuge—from responsibility. You'll miss them. But into their places will come words that live and sing and create. You'll love them more—and lastingly!

Father, I thank Thee for my long-delayed funerals. They're over. And I am free from the dead—free to live. Amen.

AFFIRMATION FOR THE DAY: *I am free to live, not at my best, but at His Best—and what a Best!*

"THERE'S SOMETHING ALWAYS SINGS"

We now take the next step toward the positive.

Fifth, *Now that you have cleansed your vocabulary from all negativisms, give out the positive and only the positive.*

Someone has put it this way: "Give others sunshine. Tell Jesus the rest." There will be negative, disagreeable things—bound to be; then tell these things to One who can find a positive in every negative, an Easter morning in every Calvary. If you repeat them to yourself, this tends to fix them within you. The habit of being negative comes out of a number of repeated negatives. But when you repeat these to Jesus, there they are transformed from the backward-looking to the forward-looking, from the yesterdays to the tomorrows. Since He transforms your thinking and your attitudes, talk these transformations. This tends to fix them. All expression deepens impression. So the expression of the positive deepens the impression of the positive.

The lilac sets its green buds in the fall, awaiting through the long winter the coming of the spring. When spring does come, the lilac is one of the first ones out. It keeps singing of the spring and feels the warmth of it amid winter's chill—feels it by anticipation.

> In the mud and scum of things
> There's something always, always sings.

Sing out of the mud and scum, and soon there'll be no mud or scum. For where there is life, the mud and scum are being taken hold of by that life and transformed into its image—the mud into the lily, the blackest into the whitest.

It is the law of salesmanship that you can sell a product only if you love it. No one will take it unless he sees you love it yourself. Well, you can't love the negative. You may tolerate it, but you can love only the positive. Now you will begin to love the positive, outgoing words and attitudes. And others will begin to love them too. You will become the contagious center of the positive and the creative. People will follow the positive, yea-saying person. They soon tire of the negative, nay-saying.

O Christ, I thank Thee that I have my feet upon the Way—the Way that leads forward, not backward. Amen.

AFFIRMATION FOR THE DAY: *I am committed to the "Can be," not to the "Can't be." I'm committed to Tomorrow.*

"THE PATTERN SHOWN THEE IN THE MOUNT"

We come now to the last step out of the negative into the positive.

Sixth, *"See . . . that thou make all things according to the pattern shewed to thee in the mount"* (Heb. 8:5). This was spoken to Moses when he was about to build the tabernacle. It applies today. Build your life according to the pattern you see at your highest spiritual moment—when you are on the mount. Don't build it according to the pattern you see when you are in the valley of depression, when you are negative and down. Many do. They make their decisions when they are defeated and discouraged, and the product is a sorry product. If you are depressed and down and negative, then hold things; don't do anything according to that pattern. If you do, you'll build your negativisms into the house of man-soul. Wait until you are on the Mount with God—wait until you see things clearly and see them whole. Then from your highest spiritual moment begin to build. For your highest moment is your most real moment. The others are the unreal.

Paul could say: "I was not disobedient unto the heavenly vision." He built his life around something that came from heaven; hence he lived a heavenly life and left a heaven in his wake. Many build their house of life according to the pattern they see not from heaven, but from earth. They take their cue from what others do. Earth, not heaven, determines them. Hence they build a life which is of the earth, earthly, and with the earth it perishes. But if you build your life according to the heavenly vision, then earth may pass and decay, but your life built upon eternal foundations lasts for eternity.

Here is a life built upon the negative: "I have a few jitters or spasms in my stomach. I do not need to stay in bed all the time, but I can't seem to get any definite guidance, except I do not seem to want to make myself do anything." Her foundations were negative; hence she remained an invalid.

Build when you see Jesus clearly. Then you'll have a house that will be eternal. Build from the positive.

O Christ, take me into the Mount and there show me the pattern for my life, and I shall build it from that and that alone. Amen.

AFFIRMATION FOR THE DAY: *I'm building my house from what I see on the Mount of Transfiguration.*

GROWTH IN THE FRUITS OF THE SPIRIT

We now turn in our meditations to growth in the fruits of the Spirit. Paul says they are nine: "Love, joy, peace, good temper, kindliness, generosity, fidelity, gentleness, self-control" (Gal. 5:22, Moffatt). Phillips translates "gentleness" as "adaptability."

These nine qualities of life are the natural outcome of the Spirit within. Now note that every one of these is a moral quality and not a magical power. To be filled with the Spirit is often looked on as making one a seven-day wonder—healing the sick, stopping tornadoes, changing the weather—signs and wonders. The Spirit-filled person becomes a dispenser of miracles. Now miracles do happen in the Christian impact; the sick are healed, and unexpected things do happen, but nowhere as a central emphasis. They are by-products of something deeper. When you emphasize the by-product and underemphasize the product, you will lose both the by-product and the product. The product is life characterized by nine qualities, all of them moral, not one of them magical. The emphasis therefore is thrown—and rightly thrown—on the moral and spiritual instead of the magical and wonder-working. This is sound. This keeps the Christian impact redemptive, functioning as moral and spiritual changes in character instead of miracles in nature.

This fits in with what Paul says were the corroboration of his ministry. There are twenty-eight things spoken of in II Cor. 6:4-10 as proving he was a "true minister of God." And every single one is a moral and spiritual quality of life and action—not one mention of performing any miracle. He did see miracles happening around him, but he knew that the central miracle was happening within him. And there is where he threw the emphasis.

It is well to note that when Paul speaks of "the works of the flesh" in Gal. 5:19-21, he calls them "works," but here he calls the fruit of the Spirit "fruit." Is there a difference here? "Works" point to something manufactured, not natural; "fruit" points to something coming out as a natural outcome. Evil is alien. Goodness fits us; it is the thing for which we are made—a natural.

O God, our Father, I thank Thee for the possibility of being fruitful in moral qualities that enrich me and my relationships. Amen.

AFFIRMATION FOR THE DAY: *I am keeping my channels open so the fruits of the Spirit may grow and grow.*

THE FIRST FRUIT IS LOVE

Moffatt speaks of the "harvest of the Spirit," pointing to the finished product, the outcome. These are the things that remain after the preliminaries—the bud and the flower—have dropped away. The "harvest" is the important thing. What do you finally reap as the outcome of a course of outlook and action? The pay-off determines the worth. Not what happens along the way in the form of pleasurable or painful emotions, but the end of the way, is the thing that matters.

And the end of the way here is not heaven as a reward, an outer gift, but a quality of being. The pay-off is in you—is you. And this is the only thing that matters. No amount of outer reward can cancel out that which is within. The within finally determines the worthwhileness of a life. Jesus said: "But love your enemies, and do good, . . . and your reward shall be great, and ye shall be the children of the Highest" (Luke 6:35). "The rich reward" is a quality of being—"ye shall be the children of the Highest"—"ye shall *be.*" The being is the outcome of the doing. And the goodness or badness of an act is determined by what it does to you. Does it lower or heighten the moral and spiritual *you?*

Having the Spirit within results in a quality of being with nine characteristics. And the first one is "love." This emphasis on the firstness of love fits in with Paul's emphasis in I Cor. 13:13 (Moffatt): "Thus 'faith and hope and love last on, these three,' but the greatest of all is love. Make love your aim, and then set your heart on spiritual gifts." The primacy of love in the spiritual life is not an arbitrary, imposed condition; it is inherent. If you have the Spirit, you have love, and if you do not have love, you do not have the Spirit. And this love is not an occasional attitude manifested toward those who love you, but a characteristic attitude of life. Love is the first outcome of the Spirit within, and if it is lacking, everything is lacking.

To grow spiritually is to grow in love. Without love all other growth is a cancer growth, consuming instead of constructing.

O Father, help me to grow in love as my primary growth. Reinforce me there and then I shall truly grow. Amen.

AFFIRMATION FOR THE DAY: *I make love my life aim. I cannot be less than love and live.*

"LIVING IS LOVING"

If we grow in love, then we grow. If we don't grow, then we simply go, not grow. And it is a very barren going.

> Living is loving,
> Loving is giving,
> Giving is growing,
> Growing is God.

Without growing in love we cannot grow in God, for His essential nature is love. Paul speaks in a telling passage of: "till we should all attain the unity of . . . God's Son, reaching maturity, reaching the full measure of development which belongs to the fulness of Christ—instead of remaining immature . . . ; we are to hold by the truth, and by our love to grow up wholly into Him" (Eph. 4:13-15, Moffatt). Note: "by our love to grow up wholly into Him" —there is only one way to grow up wholly into Him, and that is "by our love." We remain immature if we are immature in our love. If the love is ingrown, centering on itself as the focus of its love, then the result is an immature personality. If the love is selectively applied to certain groups and classes and races, again the result is an immature personality.

And modern discoveries in psychology would agree with this conclusion. Dr. Karl Menninger, the famous psychiatrist, was asked at a forum what one was to do if he felt a nervous breakdown coming on. You would have thought that he would have replied, "Go to a psychiatrist," but instead he replied: "Lock up your house, go across the railway tracks and find someone in need, and do something for him." That was very illuminating. If you are on the verge of a nervous break, you are centered on yourself. The only way to break the downward slide is to go and get interested in and love someone other than yourself. Further note: It was not an abstract love he recommended—it wasn't the love of love; it was the love of concrete people in concrete need. The word of love must become flesh in a concrete love of persons.

O Father, I see, I see that I am to catch this spirit of love if I am to grow. Help me to grow there—today.

AFFIRMATION FOR THE DAY: *The word of love shall become flesh in me in every situation I am in today.*

LOVE IS AT THE BASIS OF CREATION

To grow is to grow in love. All other growth, without growth in love, is sucker growth, growth that bears no fruit. Phillips puts it this way: "While knowledge may make a man look big, it is only love that can make him grow to his full stature" (I Cor. 8:1).

Our whole emphasis on knowledge in our educational systems points the other way. "Know facts and their relationships, and that will redeem you," says modern educational theory. And then comes the disillusionment—we know the facts of atomic energy, and without love we have a problem on our hands instead of infinite possibility. Love could transform this knowledge into redemption of ourselves and others. We thought that if only the facts of the inner life, including the subconscious, were known, then all would add up to harmony. And then came the disillusionment—we knew everything about life except how to live it. We picked life to pieces and didn't know how to put it together again. Our probing resulted in problems.

I know of a woman who has been probing herself for fifteen years trying to find the depths of her problem; if she would go out and begin to love someone in need, she would find the depths, and when she did, there would be no problem. The problem would be not solved, but dissolved, by love. Knowledge looks big, but it is big barrenness unless love is behind it.

Loise E. Cone comments: "If we do any material or man-made things of life in excess we invariably come to harm, but we can never do God's laws in excess, and if we could, there would be no harm in doing so. Love is like water. If it moves over an incline and strikes a wheel it creates; if it touches a plant it gives life; or just put it into use in any way it benefits, but put it in a vessel and set it on a shelf and it only evaporates." Love is at the basis of creation, human and divine. Therefore if we have love, we are creative; if we don't, then we are constrictive. And the constriction constricts us and others around us unto death.

Father, I pray Thee deny me all gifts if necessary, but not the gift of love. For without it I'm nil. Amen.

AFFIRMATION FOR THE DAY: *I shall think out ways in which I can make love operative today.*

123

SMASHING AND MELTING

According to the Christian faith all motives of life, if they are to be sound, are reduced to one motive—love. And this love must not be love in general; it must be love of a specific kind—the love of Christ. The greatest of Christians said: "I am controlled by the love of Christ." This cuts deep. It is possible to be controlled by the love of achievement, of success, of a cause, of one's fight. To be controlled by the love of Christ is different not only in degree, but in kind, in quality.

We went past a village in a mountain district in Japan called "the Place to leave your Mother." In the feudal days the old who had reached seventy were brought here to die. A young man carried his mother up the mountain to leave her there. He noticed she was breaking the twigs as she went along. Asked why, she replied: "I don't want you to lose your way in coming back." The young man could not leave his mother after that. He brought her back and hid her in his home. The feudal lord gave difficult orders to the people—orders which the mother by her wisdom helped them to fulfill. When the people heard where the wisdom was coming from, they changed the custom of exposing mothers. Her love changed a custom.

There are two courses to take to get rid of a block of ice. One is to try to smash it with a hammer, in which case you only succeed in scattering it, not destroying it, and other is to melt it, in which case you really do get rid of it. The Christian doesn't smash situations and people; he melts them.

Jesus on the cross is God not smashing His enemies, but melting them. There is only one way of getting rid of your enemies, and that is to turn them into your friends; and the only possible way to turn them into friends is to love them. Gandhi didn't smash the British; he melted them—melted them with his capacity to suffer. "I won't give suffering, I will take it, and I will match my capacity to take suffering against your capacity to give it. I will wear you down with my love." And he did! He won the freedom of three hundred million people by embodying love in a movement for freedom. Gandhi won his freedom and then won the people from whom he won the freedom.

O Jesus, teach me Thy way—the way of Love. Help me to melt every situation by love—Thy love. Amen.

AFFIRMATION FOR THE DAY: *What I cannot get around I shall melt with love. And what I cannot melt with love I shall give more love.*

LOVE IS POWER

Islam believes in smashing your enemies. It succeeded for a while, and then the sterility of an eye for an eye and a tooth for a tooth set in; a sterile civilization resulted. A Mohammedan became a Christian —the only Christian among his group. Two factions in this group began a fight with metal-tipped bamboo poles, and heads were being cracked. The Christian ran among them unarmed and got the blows from both sides on his own head. When both sides saw the blood drenching the white garments of their beloved teacher, they stopped the fight and attended to the wounds of the stricken man, got a doctor for the wounded on both sides, and became friends again, right then and there. Usman, my friend, didn't smash them; he melted them.

This love is power. As Weatherhead says, "Those who oppose love take up arms against the whole universe. They will be broken, not love."

Lecky the historian says that the simple story of Jesus has done more to soften and moralize humanity than all the disquisitions of philosophers and moralists put together. The philosophers tried to convince humanity; the moralists tried to bludgeon humanity; Jesus melted humanity. They gave words, and Jesus gave the Word made flesh. One talked of love, and Jesus was love.

A friend of mine was a convert from a wealthy Hindu family. When he became a Christian, the other members of the family combined to take away his share. He let them. Then the family got to quarreling over his share, and when they got into a jam, they asked him to mediate, as he was the only one everybody could trust. He did —he mediated over the distribution of the property stolen from him. Did he become everybody's door mat or everybody's temple of refuge? He was everybody's temple of refuge—he became the prime minister of that Indian state.

Each little act of love prepares one for the larger responsibility that love inevitably inherits. For the loving are the cement of any situation, and without them no situation will hold together. The loving are the inevitable rulers in any situation.

Father, help me to love everybody and everything this day, even the unlovable. Amen.

AFFIRMATION FOR THE DAY: *The unlovable are in special need of my love, for they are so unhappy in their lovelessness.*

"THEY HOLD THE WORLD TOGETHER"

Here is how the cross melts men: "T. V." is the greatest living Tamil scholar, author of sixty books. He says:

I took delight in debating with everybody. In logic, in argument my opponents feared me and I was successful everywhere. But today I see a humble man stretched on the cross and his enemies nailing him. This victim is saying "Father, forgive them." This was a new experience to me. At the sight of this, gone is all my debate. I am down. Various war lords drew their swords and slew millions. They are all gone. Here is one who threw away the sword and was slain. He lives. Well, I have found the way to live. It lies at the feet of Him who was slain and yet lives. . . . I am not a Christian. No Christian padre ever taught me Christianity. Yet I tell you the truth, Go to the foot of the cross or you perish.

And the cross melts social barriers. "I used to pick and choose my friends, but now I let God choose them for me," said a woman who before her conversion moved in a very exclusive society. Her new-found love broke a barrier that many had tried in vain to crash.

The enemies of the early Christians complained that "these Christians love each other even before they are acquainted." They did. They couldn't help it. For the very nature of the faith they had embraced was love. A corollary of the statement "Behold how these Christians love one another" was this one: "Heavens, what women these Christians have!" And they could have said: "What men!" For both men and women, loving widely and deeply, became tall in stooping to the lowly, and they became great in greatly loving. No wonder the Epistle to Diognetus says: "What the soul is to the body, so the Christians are to the world. They hold the world together." They did then, and they do now. For without love no personality, no situation, will hold together. Love is no mere luxury—something we can have or not have and nothing happens. If you love, you live; if you don't love, you don't live. To grow is to grow in love.

O Father, I thank Thee that Thou art bringing me to the very crux. Hold me to it. For I would grow. I must grow in love. Amen.

AFFIRMATION FOR THE DAY: *The crippled in soul are crippled because of a lack of love in themselves or others. I shall give them love.*

STEPS IN GROWTH IN LOVE

We now come to the steps we may take in growing in love.

First, *Let us remember that the capacity and necessity of love is inherent within us.* We stress the inherent self-interest of the child, but the other-interest is just as inherent in the child. This is obvious from the fact that if the child is only self-interested, turning to selfishness it is automatically an unhappy child. The happy child is the other-interested child. We are destined to love and this destiny is written within us. We can live against this destiny and be unloving, but if we do, we are automatically unhappy and automatically make those around us unhappy. This passage tells us of our destiny: "destining us in love to be his sons through Jesus Christ" (Eph. 1:5, Moffatt). We are destined to be Christians, to be His sons, and that destiny came through His love—"destining us in love." If that destiny came out of love, then it must hold within it a destiny to love.

When you decide to be a man or woman of love, you are deciding to live with the grain of the universe, not against it. You are fulfilling your own destiny.

Second, *Since to be a man or woman of love is your destiny, then do what Paul suggests: "Make love your aim," your life purpose* (I Cor. 14:1, Moffatt). This will take the business of love out of the occasional and the spasmodic and will make it the central controlling purpose of your life. Then you will not be a person who occasionally loves when it is convenient, but a person whose controlling life purpose is love. Love will be the organizing motive and power in your life. In that case if love be hindered here, it will break out there; if it is thwarted here, it will find a way there. "Love never fails," for it always finds a way of expressing itself; and when it expresses itself, itself is the success. For in expressing itself it makes the person more loving, even if the other doesn't accept the love.

Your life purpose is fulfilled even if you see no results of your loving, for you have become a loving person. There is nothing higher.

O God, my Father, I thank Thee that the real thing, love, has taken hold of me. Let it possess me. I consent. Amen.

AFFIRMATION FOR THE DAY: *I cannot fail if I love, even if my love fails to accomplish its ends.*

"THE LOVE OF GOD IS UPON ALL FLESH"

Third, *Since love is now your aim, your ambition now is to excel in love.* I have quoted Paul: "The Lord make you increase and excel in love . . . , so as to strengthen your hearts" (I Thess. 3:12, Moffatt). There is room for competition in Christianity—the competition is over who can excel in love. This would be a healthy competition.

And the result is not only contributive and constructive to others, but there is a deposit left in you: "So as to strengthen your hearts." The heart that loves is not a weakened heart—weakened by the giving; it is strengthened—strengthened by the very giving. The giver and the receiver are both strengthened, for love itself is strength, the only strength.

This competition, which we might call the higher competition, harnesses competition to higher ends with higher motives and with higher results. It is the redemption of an elemental drive and its redirection for Kingdom ends. The more you excel in love, the more everybody is benefited.

Fourth, *The pattern for your loving is God's loving.* God loves us not merely for what we are, but for what He sees we can be. He loves that foreseen person into being. He therefore can love the unlovable, for He sees the possible lovable. We can love the same way. We can love people not for what they are, but for what we see they can be. And by our love we tend to produce the person we see—we love it into being. Michelangelo saw a David in a rejected piece of marble and patiently loved it into being. Jesus looked at the inwardly clashing, tempestuous Saul and loved into being the dedicated and harmonious Paul. Love is creative—it faiths faith out of the faithless, believes belief out of the beliefless, and loves love out of the loveless.

Ecclesiasticus says: "The love of a man is upon his friends, but the love of God is upon all flesh." For the love of God turns flesh into spirit and turns spirit into creative spirit. Then love all, despair of none; and if we are let down, we are not let down, for we end up more loving.

O Christ, give me Thy love—Thy love for everybody and everything—and then help me to manifest it this day. Amen.

AFFIRMATION FOR THE DAY: *My love shall be as prodigal and indiscriminate as God's love—and as redemptive in my small way.*

LET CHRIST LOVE YOU INTO LOVING

We come now to the next step in growing in love.

Fifth, *Do everything for the love of Christ.* To do everything for the love of Christ transforms the menial into the meaningful, the sordid into the sacred.

One of the richest meanings of the Incarnation is here. The carpenter's bench, the struggle in the wilderness, the healing of the sick, the feeding of the hungry, the torture of the cross—all these were not obstacles but opportunities for showing the love of God. Everything and every situation was an opportunity to demonstrate the Word become flesh. Then everything becomes big, not because it is inherently big, but by the significance we put into it. It is big because it illustrates the Big. The love of God is the biggest thing in the universe, and when that love is incarnate in a deed, then the deed is big.

And doing everything for the love of Christ will dull the edge of disappointment and make us invulnerable to lack of appreciation.

> Love is not love
> Which alters when it alteration finds,
> Or bends with the remover to remove.
> O, no! it is an ever-fixed mark,
> That looks on tempests and is never shaken.

Doing everything for the love of Christ will help us to love those with whom we differ. For our love is not a give-and-take on a level of reciprocity; it descends from above and is showered on the deserving and the undeserving, the agreeable and the disagreeable.

Sixth, *Don't strain to love, but let the love of God love within you.* John puts it this way: "Yet if we love each other God does actually live within us, and His love grows in us towards perfection" (I John 4:11, Phillips). Note: "His love grows in us toward perfection." We don't try to love; we just let Love love. And as we do, we grow in love toward perfection. His perfect Love perfects our love and perfects us in the process.

O Father, I thank Thee, that all I have to do is to surrender to Love in order to become a perfected being. Amen.

AFFIRMATION FOR THE DAY: *God's love grows in me toward perfection; then no blocking of that love today.*

"THERE IS NO FEAR IN LOVE"

We come now to the next step in growing in love.

Seventh, *Go out today and find someone who needs your love, and give it and give it generously.* You cannot determine to love in general; you must love specifically. The word of love must become flesh in a specific deed of love. "Broadcasting love" is good as an attitude in general, but it may become a snare and a delusion if it remains merely general. It may become a cheap substitute for loving in particular. For it costs nothing but sentiment to love in general, but it really costs to love in particular. So don't broadcast love; beam it to a particular person in particular need. And do it today.

Eighth, *If you are afraid of people and situations, the best way to get rid of fear is to go and love.* "There is no fear in love; but perfect love casteth out fear" (I John 4:18). Let this phrase burn itself into your mind and heart—"There is no fear in love." When you have love, you do not have fear. So don't fight your fears; go out and love —love the loveless, and soon you'll find your fears are gone. They will be dissolved in love. It is a sure remedy for fears. For the fearful are always thinking about themselves, and that makes them more fearful, for the self-centered are invariably fearful; they know instinctively that they are off-center. Love changes the center of interest from oneself to another, and by this very change the fear drops away, for to have the other-interest is the right center. Hence life feels a sense of well-being, since it is right-centered.

And this is a sweeping remedy—"perfect love casts out all fear"— not some fear, all fear! So the way to get rid of that last remnant of fear is to perfect the love. Don't tinker with the fear—it will grow with attention—but develop the love, and the fear will disappear.

> Look up! and not down;
> Out! and not in;
> Forward! and not back;
> And lend a hand.

O Father, I thank Thee that Thou hast a simple remedy for everything—love. Help me to take it. Amen.

AFFIRMATION FOR THE DAY: *My remedy for every situation: love, and more love, and yet more love!*

LOVE IS THE MASTER KEY

We continue the steps in growth in love.

Ninth, *In loving we not only get rid of fear in general; we get rid of the fear of failure.* Love gets rid of deficiencies of various kinds, for a loving person succeeds where a merely efficient person fails. The love is the success. You can put up with a loving person, for love hides a multitude of sins and deficiencies. There are thirty-one wrong things the disciples did in the pages of the New Testament, and yet they succeeded, for they loved—they loved the Lord centrally and loved people as a consequence. That carried them over and beyond their mistakes. But if you don't love, then no amount of efficiency can atone for that; the apple is rotten at the core. A management engineer told me he could increase the output of a plant 10 per cent with no change of machinery, by straightening out relationships between the men. The good will put oil in the machinery. Ill will puts sand in the machinery. So love is efficiency.

Two sons were always fighting and quarreling with each other. The father did everything he could to straighten them out. He failed. Then he called them to the proverbial woodshed for a whipping. But instead of laying the whip on them he handed the whip to them, bared his back, and said: "I must be a very poor father indeed to have such bad-tempered, quarrelsome sons. I have been a failure as a father. You lay the whip on my back." The boys looked at each other, burst into tears, made up their quarrels, and became fast friends from that moment on. The love of the father succeeded where other remedies had failed.

This is an interesting passage. "He has won the power of opening" (Rev. 5:5, Moffatt). Jesus won the power of opening because He was the Word of Love become flesh. Where others failed, He succeeded, for where knowledge knocks in vain, love enters in by lowly doors. Where other keys get jammed, love opens the doors, for it fits the heart—every heart. It is the Master Key. Paul says: "Love never fails" —it never fails, for if it is not received, then one is more loving for having loved. This is the victory—just being love.

Dear Father, my way of life won't work unless it is the way of Love. Help me to take that way—and take it today.

AFFIRMATION FOR THE DAY: *I shall try the key of love to unlock every difficult person or situation I meet.*

131

"ONE REMEDY—SELF-SURRENDER"

We come now to an important step in growing in love. Tenth, *Surrender yourself completely to God, for without this surrender there is no love.* A woman came up to me at the close of a meeting and said: "I've found you out. You've got only one remedy—self-surrender." I laughed and told her that she was right, for I had found myself out; that I did have only one remedy. As the long experience of a doctor makes him prescribe certain basic remedies, life had driven me to prescribe in most cases a simple remedy, self-surrender. Psychology comes out to the same place. A psychologist has written a booklet entitled *The Therapeutic Value of Self-Surrender.* He found by actual experience that the unsurrendered are the unreleased. They are tied up until they let go of themselves. If you understand the meaning of the attitude of losing yourself in the interests of others, you know how to live. Life takes on rhythm, harmony. If you don't know this self-losing, then life gets tangled in the flypaper of its own self-interest.

Love can take place only where there is self-surrender. Between persons no love can spring up unless there is mutual self-surrender. If either one withholds the self, then love cannot come into being. It is automatically blocked. If this is true between persons, it is also true between the Divine and the human. You cannot love God unless you surrender to God. And you cannot love Him perfectly unless you surrender to Him perfectly.

And this is psychologically sound. For love is an emancipating passion. It breaks the tyranny of self-preoccupation and frees the powers by getting them outside themselves. But while it emancipates from self, it also gives a self back to itself. And now it is a self you can live with—it is a lovable self because it is a loving self. The love of others is not an arbitrary requirement; it is inherent in the nature of reality.

Christianity therefore makes possible self-love. "And each with an eye to the interests of others as well as to his own" (Phil. 2:4, Moffatt). You do have an eye on your own interest when you have your eye on the interest of others. It's a double pay-off.

Father, help me to love widely and deeply so that I can live with myself and others. In Jesus' name. Amen.

AFFIRMATION FOR THE DAY: *I can now love myself safely and wisely, for I love something more than myself—God.*

LOVE'S BURDEN IS LIGHT

We now take the last step in growing in love. Eleventh, *Remember that while love involves a self-surrender and therefore seems the way of sacrifice, it is really the easy way.*

While love takes on itself impossible tasks, yet it finds that love lightens all loads. It is the same burden that wings are to a bird, sails are to a ship. Nothing is hard if done for love's sweet sake. The yoke of love is easy; the yoke of duty is hard. There is all the difference in the world between being drawn by love and being driven by duty. The task may be the same, but love makes everything light, and duty makes everything drudgery. These are two worlds.

The way of love is therefore the easy way. The way of loveless duty is the hard way. And harder still is the way of loveless living. Everything without love is drudgery.

There is an old story of a little girl who, when carrying her little brother, was asked by a kindly gentleman, "You have quite a burden, haven't you?" She replied, "He's no burden. He's my brother." Love made the burden light.

I've traveled in all continents and have seen missionaries in many lands often living under trying conditions, but always with the same sense of privilege, of special favor in being able to live so. The sacrifice would be in not being able to do it. I asked a missionary in Manchuria some years ago how they met this crisis, for I felt there was a crisis on when I could hear the rattle of machine guns while I was speaking; and she smiled and said: "Which crisis? We've been in one for twenty-five years, and we can't tell when one ends and the other begins." And she said it with a gay laugh, as one who was having fun in facing a crisis for the love of Christ. There is fun and freedom in loving, and the more widely and deeply you love, the more fun and the greater freedom you have.

To grow in love is to grow in life. You begin to be alive to your fingertips. And your fingertips begin to be healing. You heal everything you touch, and you touch everything.

O Father, I know this is it. Help me to bring love into every area of my life and into all my contacts. Amen.

AFFIRMATION FOR THE DAY: *Love makes everything easy. Even sacrifice seems joy when we love.*

"INCORRIGIBLY HAPPY"

We now turn to the second fruit of the Spirit—joy. It is no mere accident that "joy" follows the first, love. Joy is a by-product of love.

If you seek joy first, it will elude you. But if you go out to love everybody in the name of Jesus, joy will seek you out. You will be automatically joyful.

Everybody wants to be happy, but most people are intensely unhappy. Why? For one thing, they seek happiness in happenings. And happiness comes from inner relations, not from happenings. Westbrook Pegler says: "On my vacations, I drink, gamble, and carouse. How do the drys have a good time?" The answer that sprang to my lips was, "If the drys are Christians, they just have a good time." They don't try to have a good time; they just have it—constitutionally! I passed a place in Los Angeles with this sign on it: "Jones Jolly Joint," and I laughed and said: "That's me—on the inside;" And I didn't have to attend a "joint" to be jolly. Some psychologists made an investigation of the motive behind people's drinking, and the conclusion they came to was: "To get drunk." And why do people want to get drunk? To forget the emptiness of their lives, or to forget guilt, or to escape inner and outer dilemmas. But the Christian doesn't want to forget his emptiness; he rejoices in his inner fullness of life. He doesn't want to forget guilt; he remembers with joy the divine forgiveness. He doesn't want to escape inner and outer dilemmas; he has already escaped into the arms of God, and there he has learned how to resolve inner dilemmas and to use and make something of the outer ones. In short, he has learned how to live—to live! And out of this consciousness joy springs automatically. The pressures of life only squeeze the basic joys out of him. He has a laughter that is born of the consciousness that life approves of him, that it backs him and sustains him and furthers him, no matter what happens. He is incorrigibly happy. "Why don't you get stomach ulcers from the unjust criticism you are constantly getting?" A pastor asked me. And I laughed and said, "Why, I've learned how to laugh." And when you have a basic laughter, not an escapist one, then you're immune.

Dear Father, I thank Thee for this incorrigible joy—a joy that can laugh at hell and high water. I thank Thee. Amen.

AFFIRMATION FOR THE DAY: *Inwardly I shall laugh at everything today, especially at myself.*

"WE ENJOY OUR REDEMPTION"

We continue to look at growth in joy.

Joy is one of the central characteristics of the Christian. And yet a lot of Christians know little or nothing of Christian joy—they are under the lash of duty, not under unabashed delight. They are artificial, not artesian. They creak in soul and body joints on the way to glory. "To glory"? No, they don't walk the glory road now.

And some not only don't expect joy; they don't want it. One grim New Englander had put on his tombstone: "He was a Christian, without emotion." As if one could be a real Christian without emotion! The total person is redeemed and is lighted up in the process of redemption, and because he is lighted up, he sings.

This is being written in a crowded third-class compartment in Japan. A large contingent of travelers is going to a shrine to pay tribute to the war dead. They have sashes around their necks telling of their sad pilgrimage. Some sit in glum silence. Some are trying to forget and be gay through drink. Some are chanting praises to the founder of a Buddhist sect. But that song is a funeral plaint—life is suffering. There is not one lighted up spot in the whole thing, for the simple reason that there is no Easter morning in their faith. There is no inherent joy. The Christian has inherent joy. It is the very essence of his faith. If there is no joy, there is no Christianity, for Christianity is joy. The empty tomb takes away our empty gloom. When we can sing in the face of death, we can sing in the face of everything.

These passages show our privilege of being joyful. "Let us enjoy the peace we have with God" (Rom. 5:1, Moffatt). Some have peace with God but don't enjoy it! Their peace is not peace with a bubble in it—it doesn't boil and overflow. Another passage: "We enjoy our redemption" (Eph. 1:7, Moffatt). To be redeemed and not enjoy that redemption is a contradiction in terms. Again: "We both enjoy our access to the Father in one Spirit" (Eph. 2:18, Moffatt). And finally: "We enjoy our confidence of free access" (Eph. 3:12, Moffatt). Here joy seems to be overflowing because of peace, redemption, access to the Father, and confidence of free access. Joy is inevitable!

Gracious Father, with all this as the basis of life, how can I help but offer the tribute of my joy? I do. I do. Amen.

AFFIRMATION FOR THE DAY: *My greatest joy is in something beyond joy, but which includes joy—free access to the Father.*

"NEVER ASSOCIATED GOD WITH JOY"

We continue to meditate upon Christian joy. We saw yesterday that it is an inevitable part of the Christian expression of life. And yet so few expect or enjoy it. A Roman Catholic who came into a sound experience of spiritual conversion said in surprise, "Strange, but I never associated God with joy before." But now, in an almost impossible home situation, she describes herself as "happy as a lark." She is happy *in spite of!* That is real happiness.

And happiness is not a luxury; it is a necessity. A doctor told me that he told his patients that the most dangerous disease of the world is "unhappiness." It spreads chaos not only in the mind and soul and in one's relationships, but in one's body as well. It probably causes more sickness than any other thing. Here was a woman who wanted to go back to Texas to live, was very unhappy living in Arizona. She suffered from asthma. She went to Texas and was free from asthma. Then she adjusted herself to Arizona and began to live there happily. Her asthma disappeared. A little boy of eight was very unhappy at my leaving his home. He went upstairs, cried, and lost his dinner. His unhappiness upset his digestion.

A nurse was working in a women and children's section of a hospital. That section she said was called "The Clinic of Delinquent Husbands and Fathers." The delinquencies of the husbands and parents produced illnesses in the wives and children. Here were two daughters who had the same family problem. One reacted badly to it, was full of conflicts, wouldn't let anyone speak of her parents, and finally lost her reason. The other met it well, became a matron of a school and was loved and honored and happy. One was the center of gloom and the other of glory.

The head of a trucking firm said that in tracing the cause of accidents he almost invariably ran into an unhappy home situation on the part of the truck driver. The unhappiness produced a conflict which lowered his efficiency as a driver. So the Christian redemption from unhappiness is a needed redemption. If we are not redeemed from unhappiness, we are not fully redeemed.

Father, I thank Thee that redemption extends to the roots of our unhappiness. We can be changed there. Amen.

AFFIRMATION FOR THE DAY: *My happiness is not dependent on happenings, but upon relationships that persist amid happenings.*

"REJOICE AT ALL TIMES"

We continue to look at growth in joy.

Many do not expect their faith to make them basically and fully joyful now. That is reserved for the hereafter. Against this, look at this passage: "Who richly provides us with all the joys of life" (I Tim. 6:17, Moffatt). Note: *all* the joys of life." You do not have to go outside Christ to have all the joys of life fulfilled. And this in no meager, half-starved way—"who richly provides us"; it is abundant living and abundant joy in that abundant living.

A very cultured but unhappy woman said: "If I had what you have, I wouldn't be in the mess I am in." She surrendered the "mess" to Christ and was transformed. She writes: "Every day I have strength and fun to spare." Strength and fun to spare—"He provides us richly with all the joys of life." No meagerness here—strength and fun to spare! And this strength and fun are not because she is not meeting difficulties and opposition. She has both, but she writes: "I grow best under the lash." Her joy is in spite of! The Christian position and privilege is this: "Rejoice at all times" (I Thess. 5:16, Moffatt). Note: "at all times." The Christian can rejoice "at all times," for if nothing else is the cause of his rejoicing, he can find a cause for rejoicing in his own growth. He grows under the lash. So even the lash contributes.

Another verse: "Thank God for everything" (I Thess. 5:18, Moffatt). For everything furthers the Christian if he knows how to use it. But if you thank God for everything, you must see God in everything. Not in its genesis, but in its exodus. It may have begun with the devil, but by the time it gets to you and through you it has a divine destiny running through it. An old lady was praying for bread. Some boys, hearing her, decided to play a trick on her. They threw some loaves down the chimney. The old lady began to shout. The boys said, "But we threw it down, not God." She replied: "The devil may have fetched it, but God sent it."

So wherever an event may come from, by the time it gets to you it has passed the will of God for you and is a source of blessing.

O Father, this kind of Joy is the kind that transforms everything into something else. We thank Thee, thank Thee. Amen.

AFFIRMATION FOR THE DAY: *My joys have their roots in God; therefore they have their fruits no matter what happens.*

"THERE IS SOMETHING WITHIN"

The Christian springs of joy are deep within and can exist whatever the outer may or may not be.

"Your life is hidden" (Col. 3:3, Moffatt). The springs of it are out of sight. The man out of Christ is the man whose life is obvious. His are the wet-weather streams, full when outer circumstances are favorable, but dry when these outer circumstances change. But the Christian's springs are deep in God and never run dry.

This letter expresses it: "I have been reading your books. About four years ago I got hold of *Abundant Living,* and after that I got hold of *The Way.* But I was still confused. Some people said God would not save me in the Baptist Church. So I read *Is the Kingdom of God Realism?* and something happened down in me, and I am not confused any more. I just want you know something happened on the inside, a great change. I don't have that inferiority complex any more. I am changed to the fingertips. I can't tell you how I feel, but I feel good. I just want you to know. There is something within." She has it. That woman knows the secret. There is something within!

And yet people, when expressing well-being, say: "I feel like a million," as if a million would insure happiness. In the Edgewater Beach Hotel, Chicago, twenty years ago there sat seven men who among them controlled more wealth than was in the United States Treasury. But the years went by. One died, living on borrowed money; one was let out of prison to die. Three of them committed suicide, all of them failures. And yet we still say, "I feel like a million." The Christian has more joy to the square inch than others have to the square mile. And it is pure unalloyed joy without a kickback in it. And no hangover! I won't get up tomorrow morning saying: "Stanley Jones, why were you a Christian last night? What made you do it? I'll get up with a grin; some get up with a groan!" "It is superbly wonderful to be a Christian," said a Japanese Nisei girl. Another Japanese Nisei, greeting me on the high-school steps in Hawaii, said: "I'm a Christian, and I'm glad I'm a Christian." Many are Christians, but not glad Christians.

O Christ of the glad heart, impart into our depths Thy gladness, Thy unconquerable gladness. In Thy name. Amen.

AFFIRMATION FOR THE DAY: *I am a gay Christian walking the glory road, because my life is centrally adjusted to God.*

"NOTIFY YOUR FACE"

I woke up early one morning in Sat Tal in India. My custom is to turn this early awakening around 3:30 or 4:00 into a Listening Post. I ask the Father: "Have you anything to say to me?" And in the quietness He tells me to correct this, that, and the other. It is all very quietly searching. But that morning when I asked Him whether he had anything to say, He said: "No, I love you. Go to sleep." Lovely? Well, one morning, after a very hard day in which everything had seemed to go wrong, numerous difficulties piling into the day, I said to Him at the Listening Hour: "Father, thank you for the troubles of the day. I can just feel myself grow under them."

The Stoic endures trouble; the Hindu accepts; the Mohammedan submits; the Buddhist takes it as inevitable; only the Christian exults in the midst of trouble. For he makes his troubles make him.

A Christian policeman as a traffic officer at a busy intersection was spoken to condescendingly by someone: "Yours must be a dog's life," and he replied: "It would be if I were a dog. But I'm not a dog. I'm a saver of lives. Already I have saved three today, right here at this corner. How many have you saved?"

The Christian is incorrigible. If life hands him a lemon, he adds some sugar and makes it into lemonade. But the point is in adding the sugar. Some add more lemon—the lemon of complaint and resentments. This only makes a sour soul and a sour countenance. A Japanese, not knowing English too well, wrote to a friend in America: "The Lord bless you and pickle you." Some look as though they were pickled rather than preserved! I saw a sour-visaged leader of song trying to get a group of people to sing joyously. His face canceled out everything he said. Many of our faces undo all we try to do. I often ask an audience singing a joyous hymn in a melancholy way: "Are you happy?" And when they say, "Yes," I suggest that they notify their faces! The Psalmist says: "Make a joyful noise to the rock of our salvation." If you do, then from that Rock you get a joyful echo in return. You get back from life what you give.

Gracious Father, make me gracious. Fill me with Thy joy, for the world is sad, and I must not add to its gloom. Amen.

AFFIRMATION FOR THE DAY: *I shall make a joyful noise to the Rock of my salvation and get back the echoes of joy I have produced in others.*

"THE SOLID GLORY"

The Christian's joy is not in what he possesses, nor in what he does, nor in what others do for him. It is in relationships that abide amid the flux of possession and nonpossession, of success and failure, of good treatment and ill treatment. The Christian can do without anything on earth—even life on earth, for he has a permanent eternal life now which is rooted in eternity.

Rendel Harris says: "Joy is the strength of the people of God; it is their glory; it is their characteristic mark." And when the mark is absent, then the characteristic of a Christian is absent. Joy is the natural fruit of Christian living. And because it is natural, it finds joy in simple things.

There are two ways to be rich; one is in the abundance of your possessions, and the other is in the fewness of your wants. Jesus said of himself: "Foxes have holes, and birds of the air have nests; but the Son of man hath not where to lay his head," and yet "He thrilled with joy at that hour in the holy Spirit" (Luke 10:21, Moffatt). His joy was not in His circumstances, but in His inner-stances. They remained the same no matter what happened on the outside. Therefore His joy was invulnerable.

Here is an important passage: "I have told you this, that my joy may be within you and your joy complete" (John 15:11, Moffatt). This points to the fact that His joy and our joy are not different types of joy—they are not alien, but allied. You cannot take His joy without finding your own joy complete. For we are made in the inner structure of our being for His joy. His joy completes ours. Therefore the idea that the Christian joy is an imported joy as a reward in heaven instead of an intrinsic life joy now stretching out into heaven, is false. The Christian joy is a joy from a sense of well-being, of harmony with the sum total of reality, of feeling the music of the spheres singing its way through our own souls, of direct and immediate contact with His joy.

O Father, I thank Thee that I have found an ultimate joy, unshakable, immeasurable, and eternal. I thank Thee. Amen.

AFFIRMATION FOR THE DAY: *My joy will outlast all earthly joys and will still be singing when they are silent and gone.*

STEPS TO GROWTH IN JOY

We come this week to take the steps to joy.

First, *Make up your mind that joy, not gloom, is your birthright as a child of God and is the natural way to live.* You are made for joy, and if there is gloom, there is something wrong. Joy is blocked. Clear away the blocks, and joy comes automatically. If you are gloomy, then don't look around for the cause; look within. If you have an unhappy home, explore the possibility of the cause being in the person your mate married. Stop blaming your circumstances.

Here was a very cultured woman who lost her husband. Every day she went out into the yard and listened to a bird that seemed to say, "Poor Helen, poor Helen." She took a morbid interest in the sympathy of that bird. It boosted her self-pity. Then one day at the Ashram in Canada as I spoke at a vesper service at the side of a pond, a large, deep-throated bullfrog kept punctuating what I said with a loud, "So what? So what?" She caught its message and stood up in the closing meeting and said: "I've been listening to the bird saying, Poor Helen; now I'm through listening to him. I'm going to listen to that bullfrog saying, So What? I'm through with gloom. I'm accepting gladness." When she made up her mind to live a life of gladness instead of gloom, she did. Lincoln once said that "a person is about as happy as he makes up his mind to be."

Someone has put it this way: "I am an optimist. My favorite motto, which is embroidered on a pillow I carry with me when I travel, is, 'Never complain. Never explain.'" Remember that portion "Never complain." We can make life woeful or wonderful according to the way we take it. You're natural if you're joyous and happy; you're unnatural if you're unhappy and gloomy. As someone has said, "It takes sixty-two muscles of the face to frown, but only thirteen muscles to smile. Then why overwork your face?" You're made inherently to smile rather than to frown. Then be natural. A man said, "I prefer the east-west face, rather than the north-south face." If you've had a north-south face, turn it into an east-west face. It's easier on you and others!

O Father, help me to take my birthright of joy and live the life for which I'm made. I will cease being unnatural. Amen.

AFFIRMATION FOR THE DAY: *My joy is a simple, natural, spontaneous joy based on right relations to God and myself.*

"LIMP IN AND LEAP OUT"

Second, *Make up your mind where your joy is going to center— it's going to center in God.* If you continue to think that your joy is going to center in this thing, that thing, or the other thing, you're doomed to disappointment. It will let you down. Only in one place in this universe can you put your whole weight down—on God. Everything else is a staff upon which, if you lean too hard, it will break and pierce your hand—and your heart. But you can lean on God, absolutely, and He will hold you, absolutely.

Here is the judgment of one who tries to live without God: "This living is a road that leads to a dark forest—that dwindles to a morass. A wall beyond which is an abyss, and a horizon, beyond which is nothing." In Christ you don't end with "nothing." You end with everything! Now and forever! It holds! Now and forever! Make up your mind that there is an absolutely trustable spot in the universe, and only one—and that spot is God.

Third, *Since you have decided that God will be the center of your joy, now surrender yourself and all you have into His hands.* If He is going to make the total you joyful, He must have the total you. Let Him make you over from the ground up. I saw a sign over a garage which specialized in repairing broken car springs, saying: "Limp in and leap out." That's what surrender of yourself and your sorrow and gloom to God will mean; you will limp in, and you will leap out! If you've been bumping through life on broken springs of joy, come to Him and try a full surrender.

There is this passage: "And they called the name of that place Bochim [Weeper]; and they sacrificed there to the Lord" (Judg. 2:5, R.S.V.). Many sacrifice at the place of weeping. You need not. You can sacrifice at the place of joy. When you do, then you fit—fit into the purpose for which you are made. His will is your freedom. When you are most His, you are most your own. So the surrender is not a surrender; it is a swap—a swapping of conflict for concord, of all-in-pieces for all-of-a-piece, of hell for heaven. You limp in, and you leap out.

O Father, help me not to withhold myself and thus impoverish myself. Take me. I give all freely and gladly. Amen.

AFFIRMATION FOR THE DAY: *I am not withholding myself; God is not withholding Himself. Where these two meet, joy is inevitable.*

142

"SENT LEANNESS INTO THEIR SOULS"

We take the third step: *Third, in making the surrender be sure that no areas of conflict are left behind.* More failures come at this place than at any other. The rock on which the joy of many flounders is the rock of compromise. We give and then withhold. And the thing withheld cancels out the rest. The joy dies.

Judas got what he thought he wanted—money. And then after he got it, he found he didn't want it and threw it down. You will not like anything you take in the place of Christ. You will inwardly or outwardly throw it down. George Bernard Shaw once said that "there are two tragedies in life: One not to get your heart's desire, and the other to get it." And the biggest tragedy is to get your heart's desire if you get it in lieu of God's desire for you. God's desire is your real desire. Any desire against His desire is a false, spurious desire that will turn sour on your hands.

This passage is vivid and very true: "The sins of other men are not apparent, but are dogging them, nevertheless, under the surface" (I Tim. 5:25, Phillips). "Not apparent, but are dogging them, nevertheless, under the surface"—this is the description of the inner life of many a man who has taken something into his life other than, and against, God's will.

There are many who build their lives on the flesh instead of the spirit, and then the years come and go, and the flesh is unable to sustain the pleasure any longer. It fades out and with it the pleasure. There is the picture of a man who is sniffing the empty perfume bottles in an apothecary's shop. Many men and women, who have lived a life in the flesh, are reduced in after years to sniffing the empty bottles of their lusts as they try to live over again in memory their flesh life. It's a sorry spectacle. They took pleasure for joy, and pleasure lets them down—and how!

It is said: "He gave them their request; but sent leanness into their soul." The saddest sad sight on this planet is a person who has had the desires of his heart but has found not fufillment, but leanness of soul.

O Father, I thank Thee that Thy joys are joys—full stop! And they last. And they get richer and fuller all the time. Amen.

AFFIRMATION FOR THE DAY: *My joys are growing richer in content, wider and deeper in extent, because purer in intent.*

SORROW WILL GET BEHIND OUR ARMOR

Fourth, *Don't try to protect yourself against sorrow, for it is bound to come. Face it in Jesus' name and turn it into joy.* The attempt to stop up all the holes against sorrow is bound to fail. It will get behind our armor in spite of all that we do.

Gautama Buddha as a youth in a princely palace was protected from all signs of decay. When he was taken into the garden, maids were sent out to take away all decaying flowers, all fallen leaves, so he would be protected against all signs of suffering and death. Then from that protected situation he went out one day and saw a corpse. It shocked him. His reaction was spiritually violent, and later he came to the startling conclusion that existence and suffering were one. His whole system was founded on that. When he was about to die, he asked for some leaves, fallen leaves, and calling his followers, he said to them: "Take these leaves, there are more, spread them." So they went out with dead leaves in their hands to spread the message that life is fundamentally suffering, that the only thing to do is to escape it into Nirvana, the state of the snuffed-out candle—extinction of personality.

Here was a dramatic and tragic example of trying to protect oneself from suffering. The result was a system of philosophy based on a vast pessimism. The Christian faith is the opposite of that. It exposes one straight off to the very heart of suffering, to a cross. And then it proceeds to take that suffering and turn it into salvation; the cross becomes an Easter morning. The worst is met and changed into the best. Pains are turned into paeans. A singing optimism is won out of a dark pessimism. The Christian sings in spite of.

"Although they may in the usual way slander you as evil-doers yet when disasters come, they may glorify God when they see how well you conduct yourselves" (I Pet. 2:13, Phillips). Note: "when disasters come"—they are bound to come to everybody, and the Christian is not exempt. He is a part of a mortal, decaying world. But he exults in the face of it. Upon his heartstrings sweeps the bow of God's joy, and then, the music, the music!

Father, I thank Thee that everything furthers those who follow Thee, that pain too can make us sing the sweeter. Amen.

AFFIRMATION FOR THE DAY: *When disasters come, I shall make them doors—doors into richer, fuller, more effective living.*

THE BEST OUT OF THE WORST

A young woman was bitter against her mother because the mother, a member of a cult telling people that all is sweetness and light, had let her down. Life was not all sweetness and light; it could be, and was, tragic. But the mother had not prepared the girl for this; hence the bitterness.

A woman put it this way in one of our Ashrams: "I have been going to the cults. They all begin with me and my happiness. But I feel instinctively that I'm not the place to begin. Here you told us that the first thing is to 'belong.' That starts things in the right place and puts me in my place. Now I am safe." And since she was safe, her happiness was safe too. For she could now stand anything that could happen. She had lost herself—what else could she lose? Nothing!

All others are baffled when life is tragic. Only the cross has a saving word then. For then wounds answer our wounds and heal them. For out of the worst He wrings the best and makes life most victorious when life is most victimized. This is joy indeed.

The account says: "When Jesus heard that John had been arrested. . . . From that day Jesus began to preach, saying 'Repent, the Reign of heaven is near'" (Matt. 4:12, 17, Moffatt). Or, as Mark puts it, "After John had been arrested, Jesus went to Galilee preaching the gospel of God" (Mark 1:14, Moffatt). At the darkest moment, when His forerunner had been arrested, foreshadowing the fact that His turn would also come soon, He went out and preached the good news about God! "About God"—why didn't God interfere and save John? That's what He would have to do according to the cults that proclaim exemption from suffering for the Christian. But He didn't! He did something better. He made the beheading of John and the crucifixion of Jesus redemptive—turned them into other and higher purposes. When you can do that, then you have a joy which is joy indeed!

O Father, Thou hast given me a safe joy, a joy that can stand anything because it can use everything. I thank Thee. Amen.

AFFIRMATION FOR THE DAY: *Everything that kicks me today shall kick me forward. I shall determine the direction.*

GETTING BACK THE ECHO

Fifth, *Go out and give joy, and joy will come back to you.* Joy is a gift of God to you, and having freely received, you must freely give.

Some put it on a legal basis: "I have a right to be happy—the world owes it to me." This type of mentality is always unhappy.

To get happiness, you must forget it. The happiest people in the world are the people who deliberately take on themselves sorrow and pain in behalf of others. In the midst of their labors they catch a strange, wild, deep joy.

Those who take joy as the gift of God are the truly joyous, sometimes the hilariously joyous. A Salvation Army convert, now playing the horn for God, said in a moment of ecstacy: "I feel so full of joy I could blow this horn out straight!" Only the Christian knows that kind of joy—joy uncontainable!

Now that it is a gift, then the only thing to do is to go out and share that gift. And when we share it, it multiplies on our hands like the five loaves and two fishes in the hands of Jesus. We give five loaves and two fishes and then gather up twelve baskets of joy!

Mary, whom I shall mention later, gives vent to her joy. She goes out on a hilltop on her farm and calls toward the house and barn, "Praise the Lord," and the house and the barn echo, "Praise the Lord." She gives out one voice and gets back two! Then she varies it: "I love the Lord," and the house and the barn reply, "I love the Lord. . . . I love the Lord."

A woman went to see a famous woman, and as she came away, she said: "I felt as though after talking to her I wanted to go into a church and pray." Some people do that to us. When we leave them, we find a song singing its way into our hearts. Their joy kindles our joy. Just as we can "smile a smile out of the baby," so we can joy a joy out of the joyless and a song out of the songless. A young man expressed this when he said: "When I went to him, I was looking down; when I left him, I was looking up." It is our privilege to light a candle in the darkness and to sing a song out of the heavyhearted.

O Father, I thank Thee that Thou hast given me the most joyous of tasks—to spread joy. Help me to begin. Amen.

AFFIRMATION FOR THE DAY: *A sorrow shared is a sorrow halved; a joy shared is a joy multiplied. I shall multiply my joys today.*

"DON'T BOTTLE IT"

We come now to our last step in growing in joy.

Fifth, *Substitute for all gloomy words joyous ones; replace scowls with a smile and long looks with laughter.* For the expression deepens the impression. The use of pessimistic words tends to produce pessimistic moods. A scowling face tends to produce a scowling spirit. And if you set your face for laughter, it induces the laughing spirit. Not necessarily, but the physical expression tends to produce the spiritual counterpart. This doesn't mean that we are pleading for a Cheshire-cat type of perpetual grin. Nothing is more irritating than that. But the physical does influence the spiritual. Set the physical for joy. Expect joy; exude joy.

As someone has said, "Laughter is a fine tonic. Don't bottle it." For if you bottle it, it will evaporate.

A brilliant woman, a psychologist, made a complete surrender of all her problems to God, and at the end of the first day of release she said: "My face muscles are actually sore from being held up so much by smiles and laughter." She had a face lifting from within.

The deep-down laughter of essential harmony will produce the outer manifestation. "The cup that is filled with sweetness will not spill bitterness no matter how hard it is knocked."

Mary had an aunt come with her when Mary's boy was to undergo brain surgery of a very severe type, a matter of life and death. After the aunt had been with her for an hour, she said: "Well, I might as well have stayed at home, for you certainly don't need any comforting, and besides you are helping me through this—instead of my helping you through, as I came to do!" Mary's joy made her incorrigibly happy in the very face of possible calamity. Her joy was from the inside out.

But while this is profoundly true, nevertheless it is a two-way traffic: it can work from the inside out and from the outside in. So when you get to taking yourself and life too seriously, deliberately go to the looking glass and burst out laughing. I often do it. It's contagious. The inside catches it.

O Father, I thank Thee that Thou hast set laughter in our hearts and on our faces. Help me to use Thy gift. Amen.

AFFIRMATION FOR THE DAY: *A ban on all joyless words, attitudes, and thoughts; a green light to all joyful words, attitudes, and thoughts.*

GROWING IN PEACE

We pass now in our meditations from joy to peace. The third fruit of the Spirit is peace. This order is an inspired order: First, love—love is pre-eminent; then joy—joy comes as a result of love; and then peace—peace is joy grown quiet and assured. Joy simmers down into peace. Joy is peace with its hat in the air, and peace is joy with its arms folded in serene assurance. We cannot live all the time in ecstasy; we must simmer down into quiet peace. Sometimes He

> Takes away my trouble
> And gives me a bubble.

But He also lets the bubble quiet down, and we feel the depths of peace—and how deep those depths can be!

Before we go into the matter of growth in peace, let us get one thing straight. It is important to settle whether we are going to find peace instead of a pseudo peace. There are many who look on religion as a device to give them peace of mind. An able minister put it this way: "I was using Jesus. He came to bring me peace of mind." This using of God to give us peace of mind and to make us healthy is a species of self-idolatry which is very prevalent and very popular —and very shallow. It makes God serve us instead of our serving God. We are the center, and God is the cosmic bellhop to supply our needs. We use God, and everything dances attendance on us, including God.

The phrase "peace of mind" in itself reveals the shallowness of the quest. You cannot have peace of mind unless you have something deeper than peace of mind. When you have peace at the depths of your spirit, then peace of mind is an outcome of that deeper peace. You cannot have peace in the mind if there is conflict in the spirit. So your quest, while it includes peace of mind, must be deeper—it must be peace in the essential you. You yourself in your essential make-up must be a harmonized person. Then and then only will there be peace of mind. To tinker with the mind and let the depths be untouched is just to tinker.

O Father God, give me the peace that passeth knowledge—a peace that I do not possess, but that possesses me. Amen.

AFFIRMATION FOR THE DAY: *Peace shall not be my quest, but the by-product of my relations to God and life.*

148

A PAGAN AND A CHRISTIAN PEACE

We are studying growth in Christian peace. I call it Christian peace in contrast to a pagan peace—a peace that is attempted by dealing with thought processes of the mind without reference to God. The Scripture says, "There is no peace to the wicked," and we may add, "There is no peace to the pagan," though he may be moral according to accepted standards and not wicked. Why? Because peace comes from adjustment—adjustment to reality—and there can be no adjustment to reality without adjustment to God. Peace of mind breaks down if at the center of it is eating the worm of doubt about that ultimate adjustment. A calamity will push it over.

This is what I mean by Christian peace, a tough-fibered kind of peace that can stand anything that can happen.

Although I was born of Jewish parents, I was not interested in Judaism or Christianity. So I turned away from all religion and tried to get as much pleasure as possible out of life. I often pondered: "What is life all about? Our bodies are getting weaker, our teeth will decay; what anyway is the purpose of life?" I treated someone mean, and I felt the guilt before me. My older brother was converted, and I began to read the New Testament. This struck me: "Ask, and it shall be given you; seek, and ye shall find." When I read this, a miracle happened. God lifted me into a different world. I could feel the love of God as one can feel the warm sunbeams shining. I slept well that night, and early in the morning I walked outside into a different world. . . . The burden of sin and guilt had rolled away. Also my attitude in life changed. Before my conversion I was 100 per cent selfish. Now I wanted to help people. Before I was restless; now I know a peace that passeth understanding.

While this man was carrying on his work in jails and hospitals, he was stricken with an incurable disease that gradually made him more and more helpless. His spirit is serene and calm and joyous. In a wheel chair he said to me laughingly, "I'm going to walk all over God's heaven." Here was peace, perfect peace, in the face of growing helplessness. He calmly looks life in the face and says: "Do your worst or your best. I have peace, adequate peace, within."

O Christ, Thou art Master of time and tide and turmoil. Thy will is peace, perfect peace, when perfectly obeyed. Amen.

AFFIRMATION FOR THE DAY: *"Thou wilt keep him in perfect peace, whose mind is stayed on Thee."*

"THIS TOO WILL PASS"

We are studying a Christian peace. This peace cannot only stand anything that comes upon us; it can use everything. When you can use everything that comes, you can calmly await everything, sure that you can turn it by the grace of God into something else.

A motto on a wall of a pastor's house said: "This too will pass." This is good and very true, for everything including pain and sorrow will pass. But the Christian can make that motto read: "This too will pass into something higher." For the Christian has the strange alchemy of changing the base metal of human events, including pain and sorrow, into the gold of the Kingdom. Therefore his peace is based on a solid security—the security of knowing that every hurtful thing can be turned into a helpful thing, every injustice into an opportunity for witnessing. This brings what Peter calls "serene assurance": "Be eager to be found by him unspotted and unblemished in serene assurance" (II Pet. 3:14, Moffatt).

Any peace based on mental tricks will let you down. This will hold you up because it has the universe behind it. This is solid peace.

It is the kind of peace Jesus had: "Peace I leave to you, my peace I give to you; I give it not as the world gives its 'Peace!' Let not your hearts be disquieted or timid" (John 14:27, Moffatt). That last phrase, "or timid," implies a spirit that can walk straight up to life confident that it can find some good in the worst that comes. This verse emphasizes that: "I have said all this to you that in me you may have peace; in the world you have trouble, but courage!—I have conquered the world" (John 16:33, Moffatt). And within that world which He has conquered is included every single thing you have to meet in your life. Therefore, if you remain in Him and accept and use His victory over the world, then you are secure, absolutely secure. Then you can say: "All that I am, and all that I hope to be, I place lovingly in the hands of my Father, knowing full well that that which is for my best good shall come unto me, and no power on earth can prevent it." Then you have unshakable peace.

O Jesus, I know that in Thee I have peace. Help me to abide in Thee, knowing that together we can meet anything that may happen. Amen.

AFFIRMATION FOR THE DAY: *My security is not in securities,, but it comes from being secure in God, who changes not.*

THE SUBCONSCIOUS AT PEACE

We ended yesterday by saying that when we are "in Christ," we are secure. I saw a bird's nest hollowed out of a prickly cactus tree in the deserts of Arizona. It was surrounded by thorns, but among these thorns it had hollowed out a place of security and peace. I said to myself: "In the midst of a thorny world I can find a place of peace in the very heart of God."

And that peace is available in the hour of crisis. Here was a woman who put up with a drunken husband when he used to lock her out of her house for days. He came home one day and in a drunken fit choked her until she was getting blue in the face, when the Inner Voice said: "Relax." She did, and as she did so, she slumped out of his grasp and sank upon the floor—saved.

Her subconscious mind was at peace and could be spoken to in a crisis. For the subconscious is included in this peace, and included especially. If the subconscious is not redeemed from clash and chaos, then that unpeace of the subconscious will spill over into the conscious and will trouble it. A research scientist was showing me around a raja's palace now converted into a science laboratory. He said: "I can convert the upper stories into an All-India Drug Research Laboratory, but the cellar with its many subterranean passages seems impossible to convert." The subconscious mind is like that cellar—difficult to convert from old ways. But not impossible. For Christ can save to the uttermost, and the uttermost means the deepmost.

If we have unsurrendered fears and anxieties and conflicts down in the subconscious, then there is not much use in our trying to mop them up in the conscious by various expedients. The subconscious is the place of peace or unpeace. Tackle it there at the source, and then the stream will run peace. And how do we tackle it there? By the one real remedy—surrender! Turn over all you know—the conscious—and all you don't know—the subconscious, and the Holy Spirit will take over the subconscious and will cleanse and co-ordinate and make it peaceful and calm with His presence and His power.

Father, I thank Thee that there can be a total redemption from unpeace. Heal me at the depths, and then I shall be healed. Amen.

AFFIRMATION FOR THE DAY: *My depths are held by peace. The surface may be disturbed; it's the depths that count.*

"THINGS FALL APART"

We saw yesterday that even the subconscious can be full of peace if fully surrendered.

But there is another condition upon which continuing peace depends: "Thou wilt keep him in perfect peace, whose mind is stayed on thee: because he trusteth in thee" (Isa. 26:3). It is not enough to have the subconscious cleansed and controlled by the Holy Spirit; there must be a conscious centering of the mind on God—"stayed" on God. He must not be the place of occasional reference; He must be the center of our affections and our loyalty. And further, He must be the center of our trust—"because he trusteth in Thee."

The lack of trust in God is found in these lines by W. B. Yeats:

> Things fall apart; the centre cannot hold,
> Mere anarchy is loosed upon the world,
>
> .   .   .   .
>
> The best lack all conviction, while the worst
> Are full of passionate intensity.

Things fall apart because the center cannot hold, for the simple reason that the center is not stayed on God. We thought the accumulation of things could stay off anxiety, only to find that it increased it. I have mentioned that it is estimated that five million people go to sleep every night with the aid of sleeping tablets, but one man was so addicted that he set his alarm clock at twelve every night to wake himself up so he could take his sleeping tablets!

Dr. A. J. Gossip says that after Stevenson had published several volumes of hope and joy, a certain critic said that the work was obviously that of some sheltered man, protected from the grim realities of life. "Let this exasperatingly happy person have one touch of rheumatic fever, and he will quickly change his tune." All the while Stevenson was suffering from sciatica and was all but dead from hemorrhages. But he refused to let the medicine bottles on the mantelpiece be the limit of his horizon.

Father, Thou art desirious of giving peace at the depths. Help me to open my depths to Thy healing peace. Amen.

AFFIRMATION FOR THE DAY: *The peace of God helps me; the peace of God holds me; the peace of God controls me.*

WANTS AND NEEDS

In the night hours of wakefulness, instead of worrying about not sleeping, if we turn the whole episode into a Listening Post where we listen to God instead of to our fears, He will probably show us plans where we can change things that rob us of our peace.

A man said to a friend of mine:

I've been in trouble. I've been in debt and didn't seem to be able to pay up. I was always buying things I couldn't pay for. I went to my knees, and God said, "The trouble with you is that you don't know the difference between your wants and your needs. Now what do you really need?" And I replied: "I need a home and a job and transportation." And now I own a parking lot, and I have a home and a job, because I promised God I'd confine myself to my needs and not be led astray by my wants. Now I have peace.

A man came up to me and said: "You said something years ago that has stuck in my mind ever since: There are two ways to be rich —one is in the abundance of your possessions and the other in the fewness of your wants." It is a simple way to be rich—just reduce your wants to your needs. And the needs of life are few—very few. But if you get the disease called gadgetitis, the disease that makes you feel you will be unhappy unless you get that next gadget, then you'll be perpetually uneasy, for the new gadgets make the old ones obsolete.

A man was visiting in the mountains, and as his host gave him a kerosene lamp, he showed him his bed in a lean-to portion of the house and said: "Now if there is anything you want, let us know, and we'll come and show you how you can do without it." He had learned a precious secret—the secret of how to get along without things.

But some people seem bent on worrying over either what they have or what they have not. Here was a man who was worried over being left bereft in old age. He had several hundred thousand dollars laid up, and he was then seventy-six. Afraid of being bereft in old age! School yourself to your needs, and worry will disappear.

O Jesus, Thou hast shown us how to live in simplicity and in great peace. Give us Thy secret, and we will follow. Amen.

AFFIRMATION FOR THE DAY: *Schooled to simplicity, I know life will give me what I need. What more do I need?*

"A SOUL BREATHING PEACE"

Someone has said: "He only is advancing in life whose heart is getting softer, whose blood warmer, whose brain quicker, whose spirit is entering into living peace." "Whose spirit is entering into living peace"—peace, to be peace, must be a living peace, not a dead peace of retreat out of responsibility, or an incasement into insensibility, but a peace of quiet within in the midst of activity and responsibility.

I have mentioned Heb. 4:1, 3 (Moffatt), where there is a kind of rest spoken of as "his Rest"—"the Rest." His Rest is the rest of seeing the end from the beginning, of being adequate to meet it all. This becomes *"the* Rest" for us—the rest of adjustment to God, to yourself, to reality—to everything except evil. We enter this rest by ceasing from our own works—self-dependence (v. 10)—and by receptive faith (v. 3). This rest is called a sabbath-Rest because the Sabbath was a day of ceasing to work and struggle, a day to accept the gifts of God, to be quiet and receptive.

Conversion gives rest from our sins; this experience of entering into His Rest gives rest from ourselves. Here by self-surrender we learn how to renounce all self-dependence and enter into God-dependence and hence into His Rest.

Jesus describes this state of mind and heart thus: "Then, if there is a soul there breathing peace, your peace will rest on him; otherwise it will come back to you" (Luke 10:6, Moffatt). "A soul breathing peace"—he breathes in peace, and he breathes out peace, the rhythm of the intake and the outgo of peace. There must be both; you take in peace by receptivity and give out peace by response. Peace becomes as natural as breathing. It is not an artificial importation; it is the very breath of one's life.

"Jesus then repeated, 'Peace be with you!' . . . And with these words he breathed on them, adding, 'Receive the holy Spirit!'" (John 20:22, 23, Moffatt). His breathing peace on us is the breathing of the peace of the Holy Spirit within us—the peace of adequacy and power, the peace of the Divine Presence deep, deep within.

O Christ, breathe upon my waiting heart Thy best gift—the gift of the Holy Spirit, the Spirit of adequacy and power. Amen.

AFFIRMATION FOR THE DAY: *I am calm in God. I am at home in God. I am at rest in God. I have everything in God.*

STEPS FOR GROWTH IN PEACE

We come now to the steps we are to take to grow in peace.

First, *Growth in peace is growth in adjustment, and growth in adjustment is growth in maturity of character. Therefore growth in peace is the acid test of growth.* Peace is not a luxury to be added to life; it is a sign of a growing life. If I am not growing in peace, I am not growing in life.

Second, *Fix in your mind that growth in peace is possible and is possible for you.* A great many people hold that life is struggle and tension and antagonism, that without these there is no growth. But Jesus taught the opposite of this. He said: "Which of you by taking thought can add to his stature one cubit?" (Luke 12:25). You cannot grow by growing tense and anxious and becoming troubled about growing. He cites the birds and the lilies: Consider the lilies of the field how they grow; they toil not, neither do they spin; and yet I say unto you, That even Solomon in all his glory was not arrayed like one of these" (Matt. 6:28-29). The most splendid was the least striving. It was all effortless assimilation. Open channels brought open possibilities. The plant links its smaller life to the infinite life around it, assimilates it, and grows effortlessly. Learn the art of receptivity, says Jesus; learn how to take in, and then the amount taken in will be the measure of your growth. The tense do not take. They try to grow by expenditure of energy and struggle. This is self-defeating because self-contradictory.

Jesus said: "Keep your loins girt and your lamps lit" (Luke 12:35, Moffatt). Many have their loins girt—the symbol of readiness for tense action. A youth conference had a motto in front: "Courage, God, we are coming." They had their loins girt for action, but whether their lamps were lit was another question. They were going, but where? They hadn't thought about that. Their lamps were not lit.

When we have the inner life lit by the lamp of a quiet peace, then our going is a going with directions certain. First peace, then pace. But pace without peace will leave us in pieces. Don't struggle to grow; surrender to grow. Empty your hands and take the gift.

O Father, all my futile striving leaves me exhausted. All my fruitful receptivity leaves me exhilarated. I thank Thee. Amen.

AFFIRMATION FOR THE DAY: *My lamp shall be lit—adequacy—and my loins girt—readiness for any task.*

155

"REDUCED MY MIND TO A TEACHABLE FRAME"

If peace is an attainment instead of an obtainment, then peace may not be yours. But if it is an obtainment, then it is open to all. This puts the latchstring low enough for the least and the lowliest to reach.

It is not our blood that obtains the peace, but the blood of Jesus that whispers peace within. Many try to obtain peace by their own blood, their own struggles and sacrifice; but it's not by our blood, but His! In an impetuous moment I once said to God: "Lord, I'll give my right arm to get this." And He replied: "Not the gift of your right arm, but give me your right hand, and I'll lead you into it—free! It's a gift!" That changed my whole universe. It became a universe of open and infinite possibilities, for my power to receive was infinite. So the steps become: Relax, Receive, Release.

Third, *Make peace possible for you.* Since peace is possible, then the next step is to make it possible for you. Stand in the way of allowing peace to invade you. Peace is knocking at the door. Lift the latch and let peace come in. Here is what one man said of his own acceptance: "I was afraid to live and afraid to die. I feared people. I distrusted everyone. I found that if we surrender ourselves and our fears to God, all these things will drop away. I've gotten rid of fears and inadequacies." And all he had to do was to stand in the place where Jesus could breathe on him—the place of surrender and receptivity. Calvin put it this way: "God in a sudden conversion reduced my mind to a teachable frame." "A teachable frame"—a frame where you are receptive. There anything can happen; everything can happen. "Thy will is our peace," and when we bring everything into submission to that will, our peace begins and is assured. The Phillips translation puts it this way: "Let the harmony of God reign in your hearts" (Col. 3:15). God is harmony, and when we are in harmony with God, we are in harmony with harmony. "Chaos is God saying, 'No,' to what we are doing in pride and ignorance"; harmony is God saying, "Yes." And when we fully align our lives to God's will, then we live in a state of "Yes"—we have approval from God and ourselves.

Father, I thank Thee that Thou dost will my peace. Help me to accept the will that wills my peace. In Jesus' name. Amen.

AFFIRMATION FOR THE DAY: *Harmony within will tend to produce harmony without; if not, it comes back as greater harmony within.*

"PEACE THAT PASSETH UNDERSTANDING—
AND MISUNDERSTANDING"

Fourth, *Go over your life and root out all things that cause discord.* Go over your relationships and see if there is anything that causes discord between you and others. See how far that discord is your fault. Have you been confessing the sins of others instead of your own?

I came into a home where the husband and wife were quarreling. I got them sufficiently quiet so we could have prayer. I prayed for the wife first. The husband burst into my prayer with this comment: "Yes, Lord, she needs it." He was confessing her sins, not his own. And hence the discord. Paul says: "As much as lieth in you, live peaceably with all men." Note: "as much as lieth in you." You may not be able to live peaceably with all men—the fault may lie in the other person. But as far as it depends on you, you are to live peaceably.

A husband and wife made an agreement that they would not leave the room where a quarrel had taken place until the quarrel had been settled and reconciliation effected. Years later I saw them, and one could see that they were at peace and deeply in love, and their agreement had worked. They planned for peace.

Perhaps the cause of the inner unrest is not in your relationships with one another, but in your relationships with God. A missionary said in one of our round-table conferences: "God and I are not getting on very well together. We seem to be at cross-purposes. And my life is getting more and more dull and unhappy and restless." Of course, for if you won't live in harmony with God, you can't live in harmony with yourself. But when you have no discord with God, you have no discord in yourself. Peace reigns.

And what a peace! It is "a peace that passeth understanding"—and misunderstanding! It is the peace that Wesley had when a mob stoned a building and expected to find him buried and mangled and frightened. Instead they found him leaning against a pillar with stones all around him, asleep. He was at peace with God and had therefore a peace that passed understanding.

Father, help me to let go that last thing that upsets my peace. For I can't afford to live a conflict. In Jesus' name. Amen.

AFFIRMATION FOR THE DAY: *I can become so peaceful that I become peace, so harmonized that I become harmony.*

DISCIPLINE YOUR THOUGHTS

Fifth, *Discipline your thoughts to think thoughts of peace.* Here is the classic passage on this discipline:

Finally, brethren, whatsoever things are true, whatsoever things are honest, whatsoever things are just, whatsoever things are pure, whatsoever things are lovely, whatsoever things are of good report; if there be any virtue, and if there be any praise, think on these things. . . . And the God of peace shall be with you" (Phil. 4:8, 9).

Among the things the inspired writer suggests thinking upon, not one is negative; all are positive. If you constantly think upon the untrue, the dishonest, injustice, impurity, the ugly, things of evil report, vice, and the unpraiseworthy, then the very disharmony of these things will invade you and pervade you. Your peace will be gone. But if you do as Paul suggests then, "the God of peace shall be with you."

I described previously how I had accustomed myself to turning a wakeful period into a Listening Post. When I awake and get what message I can from the Father, then instead of being impatient and upset over the interruption of sleep, I keep repeating to myself these phrases: "There is no fear, no anxiety, no conflict—only faith and harmony and peace." And soon I am back to sleep again.

Here is what a badly crippled invalid wrote and now keeps repeating to herself. Before arthritis laid her low, she was, of all things, a scout for a major-league baseball club, the only woman professional scout and a good one, having discovered some outstanding players.

> Dear Lord, if it be Thy will,
> Remove this suffering and pain
> That undermine and seek to kill
> Fond hopes that may not rise again.
> But if Thou hast a better way,
> Pray give me strength these things to hide
> Behind a smile throughout the day,
> And always, Lord, near me abide.

O Father, help me to think peace and breathe peace so that those that come near me today shall feel my peace. Amen.

AFFIRMATION FOR THE DAY: *There is no fear, no anxiety, no conflict—only faith and harmony and peace.*

158

CONSTRUCTIVE TENSIONS

This story illustrates a Christian peace: Some Christians in the early days were in prison, and the guards came and told them that the next day they were to be beheaded. They were playing chess. One said to the other: "They have come to destroy our peace. They can't do it. The next move is yours." That is peace—real peace.

That leads us to the next fruit of the Spirit: "good temper" (Gal. 5:22, Moffatt). The King James Version puts it "longsuffering." Someone has suggested that longsuffering is love stretched out. It is so elastic and tough that it doesn't break down into bad temper. It maintains good temper amid the flux and flow of human events.

But good temper must not be confused with "apathy." The Stoics made apathy a virtue, and early Christianity tried to Christianize this conception. But it couldn't be done. For apathy, coming from *a*, "not," and *pathos*, "suffering," meaning nonsuffering, leaned in the direction of indifference, and the Christian wasn't indifferent. So apathy could not be assimilated. The Christians cared, and because they cared, they suffered, but they found their equipoise and consequent good temper amid the suffering.

Moreover, just as the Christians were not free from suffering, they were not free from tensions. The violin string free from the violin is free from tensions and hence incapable of music.

Jesus had tensions. "What a tension I suffer, till it is all over." (Luke 12:50, Moffatt). But His tension was a tension harnessed not to fear and anxiety and self-interest, but to redemption. He was on His way to a cross, and that tension was not loosed until He said: "It is finished." That tension did not leave Him frustrated and bad-tempered; it left Him calm and composed with a prayer for forgiveness upon His lips for His enemies. It drove Him, not to pieces, but to peace—the peace of achievement and victory. This was so because the tension was harnessed not to self-will but to God's will. Hence it was a constructive urge. Many of our tensions drive us not to goals, but "drive us nuts." They are harnessed to our fears, to our self-interests, to our resentments.

O Father, harness my tensions to Thy purposes, and then they shall pass into rhythm and song. In Jesus' name. Amen.

AFFIRMATION FOR THE DAY: *All my tensions, redeemed from selfish conflicts, will be harnessed to Kingdom purposes.*

DID THE POISE OF JESUS SNAP?

We saw yesterday that Jesus had tensions. He had a terrific driving force, for His tensions were God's intentions. Hence He was calm and peaceful amid the strain. The strain was not drain; it was recuperative. For we are made for creative achievement, and there can be no creative achievement without tension. But that tension can be peaceful tension.

The question arises, however, Didn't the peaceful tension of Jesus snap when in the synagogue He looked around on them in anger? And also when He blistered the souls of the Pharisees with His burning words of "Woe unto you"? Were these manifestations of bad temper? Hardly. This luminous phrase lights up the situation in regard to looking around upon them in anger: "being grieved for the hardness of their hearts." The anger was grief—grief at their insensibility to human need. It was a grief at what was happening to someone else and not personal pique at what was happening to Himself. That changed the anger from destruction to construction.

In the case of the Pharisees His burning words were an uncovering of the sordid depths of a self-seeking, soured religion. This had to come, for as He lifted the veil from God, He had to lift the veil from the hearts of men. They would never see God unless they saw themselves. So his words were redemptive. His words were like a surgeon's knife—the cutting was not to hurt, but to heal. That this was so can be seen in the climax. He turns from "woes" to weeping. "O Jerusalem, Jerusalem! . . . How often I would fain have gathered your children as a fowl gathers her brood under her wings!" (Matt. 23:37, Moffatt). This redeemed the woes from personal spite into collective salvation.

Usually our temper is bad temper. The ego is wounded and lashes back, not in redemption, but in retaliation. The redemptive temper burns with a steady fire of redemptive intention; the retaliative temper simply burns you up. Note that I say "burns *you* up"—it was intended to burn up the other fellow.

O Father, give me the redemptive intention in all my attitudes and acts. That will save me and them. Amen.

AFFIRMATION FOR THE DAY: *All my temper shall be tempered to Kingdom purposes and to Kingdom purposes alone.*

TWO WAYS TO HONK A HORN

Temper turns to bad or good according to what is behind it. There are two ways to blow the horn of a car—the Christian way and the unchristian. The Christian way very gently calls attention to a situation; the unchristian way not only calls attention to a situation, but it also calls attention to what the honker feels about the situation.

One man put on the back of his car a sign which read: "Honk away, it's your ulcer." The ulcer is usually the visible sign of an ulcerated spirit—ulcerated by fear or resentments.

A lecturer, a Western convert to Hinduism, was lecturing on the occult peace and poise of Hindu mysticism. The lamp on the table came near toppling over as he struck it with a gesticulating hand. He completely lost his temper. He lost his temper and his audience at the same time. A psychiatrist was interviewing a man full of conflicts. In the midst of the interview the phone rang, and because of a mistake in the phone number the psychiatrist swore at the exchange girl. He lost his patience and his patient. For the patient saw that he had little to give except verbal advice.

But when we lose our tempers and take it out on people around us, we do something to ourselves. We give people a piece of our minds and lose our own peace of mind in the process.

The fact is that this taking it out on people around us is usually the projection of an inner conflict with ourselves. The one who is out of patience with the family or business associates is usually out of patience with himself. He projects his conflicts. The cause and the remedy are within himself.

As I walked into a new church, I saw this statement engraved in the stone over the door: "Let every Christian begin the work of union within himself." That is the place to begin—within yourself. For as the Chinese saying puts it: "He who has peace in himself has peace in the family; he who has peace in the family has peace in the world." A prominent man in our country says he is dedicated to peace, but when he lost his temper and wrote a stinging letter, his advocacy of peace was blurred.

O God, give me the temper that is unperturbed amid provocation and remains sweet amid surrounding bitterness. Amen.

AFFIRMATION FOR THE DAY: *I shall be the peaceful exception amid disturbed surroundings, at rest amid restlessness.*

THE RESTRAINT PAID

The greatest single influence in changing bad temper to good temper is the grace of God. A Christian businessman tells how he started life on a small farm in Mississippi. He had a high temper and would get mad and rave and rip when things went wrong. He went to an altar one night and was converted. The next day he went back to plowing new ground with a mule. When the roots hit him on the shins and the plow hit rocks, causing the handle to gouge him in the side, instead of cursing and yelling and beating the mule he just said: "Lord, help me." This went on for some time, and finally the mule of his own accord stopped, twisted around in the traces, and just looked at him in surprise! Later a neighbor who was working in another field came over and said: "Charley, I saw you plowing, but I couldn't hear you. Are you sick?" "No," he replied, "I'm not sick. Got saved last night."

Here is what a schoolteacher says of her change: "I'm still as happy as can be in spite of getting up at six o'clock each morning, I haven't taken a pill since I came home; neither have I felt tired. The children have been bad, and I used to come home exhausted. It is wonderful. What a fool I've been all these years!"

Here was a great moment in the life of Saul: "But some worthless fellows said, 'How can this man save us?' And they despised him, and brought him no present. But he held his peace" (I Sam. 10:27, R.S.V.). Had Saul kept that spirit, he would have been a great man.

Many feel they have to show bad temper to get things done for God. But this passage makes the matter plain: "For man's temper is never the means of achieving God's true goodness" (James 1:20, Phillips). It is the case of the wrong means trying to get to right ends. Wrong means get to wrong ends, inevitably. A pastor thought of writing a stinging reply to one of his members who criticized a friend. He resisted it. Then another criticism came. This time he wrote a stinging reply but decided to tear it up. When for the third time he got a letter from the man, he hated to open it. But when he did, he found in it a check for a thousand dollars for missions.

Father, help me to meet all impatience with patience, all hate with love, all grumpiness with joy. In Jesus' name. Amen.

AFFIRMATION FOR THE DAY: *My temper shall be so tempered it shall produce no tempests—only tender concern.*

BURYING THINGS

A pastor asked a man if he were a Christian, and the man angrily replied, "It's none of your business." The pastor replied, "This is my business. I'm a pastor." And the man snapped, "Then go about it." The pastor held his peace and refrained from "the last word." Two years later this man called up the pastor and apologized for what he had said to him and added that he would like to join his church and take Communion. The pastor did have the last word, and what a word!

A very radiant and spiritually triumphant woman writes: "My family gives me digs now and then. They are only succeeding in disciplining me. I always have the last word. My last word is silence." Her last word in controversy is silence; but when she speaks, people listen, for she speaks out of the depths of silence.

It is possible to retreat into a favorite verse of Scripture and there be held steady when provocation comes. The verse environs us and holds us within its loving embrace. We cannot betray the verse, for it has been a tower of strength to us.

Many people "bury the hatchet," but they leave the handle sticking out. And at the slightest provocation they pull the hatchet up again.

But having the last word usually does not end in having it, for it usually precipitates a debate within you—between you and your conscience over that last word. And then conscience will always have the last word. So this last-word business is a losing business. But letting love have the last word is always a winning business. It is interesting to see how the Old Testament last word is "a curse" (Mal. 4:6), and the New Testament last word is "the grace of our Lord Jesus" (Rev. 22:21). One ends with a "a curse" and the other with "grace." And the last word of grace draws more people to it than the word of a curse. It always does. Honey draws more bees than vinegar. Mary, of whom I shall write later, wrote: "The world ought to be grateful to you, for it has been receiving much better treatment from me since you gave me the gospel." She always has the last word, for that word is love, and love never fails.

Dear Father, let me have the last word always, and may that last word be love—always. For Jesus' sake. Amen.

AFFIRMATION FOR THE DAY: *The world is going to get better treatment from me today because I've had such treatment from Christ.*

STEPS IN GROWTH IN GOOD TEMPER

We come now to the steps in growing in good temper.

First, *Fix it in your mind as an axiom that bad temper is self-defeating—it gets you nowhere except backward.* The bad-tempered can't win, for the bad temper itself is defeat. Two bitter last words never made a sweetheart or a sweet home.

Second, *Cultivate good temper as a life policy.* Good temper is not a luxury; it is a necessity. You can't go through life on any other basis and go through. You will always be up against opposition and hate if you manifest bad temper. "A soft answer turneth away wrath: but grievous words stir up anger." If you give out anger, you will live in an angry world.

So fix it as one of life's basic decisions: no bad temper ever, good temper always.

Third, *Remember that your keeping of your temper is the victory.* You have lost if you lose your temper. No matter what temporary advantage you may have gained, you have lost your case if you lose your temper. If you control your temper, you control the situation.

Fourth, *Breathe a prayer for those with whom you are about to lose your temper.* That prayer will be the pivot on which impending defeat will turn to victory. If one were to pick out the three greatest Christians in the New Testament, the choice would undoubtedly be Jesus (Some say: "The only Christian who ever lived!"), Paul, and Stephen. And if one were to pick out the greatest facts in their lives, the choice would be the fact that all three died with a prayer for forgiveness of their enemies upon their lips. Jesus died praying, "Father, forgive them"; Stephen died praying, "Lord, lay not this sin to their charge," and Paul, writing his valedictory, said: "The first time I had to defend myself, I had no supporters; everyone deserted me. (God grant it may not be brought up against them!)" (II Tim. 4:16, Moffatt). These were the crowning acts of their lives. Prayer for enemies, potential or real, is the crowning act of prayer. And when you pray for your enemies, it proves to be a catharsis for yourself.

Father, put prayer upon my lips instead of bitter words—and deeper: put prayer into my heart for my "friends." Amen.

AFFIRMATION FOR THE DAY: *I shall meet all unpleasantness with a barrage of prayer and love today.*

MEET RISING TEMPER WITH A PRAYER

We come now to the next step in growing in good temper. The last step was to pray for others with whom you are tempted to lose your temper.

Fifth, *Breathe a prayer for yourself when you are about to lose your good temper.* For you are the center of the problem at that moment. Jesus said: "Take heed to yourselves: If thy brother trespass against thee, . . . forgive him" (Luke 17:3). Take heed to yourself at a particular moment—at the moment when your brother sins against you. For your reaction to what he does to you may color and determine your whole life for good or ill. Your actions are important, but your reactions are just as important. Many are correct according to actions, but they react badly to what happens to them. They are converted in their actions, but not in their reactions.

Here is the way a woman reacted to an impending calamity. "I had glaucoma of the eyes with a short time of sight left. You counseled and prayed with me, and out of that came a time of peace, a surrender to the will of God that has recently brought an amazing result. On last examination about a month ago the doctor found the tension entirely gone—negative."

Mary, a radiant Christian of whom I shall write more, writes:

I went out to shut the chickens up for the night and found the boys had closed the door and turned out the light, and all the chickens were on the outside. Perhaps you know that chickens can't see in the dark if you shine any light on them—it blinds them. Well, three years ago I would have gone in and given the boys a good spanking and made them get the chickens in. Tonight when I saw what was wrong, I didn't even *stop singing!* I just went inside the chicken house to turn the light on, but found the bulb was burned out! And instead of being more disgusted, as I would have been (B.C.), I just got a new one and then, with a patience I had never known before, I worked those chickens in with tenderness and kindness and never even mentioned the fact to the boys! And when the last chicken was in, I bade them all good night and thanked Him for helping me get them all in so easily by simply *not controlling the chickens, but me!*

Dear Father, help me in the hour of pressure and crisis to react by word and act in a truly Christian way. Amen.

AFFIRMATION FOR THE DAY: *I shall wear down all hate by love, all disturbance by the unperturbed heart.*

THICKEN YOUR SKIN

Sixth, *Thicken your skin deliberately so you will no longer be a touchy individual.* Many find themselves very thin-skinned. I was once one of them. On board ship going out to India forty-six years ago I would deliberately stay down in my cabin rather than walk on deck, lest someone would say something about me. Believe it or not, I was shy. But through the years I've had to toughen my skin, so now I wonder if my skin isn't a rhinoceros hide! I've had to thicken it to survive in a thorny, critical world.

Someone remarked, "I don't believe you know when you are insulted." And I replied, "Well, I suppose I don't. For my soul is too glad and too great to be the enemy of any man."

Don't go around with a chip on your shoulder. If you do, it will probably be from the block above!

Don't go around with a chip on your shoulder, but with a Hand on your shoulder. Have a sense of mission, a sense of working out a plan, a divine plan; and then you won't mind these hurts that come, for you are working out something big and important. In the light of that, what is a scratch or two! We fought a forest fire in India for twelve hours. When I came back, I found my big toenail was black with a smash from a falling rock, so badly smashed it eventually came off. But I could not even remember when the hurt had occurred. I hadn't felt it, for the putting out of the fire had absorbed me. Have a task so big that you'll not even feel the hurts along the way.

I received a letter from a woman who is very able and could do great things, but she has a complex that the world is conspiring against her to ruin her. And no one is ruining her except herself!

Inoculate yourself with mild doses of self-criticism, so that you'll be immune against the criticism of others. When criticism comes, you can say. "That isn't anything. I've said far worse things about myself."

Someone said of a certain man, "He is the best oiled and smoothest running bit of human machinery I have ever seen." One of the reasons for that smooth-running machinery was that he oiled his machinery by a daily self-criticism.

Father, help me this day to go over my life in Thy presence with such a severe self-criticism that nothing else will matter. Amen.

AFFIRMATION FOR THE DAY: *I shall inoculate myself against all criticisms by being more critical of myself than others can be.*

HAVE A MEMORY THAT FORGETS

This is so important that we take another step to good humor.

Seventh, *Have a convenient memory—a memory that easily forgets hurts and slights.* Some people have long memories for slights and hurts and short ones for the blessings and good things of life. A college turned down Dr. George Washington Carver when it found he was a Negro. Years later when Dr. Carver became famous, I asked him what college it was, for he had never mentioned the name. He brushed it aside and said, "Oh, that doesn't matter." And he would not tell me! And rightly so, for if he had mentioned it, it would have fixed it more and more in his mind.

I said to a boy who had lost his foot in Korea by stepping on a hidden mine in the snow: "You paid a real price—you lost your foot." "Oh," he replied—cheerily, "I got off pretty well. I only left a foot. Others never came back at all. I was lucky." Keep your eyes on your blessings, not on your blightings. And your very spirit will heal over the blights, and heal them over quickly.

Have a convenient forgettory. On the wall of a room in a church was this motto; "Forget, Forgive, For God." But the first thing is "forget." Don't take your hurt to bed with you. Drop it into the love of God and bury it there. A pastor suggests an added collection in which we pass the collection plate and drop into it our fears and anxieties. And our hurts, I would add. Then take them to the foot of the cross and bury them. Wipe them out of your memory.

When these thoughts come back, perhaps in waking hours, do what I found myself doing one morning in an early waking hour. Repeat these words: "The love of God invades me, the peace of God pervades me, the will of God persuades me, and I am wholly His." Then there will be no room for hurt feelings, or real or imaginary slights.

When Dr. George Washington Carver heard the news in a classroom that his life earnings had been wiped out, he went on with his teaching as though nothing had happened. And nothing really had happened. He and his lifework were still intact. He remembered that and never looked back.

Father, I thank Thee that Thou hast given us the power to forget. Help me to use it this day on everything unpleasant. Amen.

AFFIRMATION FOR THE DAY: *I bury my slights and hurts in the sea of gratitude for what Christ has done for me.*

CULTIVATE THE POWER TO LAUGH

Eighth, *If you are to grow in good temper, you must grow in good humor.* God has given us the power of laughter not only to laugh at things, but to laugh off things. There is no good in a movement or a person where there is no good humor. For good has laughter as a corollary. There is something basically wrong with a person who doesn't know how to laugh.

A friend of mine was a Communist leader in India for ten years, most of this time underground. When the Politburo decided that he should sabotage a train, his background Christianity revolted. He renounced Communism. He stayed with a Christian friend of mine whose wife said, "For two whole weeks he never smiled. Only at the end of two weeks did he manage to smile." Explaining this afterward, he said: "We were in a grim business—plotting against society, here and there and everywhere, and distrusting everybody. There was no place for a smile." Depend on it, where you cannot smile, you cannot live. For Life is basically disapproving of you.

I have watched groups as they come into an Ashram. Many are tied up with fears, resentments, self-preoccupation, and guilts. We ask them to tell their needs. They do. They get up and out these inner conflicts and learn the art of receiving grace. Then the laughter begins. They grow progressively gayer as the week goes on. By the end of the week they have a hair-trigger laugh. They are ready to laugh at anything, even themselves. The art of laughing at yourself is the highest kind of laughter.

And yet the Christian faith is often looked on as a gloomy thing. There is a story of a minister coming to his new parish. A group at the railway station went up to a man who looked like he might be the new minister and asked him if he were. "No," replied the man, "indigestion makes me look this way." There is something basically wrong with a faith which doesn't make you progressively gayer.

And the good humor will make you good-tempered. Laughter will become a settled habit. And it will be real laughter too.

O Jesus, Thou wast "annointed with the oil of gladness above Thy fellows." Teach me Thy secret of holy laughter. Amen.

AFFIRMATION FOR THE DAY: *Since I am under redemption, I shall talk redeemed, think redeemed, and look redeemed.*

GROWTH IN KINDLINESS

We come now to the next fruit of the Spirit—kindliness.

This is a very homely virtue, homely in the British sense of belonging to the home—a very commonplace, ordinary virtue. And yet it is ordinary as salt, and as essential. Without kindliness there is no virtue in the other virtues. It puts a flavor into all the other virtues; without it they are insipid and tasteless; or worse, they degenerate into vices. Love, joy, peace, good temper, without kindliness are very doubtful virtues. So it is no chance that this is the middle virtue of the nine, putting flavor into all the others.

So to grow in kindliness is to grow in virtues that are flavored with a certain spirit. The spirit of kindliness pervades everything. The Old Testament, especially the Psalms, uses the expression "lovingkindness." A little boy explained the difference between kindness and lovingkindness: "Kindness is when your mother gives you a piece of bread and butter, but it is lovingkindness when she puts jam on it as well."

But in the New Testament a content has gone into kindness that made the adding of "loving" unnecessary. We have quoted a passage into which the content of Jesus has gone into the words: "Treat one another with the same spirit as you experience in Christ Jesus" (Phil. 2:5, Moffatt). Not merely the same actions, but the same spirit in the actions as was in Jesus. This is the high water of morality in this universe. Beyond this the human race will not, and cannot, progress. This is a character and conduct ultimate. This gives kindness a plus—an infinite plus.

And this saves kindness from mere maudlin sentimentality. It can be very severe—severe because He loves so deeply that He often has to save us by hard refusals. And His kindness can cut—it can cut when, like a surgeon, He insists on cutting out of us moral tumors and cancers. But always His severity is security. It is redemptive. He loves us too much to let us go.

O Christ, show Thy kindness to me this day even if it be a cutting kindness, for I don't want leniency; I want life. Amen.

AFFIRMATION FOR THE DAY: *I want God to be kind to me in the form that my deepest necessities demand.*

THE KINDNESS REMAINS

We left off yesterday when we were considering the fact that Jesus can be as hard as flint at the very moment He is as tender as a mother. He can be tenderly terrible and terribly tender. A little orphaned boy was practically adopted by a soldier during the war. One day he let slip a swear word, and when he did, he looked around for the disapproval and rebuke of his adopted guardian. But instead the soldier laughed and said, "Never mind, Sonny, say all that kind of thing you want." The little fellow thought a moment and then burst into tears and said, "If you were my father, you wouldn't say that." He felt he wanted and needed something more than sentimental kindness. He wanted to be saved by hard refusals.

With this redemptive content put into kindness we now consider our growth in kindness. Perhaps now we can quote these lines, since we have put into kindness a higher meaning:

> So many gods, so many creeds,
>   So many paths that wind and wind,
> When all that this sad world needs
>   Is just the art of being kind.

That kindness is important is seen by the fact that we remember an act of kindness when all events slip out of memory. The kindness remains. At a time when bitterness was strong between Britain and India, I found a prominent Indian wearing a white flower in his buttonhole each day. He explained to me that when he was in Britain studying, the English landlady used to put a white flower in his buttonhole each day. The kindness stood out like a star on a dark night of bitterness.

The Finnish people have treated me with many honors—large crowds, eager listeners—but the one thing that stands out is the act of an unknown Finnish lady who ran out into the street in the snow, stopped the car and handed me a flower through the window. That flower blooms fresh and fragrant in my grateful memory.

O Father, help me this day to do some little act of kindness that may live in somebody's memory forever. Amen.

AFFIRMATION FOR THE DAY: *I cover all ugly unkindliness with the same robe of kindliness with which He covers my uglinesses.*

"THE NATIVES SHOWED US UNCOMMON KINDNESS"

We were speaking of how an act of kindness sticks in the memory. An act of unkindness also sticks.

A writer tells of going down a lane with a nursemaid in England, when two village children ran out and shyly offered him some wild flowers they had plucked. He remembers bitterly how he haughtily rejected the flowers and ran and took the hand of his nursemaid. When he looked back, he saw the two children still standing and looking at him, and tears were running down their faces. "There," said the writer, "I first authentically rejected the Kingdom of God."

On the other hand, a certain Negro will not forget this: A bus was crowded in a Southern city, and the Negro section was overcrowded, so a Texan white man invited a Negro who was standing to share his seat in the white section. The bus driver objected, and the Negro got up. And then the white man in protest stood up with him, refusing to be seated while the Negro stood. If the Negro doesn't remember— but I'm sure he does—then I cannot forget. That deed shines against a dark background.

It does something to you while traveling in Japan to have the train pull out to the accompaniment of music over the loud-speaker. Then when you arrive at your destination, over the loud-speaker a voice graciously says, "You must be tired. We are sorry the train is two minutes late. Please see that you have left no parcels. Good-bye." It makes you feel that there is something more to traveling than mechanics. And as you wash your hands in the train lavatory, there is a bunch of fresh cut flowers, probably carnations. These touches touch you. A lot of it is superficial, but superficial or not, it puts a good taste in your mouth. And then the personal contacts: I smiled once at a little girl and boy as they came through the train in Japan, and then they came through the car again and again to get another smile —and give a bigger.

Paul, looking back upon the shipwreck experience on Malta, remembered one thing especially: "The natives showed us uncommon kindness" (Acts 28:2, Moffatt).

Dear Father, help me today to search out someone who needs my kindness and give it and give graciously. Amen.

AFFIRMATION FOR THE DAY: *Severe with self, generous and kind to everyone, especially the unkind and ungenerous.*

HANDING BACK THE IRON

The Japanese were brutal, in many cases, during the war, because they were in a framework of militarism. But in the framework of their own social customs they are a very gentle, kindly people. This demands kindness. One custom is striking: If a man's house burns down, he will immediately go to his neighbor and present him with a present, saying: "I am so thankful that your house didn't burn down." Overdone? Perhaps. And yet that spirit of kindness pervading social customs does something to human relationships. I said to a missionary, after traveling through over seventy cities in Japan, "Do you know I haven't seen two Japanese fighting or quarreling?" He replied, "I've been here forty years, and I haven't seen a Japanese quarreling in public. It isn't done." Kindness was built into a social system.

All my life I've been a traveler, by necessity. And many things happen on journeys, interesting things. But do you know the thing that stands out as an Everest among the peaks of happenings? I was riding on an elephant through the streets of Hyderabad, India. The mahaut was prodding the elephant's neck with a sharp pronged iron to make it go faster. The iron fell out of its wooden handle onto the street. The elephant, without any apparent signal from the mahaut, turned around, walked back, picked up the iron in its trunk, and handed it back up to the mahaut and then resumed his journey. Handed back an instrument of torment to his tormentor! That was doing good to those who despitefully use you!

And Communists are supposed to be hard and impervious to mere kindness. But they are not. A Christian of Travancore, India, became a Communist, and for ten years he was a leader in the underground movement. He was put under house arrest. A Syrian bishop and I went to see him. And fortunately, instead of berating him for leaving Christianity, we treated him with respect, even kindness. Years later when he left Communism, he said that one of the things that made him come back was that visit. "Would I visit one who had turned his back on Communism, and talk to him kindly? That simple kindness was one of the things that brought me back to Christ."

O Father, help me to overlook no opportunity this day of being kind to everybody in every situation. In Jesus' name. Amen.

AFFIRMATION FOR THE DAY: *Kindliness pays, in little ways, for it always says what can't be said.*

1/2

STEPS IN GROWTH IN KINDNESS

We must now look at the steps in growth in kindness:

First, *Fix it in your mind that kindness is not a luxury virtue, but a moral and spiritual and physical "must."* Kindness, to be kindness, by its very nature is an outgoing attitude. It breaks the tyranny of self-preoccupation and gives you the attitude of other-interest. And other-interest is psychologically healthy. A doctor wrote out a prescription for a sick man—emotionally sick, hence physically: "Go down to the New York Central Station and find there someone who needs you and do something for him." The businessman thought the doctor crazy but didn't know what else to do, so he went. He found a woman in a corner seated on her suitcase weeping. He asked her if he could do something for her. She replied that her daughter was to have met her but hadn't, and she didn't know her address, and she was frightened by this great city. The man got the daughter's address from the telephone directory, got the mother into a taxi, bought some flowers for her on the way, delivered her to the daughter amid the tearful gratitude of both, and then came back and called up the doctor and said, "Say, Doc, that was great medicine! I feel better already."

So kindness is a "must." If you're unkind to anyone, you are a sick man, or you are on the road to being a sick man. Unkindness is spiritual sickness and will possibly issue in physical sickness.

Second, *Put kindness into your life, not as an occasional deed, but as a life attitude.* In the unforgettable description of a model wife in Prov. 31, there is this statement, "She openeth her mouth with wisdom; and in her tongue is the law of kindness" (v. 26). Note: "the law of kindness"—she has passed an inner law in the legislature of her well-ordered soul that everything she says will fit into the law of kindness. Then kindness is not something set in changing emotions; it is set in her will, a life attitude. No wonder it is said: "She openeth her mouth with wisdom." For the kind thing is always the wise thing, and the unkind thing is always the unwise thing.

O Father, on bended knee I pass in the legislature of my heart the law of kindness. I come under its sway, forever. Amen.

AFFIRMATION FOR THE DAY: *You can never heal a hurt with another hurt. Kindliness is the one and only balm.*

"IS IT KIND?"

Third, *Remember that no other things done can atone for a lack of kindness.* Many people excuse themselves for a lack of kindness by pointing to the things they do for someone—"I am working my fingers to the bone for him." Yes, but the fleshless fingers will not atone for unkind words and attitudes.

Even ministers who work hard but lack this essential kindness are no exception. Paul says: "I prove myself at all points a true minister of God," and in the twenty-eight things he names, he puts as the fourteenth "kindness" (II Cor. 6:4-10, Moffatt). At the very center of all his proofs was "kindness." If at the center of all our proofs of our being true ministers and workers for God is not kindness, then all the rest is sounding brass and tinkling cymbal.

A prominent man, very ardent and very able and in every way outstanding, was divorced by his wife on the simple statement: "He crushed my personality." There was an apparently central unkindness. And nothing else could atone for that.

Fourth, *Beware of the attitude of criticism which will dry up the springs of kindness.* If you take the attitude of criticism, it will put you on the defensive, and you'll have to set yourself against kindness to justify your criticism. In an atmosphere of criticism, kindness withers and dies. So kill the criticism before it kills the kindness.

In our Ashrams we have this motto among others:

"When about to criticize another, ask:

Is is true?	Is it redemptive?
Is it necessary?	Is it kind?"

If the criticism doesn't pass the test of kindness, it is unjustifiable.

There are those who feel they are called of God to criticize people into goodness. The Pharisees sincerely tried this and ended in producing not goodness in others, but Pharisaism in themselves. Setting yourself up in judgment produces not the very good Christian, but the very good Pharisee. And the very good Pharisee is an ugly character. Jesus made the very good Pharisee forever unrespectable.

Dear Lord, as I know my own faults, help me to be kindly toward the faults of others. In Jesus' name. Amen.

AFFIRMATION FOR THE DAY: *I can never criticize another into goodness, for I make myself bad in the process.*

KINDNESS BRIDGES CHASMS

We come now to our last step in growth in kindness.

Fifth, *Since kindness is power, I'm going to exercise this kind of power, and only this kind of power, in every situation.* Many wonder if kindness is power. They try to rule situations by threats. But threats soon wear out. No one is ever really changed by threats. Only by kindness can people be changed. Look back over your life and see who are the people who have influenced you and how. You'll find kindliness at the basis of all influence over you.

A German pastor stood looking out over the ruined city of Frankfurt, now slowly rising again. His eyes were wet with tears as he told me of a pastor and his young people who came to Germany from America for the summer to help rebuild the ruins. They were obviously not used to this hard manual labor, but they heroically toiled beside German laborers. Some of the girls, dead tired at eventide, would throw themselves upon their beds and go straight to sleep. The German workmen were at first uncommunicative, but gradually they saw the motives behind it all. Then one day, said the pastor, he saw a German workman take out of his pocket a piece of precious cake and offer it to the pastor. It seemed to echo the word of Jesus long ago: "Take, eat." "And there," said the pastor, "I saw the chasm of hate and fear bridged—bridged by this incarnate kindness of the pastor and his group." Kindness is power. Use no other.

Some Quakers were feeding people in Poland during the war. A Polish woman came up and said to them, "You feed everybody?" "Yes." "Poles, Russians, Germans?" "Yes." "Jews, Catholics, Protestants, Atheists?" "Yes." She drew a deep sigh and said, "Well, I knew there ought to be people in the world like that, but I didn't believe there were." And that proved to be power. For as someone said, "There were only two who came out at the end of the war with enhanced reputations—Christ and the Quakers." And they both used kindness against the background of hate and force.

Gracious Father, help me this day to be clothed with kindliness. May the first thing people see in me be kindliness. Amen.

AFFIRMATION FOR THE DAY: *God lets His kindly rain fall on the evil and the good. I too shall rain kindliness on all, regardless.*

GROWTH IN GENEROSITY

In the fruits of the Spirit six out of the nine are related to our attitudes toward others—love, good temper, kindliness, generosity, fidelity, gentleness. Only three can be said to refer to oneself alone—joy, peace, self-control. Does this mean that there should be twice as much interest in our outside relationships as we have in our own? Jesus said that we are to love our neighbor "as" ourselves—the self-interest and other-interest are to exactly balance. And Paul said that each of us should have "an eye to the interest of others as well as to his own"—*as well as*. Here they exactly balance again.

But in this surrendering to the Spirit and letting the Spirit have sway over us, does it turn out that we find ourselves twice as interested in others as ourselves? Is this the second-mile attitude in human virtues? And if we do go the second mile, do we become lopsided personalities? One would think so. But strangely enough, No. The more we love others, the more beautiful we become in ourselves. The loving are the living—in themselves!

So Paul turns the many-sided Christian character to the facet of generosity. This leads us to look at a verse from Jesus, previously quoted,

> If your Eye is generous,
>   the whole of your body will be illumined.
>   (Matt. 6:22, Moffatt)

If your Eye—your outlook on life, your whole way of looking at things and people—is generous, then your whole personality is illumined, is lighted up.

Jesus was generous toward all—the poor, the meek, the sinful, the unlovely. And His whole personality was full of light. And Jesus generates that generosity within us. We begin to see everything and everybody with the generous Eye.

O Jesus, Thy generous Eye saw in me what wasn't there, and lo, it was there! Help me to thus create what I see. Amen.

AFFIRMATION FOR THE DAY: *My generous Eye will generate generosity in others; if not, I'm more generous for giving unmerited generosity.*

THE GENEROUS EYE

The generous Eye and the generous attitude are at the basis of all sound human relationships.

The Norwegians and Swedes live together as brothers. They are different, but underneath is an unbreakable tie that binds them as one people. Why? Well, when Norway wanted her freedom, Sweden gave it, gave it out of the Christian spirit behind the ruling family in Sweden. That generosity, in giving freedom without war or bitterness, has created a basic soundness that flavors all their relationships.

Why are the relationships between Britain and India basically better than with probably any other foreign nation? A few years ago those relationships were bitter, not better. For one thing, the pressure of the Gandhian movement, the spirit of which was expressed in the statement of one of the Gandhian leaders at the time of the height of the struggle: "We can thank our lucky stars that we are fighting the British and not some other nation, for there is something within the British we can appeal to"; in other words, they were trying to see something good within the British character to which they could appeal. A new kind of warfare—looking for good in your enemies! I wrote to the commission arranging the transfer of power: "I can see in your patience and generosity what I would call nothing less than the Christian spirit in public affairs." That double generosity in the British and the Indian made it possible for India, when given her freedom, to decide to stay within the British Commonwealth.

The race relations which I consider the best in the world are between the New Zealander and the Maori. These relationships were laid by the wise statesmanship of a Christian governor and a bishop. They put through legislation that made it impossible for the Maori to alienate his land to the white man, saving him from being a landless pauper. Generosity laid a sound economic basis under their relationships, and so today these two races live side by side in mutual respect and love. A Maori was the Prime Minister of New Zealand, honored and respected. The generous Eye filled with light the whole body of human relationships between two diverse races.

O Jesus, help me this day to lay generosity at the basis of all my dealing with everybody, everywhere. Amen.

AFFIRMATION FOR THE DAY: *I shall be the channel, and not the stopping place, of all God's generosity to me.*

GENEROSITY GENERATES

I wrote yesterday about the generosity of the two white men toward the Maoris of New Zealand. But the Maoris too were generous, even when bitter fighting was going on in the early days. The Maoris sent word: "White man hungry. Cannot fight well. So we are sending some food to the white man!" The white men couldn't forget, hence one reason for the wise legislation.

One of the most potent forces in the healing between the North and South was the spirit of Abraham Lincoln. He refused a triumphal march into Richmond after the victory. When he arrived on foot, he went to the room where Jefferson Davis had governed the Confederacy and for a long time sat at the desk with his head bowed on his arms, weeping—weeping for the fallen on both sides. That sight of the weeping President broke down more barriers and healed more wounds than all the exhortations to a resumed brotherhood.

It was Ananias who, as a potential victim of Saul's rage and hate, put his hands on the stricken Paul and generously said, "Brother Saul"—"Brother Saul" to one who had come to murder him! That generosity opened the gates of life to the broken man and started the greatest Christian of the centuries on his way.

A Congregational and a Methodist church formed a Federal Union in a local situation, each with its separate pastor and each with its emphasis, but over them there was formed a parish assembly made up of representatives from both the branches. Among the ten things they were doing together, through the parish assembly, was a joint budget. The stronger branch, the Congregationalist, said to the weaker branch, "You have only a student pastor. Put enough in your budget for a full-time pastor, and we'll go out together to the community to get it." They did. Result? The stronger branch increased its income 48 per cent and the weaker 128 per cent. Both benefited, but, more, the body of relationships between the two bodies became full of light.

Father, I see that only as I am generous do I win, for the being generous is the victory. Help me to that victory today. Amen.

AFFIRMATION FOR THE DAY: *The first mile doesn't register. It's the second mile that counts. I'm a second miler.*

GENEROSITY APPLIED TO MONEY RELATIONSHIPS

We have been looking at the generous Eye in general. We now come to the generous Eye as applied to money relationships.

In China there is a Christian group striving to build their lives on the New Testament pattern of the second chapter of Acts. When the Communists took over, they said to these Christians: "You are doing better than we are. You are doing by love and consent what we are trying to do by hate and force." But later the Communists, true to their outlook and principles, told the "Jesus Family" they wanted their buildings as headquarters, since they had the best buildings in the town. The Christians went out, leaving everything to the Communists—went out empty-handed. This aroused the townspeoples: "If they do this to the best, what will they do to the rest of us?" The Communists were losing the sympathy of the people, so they had to ask the "Jesus Family" to come back and take over their buildings again. Later some investigators were sent by the Communists to investigate a member of the Christian group. He stayed a few doors away. One day a hen came over into the compound of the "Jesus Family" and laid an egg. Not knowing whose hen it was, they tied a currency note, covering the cost of the egg, to the leg of the hen and let her go. She went back to the house where the investigators were staying, and they said: "Well, what's the use of talking about investigating a people as honest and as generous as that?" They called it off!

The principle of generosity works everywhere. Here is an incident out of our capitalistic society. A man lost all his property during the depression—all except $25,000 which he had given to the church. When he went to church, he said, "Nobody can take this away from me now." Now he is building up his fortune again, and almost as fast as he makes it, he is giving it to a Methodist college, for he says he doesn't want to leave it to his one daughter to burden and perhaps ruin her. He found that generosity is a good investment—the only safe investment.

O God, Thou hast invited us to put our money in purses that wax not old—the purses of human character. Help us to invest. Amen.

AFFIRMATION FOR THE DAY: *I shall bank heavily today in the bank of human character—my one safe investment.*

STEPS TO GROW IN GENEROSITY

Let us come now to the steps we are to take if we are to grow in generosity.

First, *Decide that you own nothing. God is the owner, and you are ower.* This puts God in His place and you in yours. You are not free to manage your material possessions as you like, but as He likes. This gives you a sense of accountability to Another. You get your life orders not from whim, notion, self-impulse, but from God.

Second, *Since God is owner, go over your life under His guidance and see what belongs to your needs and what merely belongs to your wants.* Your needs are important. He has promised to supply them— them, not your wants. And what are your needs? You need as much as will make you more physically, mentally, and spiritually fit for the purposes of the Kingdom of God. Beyond that belongs to other people's needs.

How can you decide what belongs to your needs? No one can decide it for you; you are accountable to God. Then in His presence go over your life, and item by item decide which belongs to which. Where does society come in? Has society no say? Yes, it has, for you are primarily responsible to God, and secondarily responsible to society, for society is affected by your choices. Then go over the matter with some member, or members, of society, who have a similar sense of accountability to God and man, and check up with him or them. But the final decision must be with you.

Third, *Since the central issues are fixed as to ownership and as to need, now decide to have the generous Eye toward people and things.* You now have a framework for generosity. The basis of your life is fixed; now within that fixed framework let your love operate as generosity. This will not now be so difficult, for generosity is the native air of this framework. In it you will live and move and have your being. It is the homeland of your soul.

Decide that your very outlook on everything and everybody will be to find the good, further the good, and to do good in every situation with every thought and act. You're naturalized in generosity.

O Father, I thank Thee that the basis of my life is fixed in Thee and Thy plans; help me now to give with the stops out. Amen.

AFFIRMATION FOR THE DAY: *I shall take out of my earnings what I need. The rest is at God's disposal.*

TITHE YOUR EARNINGS

Fourth, *Fill in this framework with specific attitudes and habits— give a tithe of your earnings.* The giving of the tithe, or one tenth, is a symbol of acknowledgment that the nine tenths belongs to God. Just as you give rental as an acknowledgment that the rented house belongs to another, so you give one tenth as acknowledgment that the nine tenths belongs to God. The Hebrews waved the first fruits of the harvest before the Lord as acknowledgment that the coming harvest belonged to Him and that they would use it as such. That didn't always happen, but that was the purpose. Often they did according to a modern Jewish custom of offering a chicken to God, then placing their sins on the chicken and throwing it under the table. From there it disappears and comes back on the table to be eaten! This is basically in the interests of self, hence self-defeating.

On the other hand, when one sincerely gives within this framework of generosity, something happens. Hyde of Mentholatum is an illustration. He took God into partnership and lived according to that pact. He gave a larger and larger percentage of his earnings. Among other things he gave to Dr. Vorhees, head of a self-sustaining missionary project in Japan, called the Omi Brotherhood, the right to manufacture Mentholatum and contributed the machinery. It sustained the Omi Brotherhood during the war, and at the close of the war Dr. Vorhees became the go-between between the Occupation and the new Japanese government. He also had a vital part in the Emperor's announcement that he was not divine, one of the most important things that has happened in the postwar period. It laid the foundations for a new Japan. Back of that vast change as a contributing factor was Hyde, the steward of God's intrustment to him.

In the same way the Ashram movement in America, which has transformed thousands of lives, began in the generosity of my friend, E. V. Moorman, who underwrote the initial expenses of their establishment. The dedicated money was transformed into dedicated men.

O Father, that my money and property may not be dead money and dead property, I dedicate them to Thee. Amen.

AFFIRMATION FOR THE DAY: *My property is the extension of my person. My person belongs to God; so does my property automatically.*

SUPPOSE HE HAD REFUSED!

We come now to the last step in growing in generosity.

Fifth, *Remember that what happens to your money happens to you.*
Your money is an extended or a contracted you. If you pile up your
money with no purpose behind it, you clutter up yourself, and it
becomes a purposeless self, hence an unhappy self.

Suppose when Jesus wanted to feed the hungry five thousand and
blessed the loaves "to serve out," the disciples had said to themselves,
"Let's not serve it out, let's save it up, we'll corner this abundant
food supply and make the multitude, driven by hunger, pay high
for it. We'll cash in on their hunger." What would have happened?
The connection with heaven would have been broken, the supply
would have stopped, and we would never have heard of the disciples again.

Suppose the man who owned the colt, when the disciples said to
him, "The Lord hath need of him," had replied, "I also have need
of him; you can't have him"—what would have happened? For the
balance of his days he would have had an inner debate over that
colt, always trying to justify the unjustifiable. But after he gladly let
Jesus have it, that colt came back the most famous colt in history.

Suppose the little boy had refused to let Jesus have the five loaves
and two fishes, saying they were his and he wouldn't let them go?
The rest of his days he would have kicked himself for the refusal.
That little boy became the center of gratitude of five thousand people
and the center of peace within, and incidentally the most famous
boy of history.

Japan needs a place for her surplus population. Eighty-five million
people cooped up in these small islands are bound to resent unoccupied spaces. If New Guinea, one of the unoccupied spaces of
the world, were given to Japan, under UN auspices, it would do more
for the peace of the Far East than any single thing. Generosity
would generate peace.

**Father, Thou hast opened the doors of life to me, provided I open the
doors of my heart to others. Help me to do it. Amen.**

AFFIRMATION FOR THE DAY: *My money is God's intrustment to me;
I shall be faithful to this intrustment.*

GROWTH IN FIDELITY

We come now to the next fruit of the Spirit: fidelity. We would have expected this fruit to be among the first, or at the very first. The Moral Rearmament movement makes it the first of its four absolutes—absolute honesty, absolute purity, absolute unselfishness, and absolute love. In a way it does belong there, for if there isn't basic honesty with God, ourselves, and others, then nothing else can atone for that lack of basic honesty.

And yet Paul, instead of putting honesty first and love last as Moral Rearmament does, puts love first and fidelity toward the last. Is he right? Yes, for the primary basis of the Christian faith is love. The first and second great commandments begin, "Thou shalt love." The primary question is: What do you love supremely?

If the primary thing is honesty, then the root of religion is in the will. But if the primary thing is love, then the root of religion is in the emotions. If the center of religion is an act of the will, then religion means a whipping up of the will—a demand of duty. But if the center of religion is not in the will, then we surrender the will to the object of the emotion—God. Then religion is not a straining to be good; it's a surrender to Goodness.

So Paul puts fidelity as a fruit of surrender to the Spirit. Jesus said:

He who is faithful with a trifle is also faithful with a large trust,
and he who is dishonest with a trifle is also dishonest with a large trust.
So if you are not faithful with dishonest mammon,
    how can you ever be trusted with true Riches?
And if you are not faithful with what belongs to another,
    how can you ever be given what is your own?
                    (Luke 16:10-12, Moffatt)

Here the basic principles are laid down: If you are not faithful in a trifle, you cannot be trusted with the tremendous. If you are not faithful with the material, how can you be intrusted with the spiritual—"true Riches"?

O Father, Thou art letting me be tested day by day with the little. Help me to be faithful there. Amen.

AFFIRMATION FOR THE DAY: *Fidelity in thought and deed shall be the hallmark of my character.*

THE UNIVERSE IS MADE FOR TRUTH

We left off yesterday when Jesus equated "true Riches" with "that which is our own." Is true Riches—a richness so rich you have to spell it with a capital "R"—something inherently ours?

Is the Kingdom of God, which is the "true Riches," our own? Are we made for it as the lungs are made for air? When we find it, do we find ourselves? With all my heart I believe so.

Both the universe and we are made for truth and honesty, and both the universe and we are alien to untruth and dishonesty. The universe is made for the same thing we are made for—namely, righteousness. Not only the face of the Lord, but the face of the universe, is set against evildoers.

The universe is not built for the success of a lie; a lie breaks itself upon the moral universe, maybe not today, nor tomorrow, but the third day—Yes! The Tamils of South India have a saying: "The life of the cleverest lie is only eight days." The Germans have a saying that "lies have short legs"—good in the short run, but bad in the long run. But during the war they changed that saying to: "Lies have one short leg," for Goebbels, the propaganda minister, had one short leg. The best concocted lie had a life of only eight days!

A speaker said: "In our fight with Communism we are handicapped by our decency. We can't do what they do." But is decency a handicap? Indecency is a handicap! For every indecency becomes a handicap that binds us inwardly and outwardly. We are up against a strange imponderable—the moral universe.

I would like to make a prediction: Communism will be broken from within; it will flounder on the rock of its own amorality. It dismisses the moral universe and sets up its own goals as determining right and wrong. On that it will break. Listen to what the years and the centuries say against these hours.

So no one gets away with anything in this universe. "There is nothing covered, that shall not be revealed; and hid, that shall not be made known."

Gracious Father, help me not to try to fool myself and others, lest I turn out to be a simple, plain fool. Amen.

AFFIRMATION FOR THE DAY: *Today I shall work with the moral universe and get results; if not, I get consequences.*

DISHONESTY DOESN'T PAY

We continue our study of fidelity. The ultimate question about a man's character is this: Will that man lie? Are there any circumstances under which he will lie? If so, the rest of his character is worthless. For basically he is unsound.

Here was a Christian worker, a deaconess, who would work her fingers to the bone for people at any hour of day and night, and yet she would lie and steal. That basic falsity canceled the rest.

In an ancient church in South India the priests decided to devaluate the valuable gold cross in the tax return so as to escape a heavier taxation. Later the cross was stolen and cut up into bits. It was recovered by the police. But the judge decided that this gold did not belong to the stolen cross, for the record showed that the stolen cross was of a lower carat than the recovered gold. So the gold was confiscated by the police.

The limousine was waiting at the airport for a woman who insisted on making a long-distance call from the airport before departure. She explained her delay to the passengers who waited for her: "You see, I called myself up at home, and of course was told that I was not there. That allowed my family to know that I had arrived safely, but I didn't have to pay for the telephone call." She thought herself clever, but she was only a clever fool, for calling herself up in this way started a series of calls to herself on the inside of herself—calls that she had to justify to herself. She lost her inner self-respect for two dollars. She sold herself—cheap!

I sat in Madras and watched a man driving a cow and calf from door to door and milking the cow in the presence of the housewife. Why did he have to trudge in the hot sun day after day in this clumsy way of delivering milk? Simple reason—he could not be trusted. He would water the milk unless he milked it before the eyes of the housewife. So his dishonesty doomed him to this drudgery! The moral universe had the last word. Dishonesty puts sand in the internal and external machinery of life. Honesty and fidelity put oil. You can choose to live with sand or oil in your inner mechanism.

O Father, I thank Thee that Thou hast made me for **truth in the inner parts.** Help me not to violate my being. Amen.

AFFIRMATION FOR THE DAY: *My moral joints shall not creak with dishonesty; I shall oil them well with honesty.*

HE OPENED HIS ARMOR!

At a certain period the Travancore government of South India was suppressing minorities, especially the Christians. The secret police took down everything I said at a Christian convention. Afterward I received a letter from the superintendent of police asking if I had said certain things, among them: "Did you say that any dishonest official was a traitor to his country?" I wrote after this question: "If I didn't say it, I ought to have done so." I never heard from him again! He opened his armor. What was the result of such a mentality that made such a statement? That government has been replaced by a new one.

Where there is corruption, there the clean-up squad of the moral universe will gather to clean it up. For the moral universe cannot stand corruption. It stinks to high heaven, and high heaven sends its clean-up squads to remove it.

The Chinese have a saying: "Nations first smite themselves and then others smite them." This takes place when one can write of a government as one writer has done: "There are two major principles for getting and keeping power: (1) Let nothing, least of all truth and honor, interfere with success. (2) Be honest and trustworthy in the little things, but boldly dishonest in the large ones." Result? Like blind Samson they pull down the pillars of state and bury themselves and others amid the wreckage of things.

It is the ten righteous men who spare Sodoms, ancient and modern. The men of fidelity are the ones who hold together the situation long enough for the men of infidelity to practice their infidelity within that situation. Take them out and make evil pure evil, and it will destroy itself. For all evil is a parasite upon the good.

An American colonel in occupied Germany stole the rich furnishings of the house he took over, and sent them to America. He succeeded only in surrounding himself with the objects of his perfidy, reminders of how he had betrayed his country and himself. They became his silent but eloquent tormentors.

O Father, help me to be honest with Thee and with myself and with all whom I meet this day. Amen.

AFFIRMATION FOR THE DAY: *No dishonesty is worth the price I will have to pay for it—inward conflict and unhappiness.*

STEPS IN GROWTH IN FIDELITY

We come now to the steps in growth in fidelity.

First, *Determine to be basically honest and faithful in thought and speech and act.* Lay this down as a basic cornerstone of your life. Begin building from there. And admit of no exceptions.

The question of whether it is ever right to lie can be settled once and for all by this fact: God cannot lie, and He cannot delegate you the privilege of lying for Him. The New Testament is flat-footed on this matter: "Lie not one to another." And the same New Testament ends by declaring that "all liars . . . have their part in the lake which burneth with fire." When you take lies and dishonesties into your bosom, you take fire into your bosom, here and hereafter.

Second, *Fix it as an axiom in your thinking: Nobody gets away with anything, anywhere, at any time, if that "anything" is dishonest or untrue.* The whole history of humanity is a commentary on this. The first lie uttered by Satan was this: "You shall not surely die." And he keeps repeating that well-worn but discredited lie to every son of Adam. But something does die the moment you are dishonest. Self-respect dies within you. Death is eating at your heart the moment dishonesty comes in. You are not so much punished for sin, as by sin. Perhaps we can put it this way: You are punished by sin, for sin. Sin is its own punishment.

Third, *Where you have been unfaithful and dishonest, face it frankly with yourself and God.* Don't suppress it, for that only drives it into the subconscious, where it festers. Psychology and religion both say: "Bring it up and out and look at it honestly and settle it." There is absolutely no other way to get rid of it. Every other way leads to a road with a dead end. Here is a letter a man wrote to his former employer: "I've been converted. I'm restoring this $100 I stole while I was an employee in your service." A man came to me in Travancore after a service and said, "I'm a rogue. I've been a toddy contractor. But I'm coming to the cross. I'm giving thirty-six acres to the landless." Both of these men were freed by open honesty. They walked into the open arms of God.

Dear Father, give me the strength to take the hard way, for the hard way turns out to be the easy way. Amen.

AFFIRMATION FOR THE DAY: *A dishonesty suppressed is a dishonesty expressed in harmful ways of conflict and ill health.*

FIDELITY IN GOD'S INTRUSTMENTS

Now the next step: Fourth, *Fidelity will mean to me not merely the absence of dishonesty but fidelity in handling God's intrustments to me.* All my powers and possessions are God's intrustments to me. I shall be a faithful steward of time, talents, possessions.

Weatherhead tells of a man who said that when he got a thousand pounds ahead, he would be secure enough to begin tithing his income. He got the thousand pounds and found he wanted another thousand. Now he is getting a thousand-pound income a year, but he has not made a start to fulfill his promise to God. This is the meaning of "the deceitfulness of riches."

To handle God's intrustments means that though the intrustments may not be large, nevertheless they will be God's! The great work in the world is done by small-talented people using those talents for God's purposes. "You have small talents," said someone to a very useful man, who replied, "Yes, but I have a great God." God and he were linked up, and there was a plus to all he did.

An Indian Christian switchman saw his little boy on the railway track, and he had to decide between letting his boy be killed or wrecking a whole train. He decided to throw the switch that saved the train but killed the boy. He was faithful to his trust, and his name will be remembered by thousands as the man who performed his duty at deep cost to himself. Fidelity is written across that deed!

Here was a woman in very poor circumstances who walked back and forth from the church instead of riding on the street car, so she could save the fare. When a call was made at the church for a dedication of life and substance, she came forward at the altar and knelt and offered her two streetcar fares she had saved by walking. It so touched the rest of the members of that church that thousands of dollars came flooding in for that cause. That poor but rich woman, faithful in the little, loosed the big and furthered a great cause. Faithfulness in the little becomes fruitfulness in the big.

It doesn't take much of a person to be a Christian, but it takes all there is of him—person and possessions.

Dear Father, like the little boy with the five loaves and two fishes, I offer what little I have. Take it, break it, distribute it. Amen.

AFFIRMATION FOR THE DAY: *God will make my little into the much, my insignificant into the significant—for He has it.*

LOOK FOR LOOSE ENDS

We come now to the last step in growing in fidelity:

Fifth, *Fidelity will mean that I will carry through in God's intrustments to me; I will keep faith until the end.*

When I asked the leading members of a large church what was the outstanding need of their church, they replied: "Fidelity." Fifty per cent of church members are hangers-on, getting a free ride, contributing nothing from purse or person; twenty-five per cent promise to do something and then after a few stabs at it drop out. They lack fidelity. The life of the church is carried on by the remaining twenty-five per cent.

A church had a weather vane put on the steeple, says George A. Buttrick, with the words, "Thy will be done" on it. A scoffer asked if that meant that our obedience is as variable as the wind. "No," came the reply; "it means that whatever the wind, or the weather, we must obey."

If we could get people who put their hand to the plow and never look back, who have inner compulsions and go on no matter the wind or the weather, we would have a growing people.

Go over your life and see where there are loose ends, broken promises, half-fulfilled tasks; and begin to complete the incomplete, fulfill the half-fulfilled, and gather up the loose ends; and when you do so, there will be a sense of well-being, a sense of being whole.

In a radio station there was a motto on the wall: "Don't do it today. Put it off until tomorrow, and get stomach ulcers." Unfulfilled tasks, broken promises, feints at doing this, that, and the other, bring a sense of tenseness, a sense of the half-done hanging over one. Don't live under that haunting sense of the incomplete. Don't take up too much, but what you do take up, complete. Jesus said: "As for the seed in the good soil, that means those who hear and hold fast the word in a good, sound heart, and so bear fruit steadfastly" (Luke 8:15, Moffatt). Note: "so bear fruit steadfastly"—only the steadfast are the finally fruitful.

O Father, I am good-intentioned and weak-willed. Take my intentions and turn them into driving convictions. Amen.

AFFIRMATION FOR THE DAY: *My half-finished jobs shall all be finished today, for I don't want to be a half-finished person.*

GROWTH IN ADAPTABILITY

We now come to another fruit of the spirit—"adaptability" (the Phillips translation).

This seems a strange fruit of the Spirit. Is it thrown in as a second thought or is it integral to the spiritual life? I am persuaded it is integral and fundamentally necessary to the best human living, individual and collective.

Toynbee says that when a nation meets a new situation, which precipitates a crisis and demands an attitude and action toward that situation, that nation is liable to take one of four attitudes: (1) It may retreat into the past and glorify and rest in past achievements. (2) It may try to leap into the future and dream of what it will do sometime. (3) It may retreat into inner states of mind and there try to exist on mysticism, apart from the pressing issues. (4) It may boldly take hold of the situation and transform this new situation into opportunity for life on a higher level.

The first three adapt themselves negatively and downwardly. They perish. The fourth adapt themselves positively and upwardly. They survive.

We always have to adapt ourselves to a new situation—destructively or constructively. We adapt. But how?

Some adapt to their surroundings by succumbing to them; they fit in and echo. They don't stand for anything, and hence they become nothing. They have all morality and spirituality flattened out of them. This is the wrong kind of adaptability; it is adaptability downward. Those who adapt in this manner perish morally and spiritually.

While this kind of adaptability is out for any person who wants to grow, nevertheless we must have adaptability. While we refuse to compromise the center—the citadel—of our moral convictions, we must, however, learn to be adaptable persons—adaptable in the things which are not vital convictions, remaining adamant in the things that are matters of principle.

To put together these two things in a proper blend—this makes the strong man.

Dear Jesus, Thou didst have these two things within Thy character. Give them to me, for I too would be strong. Amen.

AFFIRMATION FOR THE DAY: *I shall have to have a trained insight to know when to be adaptable and when to be adamant.*

UNABLE TO ADAPT THEMSELVES

Those who can adapt themselves to their surroundings and yet can keep a principle of life within, survive.

The most massive creatures this planet has known, the dinosaurs, panoplied with thick armor and with massive teeth and claws, perished, not because stronger animals wiped them out, but by a simple change of climate. On the other hand, one of the most defenseless creatures on the planet, the common worm, survives on glaciers in Alaska. They are called "ice worms," for they are supposed to live on ice, but they are really common earthworms, adapting themselves to living on the scant bit of soil on a glacier, by becoming almost as thin as a hair. They survived the change of climate, while the dinosaur perished. The worm knew adaptablity.

The intellectual climate of the world has changed, and individuals and systems unable to adapt themselves to this change in climate are gasping for air—perishing. They are trying to match their armor of dogmatic assertion against a climate that demands not dogmatism, but demonstration.

For instance, the only way to beat the Communists is to beat them to it! Produce a better order for everybody, including the dispossessed —and the dispossessed especially—and Communism can't get a toe hold. Make the word "all"—"with liberty and justice for all"—mean "all" and not "some," and Communism won't get a look in. But just to tear your hair and get hysterical is like dinosaurs baring their huge teeth and gnashing at a change of climate. It is futility itself.

The climate of the world now demands a total answer to the total needs of humanity—individual and collective. Life is a unit and must be redeemed as a unit. For the church, in the face of this demand, to get red in the face and wave its arms and say that all we need is individual conversion, and the rest will automatically take care of itself, is the dinosaurs again clawing and gnashing their teeth at a change of climate.

We have a total gospel for the total need of a total humanity, and we must totally apply it if we are to survive.

Father, help me not to fight new ideas and new demands upon me. Help me to adapt constructively. Amen.

AFFIRMATION FOR THE DAY: *New ideas may be God's invitation from my narrowness to His broadness, from my littleness to His greatness.*

191

WRONG AND RIGHT ADAPTABILITY

We have seen that there are two futile attitudes to take toward the new. One is to succumb to it entirely, give way to it and become a part of it, become absorbed. Someone asked a janitor how he got along when the ladies were there, for he seemed to be having a hard time with the men. He replied, "That's simple. I just throw my mind into neutral, and I go where I am pushed." A lot of people do that with their circumstances. And soon they have no minds. They become pushed-around souls.

The other method of futility is to fight against the new demand, but without constructive transformation. This attitude is like the dinosaurs, futilely fighting a changing climate.

I saw away up in the Himalaya mountains a pack of horses going along carrying the belongings of an English official on tour. On top of the load of one horse was a large galvanized iron bathtub. Wherever he was, he must have his tub. To pour water over himself by a self-created shower bath would be to be too much like the "native," so he had to carry his tub clear up over the mountains—unadaptable.

On the other hand, C. F. Andrews, another Englishman, adapted himself to the Indian people, became part of them, and is affectionately called "C.F.A.—Christ's Faithful Apostle."

If Germany becomes a democracy, a large part of the credit must go to people like Mrs. McCloy, the wife of the High Commissioner of Germany, a lady whom the Germans affectionately called "Our Mrs. McCloy." She became one of them—their sorrows her sorrows, their joys her joys.

Into the history of a changing Africa is being plowed the name of an Englishman, the Rev. Michael Scott. The African people affectionately call him "The Listener—he listens to our sorrows and hopes." And when he listens to them, he listens to the future, for the future battleground for human rights is going to be Africa.

Ezekiel said, "I sat where they sat . . . seven days." For seven days he learned sympathy, became a listener to a captive people. They could never forget him.

O Jesus, Thou didst sit where we sit. Thou didst become The Listener. We can never forget Thee—never. Amen.

AFFIRMATION FOR THE DAY: *I shall lend my ears and my heart to human need and then ask God for supply.*

"ABLE FOR ANYTHING"

We come now to look at the adaptability of the writer of the epistle from which these "fruits of the Spirit" are taken. Did he know adaptability by experience? He did, and that made him an evangelist to the Gentiles, while Peter had to confine himself largely to Jews. Paul became "all things to all men" and as a result was powerful in his appeal to all.

Paul's greatest passage describing his adaptability is this one:

Not that I complain of want, for I have learned how to be content wherever I am. I know how to live humbly; I also know how to live in prosperity. I have been initiated into the secret for all sorts and conditions of life, . . . for prosperity and for privations; in Him who strengthens me, I am able for anything (Phil. 4:11-13, Moffatt).

This passage shows the essential greatness of the man—a man who could take both privation and prosperity in his stride, making them both contribute toward the ends for which he lived.

Some can stand one or the other; only the big man can take both. Some people go to pieces over privations. Others cannot stand prosperity. There is the story of the man who gradually turned to stone from his feet up. When the stone got to his heart, it killed him. Many are thus petrified by possessions. And when it gets your heart, it gets you.

Paul called his secret being "initiated into the secret for all sorts and conditions of life"—an initiation into a secret society!

And what was the initiation fee? The old word again: "self-surrender"! He had sustained a central loss, the loss of himself! What could lesser losses do to him now? After I went back to India at the close of the war, I had five straight nights in which I did not get over two hours of sleep a night. After that when I was deprived of a night's sleep, I would laugh and say: "What's that? One night? I've had five straight nights!"

The initiation fee is yourself. But the "secret" is worth it. Thereafter nothing can hurt you, for you've centrally hurt yourself.

O Father, I thank Thee for this glorious secret—the secret of being able to meet anything that comes. Glory be. Amen.

AFFIRMATION FOR THE DAY: *Penury or plenty leaves me undismayed; I am rich in God, very rich indeed.*

"YOU ARE LIFTED ABOVE THESE DISTINCTIONS"

As I was standing on a railway platform in India, I asked an Indian gentleman if he were going on the train about to depart. "No," he replied, "I'm not, for there is nothing but third-class carriages on it." Third-class carriages have hard wooden benches and are crowded and usually dirty. I replied, "I'm going on it." "Yes," he said, "you can go on it, for you are a religious man. If you go third class, it doesn't degrade you; and if you go first class, it doesn't exalt you. You are lifted above these distinctions. But I have to keep them up."

This being "lifted above distinctions" brings a divine indifference to everything but the one thing—one's relation to the center, God. When that holds intact, then everything is secure.

I once said facetiously to an audience in Minneapolis that I had only one need as far as I could see—the need of a second pair of suspenders, so I wouldn't have to change my one pair of suspenders every time I changed my other pair of trousers. When I went through Minneapolis again, someone met me at the station and presented me with four pairs of suspenders! "There," I said to myself, "as far as I know, I haven't a need left in the world. Except the need to know what to do with these three extra pairs I don't need!"

I am constantly moving from place to place and from country to country throughout the world. I find people infinitely interesting. I haven't seen a place on earth where I haven't felt I could get interested in the people's problems, settle down and help to settle those problems, and be at home sufficiently to spend the balance of my days there. With the exception of Manchuria! It would have taken grace to settle down there!

When Paul said, "I have learned how to be content wherever I am," he had learned the ultimate lesson in adaptability. The secret was that he had learned to find his contentment within. Finding contentment there, everywhere was home, and he was at home everywhere.

O Father, teach me the lesson of adaptability, of how to be at home with everybody, everywhere. In Jesus' name. Amen.

AFFIRMATION FOR THE DAY: *Everywhere is home to me, for Christ is everywhere and He is my Home.*

STEPS IN GROWTH IN ADAPTABILITY

We come now to the steps in growth in adaptablity.

First, *Break up some old form and establish a new one every day.* That will keep your mind and attitude flexible. Some people are afraid to change. One man came to one of our Ashrams and on the last day told of his fear of change. He said he always sat at the back so that people would not see his agitation when a new idea was presented. His soul and mind were rigid and afraid of change. But all education is change. So he ceased to be educated, for he was resisting change. And he was a schoolteacher!

Find some way to do something different today. In the church of Antioch there were "prophets and teachers" (Acts 13:1). Teachers are usually the conservators of the past, passing on the lessons that have been learned from the ancestors. Prophets are usually the radicals —they want to apply the lessons of the past to the present and the future. They press the "Is" into the "Ought-to-be." Without them we sink from the "Is" to the "Was." Keep alive the prophet in your soul.

Second, *Perhaps you are in a position to which you have never really adapted yourself. Begin to do it today.* Here was a mother who was tense and resistant against the in-laws of her son, though the daughter-in-law herself was everything she was expected to be. The in-laws were respectable people, but not of her social set. She arrived in a plane and was taken to the bride's home, and the mother of the bride met the grand lady with an apron on! She couldn't get over that apron! She made herself and everyone around miserable and uneasy by her lack of adaptability. She couldn't accept this lovely, cultured girl because of her background. When she surrendered her tense lack of adaptability, she was released.

Here is a man who has an impaired heart. If he can adapt himself to this fact and learn to live within this limitation, he will probably live long. But if he resents it and fights against it he will push himself off before his time.

If you make your happiness within, then you can live under every conceivable set of circumstances. You're immune to unhappiness.

O Father, as Paul adapted himself to a thorn in the flesh and lived gloriously with it, help me to do the same. Amen.

AFFIRMATION FOR THE DAY: *No thorns in the flesh can really hurt me, for I have none in my heart to impair me.*

ADAPTATION TO ANY LOSS

We take our last step in adaptability.

Third, *Adapt yourself to any loss that may have come to you.* If you have lost a loved one, don't lose the beauty of that love by corroding it with a morbid self-pity. That makes you lose the loved one and the love. Cherish the memory with gratitude—that saves the love, and you.

A prominent preacher was told he had a bad heart and he must stop preaching. He said to an audience: "I decided I would rather preach and die than live and listen." Instead of dying from a bad heart, he literally committed suicide. He could not adapt himself to a new fact that had arisen.

Dr. Fosdick says:

One of the adjustments most of us have to make is the adjustment to limited personal ability. We find we have small native gifts, and we realize that, in all probability, we shall have restricted personal achievements. Some individuals prove unable to make an adjustment to their limited ability and their disappointing prospects. Thus some men become embittered cynics when they cannot resolve the clash between a first-rate ambition and a second rate personal competence.

Dr. James Gordon Gilkey tells of a woman who said:

I lost my husband four months ago. He died suddenly and without warning and left me utterly alone. But I have learned this. When the day begins, all I have to do is to carry on till noon. When noon comes, all I have to do is to carry on till evening. When the day is nearly over, I don't have to face another day till another day comes. I'm taking life in little pieces. That's how I keep going.

She will get through to ultimate victory, for she has resilience of spirit, adaptability. If you have resistance of spirit, instead of resilience of spirit, you'll snap under the strain. The resilient of spirit bend, but they don't break. They have power of comeback.

O Jesus, Thou didst have power of comeback, for Thou didst make Thy cross redemptive. Give me thy power of comeback. Amen.

AFFIRMATION FOR THE DAY: *Like the bamboo, I will bend under the storms of life but I will not break.*

GROWTH IN SELF-CONTROL

We come now to the last of the nine fruits of the Spirit, self-control. The nine Beatitudes could be pronounced on those who bear these nine fruits, and there could well be special emphasis on the last: "Blessed are the self-controlled."

It is interesting that Paul puts self-control last. Most systems ancient and modern would put it first. Confucianism through self-control would strive to produce "the superior man"; Hinduism through breath-and thought-control would try to produce "the realized man"; Stoicism through will-control desired to produce "the detached man"; modern cults through mind-control strive to produce "the happy man." The Christian Way produces through Christ-control the self-controlled man. But note that self-control is not so much a means as an end. You do not gain Christ through self-control; you gain self-control through Christ.

"The love of Christ constraineth us"—or, literally, "narrows us to His way," controls us. If you begin with self-control, then you are the center, you are controlling yourself. And will be anxious lest yourself slip out from beneath your control.

But if you begin, as Paul does here, with love, then the spring of action is love for a Person, someone outside yourself. You are released from yourself and from self-preoccupation. The "expulsive power of a new affection" breaks the tyranny of self-love and releases your powers. This means that you are a relaxed and therefore a released person. When you begin with love, you end in self-control. But it is not a nervous, anxious, tied-up self-control; it is a control that is natural and unstrained, therefore beautiful.

Interestingly enough, this is the only place where the word self-control is used in the New Testament. And here it is used last as a by-product of love. The emphasis of the New Testament is Christ-control through love for Christ. "Love Christ and do as you like," for you'll like what He likes.

O Christ, let me move over and let Thee take the wheel, and then I'll get through this business of living without mishap. Amen.

AFFIRMATION FOR THE DAY: *My self-control shall be rooted in Christ-control, and therefore no longer precarious.*

CHRIST-CONTROL THE SECRET OF SELF-CONTROL

Here was a man who had spent two hundred hours in trying to help an alcoholic get control of himself. Then the alcoholic decided to get on his knees, surrender to Christ, and let Christ control him. He got up from his knees a free man. He never touched alcohol again. He found self-control through Christ-control.

I tried the Christian life as self-control. Every day I would start out with the thought and purpose that I would keep myself from sin that day. And every night I came back a failure. For how could an uncontrolled will control an uncontrolled self? A diseased will could not heal a diseased soul. Then Christ moved into the affections. I began to love Him. Then the lesser loves dropped away.

Professor Royce, in his philosophy of "Loyalty," says: "There is only one way to be an ethical individual and that is to choose your cause and then to serve it." This central loyalty to a cause puts other loyalties in their place as subordinate. Then life as a whole is co-ordinated, since the lesser loyalties are subordinated. To the Christian the "cause" is Christ and His Kingdom: We seek these first, and then all other things, including self-control, are added.

But not automatically. We have to co-operate. We have to throw our wills on the side of being disciplined. There are many who throw their wills on the other side—indiscipline, sometimes called freedom. A junior-high-school girl had on her belt this declaration of wants: "We want more holidays, less homework, more TV, and later hours for bedtime." Her crowd wanted to be free to do as they liked, not to be free to do as they ought. The result is inward and outward chaos. People who try to be free through indiscipline are "free in the sense that a ship is free when it has lost both compass and rudder." "The undisciplined person may sit at a piano," says Trueblood, "but he is not free to strike the notes he would like to strike. He is not free because he has not paid the necessary price for that particular freedom." Freedom is the by-product of a disciplined person. Then you are not merely "free from"; you are "free to."

Heavenly Father, help me to be the kind of person who is "free to"— free to do the very highest I am capable of doing. Amen.

AFFIRMATION FOR THE DAY: *Cleansed of a thousand clamoring desires, I'm now free to be the man God intended.*

"HE WOULD NOT BE PERSUADED"

An example of self-control through Christ-control is seen in the case of Paul as he neared the end of his amazing career. After all he had gone through, it would have been easy for him to say, "Well, I've suffered enough. We'll call it a day. I'm going to ease down and take things easy in my declining years." Not Paul. He knew what he was facing: "the holy Spirit testifies to me that bonds and troubles are awaiting me. But then, I set no value on my own life as compared with the joy of finishing my course and fulfilling the commission I received from the Lord Jesus to attest the gospel of the grace of God" (Acts 20:23-24, Moffatt).

And after this clear statement of purpose come the influences which try to make him swerve from it. "These disciples told Paul by the Spirit not to set foot in Jerusalem" (Acts 21:4). But the account adds: "but, when our time was up, we started on our journey." That word "but" reveals the fixed purpose within.

Again,

Agabus . . . took Paul's girdle and bound his own feet and hands, saying, "Here is the word of the holy Spirit: 'So shall the Jews bind the owner of this girdle at Jerusalem and hand him over to the Gentiles.'" When we heard this, we and the local disciples besought Paul not to go up to Jerusalem. Then Paul replied, "What do you mean by weeping and disheartening me? I am ready not only to be bound but also to die at Jerusalem for the sake of the Lord Jesus." As he would not be persuaded, we acquiesced, saying, "The will of the Lord be done." After these days we packed up and started for Jerusalem (Acts 21:10-15, Moffatt).

Here was amazing self-control in the face of well-intentioned and accurate advice. The things they said would happen did happen. He was handed over to the Romans. And that handing over meant his ultimate martyrdom. But Paul held steady, for he had not been promised exemption from trouble, but victory through it—yes, and because of it. For Paul wrote many of his most important letters while he was in Rome imprisoned.

O Father, I thank Thee that I, too, can hold steady amid all pressures. And come out triumphant at the end. Amen.

AFFIRMATION FOR THE DAY: *I am not controlled by pleasures from within or pressures from without. I am controlled from above.*

STEPS FOR GROWTH IN SELF-CONTROL

We come now to the steps in self-control.

First, *Fix it in your mind that you as a Christian cannot control the margin if something other than Christian controls the center.* Be sure that fears, resentments, self-centeredness, inhibitions, guilts do not control the center. At the center let there be Christ-control. Then you and Christ can deal with the marginal controls.

Second, *Take over the central control—control of the self.* If you find you are putting yourself at the center of conversation or situations, then deliberately plan to make others the center. Dr. Bonar once remarked that he "could tell when a Christian is growing. In proportion to his growth in grace he would elevate his Master, talk less of what he was doing and become smaller and smaller in his own esteem until like the morning star he fades before the rising sun."

They tell me that the most used letter on the typewriter is the letter "I." If on the typewriter of your life the chief emphasis has been "I," then shift to "U."

In your conversation train yourself to shift the conversation to the other person. Ask about his background, his family, and get interested in his problems. This makes the other person grateful that you are interested in what interests him, and at the same time it saves you from yourself.

The "brilliant, interesting conversationalist" is the conversationalist who talks about you. And the boring, uninteresting conversationalist is the one who talks about himself.

Third, *Don't allow conflicting loyalites in your life.* A man sat behind me in a plane and under the influence of liquor talked about himself: "I love my church. I really do. I know I drink too much sometimes, but I love my church. I love my dogs too." He had lots of loves—church and dogs and drink. And in the end the love of drink canceled out the other loves and controlled him. If you tolerate conflicting loves, then sooner or later one or the other of the loves will rise up and assume control. Have one supreme control—the love of Christ—and fit into that central love all the lesser loves.

O Christ, help me to tolerate no competing loves within me. Help me make Thee supreme and sole Ruler. Amen.

AFFIRMATION FOR THE DAY: *I have enough competition on the outside. I dare not tolerate any within.*

SELF-CONTROL IN SEX

We come to the next steps.

Fourth, *Take up the control of danger areas one by one, beginning with sex.* Controlled sex is creative; uncontrolled sex is chaotic. The people who get the least out of sex, except frustration, are the people who have the least control of sex—it controls them. Sex is the best servant we can have—and the worst master.

Here were two people who began to live together without marriage. Let her tell the story: "For awhile we thought we were happy. And then disillusionment set in. We became irritable. We couldn't live with ourselves or each other. So it broke up in frustration." This is what happens outside the marriage relationship when there is no self-control. It means a loss of the very self, disintegration.

Within the marriage relation if the other person becomes the means of self-gratification, instead of an end in himself to be respected, then again disintegration sets in. You cannot use another without abusing yourself. Your attitudes toward others become your attitudes toward yourself. If you use another for sex purposes, then sex uses you. You become an instrument instead of an end. Sex is a dedication or a desecration, and when it becomes desecration, it becomes degredation.

Fifth, *If you are to control sex, begin with the control of the mind.* What you hold in the mind passes automatically into act, if you hold it there long enough. Thoughts are motor—they are not passive things, they tend to pass straight into act if held at the focus of attention. Thoughts are destiny.

If therefore you dally with sex thoughts and imaginations, that dallying will become a doing. And that doing will become you.

As Dr. George A. Buttrick says, "We dramatize temptation in our secret thought, thus gathering gasoline for the devil's spark." And then we wonder why we blow up.

Someone has said, "What you take into your mind as meditation will stay in your life as fact." Your secret meditations become you, for good or ill. Hold nothing in your mind that you do not want to hold within you permanently.

Dear Father, help me to be a disciplined person in thought, word, and deed, especially in thought. Amen.

AFFIRMATION FOR THE DAY: *What is in my mind today as meditation will come out in my life as fact.*

SELF-CONTROL IN SPEECH

Sixth, *Have self-control at the place of the tongue.* James says:

We all make many a slip, but whoever avoids slips of speech is a perfect man; he can bridle the whole of the body as well as the tongue. . . . The tongue is a fire, the tongue proves a very world of mischief among our members, staining the whole of the body and setting fire to the round circle of existence with a flame fed by hell (James 3:2, 6, Moffatt).

The tongue, then, is important, an index of whether you have real self-control. There are three stages: impulse, consideration, speech. Many leave out the second and jump from impulse to speech. The disciplined person pauses between impulse and speech and gives himself to consideration. The amount of your disciplined self-control depends upon how long you pause at the stage of consideration. You must not pause too long, of course, lest it lead to indecision, but pause long enough to be sure that the thing you say is what you want to say.

I sat talking to one of the world's supposedly great men, a man in one of the highest positions of the world. We hadn't gone two minutes in our conversation when he suddenly jumped from impulse to word, passing by the stage of consideration. It was a half-cocked, snap judgment. He let me see his emotional immaturity. It was one of the things that led to his elimination.

If in the heat of an impulse you write a stinging letter, don't send it. Sleep over it, and see how it looks the next morning when your passion has subsided and you enter the stage of consideration. You'll probably tear it up. If not, it will probably tear you up with remorse and repentance.

A woman who was growing spiritually by leaps and bounds said that she had the hardest struggle over the middle word "consideration," for, said she, "I've lived so long on the spur of the moment I have difficulty in not jumping from impulse to word or act." Living "on the spur of the moment" is an accurate description of much of our living. The length and strength of that word "consideration" determines our maturity. No consideration, no character.

O God, help me to hold my tongue when I should and to speak when I should. Give me sense. Amen.

AFFIRMATION FOR THE DAY: *My tongue can have in it poison or power, but it cannot have both.*

SELF-CONTROL MEANS SELF-REALIZATION

We come to the last step in self-control: Seventh, *Find a self-discipline through work.*

When you give yourself to work, then this calls your attention away from yourself and your own problems, and anything that does this is healthy. So work is one of the best of self-disciplines. Trueblood says: "We are happiest when we are engaged in a task which is within our powers, but makes severe demands on our powers."

We are made in our inner structure for creation. The creative God made us creative, and when we are creative through work, we are happiest, because we are self-fulfilled. The workless person is the worthless person.

But some, cut off by illness from work in the ordinary sense, can be creative still in creating love and good will and courage around them.

A lady couldn't sleep at night. The doctor suggested that she get up and do the chores around the house when she couldn't sleep. She replied that she had a maid to do all that. No wonder she was sleepless and restless, for she had nothing to do to fulfill the creative urges within her.

We turn now to sum up the lessons of self-control. The steps through which we usually go in reference to the self are these: Self-indulgence leads to self-exhaustion, and self-exhaustion leads to self-surrender, and self-surrender leads to self-control, and self-control leads to self-realization.

The man who knows self-control knows self-realization. He *has* himself who has himself under control.

A great surgeon told me that twenty years ago he was a tobacco addict. He decided he would give it up, and stopped smoking suddenly and decisively. He said: "I felt like a man walking out of prison. I was a free man. My whole being took on new life. My color vision became better. I gained twenty-five pounds in two months. And my nerves were steadier." The self-control became self-realization. He found himself when he mastered himself. He gained a liberty through a law. He was a free man—free to do as he ought.

O Father, give me the courage to be free—free from a thousand clamoring desires that cancel me out. Amen.

AFFIRMATION FOR THE DAY: *Every habit a liberation, not a chain; every custom a course, not a curse.*

THE WORD OF CHRISTIANITY BECOME FLESH

The very center of the Christian faith is the Incarnation, in which the Divine Word becomes flesh—the Idea becomes Fact. All other faiths are the word become word, the idea projected as an idea. In Jesus the Idea walked. It spoke in human life and manifested Itself in human relationships. It transformed religion from idealism to realism.

Where this faith is sincerely tried, it becomes incarnate as fact. It works in human relationships. And wherever it is tried, it produces something so exquisitely beautiful that we stand "lost in wonder, love, and praise."

From many outstanding examples of Christian growth I am picking one, for several reasons. One is that the person is an ordinary person, with ordinary education, with ordinary abilities. The second is that she was placed in a very commonplace situation—on a farm. The third is that at first sight she seems not to be endowed with particular attractiveness—she is red-haired, freckled, and plain-looking. And fourth, she wasn't always what she is now. Her sister-in-law said: "Before her conversion her attitudes were all wrong."

And because she was average, I pick her out to let the average person see what can happen when average life is fully surrendered to God and responsive to His will.

And I pick her out because in doing so I can easily look past her and beyond her and above her to the source of her life and power—Christ. One can so easily see that attached to Christ, she has everything, and apart from Him she has little. I wrote to her one day: "Sister Mary, I hope all this attention and adulation you are getting will not go to your head, but to your knees." She wrote back: "Brother Stanley, it doesn't go to my head or to my knees. It just hasn't got my number on it. It doesn't belong to me at all. So I lay it all at His feet as fast as it comes." In another letter she wrote: "I've found I'm not the battle; I'm the battlefield. It's the Lord who does the overcoming. I simply let Him do it." But she is no mere pietistic passivist; she co-operates with all her being with all His proffered grace.

O Father, I thank Thee for those who know how to receive—to enter the Kingdom as a child and to receive fully. Amen.

AFFIRMATION FOR THE DAY: *The first, second, and third lesson in growth is to receive. Learn it, or you do not grow.*

THE ORDINARY BECOMES THE EXTRAORDINARY

A theological professor, known for his soundness of thought and emotional stability, and the last person on earth you would expect to be swept off his feet, came into his room and danced around the room with his hands up in the air after a talk with Mary and said, "For once I've seen a child of the Kingdom." She is just that—the most natural and the most naturalized child of the Kingdom I have seen in my travels around the world. Her growth in less than three years of the Christian life has been so astonishing that one very able woman said, "She is growing alarmingly." And yet you can see it is no mushroom, seven-day-wonder type of growth. It is all so natural, so sane, and so with-its-feet-on-the-ground. One woman who represents dedicated sophistication, as Mary represents dedicated simplicity, said of her, "She is the wisest and the simplest person I know." And a very skeptical doctor said, "She talks a lot, but she always talks sense." She does, and it's uncommon common sense. But it's common sense that isn't commonplace. It's all lighted up. Someone said of her, "She looks as though she has swallowed an electric light bulb." And yet she seems so utterly unself-conscious—the most natural Christian I have ever seen.

It started in a very unpromising way. She says: "I came to hear you talk about India, and you talked about God, and I found Him." And how! She walked into the Kingdom of God and took it over. Her childlike faith and simplicity fulfilled that verse: "The Realm of God belongs to such" (Luke 18:16, Moffatt). Note: the childlike do not merely belong to the Kingdom of God; it "belongs" to them. Its powers are at their disposal; all its resources are at their command. And then you see the miracle of childlike spirit becoming stronger than a giant world and playing with infinite forces—all consciously so.

Mary writes: "The easiest thing in the world for me to do is to love. I love everything and everybody. For they are lovable." And to her they are. For by her amazing love she draws love out of the loveless.

O Father, give me the simple, childlike heart that I may take over the Kingdom and become at home there. Amen.

AFFIRMATION FOR THE DAY: *In order to receive I must lose my artificiality, become open, childlike, unaffected, again.*

SMALL BEGINNINGS, GREAT ENDS

The conversion of Mary seems to have been very quiet and un-accompanied by any cataclysm. It was like the opening of a flower to the sun. A young man inquired: "Do I have to have an experience as sudden and cataclysmic as Paul's in order to grow?" The answer from Mary's case is, No. She instinctively took it as if taking her very own; it was her homeland, and at once she was at home.

Usually there is a separate and postconversion experience of the filling of the Spirit. In her case it seems all to have happened at once. At any rate her subconscious mind seems to have been Christianized. She has the most Christian reactions to every situation that arises. And the Christian reactions are instinctive and immediate. She puts it: "God seems to press the right button within me at the right time." For instance, as she sat at the table in a highly cultured family, a young man who was attending a university said in response to something Mary said: "I don't believe all that." The mother was mortified at her son's reaction, but Mary, without batting an eye, said, "But that is what is precious about you, Frank; you don't swallow everything you hear, and you shouldn't! You should keep an open mind and test things for yourself; then no one can fool you with false ideas." Frank smiled, and she had him; she had got behind his defenses, ef-fortlessly. He was her docile follower. Another instance: A woman who knifed people with her critical tongue said to Mary: "I don't want to love everybody in the world, do you, Mary?" "No," replied Mary: "I don't want to, but since this has happened to me, I can't help it." A skeptical doctor said when someone described Mary as plain: "Well, she has something I've never seen before, and it makes her beautiful." Even a little child can see it. She sat in a railway waiting room, and a little dirty-faced urchin came up and sat beside her and without a word put up his shoe to be tied. She tied it. And then he put up his other shoe to be tied. She tied it and then patted his leg. He got down, came around and patted her on the cheek, and then ran off. The spectators smiled, and some could scarcely keep back the tears. Love had become incarnate, and a child saw it.

O Father, give me that simplicity of love that the least of these will recognize it and want it. Amen.

AFFIRMATION FOR THE DAY: *Perhaps the place to begin simplification is to become simple in love, or simply love.*

SPECIALIZING IN LOVE

Mary loves everything and everybody and seems to do it effortlessly. Even her chickens see it and respond. The neighbors began to ask why she was getting bigger eggs and more of them than anyone else. Her reply: "It's simple. I love my hens, and they love me. When I go out among them, they crowd around me, and I talk to them, and I thank them for their co-operation, and do you know, they begin to lay like a house afire!" Something in it! Cornell University authorities say you must never frighten the hens by going into the hen house suddenly, as it will upset their laying for a month—you must knock before you go in, and then cluck! Everything understands love.

This is how Mary grew in her conception of love:

Paul said that once he loved God very much, and he wanted everybody else to love Him, so he appointed himself God's policeman, and he was determined to make them love Him even if he had to kill them to do it! Then Jesus came to him and showed him how to convert that destructive thing into a constructive thing. I was the same way—I wanted to convert everybody, even the converted. But Jesus said to me: "Mary, you mustn't *fight* for me, but *love* for me!" That transformed everything.

Her sister-in-law was in an accident and after eight months in the hospital was being sent home. The Jewish doctor said she would need a special nurse all the time, for she would never walk again. But Mary said, "Why can't I be the nurse?" The doctor replied, "But I hear you have two children, a house to look after, and a lot of church work." "Yes," replied Mary, "but this is my church work—to take care of my sister-in-law." "Put it there, sister," said the doctor. "You're a woman after my own heart. That's real religion." A carpenter doing some work around the house said to Mary, "You're a fool to tie yourself down to your sister-in-law in this way." "But," replied Mary, "I'm not tied; I'm cemented to her with bonds of love in my heart." And then she added: "Really the Lord ought to make me pay for the privilege of living with her. The Lord has granted me the privilege of caring for her when she needs it."

Dear God, make everything that comes my way an occasion to manifest Thy love in every situation. Amen.

AFFIRMATION FOR THE DAY: *To be simple in love is to manifest love in every simple situation and do it simply.*

THE MENIAL BECOMES A SACRAMENT

There were some things in reference to taking care of her "sister" (she never calls her "sister-in-law") that Mary didn't like—intimate things concerning the nursing—bed pans, etc. And then, she says, "The Lord said to me, 'Mary, I know you don't like to do certain things about the nursing, but I want to do them for her and can't. I haven't anyone else to do them for Me except you. Will you do these things for My sake?' That transformed everything into a sacrament. It's a joy now to do it for His sake."

And then she writes this: "I want my sister to be happy and contented as I am, and I pray God will show me all the little ways of making her serene and happy the rest of her days. He will, and has, and I've learned that to love Jesus really you must love and cherish and serve what He loves and cherishes and serves. And once His love invades your heart, it all becomes automatic, for in each small task you see an opportunity of saying, 'I love You, Jesus,' and then it's no longer a task but a privilege. Isn't it strange that B.C. a person is always seeking and worrying about his own happiness, but A.D. it is the other fellow's happiness that is important? Blessed, blessed Jesus! And then I asked Him: 'How come?' and He answered: 'I'm surprised too, Mary, that you're grown-up enough that you don't want to play Monopoly, but can take turns. Good girl!'"

Then she adds this: "There is no success in life, only fulfillment. Nothing could be more glorious and more exciting in all the world than just what I am doing right now, right here; and that is just being useful and loving to one other human being out of love for Him and gratitude for the privilege. . . . This is my mission field. I love it."

This is the word of love become flesh in a concrete situation. Pastors and others everywhere have tried to get her into their pulpits, but she almost always refuses. She writes: "Jesus said to me: 'Until the building is ready for occupancy, there should be no bell ringing in the steeple! For to what would the people come? An unfinished building and a wildly ringing bell.'" So He holds her to the little to make her ruler over the much.

O Father, help me to do the little thing in a big way—the way of love. For love glorifies all—and me. Amen.

AFFIRMATION FOR THE DAY: *I shall not ask for the big task and the big environment, but to do the little things in a loving way.*

LOOK ME FULL IN THE FACE

Mary has gone to a few pulpits, one of them in a large Negro church. She writes:

The fact that it was a Negro church was one of the main reasons for my wanting so much to go. I was so happy they would let me come and not hold my color against me. I worked two hours on the train going up there, for it was to be a great speech, and I was bursting at the seams to tell them. . . . As I stood up, I paused a moment, sizing up my audience, and do you know what I saw? I saw Jesus take my speech and tear it into tiny bits and throw them away, and then He said, "Mary, you were called to witness, not to speak. Look full into My face and tell them what you see." And the message just spoke itself, without any notes, or any effort on my part. When I finished, one of the sisters came up and took me in her arms and kissed me on the cheek. It was so tender and soul-shaking, I thought I would never want to wash that cheek again, lest I destroy the beauty of such blessing. At that moment there wasn't any question of color or race; it was just one child of God loving another and meaning it! And it came to me that this is the perfect solution of the so-called race problem: being one in Him!

She tells of another experience:

I was asked to speak in a church sixty-five miles from here on the topic (now, don't laugh!) "Pentecost." The flu had been very prevalent here, and that morning when I awoke, I had terrific pains in my stomach. On my way to the church they got so intense I felt I would surely have to go home and go to bed, as I could hardly drive the car. I prayed: "O Father, I deserve this pain, but please hold it up until the meeting is over. I want to serve You today, but I'm not well-enough trained to speak with so much pain. I'll be happy to accept it tomorrow. In any case Thy grace is sufficient for me." The pain went away. That is my *first* faith healing, for I took nothing. It just left and didn't even come back.

I am sure God must restrain Himself in telling her what to do, for she leaps at once to do it. The Father sees she needs the restraint of the reins rather than the touch of the whip.

Dear Lord and Father, give me that simplicity of heart and life that I too can take all I need of the Kingdom. Amen.

AFFIRMATION FOR THE DAY: *All doors to health and influence are open to the simple of heart who know how to love.*

209

LOVE IS DISARMING

We ended on the note of "Mary's" simplicity and her disarming, unaffected love. And people respond to it.

She writes: "For quite sometime now I've noticed that everybody I meet calls me by my first name! Recently a very austere and formal type of man, a superintendent of schools, asked me to come to his office when I had time. He kept me there two hours discussing religion. And he called me 'Mary' the whole time! He is very intellectual and kept asking over and over again, 'How?' I told him how I met Christ and of what had happened to me since. I tried every way I knew of to get that 'pill' of 'complete surrender' down him. I found that is one 'pill' that isn't even 'sugar-coated.' It's just plain bitter, no matter how you take it! He *listened,* but, of course, only he and God know if he 'swallowed' or not! He said he'd like to *feel inside* the way my face looked outside. He wants joy, of course, but only Christ within can produce that! It all seems so simple, and yet it is very hard to give it away to people. They always get to the point of 'surrender' and then try taking me down an alley instead of going one step more to the Way."

She gives this simple statement about the way she grows: "When I was talking to Him tonight, He told me He was going to help me grow inwardly. He said the most important thing to remember is always to keep my eyes on Him, and listen to Him when the going gets tough. He said He wanted me to learn to be patient when it is difficult to be patient, to be cheerful and happy when others are grouchy and sour. He wants me to learn to stop when He says, 'That's enough,' and to go when He says, 'The road is clear.' He wants me to see in each distasteful thing that I'm called on to do an opportunity to grow, and that it is for Him I labor and not for the world. He said He would never call me to do something, but that with the call will come the necessary power to do it." Simple? But very, very effective.

Her eager spirit of simple obedience is revealed in this sentence: "I don't want a thing explained now, so much as I want it revealed." The revelation is enough.

Father God, help me to be as sensitive to Thee as a blooded horse is to the touch of a whip. In Jesus' name. Amen.

AFFIRMATION FOR THE DAY: *Not God's thunder, but God's whisper, will be sufficient for me.*

SURE-FOOTED

We continue this week our study of "Mary" as an incarnate example of quick, but amazingly solid, growth. I say "solid" because there isn't a "queer" thing about her except that she's natural—plus; gay—plus; loving—plus; sensible—plus; effective—plus. A very wise Christian said of her: "Anyone who walks the heights as she does would surely make a misstep now and then. But I can't remember a fool thing she's done or said since she became a Christian." I wrote her and said: "You're as sure-footed on these mountaintops as a goat," and she replied signing herself, "Your Little Goat." Her little boy of six was overheard discussing his mother, and he said: "She can be as hard as nails, but she's human too."

She says: "Before conversion I was trying to live 'in spite of,' but after reading *Power and Poise,* the very Power you wrote about began to change the words 'in spite of' to 'because,' and everything within me began to mellow. My attitude before Christ came within me was that of defiance: 'I don't care what you do to me, life, I'm determined to live in spite of anything you can do to stop me.' But after reading *Power and Poise* you took me to what the aviators call 'the point of no return.' I didn't have enough fuel left in my tank to put back to where I started and couldn't just stay suspended in mid-air, so out of sheer necessity I had to go on—to Christ. He brought me back alive, and now I look life straight in the face and say, 'Dear precious life, I had you all wrong! I no longer tolerate you, I accept you all in all, just as you come.' Now life and I are no longer at swords' points with each other. We are friends, and the more I invest in life, the greater dividends I draw." Here is a great principle of human living: Don't be at swords' points with life, tense and anxious and defensive; accept what comes from life and make something out of it.

She writes regarding some personal attacks upon me: "I see this: Each time a barb goes deep into your heart, there flows out of this very hole the barb has made, great quantities of His love; and the bigger the barb, the greater the channel. It's a perfect example of evil being converted into good—going in evil and coming out blessedness!"

O Father, help me to take what comes from life, good, bad, indifferent, and make something good out of it. Amen.

AFFIRMATION FOR THE DAY: *Life is my friend. I will give it a friendly face and walk hand in hand with it down the years.*

BEFORE CHRIST AND AFTER

A friend writes about Mary: "She is rare indeed. All her discernments are still immaculate." They are—straight from God. Mary writes:

But in the name of Jesus, Brother Stanley, please expect big things of me and help me to pass your expectations! I'm not asking for flattery; I'm begging you to take me out of the safety zone, where nothing happens, and take me to that point of no return where everything happens. . . . There are big things to be done in this world that won't wait forever, so that's why I ask you to dream up the greatest possible thing you can think of that a woman can fill, and share your dream with me, and then hand me the pick and shovel and tell me to go to work.

During the period of gathering material for this book I wrote to her and asked her to send me any material she came across which I could use. Her reply was characteristic: "Brother Stanley, if you come across any new ideas, send them to me, and I'll put them in practice to see whether they will work. I'll be your guinea pig for ideas." And she would do just that! She wrote: "When you say to audiences that they are 'to go out and give out love and only love, and if it doesn't work, increase the dose,' they usually laugh, but I went out and did just that, and it worked."

Here again is a revelation of her spirit:

I have been studying the subject of "humility." He finds me a very difficult student, for I just don't understand the word in all its fullness. He said for me to find each day something to do that is beneath me; but there's where I'm in check, as they say in chess. I just can't seem to *find* anything that *is* beneath me. What can it be?

Her simplicity of motive and humility come out in this sentence: "I found I didn't want to use Him or to ask for special favors. I just want to love Him for nothing." "To love Him for nothing" is the pure, lambent flame of a purified devotion and love.

Father, give me such unconscious humility of heart and life that not even I shall know I have it. Amen.

AFFIRMATION FOR THE DAY: *"To be humble of heart is God's best gift"*—I shall manifest that gift today.

"NOTHING INSULTS ME"

Mary writes:

Nothing anyone says to me can insult me or hurt my feelings any more, for there is nothing anyone can say to me that I haven't already said to myself; and nothing can flatter me any more, because no matter what anyone says, there is always the picture in my mind of what I was *before* Christ, while they like what has happened *after* Christ. When God has a message to give to the world, He uses the first available instrument He finds regardless of its defects, and I found a good picture of myself in God's hands while reading Matt. 12:18-20. He wants a pen to write with; but I'm just a bruised and broken reed. Well, He'll use it until something better comes along. He wants a light. I'm just a dimly burning wick. But still He'll use me, inferior as I am.

Here again she shows that complete honesty with herself and others and her passion for improvement and growth.

I was reading about Peter's denial of Jesus, and my eyes fell on the words "for thy *speech* betrayeth thee!" I knew this was for me, so the next afternoon I cornered Brother M—— and said to him, "Brother M——, everybody up here is very anxious to point out our good points, but no one will be honest with me and tell me what is wrong that I may correct it. Will you be honest enough and kind enough to point out my weakness that I may grow?" You should have seen the look on his face! It was precious! He was afraid of offending me, but I told him he would do me a favor, and so, bless his heart, he said, "Well, it's your voice. It has a tenseness in it that isn't in your character. It is too high, and if you will try pitching it lower and speaking more slowly, you will be good to listen to." I never admired anyone more than I did him—he was willing to help me. So I went to work right away and got a book called *So to Speak,* and really I've never had so much fun nor so much hard work in anything I've tried before. But people have noticed improvement. Maybe God can make a *lady* out of me yet. I believe in miracles. In fact, I live on them.

This passion for growth and improvement does not leave her concentrated on herself. This sentence reveals her spirit: "I want to put into life everything and take out only what I need."

Dear Father, I want Thee to tell me my weak places, and then Thou and I will work at them together. Amen.

AFFIRMATION FOR THE DAY: *I shall expose my weakness to His strength, my ignorance to His wisdom, my lovelessness to His love.*

"SOME DEEP, DARK SECRET?"

We come now to look at Mary's amazing joy. She is the purest sparkling fountain I've ever seen. And as we shall see later, hers is not a surface joy; it is a joy that has met the worst and has turned it into something else, something higher.

She writes:

Brother Stanley, He is so marvelous to me that I can scarcely tell it to anyone. He amazes me with all that He gives me and does to me and with me. It is like a fairy story come true. I'm like a pumpkin that He has touched with His wand and turned into a lovely carriage. You've probably heard the story of the child who had a fan (the hand type), and she showed it to a famous painter, who said, "Let me have your fan, and I'll paint a beautiful picture on it." She grabbed it away and said, "Give me the fan. It's mine, and I'll not let you spoil it." How often we tell God, "This is my life. You might spoil it if you paint something on it." But oh, the unspeakable joy and glory that come when we learn to say, "Here am I, Lord, use me!"

And it is a joy that shows itself in loving service. Her sister-in-law was overheard telling some visiting relatives: "Mary is getting sweeter and sweeter every day. Whenever she does anything for me, she acts as though I'm doing her a favor to let her do it."

A grocer said to her, "Mary, you look happier than anyone else I ever saw. Have you some deep, dark secret you're hiding?" And she replied, "I sure have," and then whispered, "I love the Lord! And if you try it, it will put a bloom on your cheek like a sixteen-year-old."

A druggist kept watching her out of the corner of his eye. She had something different. Then he blurted out, "Why are you so darn happy?" And she told him her secret.

She writes: "Our souls must be elastic, or mine would burst with sheer joy. . . . I've learned what true happiness is—true and lasting happiness is just another name for God! . . . This will keep me from running down blind alleys instead of walking the Way!" Again she writes: "You're right about my living on my knees! But you can't kiss His blessed feet and stand! I'm so glad of that."

O Christ, at Thy feet are joys inextinguishable. Nothing—absolutely nothing—can put them out. I thank Thee. Amen.

AFFIRMATION FOR THE DAY: *My joys are beyond the reach of sorrow, for the eternal joy has invaded me.*

DOESN'T KNOW HOW TO MOURN

We continue to study Mary's amazing joy. She wrote: "I have trouble with one passage of Scripture: 'Blessed are they that mourn.' I don't really know how to mourn." And she meant it. She seems to pluck out of every happening a joy. And it is not the joy of untouched aloofness—she's in life to the depths and takes what comes. She comments: "It's friction that makes the auto tire go places. Without it the tire just spins around going nowhere." She welcomes "each rebuff that turns earth's smoothness rough."

Speaking of prayer: "Prayer always works in reverse with me. It should make me quiet and restful, but it always makes me feel that I have been injected with a tremendous dose of vitality, and I feel like going out and doing something about everything."

A very earth-bound type of minister said to her, "Mary, you scare me. Why, the world will crucify you if you go on thinking the way you do! . . . You know, you have the warmth of a Methodist; the stubbornness of a Baptist; the straightlacedness of a Presbyterian; the enthusiasm of a Jehovah's Witness; and the common sense of a Congregationalist." And she replied, "Thank you for that lovely compliment, for you have just described me as a walking example of federal union, which I believe in one hundred per cent." She is never without an answer. God always touches the right button in her.

And she has imparted this to her two boys. One of them, ten years of age, said he was raising ten hogs and would give one to India. He sent the thirty dollars the amount he realized on the hog, for India. Someone said to him, "Isn't that a lot of money for a little boy to spend on India?" And the boy replied, "Oh, I'm not spending it, I'm investing it." A real philosophy of life in that.

Her amazing joy comes out in a crisis: "Last night I was chopping the wood, and a big piece flew up and hit me right between the eyes, and, Brother Stanley, for a moment I thought I had made the grade into heaven! I saw many stars! Gee, it was *beautiful!* Now I have a small gash and a good lump to remind one of my short stay in Paradise!" She rescues something "beautiful" out of everything.

O Father, teach me to rescue out of every ugly situation something beautiful. Then I will be victorious. Amen.

AFFIRMATION FOR THE DAY: *As the Japanese make something beautiful of ugly roots, so let me make every ugly happening beautiful.*

"I HAVE TO LAUGH AT MYSELF"

Mary was nailing up some shelves, and the hammer struck not the nail but her finger and thumb and left them both purple. The boys were playing in another room, and she overheard one saying to the other, "Come on, Mom's hurt herself real bad, for she is no longer hammering, but she's singing real loud, 'Glory, Hallelujah.'" The alchemy of her radiant spirit turns the base metal of very ordinary happening into the glory of the Kingdom.

She writes:

How I love Him! Brother Stanley, several times when I was out in public with other people, I'd be praying to Him, and He'd tell me something especially precious, and before I knew it, I had said out loud, "Oh, Lord, how I love you!" People would look at me as if I were stark mad! They thought I had been listening to what they had been saying, and of course, my reply didn't fit into what they had said! But Jesus just smiles. He knows I'm crazy—crazy about Him! Once I did that in the public library, and everyone went "Sh-sh!" And they looked daggers at me! That surely must have sounded funny coming out of a clear sky in all that silence! I have to laugh at myself!

An infinite sanity runs through all she does. She writes: "As the physical grows in intensity, the mental grows in wisdom, and the spiritual grows in understanding of how to use it for growth in grace."

She makes everything contribute. This is characteristic: "Pain produces two opposites. One man rots in prison, and Paul in prison writes holy scriptures. So it is not what happens, but how we interpret what happens to us. We do have the power of choosing not what happens to us, but how we let it affect us!"

She writes: "Emotions upset us or set us up, and I am determined that all my emotions shall set me up." They really do.

Her emotions are restrained and very natural. A girl asked her if she had ever flown. She replied: "Well, yes, but not in a plane. I seem to be flying most of the time and don't even need gasoline."

O Father God, I thank Thee for the possibility of making every upsetting thing set me up. I'll try that today. Amen.

AFFIRMATION FOR THE DAY: *Every happening is a springboard to higher happiness, if I know the secret of using it.*

"THE INEVITABLE BUCKET OF COLD WATER"

Mary has an amazing amount of simple courage. And yet it was not native to her. After she was converted, she found herself afraid of a thunderstorm, so she just walked out into it and repeated the Twenty-third Psalm out loud as the storm raged. Then her fear was gone.

She writes:

At the end of every high expectation there is the inevitable bucket of cold water. There are two ways to take it. One is dodgingly. In that case you get wet, and you're resentful and angry. The other is to meet it head on, the way you take a shower bath. You step into it with expectation, and you step out of it with exhilaration.

In a state where there is segregation in buses, Mary wanted to ride home with a colored friend she had met at a religious retreat. So she determined what she would do if the bus driver objected. She said:

I've learned that when you bring in the cows from the pasture, the thing to do is to look them straight in the eye and let them know who is boss. So I determined to look the driver in the face and say, "I've got colored blood in me the same as hers,—red—and I'm obeying a law higher than the law of this state—the law of the Kingdom of God." But he just came in and glanced at us, grinned, and sat down. My colored friend said, "Thank the Lord, Honey, for the real thing that you get at the Ashram." And I replied, "If I had more of the real thing, I'd explode!"

One day going down the aisle of a train she stopped at a man who had a vacant seat beside him and said, "You've got a Christian face. Are you one?" And the man replied, "Well, I'm a minister!" She sat down, and they had a wonderful time together.

Speaking about a psychiatrist whom she met on a train, she said:

I practically recited from memory your book *Power and Poise*, and he said, "When I set up my office, I'd like you to come and be my nurse. That's the real thing you told me." I told him I read it out of a book and he could buy it for $1.50 and save going to school two and a half more years to learn the same thing! He laughed. I really threw the book at him.

O Christ, give me that simple courage of knowing that when I stand with Thee, I stand with reality. Amen.

AFFIRMATION FOR THE DAY: *Disarming frankness will be my chief and only weapon. I have nothing to cover—nothing.*

"A RIGHT TO HAPPINESS?"

We come to look further at "Mary's" insights. She heard me speak on Hegel's Thesis, Antithesis, and Synthesis, and she came up with this: "He told me this: 'There is Position, then Opposition, and then the two come together in Composition.'" I wrote her and said: "Why, 'Mary,' that's better than Hegel's." She replied: "What's Hegel's?"

She feels that she is not the source of these things but only the channel, that God speaks to her directly. And He does! She says: "A watch doesn't create time—it simply registers it. A violin doesn't create music—it simply registers the music in the violinist. So we don't create—we transmit." She is the clearest channel of transmission I've ever seen. She says: "God's whole education of me is to improve my insights through my eyesights." This is a profound saying. Some of her insights break out into clear prose and some into poetry:

> As man's created spirit,
> Up the ladder, God-ward mounts,
> He finds it isn't altitude,
> But attitude that counts.

Then this:

> If you've never felt the sorrow
> Of another person's grief;
> If you've never felt an inner urge
> To want to bring relief
> To someone who's in trouble
> By a kindly word or smile;
> If you've never loved your neighbor
> As yourself, with all your might;
> If you've never shed a tear drop
> At a pure and holy sight;
> If you've never met your Savior—
> You have nothing then to dread;
> You need have no fear of dying,
> Brother, you're already dead.

Father, give me the insights and the courage to follow Thee daily and wholly as an all-out follower. Amen.

AFFIRMATION FOR THE DAY: *"Love is blind?" Everything else is blind; only love really sees—and how!*

AMAZING REACTION TO A CALAMITY

We come now to the part of Mary's life when her way of life met the supreme test—would it hold when everything crashed around her? Everything did crash around her. This is a letter written two weeks after an auto accident in which her husband was killed and she and the two boys and the sister-in-law were smashed up. I have received many thousands of remarkable letters. This is my most unforgettable letter. Every syllable is genuine, her life since then being witness.

Claudie has a bad skull fracture and is not too good. His legs began to get stiff yesterday, and he can't turn over without a great deal of pain. They are watching him closely. How grateful I am that God healed my wounds enough so that I have strength enough to come and stay with him. My hand has a few fractures and also my ribs on the left side, but my leg wasn't broken, nor my jaws, as they first thought. I was cut with glass, but I'm still "on top of the heap." I'm still very sore and bruised all over, but otherwise just fine! I am trying hard, with grace from God, not to worry over Claudie's condition, but to just trust and keep my mind free, so I can help him all I can. He really needs a strong mother now, and I know God will help me be strong, for He has already done miracles for me.

Brother Stanley, ever since a year ago at the silent Communion service, I've understood what death really is and have tried to tell others in a small degree just how beautiful an experience it will really be. It seemed to me at the Communion service I really got a glimpse into eternity, and it was so beautiful my heart nearly broke with joy and rapture. Well, it is one thing to tell someone else something and another thing to go through it yourself, and I wondered if when my time came to "taste of death," it would hit me as an evil thing, or if it would still seem the beautiful thing it did then. Now I can tell you with all truthfulness that my original opinion is strengthened more and more! I can truthfully say that at least for me death really doesn't have any sting. This may seem strange to you, as it certainly has to so many others, especially the doctors and nurses, but even when they told me Roy was killed, I couldn't feel one bit like crying. I haven't shed a tear over it, nor do I feel like crying. (continued)

O Christ, we thank Thee for those have followed Thee wholly and have found that it wholly worked. Amen.

AFFIRMATION FOR THE DAY: *Death is not my weeping point; life, badly lived, is, for then life has ceased to be life.*

"SOUL COMPLETELY FREE"

We continue the letter of Mary, repeating her last sentence:

I haven't shed a tear over it, nor do I feel like crying, for, you see, God has been teaching me so much these last fifteen months, and He has so transformed my thinking that now I see this accident in its true light and not as a personal issue at all. The truck that caused the accident was about to pass another car, and the truck driver saw us coming toward him. He applied his brakes to slow down and get back into line, but the wheels of his truck locked and threw him sideways in front of our car, and we hit the truck square in the center. The driver of the truck was utterly helpless, and it was really *just an accident*. Roy didn't suffer, as he was killed instantly. It is not tragic just because it happened to *me*. I know that when two cars going forty-five or fifty miles per hour hit head on, it is inevitable that someone get killed. We just happened to be in the path of the truck. I certainly do know that it was not God's will that we be hurt or that Roy be killed, but since He has made us persons, He has made us free, and so we have the power to hurt or help one another. And because the laws of the universe are truly dependable laws, they work no matter who uses them or breaks them. How grateful I am *that this is so!*

But God was right there all right—I saw Him in the faces of those who wanted to help us, out of compassion of their hearts; in the ambulance driver who was so grieved when he saw it was his friends that he could hardly speak; in the doctors who instantly came to help us and worked three hours sewing us up and making us comfortable; in the friends—four hundred—who came to Roy's funeral; in Brother Loyal, who was at my bedside as soon as humanly possible; in the flowers and cards of sympathy from all over; and most of all in that "still, small Voice" that said over and over again to me: "Be not afraid, for lo, I am with you always, even unto the end of the world," and then "I am the Resurrection and the Life, and whosoever liveth and believeth in me shall never die. Believest Thou this?" I replied: "Yes, my precious Lord, I do believe that You are the one true God of the living!" And from then on my soul has been completely free of all things but His own precious holy love. (continued)

Father, we thank Thee that in Thee we are invulnerable, and not even death can touch us. Amen.

AFFIRMATION FOR THE DAY: *Death has no sting for the Christian; its sting has been pulled at the Cross.*

"LOOK DEATH IN THE FACE AND NOT BAT AN EYE"

We continue Mary's letter:

He has been with me so close every minute that I really feel as if I had wings of an eagle, and my heart is singing to the top of its voice our Ashram song: "I will not be afraid." It is a modern miracle that my dear, precious Jesus has performed in me, for while I thought it would be possible for me to accept death, little did I dream I could *rejoice* and *sing* in the face of it! But you know it was not I, but He, who made this possible. All He has asked was that I just stay "open," and He has *poured* the blessings out! Life looks just as beautiful to me as it did two weeks ago, because I have really discovered something wonderful; if you really do "keep your eyes upon Jesus," you can go through any storm life has and not have your spiritual equilibrium upset. But looking at Jesus and not at yourself is the whole thing.

I saw in the Bible these words: "Mary has chosen that good part that shall not be taken from her." I have chosen that "good part" of my husband that no one can ever take away from me. He is "one" with me now in the spirit of our Lord. It is as if he had just gone upstairs to rest, and I'll go too when I finish what I am doing, and we shall see each other again in the morning. So do not pity me. I find it impossible to pity myself.

Your prayers were certainly answered, for never have I felt the presence of God so strongly as in this past week. . . . My faith in God is twice what it was, and I feel relaxed even about Claudie, since God is even more interested in his welfare than am I, and everything will be fine.

At the hospital all the doctors and nurses were talking about what happened to me, for they had never seen anyone look death in the face and not bat an eye. When I told just what God had done for me and what I thought death was, they said they felt so much better, for they had always feared it, not understanding it. They were certain I was telling the truth because my reaction spoke for itself. They seemed to think they would like to start going to church again.

When God enters the picture, glory breaks all around!

The hardest part was telling Teddy about his daddy. It was like running a long, sharp dagger down into his little heart, but he will get over it, for he took it like a soldier. I have yet to tell Claudie when he is well again.

Your happy sister, Mary.

O God, my Father, I thank Thee for this wonderful victory—a victory impossible save in Thee. Amen.

AFFIRMATION FOR THE DAY: *In Christ I see the incredible, know the unknowable, and do the impossible.*

"I'VE SEEN EVERYTHING NOW"

We have had the privilege of looking deeply into the soul of the most radiant Christian I know. She met this catastrophe the way she meets everything, little and big, with a radiance of spirit that transforms everything.

One would have thought that she would have had a sag after that amazing triumph, an emotional reaction. It hasn't come. After a year and a half she is more radiant than ever. One discerning friend said: "Mary has no bumps, for she never lights."

She spoke of the coming operation on her youngest son. She herself wheeled him into the operating room, and the surgeon, seeing her radiant face—something he had never seen before—said, "Well, I've seen everything now. And everything will be all right." It was!

At the hospital while she was going up to the operating room for her son's operation, she saw a young woman weeping outside the door, and she asked her what was the matter and was told that her husband was dying in the room. Mary tried to comfort her, and the woman said bitterly, "Yes, but you've not lost your husband, so you can say that." And Mary told her very quietly that she had lost her husband a week before. Then the girl listened. She took the girl to the coffee shop, talked to her, and sent her back with her burden lightened and the tears dry. She did this on her way up to the operating room where her own son was hovering between life and death.

She says: "A girl who had lost her mother a year or so ago asked me if I didn't feel sad, lonely, and afraid, as she did. After she left, I wrote down these lines:

> I am not sad!
> I know the joy of a heart's full surrender,
> I am living in splendor:
> I am not sad.
> I'm not alone!
> I have God's love and His spirit to guide me.
> He is walking beside me:
> I'm not alone.

O Christ, give me the spirit that transforms everything into victorious character and achievement. Amen.

AFFIRMATION FOR THE DAY: *In Jesus everything is opportunity—opportunity to make everything into something else.*

LEGALLY, BUT NOT MORALLY, RESPONSIBLE

This pure radiance and joy of Mary is not mere moonshine. It works itself out in concrete situations as Christian living. In the settlement for the accident the lawyer said that if the senior member of the firm were associated with the junior member as a codefendant, then instead of $18,000 she could get $25,000. "But," said Mary, "he might be legally responsible, but he was not morally responsible for the accident. So I can't do it." At the close the lawyer took her up to the judge, who said: "My dear, I'm glad to shake the hand of a real Christian."

And yet her simple humility shines through it all. She writes: "It tickles me to see how God uses such big words when He talks to you and how small they are when He talks to me, 'Reticence'—gee, He never talks to me like that! But He sure 'lays it on the line' with me just as He does with you. I love Him for that."

This simplicity amid profundity shines out in this incident: She sat down in a train beside a man who was a fatalist.

I began to tell him what I believed in, and he sat up and said to me, "How old are you?" I said, "Thirty-five." He looked at me and said, "Why, I thought you were a high-school kid until I heard that philosophy of yours. That's the most amazing thing I ever heard." Well, we were real quiet for quite a while, and finally he said, "Would you mind going over that again? I never heard anyone talk or think like you, and it's hard to digest." I said "Why, it's the simplest thing in the world. It would have to be if I got it." He replied, "That's just it. It's too darn simple for me."

Her simplicity and spontaneity are sometimes disconcerting. She sat listening in a church to a very liberal speaker who said that Jesus was dead and that He stayed dead. Mary was on the edge of her seat listening, and forgetting where she was, she broke out, "Oh, no, you're wrong. He's alive. I was talking with Him this morning!" Those who knew Mary knew it was true! She had been talking with Him that morning, and the radiance lingered upon her face. But the speaker was nonplused.

O Christ, Thou art alive—alive to those who know Thee, surrender to Thee, and follow Thee—alive forevermore. Amen.

AFFIRMATION FOR THE DAY: *Today I shall feel my heart burn within me as He talks with me by the way.*

"PACKED WITH PURE UNMERITED GLORY"

The simplicity of relationship which Mary has with God is seen in the way He talks with her and she with Him. After a day in which she had walked through difficult decisions and come through with what she calls her "V" for victory, she heard Him say to her as she lay down to sleep: "Sleep well, little one. I love you. Good night." And she adds, "His love simply breaks me up. It melts me. Gee, how I love Him!"

I know it is possible to project your subconscious desires into God and hear what you want to hear. The test is the outcome. "By their fruits ye shall know them." And the outcome of all this is a life of sane and strong love, going out to everybody and everything. Recently she has been offered five different jobs, with more or less the same motive—as expressed by one man: "You may not know anything about my business, but I'd like you to come into my office and love people as they come in. I'll pay you well for it." But this can't be bought with money! It is purchased by a complete self-giving and constant obedience.

She sums up her life conclusion:

The beautiful part of it all is that every single moment of these two years and eight months of being a Christian have been so packed with joy and happiness and pure unmerited glory that if all the rest of my life were nothing but trouble and sorrow, I could honestly say to anyone that I've had more than enough to last me all through eternity.

But she was not always this way. She writes: "I do not want to tell you about the Mary before Christ, as it isn't nice to talk about people after they are dead."

But Mary is not a lone star, aloof and unique; she is an example of ordinary human nature extraordinarily responding to grace.

O Christ, we thank Thee that the latchstring is low. We can all pull it and enter, into Thy all. Amen.

AFFIRMATION FOR THE DAY: *I am through with playing "safe." My safety shall be in adventure. My adventure is Christ.*

GROWTH IN BODILY HEALTH

We now turn to the consideration of growth in bodily health. Has the Christian faith anything to do with the body, or has it only to do with the saving of the soul and getting it ready to go to heaven? If the latter is so, then it is a partial answer touching only a part of our needs.

But let it be said straight off that Christianity is not a healing cult; its primary purpose is not to keep our bodies in repair. God is not a cosmic convenience, dancing attendance on our bodily comfort. That would make us use God. And we can't use God; God must use us. And incidentally, it must be said that Christianity is not a happiness cult. Its primary purpose it not to make us happy, as many happiness cults would imply or state. Happiness does come through the Christian faith, amazing happiness beyond description. But if the end of the Christian faith is to make us happy, then we are again using God— we are the center, not God. This means self-idolatry. Happiness is a by-product of God's using us.

So the Christian faith is not a success cult, a happiness cult, or a healing cult. Its central purpose is to redeem man primarily from sin and evil, and as a by-product of that redemption it brings him true success, true happiness, and true healing. If we seek health first, we will lose it—it will evade us; but if we seek first the Kingdom of God, then all these things, including health, will be added to us.

For God wills health. Disease is not the will of God. Disease of the body is no more the will of God than disease of the soul. God is out to get rid of evil in all its ugly forms. The evil of the mind is error; the evil of the emotion is suffering; the evil of the body is disease; the evil of the soul is sin. And He is out to root out all evil from all of life, including the evil of the body, disease. The Lambeth Conference of the Church of England says: "However disease may be brought about and in whatever way it may be over-ruled for good, it is in itself an evil." And Jesus came to banish evil in all its forms.

O God, help me to co-operate with Thee in finding my way to clear views and attitudes toward health. Amen.

AFFIRMATION FOR THE DAY: *I am co-operating with the healing God in seeking the best health possible for me.*

GOD'S LAWS ARE GOD'S PREVENTIVE GRACE

I said yesterday that disease is not the will of God and that He never sends disease. This must be clarified a bit. Indirectly He does. For He has made a universe of moral and material law. These laws are His preventive grace saying: "Keep off—danger." If we break these laws, we don't just break the laws; we break ourselves upon the laws. We get hurt—physically, spiritually, morally. We get the consequences in ourselves.

If we work with the moral universe, we get results—the moral universe will back us, sustain us, and further us. We will get results. But if we go against the moral universe, we will be up against it, frustrated, hurt. We will get consequences. Some people go through life getting results; others get consequences. But we get one or the other. And those results or consequences are passed on to others, for we are all bound up in a bundle of life together for good or ill. We have the power to hurt or to help one another, and that through succeeding generations. "Just as the individual enjoys assets he is not entitled to as an individual, so he is called on to suffer liabilities which he does not individually merit."

So God, having made the laws, is remotely responsible for our suffering if we break those laws through the misuse of freedom. He is responsible for making us free and hence is responsible, remotely, if we misuse our freedom and suffer. God accepts that responsibility and discharges it at a cross. There He takes on Himself everything that would and does fall on us and suffers with us and for us. There the world's sin and sorrow "were forced through the channel of a single Heart." There He provided an open door of release from all that hurts and hinders us in any realm of life.

If we have had a bad heredity physically and spiritually, He provides us with a new heredity, straight from above. There is engrafted on us a divine nature, a new heredity that cancels or controls the lower heredity—we are born from above. So we are not caught in unchangeable conditions; there is an open door upward, always. We must learn to walk into that open door into radiant health.

O Father, I thank Thee for the open door. Help me to walk into it carefully and prayerfully and expectantly. Amen.

AFFIRMATION FOR THE DAY: *Health is God's will; it shall be my will through co-operation.*

THE BODY TO BE REDEEMED

Some people seem to look on salvation as a thing apart from the body. A Hindu sadhu, or holy man, said to me, "Sir, teach me to get rid of my body. It's an enemy dragging down my soul."

On the other hand, the French "Mother," as she is called in Arabindo Ghose's Ashram in Pondicherry, India, said to me, "Sri Arabindo is trying to achieve something that has never yet been tried, namely, not only to make his soul divine, but his body divine as well." One Hindu wanted to get rid of his body, and the other wanted to take it up and make it a part of the divine. They both failed. Arabindo Ghose died as other people die—his body subject to decay. The body is not a devil, nor is it divine; it is a God-given part of us to serve us in a mortal world. The body must break down some time or other after it has served its purpose. Then it will be replaced by an immortal body, not subject to decay. But that will be in an immortal world beyond this one. In this one the body is the mortal instrument of an immortal spirit until its work is done.

And it is a part of the redemption of Christ to redeem the body as well. But only a part. It is not the central aim or the central theme. Jesus healed people as a part of His redemptive impact upon all life. But He asked them to keep it quiet lest He be looked on as a healer only and primarily. He was primarily a Redeemer from sin and evil, and secondarily a healer of diseases. And He wanted first things first. Just as the soul is more important than the body, so the redemption of the soul is more important than that of the body.

But Jesus said to His disciples that they were to go out and say: "The Kingdom of heaven is at hand. Heal the sick" (Matt. 10:7-8). Note how closely connected were the coming of the Kingdom and the healing of the sick. A part of the coming of the Kingdom of God was the healing of the sick. Jesus didn't heal the sick as a bait to get them to listen to His good news. He healed them because healing was a part of that good news. It stood in its own right, and while it predisposed men to listen to the good news, nevertheless Jesus healed people whether they followed Him or not.

Father, I thank Thee that my body is a partaker of Thy redemption. Help me to believe it and receive it. Amen.

AFFIRMATION FOR THE DAY: *If my body is included in redemption, then I shall open every pore to God's redemption.*

INNER ATTITUDES CAN ALTER OUTER ASPECTS

We ended yesterday on the note that healing is an integral part of the coming of the Kingdom. This passage expresses it: "The body is . . . for the Lord, and the Lord is for the body" (I Cor. 6:13, Moffatt). The Lord is for the body—He made it and will keep it in repair and at its best if we will obey His laws and appropriate His grace. And the body is for the Lord—when the body obeys the Lord, it fulfills the laws of its own being. It is at its best when it obeys His behest.

He has so made the body that all right emotions, right thoughts, and right attitudes produce right effects in the body. This is important. Suppose they produced wrong effects. Then the body and morality would be alien to each other. An outstanding surgeon said to me, "I've discovered the Kingdom of God at the end of my scalpel—it's in the tissues. For the right thing morally is always the healthy thing physically." Then the laws of morality and the laws of health of the body are the same laws written by the same God for the same purpose, namely healthy and happy living.

And He has made it so that through right thinking and right emotions we ourselves can pass on right effects to our bodies. William James says: "The greatest revolution in my generation was the discovery that human beings by changing their inner attitudes of mind can alter the outer aspects of their lives." This means that they can alter them for good or ill. Wrong emotions and wrong thinking can alter wrongly the outer aspects of one's life. Right emotions and right thinking can alter rightly those same outer aspects. "As he thinketh in his heart, so is he," and so is he outwardly, sooner or later.

Someone has defined an emotion as "a change in the mind which produces a sensible change in the body." Note: "a sensible change"—an outer manifestation; the body changes for good or ill with the impact of that emotion. The British Medical Association says that "there is not a single cell of the body totally removed from the influence of mind and emotion." So the attitudes of mind and emotion do not stay attitudes; they pass over into definite physical effects.

O Father, Thou hast made us so we can damage or can deliver ourselves. Help me to see Thy way and take it. Amen.

AFFIRMATION FOR THE DAY: *All my emotions today shall bring health, not sickness, for they shall be right emotions.*

THE PHYSICAL EFFECTS OF EMOTIONS

We stressed yesterday the effects of mind and emotions upon the body. We turn "pale with fear," we "blush with embarrassment," we are "livid with rage," we "quiver with excitement." We say to ourselves, "I feel ill when I think about it." We do, for the fact we are facing upsets us emotionally and therefore physically. "He burns me up" is literally true. You hate him, and that hate burns you up physically. The emotional passes over into the physical. "He's a pill"—hard to swallow. "He drives me nuts"—he upsets your mentality.

These statements have passed into our language as expressing a fact, a very important fact: wrong attitudes toward people produce wrong effects in the body. On the other side we say, "She's a tonic"—she is, for she tones us up when we think of her or see her. "You make me feel like a million"—yes, because the reaction makes the body have a sense of well-being.

We smile about these statements, but the effects can be very real —and serious. Here was a Hindu businessman who saw a friend drop dead on a cricket field. It scared him. His fear upset his own heart. He stayed at home afraid to go to his business for fear it would be too great a strain upon his heart. He would go periodically to a doctor to be examined. In the strength of the assurance of the doctor that his heart was sound he could go for two or three weeks. The emotion of fear was upsetting his heart. It wasn't imaginary. The heart was upset, but only functionally. He was sound structurally.

A doctor friend visited the Mayo Clinic, and when he saw the streets filled and the clinics filled with people, he asked one of the doctors, "Is this a festival day?" "No," replied the doctor, "this is an ordinary day. I'll tell you what happens. John goes down the street, meets a friend, remarks to him that his heart is giving him trouble; the friend leaves John, and, thinking about it, he feels his heart is acting up too. He meets a friend and tells him about it and infects the other with the fear. And thus it spreads like an epidemic, and we get the wreckage here."

Father, teach me how to make mind and emotion contribute to health instead of contributing to disease. Amen.

AFFIRMATION FOR THE DAY: *My emotions, harnessed to God's intentions, shall be not my enemies, but my allies.*

229

"RISE UP AND WALK"

Dr. Leslie Weatherhead tells of an experiment he made on a girl who was very susceptible to hypnotism. He could even hypnotize her over the telephone. So he gathered a group of doctors, put the girl under a hypnotic spell, told her that he was touching her knee with a red-hot iron. Instead he touched her with a lead pencil. The knee was bandaged and the bandage sealed. A few days later when the bandage was removed, there was a blister with water in it. The sub-conscious mind had accepted the idea of a red-hot iron and had produced the blister out of that subconscious thinking.

Perhaps a more remarkable case still is this one, also related by Dr. Weatherhead: A woman was an invalid, paralyzed in her limbs. Her own doctor engaged her in ordinary conversation, while another doctor sat by her bedside and said to her in a low but authoritative voice, "Get up, and walk." To the astonishment of herself and others she did. And she never became an invalid again. What had happened there? Her subconscious mind had accepted invalidism, a paralysis that was probably an unconscious escape from something she did not want to face. She retreated into invalidism.

Professor C. H. Dodd said: "It appears that the authority of Jesus penetrated to the subconscious depths of personality where so many mysterious disorders of mind and body have their source." This can't account for all His miracles, but undoubtedly it was the method He used in performing some.

On American planes the cup for airsickness is hidden away, so I've seldom seen anyone sick on an American plane. People don't expect to get sick, and they don't. But in Chinese planes you are given an airsickness bag and a box of lunch when you board the plane. Suggestive! I've seen everyone on the plane get sick when it began to get the least bumpy. For the passengers would sit there holding the airsickness bag in their hands ready for use. (As I wrote the above, we were going through a storm on a plane in America. Not a person got sick!)

O Father, help me to have my mind and emotion trained to create health and not illness. In Jesus' name. Amen.

AFFIRMATION FOR THE DAY: *Today I shall by word and attitude and thought suggest health to myself and others.*

"THE SPIRIT IN TROUBLE"

The Japanese have a word for sickness: "the spirit in trouble." Very often it is the "spirit in trouble" that produces illness. A woman told me that she had what the doctors described as "anticipatory asthma." She anticipated it, became fearful, and out of her very fearfulness produced the tensions that produced the asthma.

We can't put all diseases into the category of being rooted in the mind and emotion. There are structural diseases, and they are real—the tissue is actually diseased. The disease is not merely in the function; it is in the structure. The American Medical Association is prepared to say that it is about fifty-fifty—fifty per cent rooted in the physical and fifty per cent rooted in the mental and spiritual. Medical experience would enlarge the percentage of the mental and spiritual and say that probably seventy-five per cent of the people who come to doctors don't need medicine. They are passing on the sicknesses of their minds and souls to their bodies, and they will never get well unless they change their attitudes of mind and emotion. A doctor of the Mayo Clinic said to me: "We can deal with 25 per cent of the people who come to our clinic with our instruments of science, but 75 per cent we don't know what to do with. They are passing on the sicknesses of mind and emotion to their bodies, and you can't touch that with the instruments of science." A great surgeon once said to me:

You could have headed off probably 85 per cent of the people who come to me for surgery by the kind of religion you are presenting. These cases begin with functional disturbance due to wrong mental and spiritual attitudes, and the functional disturbance passes into structural disease. Then I get them as a surgeon. But you could have headed off 85 per cent, for you could have stopped them at the place of the functional.

"The spirit in trouble" often drags the body into trouble. Therefore it is of the utmost importance that the spirit be straightened out if we are to have healthy bodies.

O God, my Father, help me to come to Thee and find the source of getting the spirit out of trouble. Amen.

AFFIRMATION FOR THE DAY: *My spirit shall not be in trouble with itself nor a trouble to my body.*

DO I REALLY WANT TO BE WELL?

We now look at the kinds of attitudes of mind and body we are to have if we are to be at our physical best.

If we have been in trouble physically, then we must first of all find out if the trouble is based in the physical or in the mental and spiritual. This would mean a physical check-up by a competent doctor. He may find structural defects that need correction. If he can find no physical basis, then we must turn to the mental and spiritual to correct attitudes which are upsetting us physically.

Step off from your life and look at it objectively, and see where you are causing functional disturbance in your system. This will not be easy, for when you come to the sore spot, you'll probably shy away and go off to some irrelevant thing instead of facing the real thing, just as a mother duck will feign a broken wing to decoy the intruder away from her nest. You will have to force yourself to become realistic.

First of all you must ask yourself the question: "Do I want to be well?" This is important. It was the first question Jesus asked the paralyzed man at the pool: "Wilt thou be made whole?" Was he using his illness to escape some responsibility he was refusing to take up? Here was a soldier who was caught in a conflict between doing his duty as a soldier and his desire to run away. To get out of this dilemma, he developed subconsciously a paralysis. The paralysis was a way out—he wasn't running away, for he would do his duty if he were well, but since he was not well, he need not do his duty. The illness was an escape.

We have seen a fundamental difference between Freud and Jung—the former found the basis of a neurosis in childhood, the latter in a refusal to accept responsibility. My experience with upset individuals confirms Jung. Where there is an illness rooted in the spiritual, it is almost invariably the result of a refusal to accept responsibility in a certain situation. If he is refusing to accomplish a necessary task, the escape into illness seems the open door. The road is a road with a dead end, but many take it rather than face up to life.

O Father, in this quest for health, real health, make me completely realistic, facing up to everything. Amen.

AFFIRMATION FOR THE DAY: *Acceptism, not escapism, will be the keynote of my life.*

THINGS THAT CAUSE ILL HEALTH

We have seen the first step in our quest for health—no subterfuges, no make-believe, no escapism, but complete honesty with yourself and others. This complete honesty is basic. Nothing can atone for a lack of it.

See if there are any fears in your life which may be upsetting your system. Here was a man whose wife was resentful because he didn't have the money his sister's husband had. She was always throwing it up to him. He retreated into illness, became a complete invalid, couldn't do a thing for himself, couldn't even dress himself. He said to an evangelist: "No one has any confidence in me." The evangelist replied, "I do." It awakened him. He began to perk up. He came to the evangelist's meetings and is now walking around. He is on the way out. He was afraid to face life in view of the demands his wife made on him. As he began to get strength from God to face that situation, he began to be well.

Then go over your life for any resentments, hidden or open. For resentments can upset the system. Dr. Flanders Dunbar tells of a diabetic woman who had suffered for seven years, not only from the diabetes but also from severe neurotic pains, from headaches and dizziness, from numbness, and from obesity. She herself had found that annoyance and rage caused her more trouble than potatoes, candy, or ice cream. In her first interview she relieved herself of many pent-up grievances; she co-operated with the psychiatrist and gained insight as to her emotional and personality difficulties; she got relief from her various pains, and her diabetes improved markedly.

Jung says that the doctor may clearly see why his patient is ill: "It arises from his having no love, but only sexuality; no faith, because he is afraid to grope in the dark; no hope, because he is disillusioned by the world and by life; and no understanding, because he has failed to read the meaning of his own existence." And he might have added that because of these things he hates life and himself. And when you do, you are ill.

O Father, help me to root out of myself all that upsets me, for I would be well in Thee. Amen.

AFFIRMATION FOR THE DAY: *None of my illnesses shall have me as their author.*

EMOTIONS UPSET THE STOMACH

We continue to look at emotions and their effects on the body.

Dr. Cannon tells of a woman who came to a clinic for examination. She was given a test breakfast, and when the stomach contents were analyzed, practically no gastric juices were found, and the food from the night before was undigested. It appeared that her husband had taken advantage of her visit to the city to get drunk and had given her a miserable time. As a result of all this her stomach refused to do its work. When their relations began again on a new basis and after a good rest and better behavior on the part of her husband, the stomach test was normal.

A man with an opening into his stomach was studied. He was observed almost every day for years, and the doctors learned to tell the state of his emotions by the appearance of his stomach lining. Once when some papers for which he was responsible were misplaced, his face grew pale, and the mucosa of his stomach grew paler by the minute, as he feared the loss of his job. When the papers were found, his stomach began to regain its normal pink color. This was a typical fear reaction. On another day he was reprimanded for failure to keep the apartment clean. He grew red in the face, but he dared not express his anger at the rebuke, although he was boiling mad, and as a result the gastric mucosa was red, the gastric acid was much increased. After his sustained resentment the doctors found small hemorrhages on the surface of the stomach lining.

So if you are going to be a healthy person, you cannot hold emotions of anger or resentment. The system is allergic to them. They do not fit—so they fight! The system is made for love and good will, not for hate and fear. Love sets up the system, and hate upsets it. Therefore you must choose. You cannot have hate and health, or fear and fitness.

If you tolerate any wrong emotions, those wrong emotions will register themselves in your body. They may not break out into sickness that can be seen, but they register themselves nevertheless. The body becomes predisposed to illness.

Gracious Father, I do choose—I choose what Thou dost choose. I give up what Thou canst not approve. Amen.

AFFIRMATION FOR THE DAY: *Hate is my let-me-down, so I renounce it and make love my pick-me-up.*

SELF-PREOCCUPATION PRODUCES ILL HEALTH

If you are to be healthy, you must give up all self-preoccupation. You must get interests outside yourself. You must love others.

Dr. Adler, a famous psychiatrist, puts his finger on our trouble: "It is always the want of social feeling, whatever be the name one gives it . . . living in fellowship, co-operation with humanity . . . which causes an insufficient preparation for all the problems of life." Jesus gave a name to that quality of life; He called it love. And love is as necessary for living as breathing is. Without either one you gasp and die—one spiritually, the other physically. And this is not sentimental. It is necessary to our make-up. Love breaks the tyranny of self-preoccupation and gives the attitude of outgoingness. This outgoingness is healthy.

This fits in with another statement of Dr. Adler: "I suppose all the ills of human personality can be traced back to one thing, namely, not understanding the meaning of the statement: 'It is more blessed to give than to receive.'" Interesting that psychiatry, after years of search for physical and mental health, fastened on this saying of Jesus as the secret of well-being. This saying is as deeply wrought into the nature of things as the law of gravitation is written into the physical universe—and just as inescapable.

A doctor was thoroughly converted. He wrote: "I had been horizontally converted, but not vertically. I had been born of water but not of the Spirit. Now I've been born of the Spirit. Now I'm going to work on the pagans of the body—cancer cells—in a new spirit." He was a cancer specialist. He called cancer cells "The pagans of the body." He was right, for cancer cells are cells turned selfish. They refuse to serve the rest and demand that the rest serve them. Hence the cancer. He said that they represented life—life turned in the wrong direction and hence destroying itself and others. He said that if he could convert these pagan cells to healthy ends, he could save them and the body.

All life is cancerous if it is turned toward itself and refuses to serve, wanting to be served.

Father God, help me to learn Thy law of self-losing as a way to self-finding. Then I shall live and live abundantly. Amen.

AFFIRMATION FOR THE DAY: *All my pagan cells of thought and attitude converted from cancer to contribution.*

GUILTS UPSET THE BODY

We are thinking of the things which we must let go if we are going to have a maximum of health. The last thing we must let go is any sense of inner guilt. For inner guilts throw sand into the machinery of human living. A filling-station attendant felt that ants were crawling over the back of his hand perpetually. It was the result of the fact that he had used that hand to steal money, appropriating what was not his own. The physical symptom registered an inner uneasiness.

So if the body is to be at its best, the soul must be clear of all haunting guilt. The most blessed fact of the Christian gospel is the offer of divine forgiveness. This is the most healing fact that can steal into the depths of personality. It pervades one as a sense of release and well-being.

A Japanese young man tapped me on the shoulder as I sat on the front seat in a meeting in Japan, and he whispered, "Are you sure I'm forgiven, Sir?" I assured him he was, if he accepted the forgiveness of God in Christ. The second time another tap on the shoulder and the same anxious voice: "Are you sure, Sir, that I am forgiven?" Again I assured him on the authority of Jesus. There was a silence, and the third time the same tap and the same anxious query. This time the message of assurance got across, for his face relaxed and broke into a smile that said the depths were satisfied. The word of forgiveness had penetrated there, and all inner tensions relaxed. How healing that was! Now nature could function normally. Until then he was tied up with tense anxiety, and nothing on earth could release that tension except the very voice of God.

When the blinded Saul heard the word of divine forgiveness, "there fell from his eyes as it had been scales," and his sight returned. The physical symptom dropped away when the spiritual tension was released. As long as he couldn't see spiritually, he couldn't see physically. The scales dropped from his eyes when the guilt dropped from his soul.

O Father, Thy healing hand is upon me, for Thy forgiveness is within me. I praise Thee, praise Thee. Amen.

AFFIRMATION FOR THE DAY: *Christ has forgiven me into forgiving.*

FORGIVENESS, THE GREATEST THERAPEUTIC

We ended up yesterday on forgiveness as the greatest therapeutic agent known. Without it the body is ill-at-ease and hence ill. "My wounds stink and are corrupt because of my foolishness. . . . There is no soundness in my flesh. . . . My heart panteth, my strength faileth me: as for the light of mine eyes, it also is gone from me" (Ps. 38:5, 7, 10).

Again the Psalmist puts it:

> When my heart was sour,
> when I felt sore,
> I was a dull, stupid creature.
> (Ps. 73:21, Moffatt)

The Psalmist again says: "My health pines away under my trouble" (Ps. 88:9, Moffatt). This is true; trouble troubles the whole person— body, mind, and spirit. But the surrender of the "trouble" to God and the release bring a health that blossoms and blooms.

Again: "My days are consumed like smoke, and my bones are burned as an hearth. My heart is smitten, and withered like grass; so that I forget to eat my bread. By reason of the voice of my groaning my bones cleave to my skin." This is the unpardoned man and the effect upon his health. Then comes the release: "Who forgiveth all thine iniquities; who healeth all thy diseases; who redeemeth thy life from destruction; who crowneth thee with lovingkindness and tender mercies; . . . so that thy youth is renewed like the eagle's" (Ps. 102:3-4, and 103:3-5).

Strength, both physical and spiritual, comes from obeying His word—the total man is strengthened. Then: "Fools because of their transgression, and because of their iniquities, are afflicted. Their soul abhorreth all manner of meat. . . . Then thy cry unto the Lord in their trouble. . . . He sent his word, and healed them, and delivered them from their destructions" (Ps. 107:17-20). God heals through lifting guilt.

O Father, I know that unless Thy word speaks to my depths the healing word, my depths are unhealed. Amen.

AFFIRMATION FOR THE DAY: *I take forgiveness with one hand, and I give it with the other.*

THE EFFECTS OF EMOTIONS ON THE BODY

We are looking at the effect of mind and emotions on the body.

Here is an account of long ago: "And Amnon was so tormented that he made himself ill because of his sister Tamar" (II Sam. 13:2, R.S.V.). His sex desires for his half sister so tormented him that he became ill. Many are ill today because of conflicting sex desires.

Here was a great missionary and a saint who was upset by conflicting emotions—Raymond Lull. When he was ready to sail to do missionary work among the Saracens, he pulled back at the last minute and let the ship sail without him. He became ill with a high temperature. He went aboard another ship, but he was put off when it was learned that he was ill. He got on a third ship, and when it actually sailed out of the harbor, the fever left him. He was well. The uncertainty because of an inner conflict about going made him ill.

Out of modern days: A missionary has a mother who has dominated her family for twenty-five years by her sweet invalidism. She wants her daughter to stay by her bed and wait on her. She will go to the bathroom on her own, then get into bed and ring for a glass of water. She can travel, but always on a pillow. Her strategy of domination is invalidism. And yet she is very religious and wants to be known as a dispenser of charities. So she tries to satisfy two urges—the urge to dominate and the urge to be known as a doer of good. The result is a vast unhappiness within her and around her.

Here was a very able and intelligent businesswoman who had a painful ankle. She began to develop self-pity over that ankle. It got worse. Then one day she found to her surprise that she had bound up the wrong ankle. When she discovered what she had done, she sat down and laughed at herself. She has had no pain since. That laugh lifted the self-pity and with it the pain caused by the emotion.

A lawyer, able and successful, was ill from various ailments for three years because he couldn't decide whether to go into the ministry or to continue his law practice. He decided to go into the ministry, and he is now a very successful pastor and for thirty years has had no illnesses. The inner conflict over the decision had upset his health.

Gracious Father, help me to direct all my emotions and thoughts toward health and wholeness. Amen.

AFFIRMATION FOR THE DAY: *I am so healthy in God that I have nothing else but health to give to others.*

OVERBOARD WITH A LOT OF IMPEDIMENTA

We come this week to meditate upon the mental and emotional attitudes we must have if we are to be healthy and radiate health.

We saw last week what we would have to let go if we are to arrest the process of decline and send life up again. A bishop tells that he was in a plane between Australia and New Zealand, and the plane was losing altitude, for one of the engines was defective. It was a tense, anxious moment. But after a while the pilot appeared and announced the good tidings that they had now arrested the descent and were gaining altitude again. They did it by throwing overboard some cargo. The passengers settled back relieved—the loss of cargo had saved them. But when they arrived at their destination, they found that the cargo was the passengers' suitcases! Costly cargo! But when they got over the shock of being stripped of suitcases, they said to themselves, "Is not life more than suitcases?" They were lighter, but they were alive.

So when we throw overboard a lot of impedimenta—fears, resentments, phobias, self-centeredness, wrong habits and attitudes, then we say to ourselves: "We've felt the loss. They have been with us so long we felt they were a part of us, but they are gone, and now we feel life—joyous, abundant life—taking their places. We've lost some things, but we are alive, alive to our fingertips, possessed by life." It seemed a slaughter, but it was a swap—a swap of old, impossible ways for God's way. And His way turns out to be the Way!

Now that these have gone, we must not leave the house of mansoul "swept, garnished and empty"; we must fill that house with the positive. Otherwise the old, finding the house empty, a vacuum, will come back again with seven other spirits of infirmity.

Health is not a vacuum, an absence of disease; it is a something which we can have and which we can give. Jesus speaks of "a soul breathing peace"—a lovely phrase! So we can be people breathing health. In breathing we take in and give out. So we can breathe in health from God and breathe out health upon others. We can be the centers of health and of health-giving influences.

O Christ, I see that no sickness invaded Thee, and Thy health invaded others. Give me that spirit. Amen.

AFFIRMATION FOR THE DAY: *I'm throwing overboard all impedimenta that causes me to lose altitude in body or spirit.*

STEPS TO HEALTH

We come now to the steps we can take in having and giving health.

First, *think health, not disease.* If our thoughts penetrate to the marrow of our very bones, then let those thoughts be thoughts of health and not of disease. You can think health or think disease into your very inmost cells. Then think health.

Is this autosuggestion? Yes, of course it is. We are always suggesting to ourselves something. Then let that something be health. That is not self-deception. The thinking of health opens the channels of your being to the permeation of health through your being. The thinking of disease ties up those channels through fear and blocks the permeation of health through you. The body in its inner structure is made for health, not disease. Dr. Cannon, the noted physiologist, says, "When we know how the body has provided for health and has provided for the throwing off of disease we will be surprised that anyone is ever ill." The body was conceived by God in health, made for health, and provided with almost every contrivance possible for the warding off of disease. So when we think health, we are not moonshining; we are sunshining. We are thinking along the lines of God laid down in the structure of our beings, so we are thinking according to the grain of the facts concerned and not against them.

But when we think disease, we are thinking contrary to nature, therefore unnaturally. When we think health, we are thinking naturally; and when we think disease, we are thinking unnaturally. When you think health, you are aligning yourself with the natural, healing forces of the universe.

On the other hand, when you think disease, you are alien to the natural healing forces of the universe. You are running counter to God's intention; therefore you are a resistant to redemption—the redemption of the total man. I know of a family who lived by recounting to one another their ailments—they thought, they talked, they lived, disease. The consequence was that they all died off before their time.

O Father God, help me to think, speak, and act health this day. And then I shall be health. In Jesus' name. Amen.

AFFIRMATION FOR THE DAY: *I shall be so full of health-giving thoughts that no disease germs will get a foothold.*

GLANCE AT DISEASE, GAZE AT HEALTH

I ended yesterday by telling of a family who lived in a state of un-health because they thought, talked, and expected disease. Whenever I visited that home, I felt I too was ill—ill by suggestion! All the members of that home died fairly early, all except two who left the home and got into healthier surroundings. They lived on.

I know it is not possible always to see health, for you may be con-stantly confronted with disease in yourself and others. But it depends on where your gaze is fixed. Glance at disease, but gaze at health. In the office of a doctor who was constantly dealing with people who had trouble with their hearts, real or imaginary, there was a model of a healthy heart right in front of the doctor as he talked to these ailing people. He constantly reminded himself of a healthy heart in-stead of a diseased one. It kept his vision clear.

Over a doughnut shop was this sign:

> As you ramble through life, my brother,
>   Whatever may be your goal,
> Keep your eye upon the doughnut,
>   And not upon the hole.

You have no right to go around spreading thoughts of disease which may produce disease in those who hear. They tell us that many medical students, when they first begin to study the heart and its diseases, develop the very symptoms they study. Then they right themselves and get their eyes on health-giving influences and begin to think health rather than disease—they get their eyes off the hole and on the doughnut.

Some people raise the moral and mental temperature of a room, and some lower it. When some people enter a room, you almost in-stinctly grab your middle—you feel the beginnings of a stomach ache. When others enter the room, you feel yourself putting back your shoulders and breathing deep breaths of health and well-being. Go out today to sell health and not disease.

O Christ, when Thou didst walk among men, the hearts of men were lifted in expectancy. Help me to lift hearts. Amen.

AFFIRMATION FOR THE DAY: *"Ask great things from God, expect great things from God, attempt great things for God."*

TALK FRESHNESS IN GOD

We come now to the second step in controlling our emotions and thoughts and making them contribute to health.

Second, *Don't talk tiredness; talk freshness.* There is a saying in Japan, a saying of sympathy: "You must be tired." I got it everywhere: "You must be tired." And since I was speaking in seventy-two cities in three months, addressing audiences from two to five times a day and traveling in between times and trying to write on a book in snatches of time, the temptation was very strong to say, "Yes, I am, very tired." But my invariable answer was: "Well, if I say I am tired, I'll be more tired, so instead I say I am fresh in God." Note "in God" —in myself I was tired, but if I could get contact with the freshness of God and let it flow into my tiredness, then I would be fresh in myself. So the "fresh in God" was an affirmation of an attitude of faith and expectancy. I was not surrendering to tiredness; I was surrendering to God. If you surrender to God and His freshness, then you become fresh. If to tiredness, then that tiredness invades you and pervades you.

Down underneath our talking about how tired we are is a perhaps unconscious bid for sympathy, a manifestation of self-pity. I was in a certain country where there was a missionary who was a shark for work. She would gather the jobs of two or three people—jobs which she should have allowed other people to share—and put them on her ample shoulders. Then, after having taken everything in sight, she would unconsciously arrange her martyr's crown for everyone to see. She came into supper after a grilling day, dropped into a chair, and announced: "I'm tired to extinction." And she was. And the temperature went down. We all felt the pull downward toward tiredness. That's what Jesus was condemning when He spoke of men fasting with long, sad countenances to gain sympathy. When you fast, said Jesus, "anoint your head and wash your face, that your fasting may not be seen by men" (Matt. 6:17, R.S.V.). And you'll feel it less too!

O Jesus, teach me the art of being open to health and freshness and thus open to Thee. In Thy name. Amen.

AFFIRMATION FOR THE DAY: *I am as fresh in God as my capacity to take from God.*

242

"HE MAKES ME TIRED"

You speak of a certain man: "He makes me tired." He does. You think of him in resentment, and as a consequence you become tired—he literally makes you tired. Thoughts of love make you lose your weariness, and thoughts of resentment make you do the opposite—become tired. For love is oil, and resentments are sand, in the machinery of the human body. We say of a person, "The sight of you is good for sore eyes." That's true. The sight of some people is healing—sore eyes get well when these people appear. For they radiate health and well-being. A person visiting a certain lady said: "After being with her an hour I felt as though I wanted to go off by myself and pray." The lady evoked reverence and prayer. There are some people who are always throwing cold water on every new idea or proposal. I know of a woman, a good woman, a well-meaning woman, whose negative attitudes cost her her marriage. She dampened the spark of love to extinction. She should have fanned it with her breezy, hopeful spirit.

A doctor who was inclined to be skeptical said of Mary, whom I have mentioned previously, "If I'm the norm, then she's off—unnatural. But if she's the norm, then I'm off—crazy. But as she is so wholesome and wonderful, then I must be off." Mary radiates love and good will until you feel you want to live and live abundantly. She is positive and creative and evocative—she evokes the same qualities in others. She "smiles a smile out of the baby." She produces in others what she presents in herself.

As I was writing the above, the pilot came into the plane as we winged our way across the Pacific and announced in a cheery sort of way, "One of the engines has gotten tired and lain down for a rest. So we are putting back to wake it up." And he did it in such a cheery fashion that not a heart fluttered, though it meant that we had to turn back six hundred miles to our last base and lose nine hours. He could have caused panic, but his cheery presentation of an ugly fact created cheer. We found ourselves laughing.

O Father, teach me to make everything into something else—upward. Give me the power of transforming things. Amen.

AFFIRMATION FOR THE DAY: *I shall present all ugly facts in a cheerful way and thus lighten their ugliness.*

A DISCIPLINED BODY

Third, *Discipline your body, especially in eating.* I once saw a man on board ship pacing up and down like a caged tiger, all out of sorts because his early morning breakfast hadn't come on time. You could see that his bodily appetites controlled him. He didn't have them; they had him. And he was fifty pounds overweight.

Someone has said that we live off half of what we eat and the doctor lives off the other half. Someone else has said that the best exercise for reducing is to put your hands on the table when you are about halfway through the meal and push hard so that you and your chair are pushed away from the table. This is the best exercise for reducing.

A woman who had gone through a wonderful healing said to God: "And now, Father, what about this overweight of mine?" And God replied: "This kind goeth not out but by prayer and fasting." She added in her letter, "God must have a sense of humor." He has!

But some of our fasting is of a very tentative kind. A man who belonged to a religious order said, "We fast on Friday, we keep silence during meals!" That kind of fasting is the kind depicted on the cover of a magazine, picturing a chef, a hundred pounds overweight, reading a book on "How to Diet" and surrounded with cakes and pastry with which he is stuffing himself while reading the book!

The nemesis comes. If we don't discipline our appetites, we have to wear around our waists a continual reminder of our failure.

I'm writing this for my readers, but primarily for myself, for I'm struggling with the same problem—a diet! But it's fun to see your weight go down and your well-being go up. It's fun to see who's boss —you or your appetite.

Fourth, *Don't try to regulate the body too much.* It is made for health and will take care of itself if we obey the laws of health. If you try to regulate the body too much, you'll give yourself "attention pains." A man discovered he had a slight affection of the knee. He became alarmed, and he and his wife spent the balance of their days attending to that knee—"attention pains."

O Father, give me wisdom in dealing with this intrustment, my body, and help me to make it the best it can be. Amen.

AFFIRMATION FOR THE DAY: *An Indian proverb says: "He cuts his little finger and considers himself a martyr." None of that spirit today.*

BE RECEPTIVE TO HEALTH

We come now to the last step in growth in bodily health.

Fifth, *Learn to accept the healing grace of God through receptive faith.* God heals in many ways—through the physician and the surgeon; through climate; through mental suggestion; through deliverance from underlying fears, resentments, self-preoccupation, and guilts which produce disease. Then He heals by the direct touch of the Spirit of God upon our bodies. This is not faith healing; it is divine healing through receptive faith. The faith does not heal, but faith opens the channels so God can heal.

Faith is the open channel through which the healing of God flows. A father told me proudly of the achievements of his brilliant son. Then with a catch in his voice he told me of the time when the doctor called him aside and said, "I've got bad news for you. Your son has leukemia, and there is no remedy. It is fatal." He said, "I went off to my knees alone, brokenhearted. I poured out my very soul to God. And out of that travail I arose with a new faith in God's healing power. A few days later the doctor said, "I can't understand it, but there's a turn—the red corpuscles are gaining on the white." They did. And the boy got well. There faith allowed the healing of God to make those red corpuscles stronger than encroaching death.

A lady writes: "There was the service of healing, and as you laid your hands on my head, I felt the power of God go through my body like electricity. I had been diagnosed as having cancer of the breast. But when I got up from my knees, I knew something had happened. That lump disappeared. I'm well."

So the power of God must not be limited to the healing of functional disease; it can and does heal structural disease as well. He who made the body can remake me.

Some diseases will apparently have to wait the final cure via the resurrection. But God will either cure the disease or give you power to use the infirmity until the final cure in the resurrection, when we get our new bodies. God is out to cure disease—now or then. Disease is not His will.

O Father, I would let Thy healing power into every pore of my being. I live by receptivity, by taking Thy Life into mine. Amen.

AFFIRMATION FOR THE DAY: *Faith is openness to God and co-operation with God. I shall have both today.*

GROWTH IN FELLOWSHIP

We come now to growth by fellowship in a group. So far we have thought only of the growth of the individual as an individual; we must now look at him in a "we" relationship. For we are made for the "we" as definitely as we are made for the "I." We are constructed in the inmost structure of our beings as social beings as well as individual beings. Just as there is no such thing as a severely individual being, so there is no such thing as a severely social being. There is only the individual-in-society and society-in-the-individual.

So if we are to grow, we will have to learn the art of living together in a group. This group may be the family, the school, the church, the club, or it may be a group specially formed for group living. We have formed such a group in what is called an Ashram, a term taken from India, but with a Christian content in it. We have established Ashrams in India and in America—six in various parts of the country. There about 150 to 300 people come together for a week with a particular purpose—to demonstrate the meaning of the Kingdom of God. We say to them, "Let us try, not to *find* an answer, but to *be* the answer in our corporate life. Let us try to be the Kingdom of God in miniature. Imperfect, of course, because made up of very imperfect people, but in some real way the new order realized—the word of the Kingdom become flesh in a group. We try to be the kind of order which, if universalized, would be what we are looking for." In order to be that order we get down barriers among classes and races; between those who work with their hands and those who do not; between the teacher and the taught; among various denominations and religions; and then finally the barriers within ourselves.

The last is the most important, for the things that separate us from God and our fellow man are within us: fears, resentments, inferiorities, self-preoccupations, guilts. These are the things that keep us from having fellowship. So we spend about five or six hours the first day we are together getting up to the surface our inner conflicts. It is a very cleansing process—a catharsis, and real results follow.

O Father, Thou hast set the solitary in families and dost bid us develop there. Help us to know how to live together. Amen.

AFFIRMATION FOR THE DAY: *The acid test of my religion is the test of my relationships.*

"I DON'T WANT TO MISS MEETING HIM"

Jesus said: "Where two or three are gathered together in my name, there am I in the midst of them." To the two or three there is added Another. A divine Plus is given. Each is heightened by the others, and all are heightened by the Other. Those who refuse that fellowship have something subtracted from them—a minus is added.

Thomas missed the regular meeting time of the Apostles: "Now Thomas, one of the twelve . . . was not with them when Jesus came; and when the rest of the disciples told him, 'We have seen the Lord' he said, 'Unless I see his hands with the mark of the nails . . . I refuse to believe it'" (John 20:24-25, Moffatt). His faith had not been kindled by the faith of the others; hence he sank into doubt. But the next week Thomas was present: "Eight days afterwards his disciples were together again, and Thomas with them. Though the doors were closed, Jesus entered and stood among them saying, 'Peace be with you!'" (v. 26). He met with the group and Jesus—result? He was at the feet of Jesus saying: "My Lord and my God!" (v. 28). His faith, kindled by the rest and especially kindled by this personal contact with the risen Lord, went far beyond anyone else in declaring that Jesus was "God." That is the first time that had been said. The doubter became the mightiest believer of them all. The getting into that fellowship had life importance in it for him. Without it he would have sunk back into incredulity and despair. With it he arose to unparalleled heights—his sight of the risen Lord sent him clear to the shores of India.

No wonder a Quaker lady, speaking of the possibility of her not being able to get to the meeting, said, "I don't want to miss meeting Him." She didn't say, "I don't want to miss the meeting," but "I don't want to miss meeting Him." She knew that He would be there "in the midst." And she also knew that she could never be the same after meeting Him—and them. When we link ourselves with "Him and them," we have our greatest source of growth.

O Father, let me know the strength and power that come from fellowship with others and with Thee. In Jesus' name. Amen.

AFFIRMATION FOR THE DAY: *In company with some two or three I shall expect to meet Him today.*

"WHAT DO YOU REALLY NEED?"

Just to sit with a group doesn't necessarily imply fellowship. Some-one has said: "Sitting in a church doesn't make a man a Christian any more than sitting in a hen house makes a man a hen." So there must be something more than being in a group—there must be a being *with* the group and the group being *with* God. So Jesus said: "If two of you agree on earth about anything you pray for, it will be done for you by my Father in heaven" (Matt. 18:19, Moffatt). The word "agree" means literally "to orchestrate," to come into harmony like an orchestra—then anything is possible.

So the first thing to do is to tune up our instruments to one an-other and to God. The discords must be taken out. So in our Ashram fellowship we ask, "Why have you come? What do you want? What do you really need?" And the very first day we spend about five solid hours answering these questions. We find that those who act as though they have no needs have the most, for all of us have needs. It is not a fellowship of the non-needy working on the needy. It is God working on us all, for we are all in need—all of us are only Christians-in-the-making. I wouldn't have believed that people would tell their needs straight off without preliminaries. But they do. Of course, we remind them that God has certain things He attends to in His private office, but we can tell our needs publicly if they do not involve others unfavorably. And so they tell, glad apparently to get hidden conflicts up and out.

Here are a number of needs which they bring up, taken almost at random: (1) "I am converted in my will, but not in my emotions. They take the reins from my hands and run away." (2) "I'm a stinker. I'm critical. I need to get rid of my critical attitudes." (3) "My trumpet makes an uncertain sound, for I'm lukewarm. I an-tagonize people, and you can't antagonize people and win them at the same time." (4) "I'm articulate, but I don't say very much." (5) "I'm tired of preaching ideas not my own. I don't know how to relate Christ to my preaching." (6) "I want to be more patient with five older ministers who don't want to change."

O Father, help me too to get up and cut every discord—everything that makes me strike false notes in the symphony of life. Amen.

AFFIRMATION FOR THE DAY: *I love life too much to spoil it by false notes and discords.*

248

BARING OUR SOULS

We continue looking at those who have knocked down barriers in the Ashram in order to grow by fellowship.

(7) "I have come here to have one big funeral—the funeral of myself." (8) "I've come here because I've never been a full-grown Christian." (9) "I have two enemies. One is myself, and the other is impatience." (10) "I need to get rid of reserve and sensitiveness." (11) "A lady went to a book seller to get a book for her parson, and she asked, 'Have you a book entitled *How to Be a Transformed Parson?*' Well, I'm that parson—I need to be transformed." (12) "I've been growing in responsibility faster than my resources." (13) "I am a sponge squeezed dry. I want to soak up some life." (14) "I am just a bad ten-year-old child that won't grow up." (5) "Ministers are supposed to be in the upper bracket of spirituality, but I want to get rid of self and fear and sin."

(16) "I am supposed to know all the answers, but I'm just a big noise." (17) "When I came here, I was installed in the infirmary—that's where I belong." (18) "I become selfish, think I know the answers, and am not happy if things do not go my way. I am here to seek relief from myself." (19) "I have found a need of which I have been suspicious. I didn't want my family to come. We had a bad time coming down in the car. I have the spirit of the elder brother, and I don't like it." (20) "I have been building my life on a wrong basis—that everything I do needs to be perfect." (21) "I'm here because I didn't want to come. I am afraid to say, 'Arise and walk.'" (22) "I spent a year in resentments because of a discourtesy. I remember the saying: 'Speak well of your enemies, for you made them.' I was so angry once I broke a baton. God has put me in a corner like a checkerboard—there's only one move to make, so she'll have to make it." (23) "In my subconscious are fears and conflicts which are causing physical upset." (24) "I want all the littleness taken out of me. I put myself on the throne, and sometimes I've put my husband on the throne." (25) "You people all overflow, but I seem to get the drippings, so I come." (26) "Prayer has meant to me a chore."

O Father God, these too are my needs. I bare them before Thee, and now show me Thy resources. Amen.

AFFIRMATION FOR THE DAY: *If I do not often tell to others my needs, I shall have to tell them to myself more often.*

"GROWTH AND PAIN GO TOGETHER"

(27) "I have a horror of being self-centered. I'm afraid of being trite, with a trite vocabulary, a trite soul, and a trite outlook." (28) "My mother says I'm poised and kindly in my job, but at home I'm not that way." (29) "I have had to take the responsibility of a home at seventy-seven years of age, since the homemaker has died. I'm afraid to begin again." (30) "It's wonderful to go to school to God. Growth is painful; growth and pain go together." (31) "I feel like I have dynamite within me, but I'm expressing it in little firecrackers. I want this thing to explode within me and blow people into Kingdom come." (32) "I know the agony of not being able to help people. It's my fault, for I have self-centeredness in all its forms." (33) " 'I have nothing to set before Him.' That's my experience."

(34) "I need to get control of my emotions. I need to know how not to fly off the handle." (35) "There is a stoppage in the fuel line—selfishness is the stoppage." (36) "I'm a big guy; I do lots of things, but I'm not Christian." (37) "I need a better balance between accepting responsibility and relaxation." (38) "I am sick and tired of having conflict in ideas and beliefs." (39) "I'm under a triple tyranny—the tyranny of self, the tyranny of things, the tyranny of people." (40) "I need patience as a pastor's wife with lazy church members." (41) "My greatest mistake is trying to please people instead of pleasing God." (42) "As ministers we feel the loneliness of leadership." (43) "I have decided to resign as Chairman of the Universe. (44) "I've come here to be a better mother-in-law." (45) "I came here because everybody was out of step but me. I had two needs—more water to put out conflagrations as they arise, and a better class of people. But that's all hell needs." (46) "I am troubled with heart, and I know it is from resentments and a desire to make my family exactly what I want them to be." (47) "I need to get rid of words. I've hurt people with words." (48) "I can help people mentally. I see what's the matter with them, but I can't help them." (49) "We keep the Holy Spirit out because we criticize one another."

O Father, help me to glance at my needs and then gaze at Thee. Thou hast the answer, and I know it. Amen.

AFFIRMATION FOR THE DAY: *To get my needs up and out is halfway to their solution. I'm on the Way.*

"I HAGGLE WITH GOD"

(50) "I'm afraid of crossing the line of assurance into conceit." (51) "I have a conflict. I've wanted to be a great educator. Now I want simplicity of purpose." (52) "I need more discipline. I also need to get rid of bottled-up hostilities." (53) "Each year I have had a need, and each year that need has been met. This year my need is to be quiet and unhurried." (54) "I have accepted God with my intellect, but in my subconscious I have conflicting desires. I need to stop struggling and striving and accept."

(55) "I am mentally and spiritually lazy. I feel guilty—I'm always behind in my work." (56) "I need a general overhauling." (57) "I'm a me-do-it person." (58) "My tongue starts nagging before my mind begins to turn over." (59) "I have been pushing people around. I have been managing other people's lives for them." (60) "I had a proud mother and a humble father, and they are in conflict within me." (61) "We bring people into the church, and there they dangle. They don't grow. They die on the vine." (62) "I've come here to get on speaking terms with God. I need direction."

(63) "I haggle with God. Eventually I do it, but I hesitate and haggle." (64) "I am producing conflicts and neuroses in my children, for I have them in myself." (65) "I'm critical and resentful and full of inferiorities." (66) "I have my course set. But my joints are stiff, and my muscles are sore. I don't run freely." (67) "I'm suffocated with pride. Pride goeth before a fall. I need to fall." (68) "I've lived a defeated life. I want to live on top of things." (69) "My sin is telling people what to do." (70) "I have high expectations and low attainments." (71) "I go through periods of discouragement and despair. I need to be on a more even keel." (72) "I need more courage. The war is on. I'm not creative. I'm afraid." (73) "I am dissatisfied with a halfhearted Christian life." (74) "I live a defeated life. I want to live on top of things." (75) "I've lost my enthusiasm. I want to regain my vision." (76) "I am critical and resentful and full of inferiority."

O God, as I disclose my needs, please disclose Thy power to meet those needs, lest I be frustrated. Amen.

AFFIRMATION FOR THE DAY: *I've seen myself in these self-disclosures, and now I see Thee, O God, in Thy self-disclosure—Christ!*

"I DON'T KNOW WHERE TO GO"

We come to our final day in looking into the soul of need as expressed in the Ashram on "The Morning of the Open Heart."

(77) "I am troubled with my heart, and I know it is from resentments and a desire to make my family exactly what I want them to be." (78) "I have found God personally, but I want to find Him in a fellowship. I want that." (79) "I can witness in the pulpit, but outside it I don't witness. Fatigue is related to my spiritual problems. I'm rather lazy." (80) "I want not only a book full of notes but a heart full of love. I've had resentments I've never spoken of in public. Confession of resentments knocks the thing in the head. Now I'm dragging it out and burying it." (81) "I have an overdose of egocentricity. I know exactly how things ought to be done." (82) "I need to be like magnetized steel. The molecules are at cross purposes, and in magnetizing they are co-ordinated and set." (83) "The best remedy for cold feet is my wife's warm hand."

(84) "I'm afraid of change—I'm afraid of being a changed person." (85) "I worry about what the church people will say and I worry about what my husband will say in the pulpit." (86) "I have a new Cadillac and a road map, but I don't know where to go." (87) "In my subconscious are fears and conflicts which are causing physical upset." (88) "Sister K—— lets God wind her up every morning. I wind myself up. But I was so changed last year and so easy to live with that my husband would have brought me here in a wheelbarrow." (89) "I felt if the Ashram would become one day late, I'd pass out. I want to swallow an electric light bulb like Sister Mary." (90) "I'm a backslidden Methodist." (91) "I know that Jesus has everything, and I'm going to keep after Him until He gives it to me." (92) "We get so wound up with programs that we get wound up with them." (93) "I learned if you don't want anything to happen to you, then you had better stay away. I love my family, and yet I quarrel with them. I want God to get a whack at me, and I find He gets a whack at me away from home." (94) "I need more reserves."

Now, Father, that we have looked at need, help us to look at supply. My eyes are there. I must tap supply. Amen.

AFFIRMATION FOR THE DAY: *My cry—Thy supply. That's all there is to it. Now I'm drawing on Supply.*

"THE MORNING OF THE OVERFLOWING HEART"

We have been looking for a week into the soul of need, and I dare say that many readers have been saying, "Why, that and that and that is my need." And now we must look at the way these same needy people got hold of resources that lifted them more or less suddenly out of defeat into victory. This was not a forced growth, but an infused life that gave birth to growth from within. These same defeated people were transformed within a week and made into a different type of personality altogether. And this transformation came largely through the group. The group itself became redemptive. People came lonely and unrelated and aloof and found themselves related, outgoing, and loving. For one of the mottoes on the wall of the Ashram is, "Here everybody loves everybody." And that very love is healing. For we are made in the very structure of our beings for this outgoing, loving fellowship where everybody gives and everybody takes. It becomes a creative fellowship. Individual growth may be growth lopsidedly, but group growth is by its very nature corrective.

We come now to what we call "The Morning of the Overflowing Heart." The last morning we share with each other what we have been finding. For the individual experience belongs to the group and, when expressed, enriches the rest. Within a week ninety-eight per cent of those who come, go away transformed and transforming. The spiritual duds become the spiritual doers.

(1) "I came here for peace of mind for a very troubled spirit. I've found it. I have given my life, and if He opens the way, I'm going to the mission field" (Young surgeon.) (2) "I can go the first mile alone, but for the second mile you have to have God. I'm going the second mile." (3) "I'm going back to be a better mother, wife, church member—and I like myself better." (4) "Jesus has become my Saviour. I saw the love of Christ in the tears of the people." (Hindu.) (5) "I had my gear shifts all squeaking. Now I've been oiled." (6) "I'm aware of a change within me. My physical handicap is not now a handicap. I'll use it."

Father, I see others entering into victory and release. I too would enter that victory and release and enter now. Amen.

AFFIRMATION FOR THE DAY: *What has happened to any man can happen to another man. I'll be that man.*

NOTES OF VICTORY

(7) "I came here all tied in knots. My healing has gone deeper than I expected. I've been able to check things off." (8) "I came here empty; now I go full. I came lonely; now I am not alone." (9) "I'm eager to get back to my law office." (10) "I've had a tension let-down. I had a lot of nagging worries, as a result of which I had a small ulcer. But the worries are all gone now, and I'm well." (11) "Now I'm going to give them the works." (12) "I've had my faith in democracy restored. Now I am assured." (Negro headmaster.) (13) "I'm the girl who had to take sleeping pills. Now I'm relaxed and can sleep." (14) "I thought the victory and release would be dramatic, but it has come quietly." (15) "I had surrendered my will but not my emotions. Now I've surrendered my emotions. I'm free!"

(16) "I've always known about God, but I didn't know Him. Last year I got a nodding acquaintance with God, but this year I've gone into God's private office." (17) "I came here with a deep wound, and now it has been healed." (18) "My wife and I are going to be easier to live with." (19) "God is teaching me to simplify my wants so I'll have more to give." (20) "I've had a double portion of fears. Now they are gone." (21) "I came here to run away from my family and found I was running away from myself." (22) "I had inherited resentments from my mother and my father, and I had added to them. Now they are gone." (23) "This is the first time I've ever stood up in public: I've been tied. Now I'm free." (24) "I came here with problems which turned out to be sins. They are all forgiven. I'm free." (25) "I've been racing with myself—trying to run away from myself." (26) "I've had a blood transfusion, according to any type." (27) "My heart has been beating like a trip hammer. I came here with nothing to lose except my chains. Now the birds are singing, and the flowers are blooming. I'm going home under entirely new management. The throne is occupied by a new Occupant." (28) "I'm going home to say, 'I'm sorry.' So many things have changed since the day of the Open Heart. Those things seem silly now."

O Father, make me to see what is important to Thee so it can become important to me. Make silly things silly. Amen.

AFFIRMATION FOR THE DAY: *I'm a candidate for the highest God has for me. Nothing less than the highest!*

"I'VE LEARNED TO USE EVERYTHING"

(29) "I've been a member of God's frozen people, but last year I surrendered to God, and now I am free." (30) "I was all bottled up, but now I'm like a fizzing bottle of soda pop. I'd explode if I didn't say something." (31) "When I came here, I felt a denominational loneliness. I came here all tied up, and I'm going away tied in—tied in to people's needs." (32) "I came here prejudiced against the Ashram, but I'm glad I came. I'm changed myself." (33) "I've been just lifting up my basket to be filled, and it's been filled." (34) "I've been going to cults. All these cults begin with me, and I'm not big enough to begin with. Here I've been told that I had to *belong,* to surrender. This has brought freedom."

(35) "Here I learned to use everything." (Korean) (36) "Here I learned to fellowship across all racial barriers. I've been an unreconstructed rebel." (37) "I have found out the meaning of casting all all your care—not cares—just bundle them together and cast them all upon Him." (38) "I've been surrendering those things that have been making me a very unsatisfactory person." (39) "I came here mad at everybody, and now I'm going away glad at everybody." (40) "I came here thinking I was a Christian. I learned I knew nothing about it. I'm going away a Christian." (41) "I've found that an Ashram is a vacation with God." (42) "I've been able to pray for people I've never been able to pray for."

(43) "Six months ago I was in a mental hospital. Today I'm well, perfectly well." (44) "I read one page of Brother Stanley's book *The Way to Power and Poise* and walked out of a mental hospital—well." (45) "For fifteen years I've tried to grasp this, but like a cake of soap it would slip out of my hands. Now I've got it. It's got me." (46) "The first day I thought, 'Have I come to an infirmary? Are all the crackpots together?' Now I see that this is what people ought to be." (47) "I've been looking at the heavens each day to see if the sun has risen—I've been discouraged. Now it has risen." (48) "I usually awake tired. Here I get too little sleep, but I wake up refreshed."

O Christ, while on others Thou art calling, call on me. Let me too touch the hem of Thy garment and be made whole. Amen.

AFFIRMATION FOR THE DAY: *"My God shall supply all your need according to his riches in glory."*

"MY SIN WAS CYNICISM"

(49) "This has been my hardest year—I lost my companion of twenty-six years. I was numb with grief. I've gained the victory over it. I'm free." (50) "I've made a resolution to spend less time with the morning paper and more with the morning prayer." (51) "My sin was cynicism. I've been critical. I now see people differently—they're beautiful." (52) "My business hasn't shown a profit. But I'm now drawing a bonus. I'm seeing Christ in everybody." (Minister.) (53) "I came with a lot of worries and confusions, and they are gone." (54) "I've been a banker, stiff and inhibited. Now I'm free and natural. When I was banker, people said to me, 'Your smile has done so much for me.' But many have said that as a preacher I was too austere and hard to get to know. I found I was not smiling. I'm now smiling." (55) "Some of the sticks I've thrown have become boomerangs and have hit me in the heart." (56) "I've been behind barriers—barriers of class, of various prejudices. But they're all down now. There is a clear way." (57) "I've had 'a dated emotion.' I've brought it up. It's now 'in the light.'" (58) "I've thought that a group could become redemptive, but up until now I've never seen it." (59) "I was tense, couldn't sleep. I've become rested, and I'm going back rested." (60) "The motto of our school was: 'To find a way out' —in other words, nothing is impossible. I've found that here." (61) "I came here seeking peace. I had lost it. I have found it."

(62) "I needed a change in my reaction. I had 'attention pains.' They are gone." (63) "It's been a spring house cleaning. I've thrown away my resentments, fears, self-centeredness:" (64) "I've got rid of a headache, because I got rid of my tensions." (65) "I came here to get self-confidence, and I've found God-confidence." (66) "I've given up one thing after another, and now it is all clear." (67) "I've been very timid; now I am natural." (68) "Christ puts a tang and zest in life—it's wonderful." (69) "My name is Cook, but on the roster its 'Cool.' Well, from now on I'm going to boil!" (70) "I didn't know there were so many little things that hindered my growth."

O Saviour, I too would let go everything that hinders my growth. Clear me of all that keeps me from Thy best. Amen.

AFFIRMATION FOR THE DAY: *My motto: all in Him and all out for Him!*

"NOW THE HOLY SPIRIT HAS ME"

(71) "Release, freedom, love, discipline—I've found them all here." (72) "I had the Holy Spirit; now the Holy Spirit has me." (73) "I came here conscious that I was guiding my life myself. Now God guides me." (74) "I looked over what I had said were my needs, and I find they have all been met." (75) "I've been impatient. I've wanted something that would settle things once and for all instead of the steps to maturity." (76) "I've taken all these negativisms and laid them at the feet of Jesus. I'm free." (77) "I came up here unhappy and alone and apart from God. But here I've found Christ. I'm through my tunnel." (78) "I've been willing to be a doctor, but to be a missionary—well, I was afraid of that. Now they are coming together." (79) "I learned here to love people and to be careful about little things." (80) "I've been a retired Christian; now I'm no longer retired."

(81) "I've spent all my life seeking God. Now I see God is seeking me." (82) "I didn't like my room, felt sore, couldn't walk up to the third floor. Now my feet have wings." (83) "I've been healed here. I didn't expect it to happen so soon. But it has happened. I'm well." (84) "Little resentments have been my trouble, not the big ones. I have found if I attend to God's affairs, He'll attend to mine." (85) "Weary of sinning, weary of repenting—that was I in the beginning. I've been resentful, critical of ministers. But it's all gone. The first night came the surrender. I've been healed." (86) "I wanted conversion, but I didn't know how to take. Now I've taken—I'm different." (87) "I've been going to church conferences all my life, but I've never seen anything like this. It's different." (88) "I came here critical of America and Christians. I thought they were hypocritical. Now I see I have been wrong in my attitudes. I've been wrong. I'm cleaned up and cleared out." (89) "I came here afraid to say 'Brother' and 'Sister.' But I go away saying it, for that's the way I feel." (90) "I came here a rumbling old wagon, and I'm going away a brand new Buick." (91) "I didn't realize I was a managerial type of person. But I've found it out. I'm going away different."

O Father, clean me up and clear me out. Make me the pure, unclogged channel of Thy grace. Amen.

AFFIRMATION FOR THE DAY: *Today all objectives clear, all fountains flowing, all channels open.*

"I'VE PRAYED ONLY TWICE WITH MY PATIENTS"

We are further privileged to listen to this paean of victory.
(92) "I was too tired to go to the third floor. Now I just go bounding up the steps." (93) "I've been saying 'I'm tired.' Now I'm going to say, 'I'm fresh in God.'" (94) "I thought I had a little halo. Now I've lost my halo." (95) "The resentments have been dissolved in me. My reconciliation with my son has been accomplished. I'm a new man. I haven't been without my glasses for thirty years. Now I can see without them." (96) "I've been full of self-credit; now I'm full of God-credit." (97) "I was a person who was always saying, 'I can't do this.' I thought I was a fool to work with my hands and now I see I was a fool for thinking so." (98) "I believed in Communism and was a part of the Communist Party. I've lost my faith in Communism—it lacks freedom and has no word about life after death. Surrender to God has done the trick for me." (99) "I've been delivered from the herd here. Now I'm going back to serve the herd."
(100) "I've got rid of my resentments and hence my sicknesses." (101) "The strain is gone, and now the drain is gone. The Christian way is the natural way—that's new to me." (102) "I was ashamed to say I was forty, and now I'm glorying in being fifty-seven. I have seen a more personal Jesus." (103) "I'm a doctor and I've prayed only twice with my patients. Now I'm going back to pray with my patients." (104) "I've been disturbed into goodness." (105) "I've been a horse trying to pull a load with his teeth instead of his shoulders. My jaws are now relaxed." (106) "I had inside me that which I hated. I wanted to be a bad man inside. Now I'm changed inside." (107) "I'm glad this is over today, for if I should receive more, I'd burst." (108) "I've never been in a place where the people have the habit of having God all the time." (109) "I was striving too hard. I was throwing myself at God instead of stretching out my hands to take. Now I'm taking." (110) "I have got rid of fears. The butterflies in my stomach have flown out. The unshakable Kingdom and the unchanging Christ did it." (111) "I've had a complete overhauling. I didn't have on boxing gloves. I've been on the defensive. I've lost that. Now I'm all out."

O God, help me to stretch out both hands to take and to take all I need and all others need. Amen.

AFFIRMATION FOR THE DAY: *I'm taking with both hands and giving with both hands.*

ONE HUNDRED AND TWENTY TRANSFORMED SOULS

(112) "I've been a worrier. I have learned I don't have to struggle and fight, but to let go and trust." (113) "My greatest sin is impatience. I'm going back serene." (114) "I just look around and feel a sense of love for every one of you." (115) "The needling I got, I hope will turn me to flannel." (116) "I came here too shallow. My subconscious was my trouble. When I heard what was said about the subconscious, I brought it all up." (Red Cap 42.) (117) "I was full of fears. I came near being an alcoholic. I was afraid to speak. But I've got rid of my fears." (118) "I've had cold feet, but my heart has been warmed, and my feet have warmed up too." (119) "I've lost five friends by suicide, I've had a broken home, and I've worked for twenty-seven years winding coils in a factory, and yet I have victory."

(120) "I came here in love—in love with myself. I was rescued from drowning, and I was scared, about as scared as I am now! I should be silent, so I'm going to sit down!" (121) "I came here with a troubled heart. Now I've been freed. I wanted to do something for God; now I want God to do something for me." (122) "I came here with resentments, and now I can walk straight up to my resentments and see victory. This is the first time I've ever spoken in public, though I'm a schoolteacher." (123) "Six years ago I was a broken personality—a pickle puss. Now I'm different." (124) "I was driven to this place. I was resenting God—'Why did you do this? Why did you do that?' But Brother Stanley wrecked my little playhouse. I sat down and wrote out my case to God. Since then I've been on top of the world." (125) "This is so simple—conversion is so simple, and growth is so simple." (126) "I've kept down things I didn't want to surrender. But this time I've brought them all up. I'm a new man."

All of this spells one thing: the Holy Spirit is not a spent force. He is available now to the degree that we will pay the price and avail ourselves of Him. He takes us on faith. He doesn't draw up a watertight legal bond for us to sign before He does anything for us.

O Father God, Thou hast called us to Fellowship, the Fellowship of the Family of God, and through that Family we are further transformed. Amen.

AFFIRMATION FOR THE DAY: *I've fellowshiped with need, and I've fellowshiped with Supply—blessed be Fellowship!*

GROWTH THROUGH PRUNING

We have just finished looking at the correction and the construction that come to the individual through the group. The group becomes the emery paper by which the rough edges of conduct and attitude are smoothed out in our characters. But after the smoothing by emery the group can then become the burnishing powder by which we are polished to shine for His glory. So the group makes us smooth and makes us shine. And further, the group makes us one in God.

This leads us to a further study of growth by pruning. "Every branch that does bear fruit he prunes, that it may bear more fruit" (John 15:2, R.S.V.). Here is growth in fruit bearing by pruning and not merely in quantity but in quality—"richer fruit." It is to be both —"more" and "richer."

The cultivatable land in Japan is so scarce, compared with the population, that what is cultivated must be intensively cultivated—everything must be at its maximum best. And it is! I have seen a man stagger through a railway station with one turnip across his back—a heavy load. Some apples were placed before me the other day, and as I picked one up, I gasped, "This isn't an apple. It's a whole tree." It was twice the size of the ordinary apple. I have measured strawberries known as "rock strawberries," grown beside rocks to hold the heat in February, and they measured three inches in length. How do the Japanese achieve such amazing results? The answer is: fertilizing and pruning. And especially pruning. Every useless branch is cut away and the whole thing set for maximum fruitfulness. When Japanese houses were rented by foreigners during the Occupation, wherever the owner could afford it, he would pay for a gardener to keep up the garden lest it grow beyond redemption. The gardener would prune it into fruitfulness and beauty. The open shears looked like a "V" for victim, but in reality they were a "V" for victory. The discipline became a delight; the letting go became a taking on of flower and fruit.

O God, I'm now looking to Thee to show me the difference between the useless and the useful and to allow Thee to prune. Amen.

AFFIRMATION FOR THE DAY: *God never cuts for the sake of cutting. He cuts only to cure, conserve, and contribute.*

"THERE IS NO PRISON FOR THE WORD OF GOD"

Many things that happen to us can be made into instruments of our pruning. Sorrows, griefs, losses, disappointments, frustrations, sicknesses, failures, business losses—these can become the pruning shears of God to make us fruitful, provided we know how to use them and make something out of them. Our inner attitudes determine the results.

Our first attitude should be that Christians are not going to be exempt from the ordinary ills that afflict humanity. If we do insist that they be exempt, then when the ills strike us, we go down like tenpins. "Why should this happen to me? I'm a Christian. God should treat me better." That is fatal. Richard Baxter wrote concerning the Great Plague: "At first so few of religiouser sort were taken away that (according to the mode of too many such) they began to be puffed up and boast of the great differences which God did make. But quickly after that they all fell alike." We must make up our minds that the difference is in the way we take what comes. Some are soured and some are sweetened by the same happening.

Paul made everything make him—and others. He says: "If I am in distress, it is in the interests of your comfort" (II Cor. 1:6, Moffatt). He made his distress contribute to other people's comfort. The distress was a pruning that made him more fruitful. Again he says: "I have to suffer imprisonment as if I were a criminal. (But there is no prison for the word of God)" (II Tim. 2:9, Moffatt). Note the word "but." That word "but" is an open door. The Christian always has a "but" to pit against any set of circumstances. "I am in prison"—but the word of God is not imprisoned; it is loosed by my very bondage, furthered by my frustration.

Note again that the criticism of Paul brought out the wonderful revelation Paul had in II Cor. 12:1-10, where he describes being caught up into the third heaven and seeing unutterable things—this would never have come out if he had not been criticized. So he made the criticism into revelation.

O Christ, I thank Thee for this way to live. This way makes everything make me and helps me to make others. I thank Thee. Amen.

AFFIRMATION FOR THE DAY: *I am not afraid of anything, for I can use everything.*

"IN EVERYTHING GOD WORKS FOR GOOD"

We are studying God's use of events and situations to prune us into fruitfulness. The events and situations in themselves may be evil, but they can be used for good. The passage "All things work together for good to them that love God" is questionable as it stands. All things do not necessarily work together for good; they may work for evil. To say that all things work together for good endows these "things" with purpose—a purpose for good to those who love Him. But "things" do not have a purpose unless we or God put a purpose within them. The Revised Standard Version puts it better: "We know that in everything God works for good with those who love him" (Rom. 8:28). The things may not be good, and may not of themselves work together for good, but "in everything God works for good." He turns the evils into good if we co-operate with Him and love Him.

Our pains, instead of being senseless, useless pain, become a discipline for us—a discipline that makes us better in character and contribution. "Pagans waste their pains," says Jeremiah (Ch. 51:58, Moffatt); they end in useless, senseless suffering. They have no purpose running through them, hence are fruitless. But the Christian uses his pains, set them to music, makes them sing. Every jolt only jolts the glory out. Every kick only kicks him forward. Even if he stumbles, he stumbles forward. Like the wall that was as thick as it was high, so that if you pushed it over it was as high as ever, so the Christian seems to be so yielding, so much a "push over," but has a strange and incorrigible way of coming up as high as ever—and higher.

He is like the apple trees which had especially fine apples on them. When asked the reason, the owner pointed to the slashes on the trunk of the tree, saying, "For some reason the trees bear better fruit when slashed and wounded in this way. So we slash them into added fruitfulness." So Christians, when they get a tongue-lashing, are only slashed into fruitfulness. They "welcome each rebuff that turns earth's smoothness rough." Their wounds, strangely enough, heal them. They make events make them, The storms only send their roots more firmly into the soil.

O Father, I thank Thee that I need be afraid of nothing, for I can use everything by Thy grace and power. Amen.

AFFIRMATION FOR THE DAY: *The creative God has made all things creative to those who know the secret.*

SLASHED INTO FRUITFULNESS

We continue to look at the glorious possibility of making every slash a slash into fruitfulness.

They tell us that the bird's-eye maple wood is made by the sting of insects. The sting is transformed into the beautiful wood, the bird's-eye maple, that adorns our drawing rooms. The tree is stung into beauty. I have seen many souls stung by daily nagging and daily pin pricks, but stung into beauty of character and achievement. Socrates had a nagging wife, who after giving him a tongue-lashing, threw a bucket of water over him, whereupon the sage quietly replied: "After the storm, the rain"; and that "rain" watered the plants of patience growing in the garden of his heart.

Wesley was like that—a nagging wife drove him into evangelism. There was nothing at home except stings, so he took to the road and evangelized Britain. That wasn't the only motive; the love of God constrained him, but the lack of love in his wife also constrained him —pressed him out into the open road to greatness and usefulness.

Here is a gracious and beautiful woman, made gracious and beautiful by a drunken husband who shut her out of her house for weeks at a time, tore up her clothes, and came near strangling her to death. Through five years of hell she kept her four children in college and got them through to responsible positions, won her husband back to sobriety and to the resetting up of his business, and then at the end of all decided to go to college herself—at the age of forty-nine! And she is keeping her job at the same time. She is a bird's-eye maple stung into beauty by five years of hell. No wonder one of her daughters said, "Mother, I don't believe you could do an evil thing even if you tried."

As I write this on a crowded Japanese train, a little girl with an unwiped nose is talking in my ear and coughing in my face, and making me illustrate what I'm talking about. So I'm sending out love to her, and I see no longer the unwiped nose, but one of these "little ones"—the little ones for whom Christ died. And my heart is warmer for the irritating contact.

O Father, I thank Thee for the joy of rescuing joy out of every sorrow and irradiation out of every irritation. Amen.

AFFIRMATION FOR THE DAY: *If situations jolt me today, they shall but jolt the glory out!*

STUNG INTO BEAUTY

A striking illustration of being stung into fruitfulness: "They discussed what they could do to Jesus. It was in these days that he went off to the hillside to pray. He spent the whole night in prayer to God, and when day broke he summoned his disciples, choosing twelve of them" (Luke 6:11-13, Moffatt). This opposition pushed Him into a night of prayer, and in that night of prayer He saw clearly that their opposition was going to culminate in His death. So before that happened, He would provide for the intrustment of His message and movement into the hands of the Twelve, who would carry it on when the storm struck Him. They furthered Him. His movement might have died if He had not chosen the Twelve to carry it on.

Here is another vivid illustration of this possibility at work:

He had loved his own in this world and he loved them to the end; so at supper, knowing that, though the devil had suggested to Judas Iscariot, Simon's son, to betray him, the Father had put everything into his hands —knowing that he had come from God and was going to God, he rose from table, laid aside his robe and . . . began to wash the feet of the disciples" (John 13:1-5, Moffatt).

Note the "though"—"though the devil had suggested to Judas Iscariot . . . to betray Him, the Father had put everything into his hands." The betrayal itself was turned into redemption in the hands of Jesus. The devil suggested to Judas and the high priests that they could stop this movement if Jesus were put on a cross. They listened and acted and did put Him on a cross. And then as the devil watched the spectacle, he must have turned pale. "What is happening? He's turning this very cross into redemption! He is saving the world through the very instrument of torture we devised! Alas, I and my kingdom are undone!" It fulfilled what Jesus had said: "The Prince of this world is coming. . . . His coming will only serve" (John 14:30, Moffatt). Did the devil "serve" Jesus? Yes, unwittingly. And when you can make the devil serve you, then you're victorious indeed.

O Father, I thank Thee that in Jesus Thou art delivering everything into my hands. All things serve me if I serve Thee. Amen.

AFFIRMATION FOR THE DAY: *I am invulnerable and invincible, for I have seized hold of a sacred secret.*

THE TRIAL PRODUCED

In walking, equilibrium is upset by every movement in order to make progress. The upset is to set us on our way. God has to allow enough upset to come into our lives to break up the equilibrium in order to make us move forward.

"Greet it as pure joy, my brothers, when you encounter any sort of trial, sure that the sterling temper of your faith produces endurance" (James 1:2-3, Moffatt). Trial produces faith, and faith "produces" endurance. The upset of your equilibrium, which trial brings, "produces"—if you will let it! Everything produces—if you will let it. Take the incident of the little Japanese girl who upset my equilibrium by her unwiped nose and her coughing in my ear. I determined I would smile at her. When I did, her mother noticed it and quickly wiped the child's nose, and then she was beautiful. So we had quite a smile fest, and I had gained a little friend, who, when she sat down in a vacant seat, continued to smile back at me. The "trial" *produced* —produced an upset of equilibrium which set me forward on the road to friendship.

Take Paul's thorn in the flesh—apparently a bad eye affliction, for he told the Galatians that they put up with his affliction, which was a sore trial to them, and that if possible they would have given their very eyes for him (Gal. 4:14-15). To have bad sore eyes was a real handicap to Paul, so He asked the Lord three times to take it away. And he had a good case for its removal—would he not be more effective as a public speaker and a writer? But the Lord answered, "My grace is sufficient for thee: for my strength is made perfect in weakness." And Paul answered: "Will I rather glory in my infirmities. . . . For when I am weak, then am I strong" (II Cor. 12:7-10). Here we see a physical infirmity throwing him back upon grace. If he was to be effective, it would be because the people saw grace instead of infirmity. He would specialize in grace. He was goaded by infirmity into grace—more grace. The infirmity served.

O Father, if infirmity is my lot, give me grace to make my infirmities into goads, goading me to Thee. Amen.

AFFIRMATION FOR THE DAY: *No infirmity shall make me infirm, for I'm firm in God.*

"THE GROWING EDGE"

We have been looking at God's prunings as God's proddings—prodding into fruitfulness.

Labine, a star pitcher, tells of this possibility: "I busted my index finger on my right hand trying to catch a pass in a semiprofessional football game. I got a bad crook in my finger. I found out afterwards that it helped my curve ball and sinker." The injury furthered him, provided he knew how to use it. That's the secret. Not what happens to you, but what you do with it after it happens to you, determines the result. You can make everything serve if you know the secret.

A bearded man with a fine face was singled out of an audience in Formosa, and I asked someone who he was. He was obviously different—and finer. He told me his story: He had been an opium addict and was ordered by the government authorities to go to a Christian hospital. He thought this was oppression. But there he got hold of a Bible, and this verse saved him: "He that *endureth* to the end shall be saved." The "oppression" opened a door!

Your sorrows and disappointments become what Howard Thurman calls "the growing edge." They become the starting points of progress. There is in Japan a movement called "The House of Growth." You can live in that house. Growth becomes the atmosphere of your life—the house in which you live and move and have your being.

Lye burns you; grease heals your burns. Lye and grease together produce soap, which cleanses you. The outcome is something different from each.

The Timking Roller Bearing Company tests ball bearings by sound. They found that the blind, not distracted by outer sights, can concentrate better and are more expert at this testing. They also are more useful, for they have the added value that they can work at night. Rubber companies have a special operation in putting a cap on tires. Put on carelessly, it comes off; great concentration is needed. They found that the deaf and dumb concentrate better, as they are not distracted by noises, so a hundred of them are employed at good wages. Their deprivations become departures into superior usefulness.

O Father, I know that Thou dost not take anything from me except to give something better in its place. Amen.

AFFIRMATION FOR THE DAY: *I am incorrigible in my faith, hope, and joy, for I'm invincible in my new-found attitudes.*

THE DIVINE EAGLE TOSSES US OUT OF THE NEST

We continue to look at God's constraints as God pushing us forward into greater usefulness—the divine Eagle throwing us out of the nest to make us fly.

The smooth stone, when it was being tossed by floods and rubbed against other stones, never knew that the hard discipline of the daily rubbing would rub it into such smoothness that it would be chosen by David as the special stone that would kill Goliath and deliver Israel.

The water which I have just passed, caught from the surrounding hillsides and confined to a pond, must feel thwarted and frustrated as it idly lies through the winter months, but when summer comes and it is freed to flow into the rice fields below and nurture the rice that is to feed a grateful people, it will see at last that this momentary thwarting is in order to a permanent thrusting into fruitfulness.

A little Japanese woman moved silently and effectively up and down the aisles and got many people to sign decision cards at Nara, Japan. She was so effective and so radiant that I asked about her, particularly as she handed us the railway tickets to our next destination. Her husband was one of the few courageous preachers who during the war dared preach against the myth of the Emperor's descent from the sun goddess. He was jailed for his courage. There he died. But his widow lived to see the Emperor himself declare he was not divine, thus exploding a costly myth and freeing a great people from myth to reality. The pastor's act must have been a part of the inner pressure upon the Emperor to denounce the myth publicly. The pastor was a seed, buried in jail, that blossomed into the freedom of a people. For the Emperor's statement was the most important thing done in postwar Japan; it brought a great people to reality. The courageous man is resurrected in the new birth of a people. In Christ we give up nothing except to see that thing come back in a larger good. The seed lost in the soil comes back in flower and fruit. The renounced soul comes back as the resurrected soul. The disciplined becomes the disciple.

Father, when I commend myself and all I have into Thy hands, Thou dost give it back into my hands—new. Amen.

AFFIRMATION FOR THE DAY: *God's prunings are God's preparations—for fruitfulness.*

"STRIP OFF EVERY HANDICAP"

I was in a plane going to Oslo, Norway, on which there was a team of American skaters going to compete in the Olympics. When the steward of the plane passed out cocktails—a vicious custom on international planes where the nondrinkers pay for the drinks of the drinkers, it being inevitably passed on to their tickets—he came to this Olympic team and remarked: "Of course these will not take any," and the coach nodded agreement. Why wouldn't they take any? Well, if they had, they would have automatically ruled themselves out of the severe competition. But if this pruning away of handicaps is good for Olympic competitors, why isn't it good for those who are in the severe competition of modern living? Cocktailers become tail-enders in every branch of life.

The writer of Hebrews says: "Strip off every handicap" (Heb. 12:1, Moffatt). Handicaps are things that cannot be classified as sin, but they handicap us in the race of life. Then, he adds, we must "strip off sin with its clinging folds"—sins that tie us up. Both handicaps and sins are to be renounced in order "to run our appointed course with steadiness."

No nation on earth needs mental pruning more than India. Its genius is its all-inclusiveness. But that strength can and does become a weakness. It can include the false and the true, the ridiculous and the sublime. Some American astronomers took a Hindu astronomer to Delhi for special observation of an eclipse. When the crucial moment came for the Indian astronomer to make the observation, he couldn't be found. He was off doing worship to the demon that swallowed the moon! His mental processes needed pruning.

A chimney in India was clogged and filled the room with eye-stinging smoke. We found that last year's birds' nests were responsible. Many lives are filled with last year's birds' nests! We need to have the chimneys of our minds, our souls, our bodies, our relationships, cleaned out—cleansed to become a channel.

O Father, I expose everything within my life to Thy searching gaze. Take away the useless, bless the useful. Amen.

AFFIRMATION FOR THE DAY: *God strips away the useless only to save the useful to greater use.*

TAKING AWAY THE GOOD FOR THE BETTER

We saw yesterday that we have to let handicaps and sins go if we are to run the race of life with any degree of credit.

We must now see the possibility of the pruning of the good for the sake of the better. Jesus said to his anxious disciples: "Yet—I am telling you the truth—my going is for your good. If I do not depart, the Helper will not come to you; whereas, if I go, I will send him to you" (John 16:7, Moffatt). What a terrific blow it must have been to His disciples to be told that He was leaving them—leaving them to a world that was hardening into opposition! Their hearts must have sunk within them with a strange sense of spiritual orphanage; they would be alone in this kind of world without Him—Him upon whom they had banked their earthly all and for whose sake they had left everything. It was all an anticlimax, and worse—a collapse of all their hopes and expectations.

But He said, My going is for your good. I will take away My presence and give you My omnipresence. I will come back to you in the Spirit and be closer to you than I am now. Now I am *with* you, then I will be *in* you. And that happened. He did change His presence for His omnipresence. He moved into the inner recesses of their hearts, burningly, blessedly near. If they had reached out to touch Him, they would have reached too far. And this meant that He was available anywhere, everywhere. They had but to drop into the recesses of their hearts, and there He was. They could commune with Him in wordless communion, a communion too intimate for words. And not only was His presence available, but His power was available—unlimited resources at their disposal at any and all times. They didn't remember Christ; they realized Him. They didn't merely call Him back to memory; they realized Him in the depths of their beings. They must have said to one another, "He's gone, but He's nearer than ever!" And they knew He was right in taking away the good of His bodily presence to give them the better of His spiritual presence—intimate, available, and within. He never takes away a good without giving a better.

Gracious Father, when some earthly good is taken away and it leaves me bereft, help me to see in the hidden better. Amen.

AFFIRMATION FOR THE DAY: *All my bad into good, all my good into better, all my better into best, all my best into His best.*

SHUT UP TO WRITE IMMORTALLY

Paul must have inwardly chafed when his liberty was taken away and he was confined to various jails—confined for no other crime than announcing the good news. The curtailment of personal liberty was hard, but it was harder still to be shut off from the opportunity of preaching his beloved good news. What could compensate for that? But as we look back, we can see that God was allowing the good to be taken away in order that the better might come. Paul's letters, mostly written from jail, have enriched the world for ages and will do so in the ages to come. But they could never have been written except in jail. He dipped his pen into the blood of His sufferings and wrote words that are deathless. Through long days and nights of pondering upon Jesus, his thoughts crystallized into immortal phrases through which men have looked into the heart of the redeeming God. And there the universal Christ grew upon him, and in piercing words he broke the remaining Jewish bonds that fettered the gospel and made it free to roam the earth, untrammeled.

Someone coming away from a meeting in which Dr. Kagawa spoke to an American audience, expressed disappointment, saying: "He didn't say anything." A friend replied, "Yes, that's true, but we go to hear him because he is Kagawa." The years spent in fighting disease, in lowly service in slums, in jails, in ceaseless toil, in unfailing love to all—all these things were silently speaking through his broken sentences and his almost ununderstandable English. The first man thought a moment and then quietly added, "Well, I suppose you don't have to say much if you are hanging on a cross." No, you don't for the cross itself speaks louder than anything we can say. The good of eloquence, taken away, becomes the better of revelation.

Now we do not think of Kagawa's speech; we think of Kagawa's Saviour. Our limitations can thus become luminous. Paul could say, "I am no speaker, perhaps" (II Cor. 11:6, Moffatt), but Christ behind the stumbling words of Paul has used that imperfect instrument to enrich the world.

O Father, I thank Thee that all my denials can become deliverances, my crosses Easter mornings. Amen.

AFFIRMATION FOR THE DAY: *If life hits me on the chin, it will but lift my face to see higher.*

MULE SENSE AND GIRL SENSE

Rufus Mosely is a man whom I have called "The saint of the South." He is God's troubadour, at eighty-six still alive with God and sparkling with a divine humor. He says that when he was on the farm, before he became a professor, he and his father went to buy a mule, and they prayed that they might be guided to the right mule. They were. The moment they saw the mule, they knew that that was the mule for them. And the mule turned out to be the best they had ever owned. Then came the time when he was looking for a wife, and he found a girl and said, "God, give me that girl. I want her." But someone else got her. Telling about it afterward, Rufus said, "I picked out the girl and asked God to get her for me, but when we went to get the mule, we asked God to pick out the mule. He did. If I had had as much girl sense as I had mule sense, I might have been married." But he has never married. The girl was denied him. And yet those who know Rufus Moseley know that that denial was a door—a door to freedom to be married to humanity through love. His love was freed from one person and given to everybody. God said to him one day: "You go out and give my love to everybody." He does.

Here is an Indian Christian, Jacob Masih, his arm and leg amputated. His stomach had a perforated ulcer, and the doctors had to put in an artificial opening. Then his lungs became infected with tuberculosis, and he was in a sanatorium for a year and a half. One lung was collapsed. He was healed suddenly after being assured by Christ that he would be healed in six months. He went to Aligarh University and stood first in mathematics in a class of twenty-five. He is now teaching in a Christian college. He took the denial of the good—bodily soundness—and made it into the better—spiritual victory.

If we live in God, then the closing of one door means that God is opening a larger one. But often we think only in terms of the closed door. So we weep before closed doors instead of turning the knob of the larger door.

Father, I thank Thee that in Thee everything is opportunity—an open door into something better. I'm grateful. Amen.

AFFIRMATION FOR THE DAY: *Not what happens to me but what I do with it determines the result.*

"TREASURES OF DARKNESS"

Sometimes we walk in darkness and wonder why. Perhaps the secret is here: "I will give you the treasures of darkness" (Isa. 45:3, R.S.V.). Are there treasures which we may find only in the dark? It would seem so. In a deep, dark well you can look up and see the stars even when people in the light above can't see them. A dark tunnel is the shortest way around a hill.

Here is a startling passage: "He [Jesus] learned by all he suffered how to obey" (Heb. 5:8, Moffatt). And he learned that "treasure" in "darkness"—the darkness of suffering. So when you get into darkness, begin to dig in the light of your flickering torch of faith, for there are "treasures" there. Milton found them in the darkness of blindness and revealed them to the world in immortal verse. Bunyan found them in the darkness of a prison and wrote the priceless story of *Pilgrim's Progress*. Helen Keller, blind and deaf and dumb, found "treasures" in the darkness of these handicaps and has revealed them to the world in her glittering spirit.

Mary woke up one morning with these words singing in her heart, "Next summer's apples are already in the tree." But it was the dead of a cold northern winter when the words sang themselves to her. The treasures of summer and autumn are already in the tree of your life, caught in the darkness of the winter's cold. Patience and warm love will bring them out.

And then will come the time when "the bursting of the petals will say the flowers are coming." The breaking of your heart will let the song out. A friend said to me very graciously: "May you have just enough clouds in your life to make a beautiful sunset."

God gives us just enough emery to make our characters and wits sharper. But emery can be an irritation if we don't know how to use it. The secret is in the learning how to make everything make you. The treasures of darkness come only to those who dig—dig for meaning.

Father, I thank Thee that all my darkness can turn into dancing delights—delights at the discovery of Thy hidden treasures. Amen.

AFFIRMATION FOR THE DAY: *When God sends darkness, He also hands us the pick to dig for treasures of darkness.*

"MINIMUM OF STRAIN, MAXIMUM OF RESULT"

The cutting of the vine is not only in order to produce added abundance in fruitfulness; it is often in order to produce another quality of fruitfulness as in grafting. God sometimes cuts us from one source of life and grafts us onto another source of life. But with this difference: in ordinary grafting the best is grafted onto the worst, but in Jesus the worst is grafted onto the Best.

Jesus said: "It is the Father who remains ever in me, who is performing his own deeds. . . . Truly, truly I tell you, he who believes in me will do the very deeds I do, and still greater deeds than these" (John 14:10, 12, Moffatt). Here is the promise that if we have our source of life in Him—not in self-interest, or society-approval, then the deeds He did we will do, and we will do them effortlessly. We will simply surrender to the life of God within us, and without strain there will be effortless fruit bearing.

When I started on my three-months' tour of Japan, going to seventy-two cities and speaking three to five times a day to huge crowds (a meeting seldom lasting less than two hours, for decisions have to be garnered at the close of the address), I was given a promise from the Father: "There will be a minimum of strain and a maximum of result." It has happened! Many days there would be over a thousand decisions for Christ, and yet there was nothing but effortless calm. Someone other than yourself was doing the work. The secret is surrender, and surrender has been defined as "a happy yieldedness to God."

But severing from the old comes before grafting into the New and then "the happy yieldedness." So the order is: Sever, surrender, succeed. If you don't allow the first, you can't have the third. But if you take the first and the second, then you have effortless fun and effortless fruitfulness, and the very fruitfulness becomes fun. It's fun to be a Christian, and the more Christian you are, the more fun you have. Life itself becomes fun. And the more fun, the more fruit.

O Christ, I thank Thee for a relaxed, released, gay way of living—this way of drawing life from Thee. Amen.

AFFIRMATION FOR THE DAY: *I am good in the goodness of Christ and gay in the gaiety of God.*

GROWTH IN GUIDANCE

We come now to an important area of growth—growth in guidance.

Many Christians know little or nothing about personal guidance from God. They go from event to event and live a kind of hand-to-mouth spiritual existence—a spiritual and moral opportunism. They have no sense of working out a plan of life under God's guidance. They have little or no sense of destiny, of mission.

This is true of the nation as well as the individual. When a nation loses its sense of mission, it is beginning to disintegrate. Someone asked President Eisenhower, before he was nominated for the Presidency, what was the greatest need of America, and he replied: "A sense of mission." A very wise and penetrating reply. Personally I believe this sense of mission for America is to be true to the last line of the pledge of allegiance to the flag: "one nation, indivisible, with liberty and justice for all." This is the thing we have been raised up to do: to give "liberty and justice for all," at home and abroad. This rules out all imperialisms—economic, social, political, military. We have been the proving ground of an idea—an economy of liberty and justice for all, apart from race and birth and religion and color and sex. We have been raised up to make the word "all" operative in all relationships at home and abroad. This is the mission of America. We must work it out—or perish. And if we don't work it out, we ought to perish—we will be a useless, amorphous mass of selfish people struggling for personal advantage.

If we as a nation go out to dominate anyone—economically, socially, politically, militarily, then our "name is mud." "Ichabod"— "God has departed"—will be written on our banners, and angels will weep. For we who began by breaking with imperialism would end in setting up one of our own—the saddest ending to the greatest beginning in human history. One of our greatest needs is a call for a national day of prayer in which we will humbly bow our knees to get back as a nation "a sense of mission"—a sense that we are working out a divine destiny in the world.

O Father, give our people the sense of being sent, the sense that we are working out a Mind and Purpose, not our own. Amen.

AFFIRMATION FOR THE DAY: *I am a commissioned officer of the Kingdom of God. I have a commission from the King.*

NEEDED—A SENSE OF MISSION

We saw yesterday that our greatest national need is a "sense of mission." Other nations feel the same. Take Japan, where this is being written. This nation felt they had a destiny—a destiny to rule. They were a divine people, with a divine Emperor, and therefore with a divine destiny to rule—to rule by force. That sense of destiny gave them drive; it drove them clear across the Pacific and to the gate of India. And then like all half-answers it broke and left a nation in ruins. A vacuum was created.

Into that vacuum are rushing all sorts of isms and cults to take over the allegiance of a great people and give it new direction and goal. When I asked a governor of one of the prefectures, "What are the five needs of Japan and in what order of importance?" he replied: "Our greatest need is to get rid of our moral and spiritual confusion. We have lost direction." And then he came before the audience a few moments later and said: "I'm a man here tonight without a faith. I wish I had a faith. I envy those of you who do have a faith. But I'm a lost sheep. I've come here tonight to gain a faith through the speaker, and I hope you will gain one too."

A nation had lost a sense of mission and direction; it had a vacuum in the soul. Into that vacuum six hundred registered cults have moved in to take possession of the allegiance of a people. Christianity is making a strong bid to win that allegiance.

John Foster Dulles says: "That which is in motion prevails," meaning that "kinetic and potential energy prevails over the static." This of course is only a half-truth. "That which is in motion," but the question is: motion in what direction? "What is our strongest point?" asked some Japanese, and I replied: "Your strongest point is that you do everything together." "Our weakest point?" "Your weakest point is that you do everything together. You may go to hell together." They had followed the military to hell together. Individuals and nations must not only move; they must move in the right direction under God's guidance.

O God, without Thy guidance we fumble from event to event without direction. Guide us lest we stray. Amen.

AFFIRMATION FOR THE DAY: *Life now is not moving with aimless feet. I'm on the Way, and He's beside me.*

GOD'S PROBLEM: TO GUIDE BUT NOT OVERRIDE

Many individuals, though Christian, know little about God's guidance. Hence they have little sense of accountability to God and little sense of His guidance in their lives. Hence their impact upon life is feeble. Only people who have a sense of mission and who are under God's guidance accomplish things.

How does God guide us? His problem, I suppose, is to guide us and not override us—to guide us, but not too much. For He must guide us and create initiative in us at one and the same time. This is not easy. In Japan horses are not usually driven from behind; the driver, or in this case the leader, walks beside the horse and leads it. The too-close leading of the horse takes away all initiative. The horse is helpless without the every-step-of-the-way leading of the man. God can't weaken us in this way. He must guide us so that we may more and more guide ourselves. Jesus said to His disciples: "Why even of yourselves judge ye not what is right?" He wanted them to be morally capable of judging for themselves. So the dictation method of guidance is out—the method which dictates what we are to do for the day. The parent who did that for the child, dictating every least thing it should do for the day, would weaken the child.

The movement of guidance seems to be from the outer to the inner. God spoke to Moses from a burning bush to go down to free His people. He guided another by wet and dry fleece. The apostles chose a successor to Judas by lot. But as men were spiritualized more and more, the guidance became inner. The inner nature was attuned to listen to God—to hear the divine whisper within.

And how do we know it is the voice of God? Mary, whom I have previously quoted, answers: "Well, when you go to the telephone and hear a voice, you say, 'Oh, this is the voice of my mother—I know it!' So I know the voice of my Father—I just know it." Jesus said: "My sheep hear my voice." We learn the divine accents. Our inner ears are attuned.

Father, I thank Thee that Thou art a God who speaks. And Thou dost speak in accents knowable. I thank Thee. Amen.

AFFIRMATION FOR THE DAY: *When God spoke through the lips of the Man Jesus, He thus guaranteed that we could understand.*

THE VOICE OF GOD TO BE CHECKED UP

We saw that when our ears are trained, we can learn to understand the voice of God within. But the voice of God within must be checked up by certain questions: Does this guidance fit in with the general guidance God has given us in Jesus Christ? Does it fit in with His spirit, and would He approve it? This is important, for God has revealed His character and purpose in Jesus. God could not guide you to do anything that cuts across that character and purpose revealed in Jesus. So put up a dozen question marks against any guidance from the inner voice which does not fit in with what you see in Jesus. It may be the voice of your subconscious mind projecting itself as the guidance of God.

How can we distinguish between the voice of God and the voice of the subconscious? Roughly, in this way: The voice of the subconscious tries to convince us, often arguing the case. The voice of God doesn't argue; it tells us, and the telling is self-verifiable. Your inmost being says: "This is it." The Voice doesn't argue; it simply announces. And there is the feel of the real and eternal upon it.

But if you are to hear the voice of God within, you must learn the art of lowly listening. You can't put up propositions to God and say, "Which do you approve?" It may be that He has an entirely different proposal. The disciples put up two men to take the place of Judas and asked God which of the two He would approve; and they cast lots, "and the lot fell upon Matthias." Well, God apparently didn't choose either; He chose Paul.

When we listen to God, then people will listen to us. We become authoritative with the authority of God. If we don't take time to listen to God, people will not take time to listen to us. We want to hear the man who has heard from God, a man who has fresh news from God. When God speaks to us, we can speak to men.

If you do make mistakes in guidance, don't be discouraged. I have mentioned that the disciples did thirty-one things which were wrong and yet they were guided into changing the world. You may slip up on marginal things and yet be centrally right.

Father, I thank Thee that Thou knowest our frame—and yet Thou dost love us still. Love me into correctness. Amen.

AFFIRMATION FOR THE DAY: *I may stumble on the Way, but nevertheless the Way leads Home.*

GUIDANCE THROUGH THE WORD

Sometimes God guides us by making some passage in the Word vital to us. We feel its authority and its relevance to our situation.

For instance, I was going through a difficult patch of criticism, most of it based, I felt, upon twisted meanings and things taken out of their context. And then one morning I read that "the Lord turned the captivity of Job, when he prayed for his friends" (Job 42:10). And who were Job's "friends"? They were people who dug into his wounds and poured salt into them by accusing him of being wicked before God, else why should this calamity have come? When Job prayed for his tormenting "friends," God released him from his own "captivity" to calamity and trouble. At this particular juncture the Spirit whispered to me: "If you'll pray for your 'friends,' letting every thought of them turn to a prayer for them, then I'll turn all your captivities—I'll release you from all your bondages." I replied: "It's a bargain. I'll do it." And I've never been so free and released.

In order for the Spirit to guide us through the Word, we must be soaked in that Word. As Emily Dickinson puts it:

> He ate and drank the precious words,
> His spirit grew robust;
> He knew no more that he was poor,
> Nor that his frame was dust.
> He danced along the dingy days,
> And this bequest of wings
> Was but a book. What liberty
> A loosened spirit brings!

What "liberty" it brings if we put our lives under the guidance of the Book and let it speak to present conditions! God must have gone into this Word, for God comes out of it; it is a revelation, because it reveals; it must be inspired, because it is inspiring; the writers must have been led, for they lead—lead us into Divine guidance.

O God, I thank Thee for Thy Word. I am grateful that in moments of crisis and confusion it becomes light. Amen.

AFFIRMATION FOR THE DAY: *"Thy word have I hid in mine heart, that I might not sin against thee."*

"ANYWHERE, PROVIDED IT BE FORWARD"

Our guidance is often forward. Livingstone once said, "I'll go anywhere, provided it is forward." The Spirit usually leads forward, and
yet He often checks to get us ready for something bigger. Mary says:

The Spirit is my check valve. I am so eager—eager to live, eager to
learn, eager to go ahead, eager to love, eager to climb the ladder more than
one step at a time! In all things the Spirit says to me: "Thus far and no
farther now!" Always the Spirit inspires, controls, and demands obedience.
When I feel that driving, burning enthusiasm deep within, the Spirit
never fails to remind me: "Proceed with caution. Take time for all things;
Rome was not built in a day!" God said to me, "Mary, I have the whole
universe to consider, not just you!" (My, how deflating to hear that for the
first time!) The Spirit said to me, "Oh, you and Job! Don't you see there
are others to be considered besides you? Don't you know it takes time to
work with multitudes as well as individuals?" Then God called me into
His private office one day and said, "If you had ten children to get ready
for school, could you get them all ready at the same time?" Then came the
dawn! I see now that God has more to get ready for a given project than
just me. When He gets me ready first, then I have to wait until the rest
are ready. Then all things work together—the perfect timing.

To talk with God,   To walk with God,
No breath is lost—   No strength is lost—
Talk on!   Walk on!

To wait for God,
No time is lost—
Wait on!

There is this passage, "He worketh for him who waiteth for Him."
We are often dammed up here and dammed up there, in order
to break out more effectively later. Jesus was filled with the Spirit at
Jordan and then sent into the wilderness for forty days to toughen his
fiber and clarify His vision.

Father, I thank Thee for Thy holding me up in order to loose me later
—loose me with sureness of direction and power. Amen.

AFFIRMATION FOR THE DAY: *If I am blocked here, then I shall break
out stronger there—in God's time.*

"HE LOVES ME INTO LOVING"

There is a phase of guidance that needs to be emphasized—guidance into loving attitudes. "May He guide your hearts into ever deeper understanding of His love" (II Thess. 3:5, Phillips).

This is a guidance which is always valid—a guidance into a deeper understanding of His love. His love, as one modern saint puts it, "loves me into loving and forgives me into forgiving." Say that to yourself over and over again: "His love loves me into loving and forgives me into forgiving." Note: The statement doesn't say, "He commands me into loving," or "He advises me into loving," but "He loves me into loving"—the word of Love becomes flesh.

Mary writes:

The boy who deliberately slaps another boy is the child who requires my deepest understanding and love. For with the one who gets slapped the sting will soon be over. But the sting within the other child, which made him feel like doing it, will not stop. It goes on eating deeper.

A lady asked me to come to talk to her and her children and the man she goes with. . . . The five of us talked about Christ for three and a half hours. . . . When a minister heard that I had gone to this house, be began to tell me a lot of things about her and the man, and I stopped him. I told him I didn't want to know anything about them personally, because it was not my business, but all I knew was that I loved these people just the way they were, perfect or imperfect. Then another man began to tell me about them and I stopped him: "I know all I need to know. I love them, and so does Jesus, and if you'll take the same energy it will take to tell me what you want to about them and just pray for them, I'm sure that will do more good than telling me things that are of no concern to me." He was amazed to find a woman who didn't want to listen to gossip. . . . God tells me that where the need is greatest the amount of love needed is greatest too; and just loving people without always being critical of them does more for them than all the preaching at them. . . . I just know He is pulling at their hearts!

O Father, Thou hast loved my poor loveless heart into loving. Now help me to give that love freely to everybody. Amen.

AFFIRMATION FOR THE DAY: *If I can be guided into loving attitudes, then all my other guidances are secure.*

"OH, NO, I DON'T WANT THAT"

We must fix in mind that if we are going to be God-guided persons, we must be willing to be guided not to our ends but to God's ends. Very often we come to God for guidance when all we want is God's stamp of approval on our decisions and our ways.

We are like the little boy who at prayer time prayed that God would make such and such a city the capital of Virginia. When his mother asked him why he prayed that prayer, he replied that he had put down that city as the capital in his examination!

Or we may be like the woman who when a pastor said to her, "Now say to God, 'Let anything happen to me that You want to happen to me,'" replied in consternation, "Oh, no, I don't want that." She thought the will of God for her would lie along the line of the disagreeable. The fact is that God couldn't will anything for us except our highest interest—couldn't and still be God. God's will is our highest interest at all times, in all places, and under all circumstances. Things may happen to us which are not primarily God's will—they come out of the will of man. Their genesis may be evil. And yet if we let God guide us, He can turn them into good.

Here was a missionary on his way to help the Chinese in West China. As he journeyed over the Burma Road, his truck and another truck turning a sharp corner smashed head on. His right arm was crushed beyond saving, and it was amputated. As he looked at the crushed arm, he said to himself, "All my life I've been taught that all things work together for good to those who love God. Now is the time to test this out. I'll find some good in this." He did. He became very skillful in using a mechanical arm and was sent to Korea on a special mission to help people who were amputees. He was so radiant that these people, who were down in morale and ashamed of their lack of arms or legs, began to take courage and interest in learning new skills as they saw him use a mechanical arm. He remarked, "If this loss had not come to me, I would not have been sent here to help these people. All things have worked together for good." God guided him into rescuing good from evil.

Father, Thy guidance is always my good. Help me then to find Thy guidance in whatever comes, turning everything into good. Amen.

AFFIRMATION FOR THE DAY: *Many things will come to me today, some of them evil. I shall make them work for good.*

GUIDANCE THROUGH CHANCE HAPPENINGS

We look further at getting guidance. Just as we must not make our decisions and ask God to approve of them, so we must not let chance happenings decide things for us; we must not see in them the guidance of God. God may or may not guide through chance happenings.

Some people in India didn't know how to vote in the recent elections. So they hung up some garlands in a temple, and they found later that the flowers had fallen on the right side, so they took that as an omen that they were to vote for the Right. They went out and voted for the National Congress. That is guidance by magic. The Christian faith moves from the magical to the moral. God would weaken us if He guided us by magical signs. We would lose moral judgment in looking for tokens of guidance. Paul says to Timothy: "The Lord will help you to understand all that I mean" (II Tim. 2:7, Phillips). You think, and the Lord will guide your mental processes. This is co-operation. For the Lord must not merely *guide* us in particular situations; He must *make* us in general.

This passage puts the end of guidance: "The aim of the Christian discipline is the love that springs from a pure heart, from a good conscience and from a sincere faith" (I Tim. 1:5, Moffatt). The aim of the Christian discipline is to produce spontaneity—a love that springs from a pure heart. Most disciplines and guidance produce suppressed resentments. This produces an expression of love and love from a pure heart—unmixed motives. This is the freeing of the emotions—emotional development. The next item is "from a good conscience"—this is the will. Then "from a sincere faith"—this is the mind. The total personality—emotion, will, and intellect—grows under God's discipline or guidance.

The prophet could say this: "Of the increase of his government . . . there shall be no end" (Isa. 9:7). For the more He governs us, the more He develops us. This is not true of other governments—social, political, religious; if pushed too far, they take away our initiative. But God's government or guidance develops us in the very guidance; hence there can be no end to the increase of His government.

Father, I thank Thee that all Thy guidance is for my development. Then guide on. Let Thy government increase. Amen.

AFFIRMATION FOR THE DAY: *God's government and my good are the same. Then let His government increase endlessly.*

CO-OPERATING WITH GOD

We ended yesterday on the statement that "of the increase of His government there will be no end." The more He guides us, the more He develops us. Then obviously we can't have too much of His guidance. So we can afford with Paul to bring "into captivity every thought to the obedience of Christ." For the moment our thoughts become His thoughts, they become most our own. We find ourselves in Him and His will.

The very uncertainty about His guidance at times makes for our development. If everything were certain, there would be no element of adventure. The very adventure develops us.

At a period in my life in India I was going through a very great crisis. My physical health was shattered, and I was on the point of giving up the ministry and the mission field to try to regain my health. It was a dark hour. Then came the release of which I wrote in *The Christ of the Indian Road.* At the darkest hour the inner Voice said: "Are you yourself ready for this work to which I have called you?" And I replied: "No, Lord, I'm done for. I've reached the end of my resources. I can't go on." And the reply, "If you'll turn that over to Me and not worry about it. I'll take care of it." And I replied eagerly: "Lord, I close the bargain right here." I rose from my knees knowing I was a well man. And I have been these years. But there is a sequel to this that needs to be told. Pauline Grandstrand, a very saintly woman of prayer, was on furlough in America at the time, and the Voice of God said to her: "Give up everything and go to prayer for Stanley Jones." The Voice persisted, and she canceled her engagements, shut herself up in her room in the hotel for a whole day, and prayed. By evening the burden had lifted. When we went over the matter and compared times, we found that at the very time she was on her knees in America the release was coming to me in India. But she knew nothing of what was the matter with me. She only knew the Voice called and she obeyed. And in that obeying she helped release me from a very *real* bondage and she set me free for these years of service—untrammeled.

Father, I thank Thee that Thy guidance is always right if we get it right. Help me to get it right. Amen.

AFFIRMATION FOR THE DAY: *I shall be a God-guided person, open to His guidance in the little and the big.*

GUIDANCE THROUGH A GROUP

Some of our guidance should come through a group. God sometimes guides the individual through a group. This was true in regard to one of the most important bits of guidance ever received by a group.

As they were worshipping the Lord and fasting, the holy Spirit said, "Come! set me apart Barnabas and Saul for the work to which I have called them." Then after fasting and praying they laid their hands on them and let them go. Sent out thus by the holy Spirit, they went down to Seleucia and from there they sailed to Cyprus" (Acts 13:2-4, Moffatt).

Out of this group-listening to God came a guidance that transformed the face of the world, for out of this came the missionary journeys of Paul which laid the foundations of Christianity in Asia and Europe and consequently in America and other parts of the world. A small group got collective guidance for two of their number, Barnabas and Saul. But the Holy Spirit made it plain that though the group was the instrument of the call and consecration of these two men, yet the group had no lordship over these men: "Come! set me apart Barnabas and Saul"—note the "me"—the Holy Spirit was to exercise ultimate lordship, not the group. And again: "Sent out thus by the Holy Spirit" —it was the Holy Spirit, not the group, that sent them out.

This is important, for often the group assumes spiritual lordship over those whom they send. One mission board examining committee asked a candidate whether he believed in superlapsarianism or supralapsariansim, and when the candidate, not knowing what either one meant, put down the wrong answer, he was rejected—rejected by the board, but not by the Holy Spirit, for he went to another country and became a great missionary.

The group may guide but not override the individual. For the cloven tongues sat on the head of each of them at Pentecost, implying that each of them was receiving the Holy Spirit as an individual. While the group too was receiving the Holy Spirit, as a group, yet the individual was not lost in the group. He had direct relationships with the Holy Spirit.

Dear Holy Spirit, Thou art making us instruments of Thy power directly, but help us to listen to Thy group guidance. Amen.

AFFIRMATION FOR THE DAY: *The most certain guidance is where the individual and the group guidance coincide.*

"TO STIR UP ONE ANOTHER TO LOVE"

The Christian cannot turn his conscience over to a group. "Stalin is my conscience" was written on the walls of a prison camp for Communists in Assam. The Christian can't do that; he has direct and primary responsibility to God.

Nevertheless the group can correct or corroborate individual guidance. An individual guidance that isn't subjected to a group guidance is liable to go off on tangents. Often we cannot see ourselves except through the eyes of a group. In Japan a pastor was leading congregational singing, and he was off key. The result was that everything was thrown into confusion. But the pastor was utterly unconscious of being out of tune. I nudged my interpreter into action, and when he arose, the pastor asked, "What's the matter?" When told he was out of tune, he was surprised. He had thought everybody else was off! The interpreter took over and guided the situation back into harmony. The group had to correct the individual.

Often the group inspires the individual. A judge was working on a farm, and a hired man said, "Judge, why don't you speak to John? I've spoken to him about Christ. Why don't you?" The judge did and won John and his family to Christ.

On the other hand, the individual can inspire and correct the group. Peter corrected a group that was about to make a fatal misstep. "Some of the believers who belonged to the Pharisaic party [an incongruous name for believers!] got up and said, "Gentiles must . . . observe the law of Moses'" (Acts 15:5, Moffatt). But Peter arose and told how God through the let-down sheet had led him to go to the Gentiles and how the Holy Spirit came upon them. That saved the group from going astray.

The interaction of the group helps and inspires both the individual and the group. This verse expresses the relationship: "Let us consider how to stir up one another to love and good deeds, not ceasing to meet together, as is the habit of some, but admonishing one another" (Heb. 10:24-25, Moffatt). The group helps the individual, and the individual helps the group.

Father, Thou hast set the solitary in families and in groups to rub off the edges of our solitariness. Help us to be grateful. Amen.

AFFIRMATION FOR THE DAY: *Paul resolved in the Spirit.*" That is co-operation—resolving the resolutions of the Spirit.

THE VOICE IS ALWAYS RIGHT

We have been thinking about God's guiding the group and the individual. Sometimes He speaks to an individual through an individual. There was a question raised as to whether I should take the trip to Japan. I received a long-distance call from Mary two hours after I had had another long-distance call from a doctor questioning whether I should go, and Mary said: "I've had a strange victory about your going to Japan. You're to go." She knew nothing of the other call and called me only after many hesitations and inner compulsion. It corroborated my own inner green light. Events have proved that she was right. So God does guide one individual through another. But usually the guided one also receives the green light within himself.

Then sometimes God guides the individual directly and personally when no other method of guidance is available. To take an illustration almost at random: I was in Nanking, China, in 1949 at a reception given by the American Ambassador, Dr. Leighton Stuart, and he pulled me aside and said that serious news had just come—the Communists would cross the Yangtze River and take Nanking on the twelfth. This was the eighth. I was to leave on the ninth to go by plane to West China, to Chengtu. If I went, I would probably not be able to come back through Nanking to Shanghai, where my next engagement was—the Communists would cut it off. I prayed, and the inner Voice said: "You're to go." Like Abraham I went not knowing whither I was going, and, more serious, I didn't know how I was going to get back! I only knew the Voice, and it was clear. While I was in Chengtu, word came over the radio that the Communists had set up the time of their crossing from the twelfth to the twentieth! I had a wonderful week in Chengtu and got back through Nanking to Shanghai on the eighteenth, two days before the Communists took over. The Voice was right.

I have not always obeyed that Voice, but whenever I have, it has always been right—sometimes unbelievably right, even when circumstance and my own misgivings made it seemingly impossible. We step on what seems to be thin air, and it turns out to be rock.

O Father, Thou hast led us through the years. Lead us to the end. Thy leadings have been my feedings. I thank Thee. Amen.

AFFIRMATION FOR THE DAY: *God's leadings are always leadings to greener pastures—rough places between often intervene.*

GUIDANCE NOT IN THE OCCASIONAL
BUT IN THE CONTINUOUS

One of the central prayers in the Lord's Prayer is this item: "And lead us, not into temptation, but deliver us from evil." Punctuated thus, it makes the prayer clear—it is a prayer for leading. This expresses a singleheartedness that means a full surrender to that leading.

I say singleheartedness. This is important. In parts of India I am told that merchants keep two sets of books—one for themselves and another for the income-tax officer. I mentioned that to a friend, and he replied: "No, they keep three sets of books—one for themselves, one for the income-tax officer, and one for their partners!" They were living in three directions, hence not living.

If we are to be guided, then that involves "surrender"—He must have *us*, and not merely our ear for a particular occasion. He cannot guide us in the occasional unless we let Him guide us in the continual.

In Sweden I told the story of the dog who at a certain time in the morning would stand before the kitchen door and wag his tail until the housewife would come into the Quiet Time with him. When she did, he would stretch out his paws, put his head between them, and be perfectly relaxed while she was having her Quiet Time. If she hesitated or delayed, he would wag his tail more vigorously as much as to say, "You know, and I know, that we will get into trouble today if we don't have our Quiet Time." A Swedish woman wrote me after the service: "I said to myself while you were talking, 'What I need is a little dog to help me keep my Quiet Time.' As we walked home, my daughter of twelve turned to me and said: 'Mommie, I'll be your little dog to help you keep your Quiet Time.' And she has. She's kept me to it." She wanted God to guide her in the continuous, so He gave specific guidance to the daughter to help her.

> His love attend thee,
> His strength defend thee,
> His peace commend thee,
> His Spirit send thee.

O Father, I thank Thee that I can come under Thy mind for direction and that Thy mind is my best interest always. Amen.

AFFIRMATION FOR THE DAY: *If God sends me, He fends me—fends me from all vital harm on the way.*

GROWTH IN PRAYER

We come now to an important area of growth—growth in prayer. This perhaps is the most important. I find I am better or worse as I pray more or less. Prayer tones up the whole of life. I can never be better in life than I am faithful in prayer. If prayer lags, life sags. If we know how to pray, we know how to live; if not, then we exist, we don't live. When I pray, I'm like an electric bulb in the socket, full of life and power. When I don't pray, then I'm like that bulb out of the socket—lifeless.

When a tiger attacks a victim, the first objective is to slit the throat of its victim with its sharp claw. When the victim is no longer able to breathe, he is done for. The enemy of our spirits does not attack us directly; he tries to get us to let down in prayer. This cuts off our spiritual breathing. Then we die easily.

A lady intended this to be a compliment with a criticism tucked away within it: "There is nothing very original in you, but you are at home in God." I've cherished that as pure compliment. The Christian doesn't originate; he transmits. God is the origin of all he has and is; he simply passes on what is passed on to him. He has learned the art of receptivity and hence of resourcefulness. He learns how to draw heavily on God and hence to hand on to man. He is as rich as his receptivity. The account tells of Jesus' withdrawing to the wilderness to pray, and it adds: "The power of the Lord was present to heal" (Luke 5:16-17). These two things follow as cause and effect—prayer and power. They are twins—Siamese twins.

Francis of Assisi had as his motto: "More than I can." That is it—we do things we can't do, think things we can't think, and accomplish things we can't accomplish. We do these things through being channels—channels through prayer.

Many think of themselves as reservoirs with a certain fixed capacity. If we are men of prayer, we are not reservoirs, but channels. We are attached to infinite resources and therefore have boundless possibilities.

My life motto: "Not able to do it, but enabled."

Father, I thank Thee that attached to Thy resources I am enabled to do what I am not able to do. I thank Thee. Amen.

AFFIRMATION FOR THE DAY: *All my capacities will be overflowing capacities—overflowing with capacities not my own.*

"MY HEART IS A PRAYER VIGIL"

We are studying growth in prayer.

The motto of a very vital group is: "When man listens, God speaks; when man obeys, God acts." And we may add: "When man prays, God empowers." The praying man is like a piece of steel in touch with a magnet. The steel in turn becomes magnetized and attracts and holds another piece of steel, provided it remains in contact with the original magnet. When the connection is broken, the magnetism ceases. The man of prayer in touch with the very magnetism of Christ becomes magnetized and magnetizes others in turn. But break the connection, and he is very ordinary steel without attraction. Prayer is the connection—break that, and you break all.

And yet many go through life prayerless, except for a crisis when they get into trouble. Then they pray. And they wonder why God doesn't immediately pull them out—making God a cosmic Grandfather! If you don't pray in the regular, you have no right to call on God in the irregular. I have watched the ground crew fill up and measure the gas put in the planes. After the ground crew has reported, one of the members of the flight crew will go the rounds checking on the amount of gas. A planefull of lives depends upon that check-up. And yet many start the day without checking the resources available to get through the day and to make a safe landing back home at night. No wonder so many crash on the way. We run out of resources, get irritable, and say and do things concerning which we have to repent and apologize. If we had taken time for prayer, we could have saved time—the time we take in unmessing the messes we get into.

Mary lives and breathes and has her being in prayer. She says, "My heart is a prayer vigil all the time," and the result is that she radiates the love of God. As she walked down the street singing softly to herself, a man turned and remarked to someone, "Well, the world is getting better." It is, as long as we can produce people who are transmitters of light and life through prayer. Of someone it was said: "His eyes are pools of silent prayer." And how deep those pools—as deep as the love of God. Prayer deepens and heightens life.

O Father, I thank Thee for the privilege of looking into Thy face each day and catching Thy mind and spirit for the day. Amen.

AFFIRMATION FOR THE DAY: *Prayer is a time exposure to God. Today I shall be constantly exposed to Him.*

PRAYER IS CO-OPERATION WITH GOD

We now come to see the elements that make up true prayers.

First, *Prayer is co-operation—co-operation with God*. It is the purest exercise of the faculties God has given us—an exercise that links these faculties with the Maker to work out the intentions He had in mind in their creation. Prayer is aligning ourselves with the purposes of God. Prayer isn't bending God to our wills, but our bending of our wills to God's will. If prayer is the purest exercise of our faculties, it is also the most natural. For when we co-operate with God in prayer, then we are working out God's intention inherent in the very structure of our beings. We do what we are made to do—made to do by our very make-up. Prayer, then, makes us natural by our very contact with the Supernatural. We work out the purposes God has worked into us. Prayer, then, is the fulfillment of our very beings. In prayer we become supernaturally natural. The supernatural works itself out through the natural and makes the natural more truly natural. There is obviously a destiny written into the constitution of our beings. We don't produce it; we discover it. And this destiny written in us is a Christian destiny. We are made in the inner structure of our beings to be Christian. Every organ, every cell, every nerve works well in the Christian way and badly in any other way. Hence we are pre-destined by our very nature to obey Jesus Christ. This destiny is not written merely in a book; it is written in us.

Prayer aligns us with God and therefore with ourselves. We are working with the grain of the universe and not against it. Jesus says, "Without me ye can do nothing," because you are not only working against Me, you are working against yourself. It is the eye fighting light—the thing for which it is made; the ear fighting sound—the thing for which it is made; the heart fighting love—the thing for which it is made. Prayer makes us stop fighting and makes us co-operate. Then infinite power works through our finiteness; an infinite mind thinks through our finite minds; and infinite love loves through our finite love. We are no longer nonplused; we are plused—a Plus is added to all we are and do.

Gracious Father, this throws open infinite possibilities to me. Help me to boldly accept them. Amen.

AFFIRMATION FOR THE DAY: *"I ask not for tasks equal to my powers but for powers equal to my tasks,"* and may they be big ones!

"BY SMALL ACCOMPLISHING GREAT"

I listened to an organist playing, accompanied by chimes. Back of the organ I could see a man with a mallet striking the long tubes— striking the same notes the organ was playing. So amid the tones of the swelling organ were the tones of the chimes, forming a beautiful accompaniment. Prayer means we are striking the same notes that God is striking. We thus become a part of a universal harmony—the music of the spheres. Our little notes are caught up and universalized. Prayer puts us in tune with the Infinite.

Here was a Japanese layman who had built up a social settlement in the slums of Okayama. One night fifty bombers passed over the city and left the city a ninety per cent ruin. He came back from the war and after a month of search found his family with one child killed. He stood with them and viewed the ashes where his buildings had stood. "Let us build," whispered God, and "Let us build," he replied. But he had nothing with which to build except the whisper. Today I looked at his hospital, school, social center—all rebuilt out of the ashes and all built out of a whisper—a whisper, but a creative whisper. He co-operated with the creative God and rebuilt with love what hate had destroyed.

Milton expressed it: "By small accomplishing great things." We do just that when we co-operate with God in prayer. The little boy offers his five loaves and two fishes to Jesus—co-operates with Him in the feeding. And how his eyes must have bulged and his heart danced as he saw his little become the big, the insufficient become the adequate!

If we co-operate with God in His plans, He will co-operate with us in His power. If we do what He says, He will do what we say. But He is first! We have mentioned that Jesus says this astonishing thing: "The conqueror I will allow to sit beside me on my throne" (Rev. 3: 21, Moffatt). Telling poor mortals that they would share the throne of the universe! Does that happen? Yes! When we co-operate with Him, then we share the ideas and powers which rule the universe. We literally share His throne! We are a part of the ruling ideas and powers which govern human development.

O Jesus, You invited me to a cross, I took it, and, lo, it turned out to be a throne. I'm humbled to the dust. Amen.

AFFIRMATION FOR THE DAY: *I share Christ's throne only because it is a "throne of grace"—only grace would share its power.*

TURNING OFF THE SUN!

I spoke to a group of Japanese and Swedish Christians gathered at the station to sing "God Be with You Till We Meet Again" and to say good-by. I repeated to them the words of Jesus: "Fear not, little flock; for it is your Father's good pleasure to give you the kingdom." No more preposterous words could have been spoken—a handful of fishermen having a Kingdom! But that has come true literally—that group of men gave the ideas that have ruled the development of civilization; they have ruled the minds of men and nations. They have had a Kingdom given them. I told this group that they had the ideas and spirit in the Christian faith which would rule the destiny of the new Japan. Their ideas would be the foundation of the future, provided they were the ideas of Christ. For He holds the future. Co-operation with Him in prayer and purpose means co-operation with Him in power and performance.

There is a breath-taking phrase used: "So let us approach the throne of grace" (Heb. 4:16, Moffatt). What a name—"The throne of grace"! He rules! But at the heart of His ruling is grace, unmerited favor—in other words, He rules redemptively. He rules men by graciously giving to men. He rules them by love. So if we love with His love, we partake of His grace, and we partake of His gracious ruling. We too rule by love. And ruling by love is the only ruling; anything else is what Jesus referred to when he said: "the rulers of the Gentiles lord it over them" (Matt. 20:25, R.S.V.). And He was right. Those "rulers" are gone and only love lives on.

I went back into a room I was leaving in order to turn off the lights. I found the light I was to turn off was the sun shining through the windows. You can't turn off the sun; you can hide yourself from it, but you can't turn it off! So you can't stop God's gentle ruling—it's there! And when we rule by love, we are always there—we can't be turned off. For back of us is the love, and hence power, that radiates from the heart of the universe.

O Father, how can I thank Thee? This glorious destiny does not puff me up. It puts me down to the dust in gratitude. Amen.

AFFIRMATION FOR THE DAY: *I am a man of destiny—a destiny that reaches to the stars and beyond. I will work out that destiny.*

"THE LIFE OF JESUS MAY COME OUT"

We have been speaking of co-operation in prayer and in power.
The co-operation works within us as well as in the world. These
verses express it: "So that the life of Jesus may come out in my
body: . . . so that the life of Jesus may come out within my mortal
flesh" (II Cor. 4:10-11, Moffatt). If we are identified with Jesus in
prayer as co-operation, then His very life comes out in our bodies,
quickening them, reconstructing them, making weak tissues and
nerves into strong tissues and nerves. The healing is from within.
This is different from the ordinary conception of healing; healing is
looked on as a special invasion from without—an act of healing on us.
But this is healing by His very presence within—His life coming out
in our mortal bodies. We don't so much ask for healing; we just let
healing course through us from within. We cultivate His presence,
and He in turn permeates us with His health. We absorb it as we
absorb food into our blood. This is continuous healing.

And yet Paul recognizes that these bodies are "mortal flesh"—they
will not last forever. But they will last as long as necessary. I awoke
one morning recently, and at the Listening Post the Father said, "As
long as you have anything mentally, spiritually worth giving, I'll keep
your body in repair to be the vehicle of that giving if you will allow
me." I added a note, "That is very searching, for it puts me on
tiptoe to have something to give. Why should God keep my body
in repair as a body and not as a vehicle for something beyond itself?"

At another Listening Post time the Father said to me, "What do
you really want in life?" And I found myself replying, "Lord, just one
thing: grace and power to win others to Thee. Give me that; I really
want nothing else." And the reply: "You shall have that and all else
you really need." Recently I was put on a diet, and the nurse, when she
handed me the diet sheet, said, "Don't read it now. You won't like it."
To my surprise I found it fun to try to live according to it in the
midst of evangelistic campaigns. And I found myself saying, "I don't
mind, Lord, if you feed me charcoal, just so the fire of witnessing to
Thee is kept burning in my heart."

Father, give me as little or as much as I need, but keep the fire
burning within so I can witness effectively for Thee. Amen.

AFFIRMATION FOR THE DAY: *Through thick and thin to witness effectively for Christ—let this be my aim, my only aim, in life.*

Luke 18:1; Rom. 8:26

I AM HIS HANDS

Sometimes Jesus' life is transmitted to others. Here is a letter:

For months I had been under a doctor's observation for a painful growth in my left breast. I had been praying about it, and when you laid your hands on my head, I felt the electricity (such is my description) of the Holy Spirit going into my body. The pains and the growth are gone, and the only time I think of the breast is when I thank God for its perfect health.

And here is another from a woman who a few years ago gave me her cigarette case, flask of liquor, and sleeping pills, when she arose from her knees a new person, not needing these crutches any more.

As for my health, you know me very well, I think, and I believe you read my desperation between the lines that tried to be casual. Physically I have been most miserable for months, and while I have gone on working, I was beginning to wonder how long it, and I could last. This last month I've improved so much that the doctor beams and just can't believe it. And yesterday a board member said to me, "You don't look like the same person who was at the board meeting last month. What has happened?" I replied, "A friend prayed for me!" I told the doctor the same thing.

When we co-operate in prayer, we extend ourselves through Him. A little girl in Denmark found a figure of Thorwaldson's "Christ" in an abandoned house. She brought it to her father and said: "But it has no hands. They have been broken off." And the father replied: "Then you will have to be hands for Him." Through co-operation in prayer you can be His hands with which He touches others; His heart through which He loves others; His feet through which He seeks out others; His very life going out to others through you. You can be an extension of the Incarnation.

Prayer is not begging for boons; it is becoming a boon to yourself and others. Prayer adds a plus to all our thinking, all our loving, all our acting. God extends His personality through us, and in doing so extends our personality. We lose and find ourselves.

Father God, Thou art offering to me breath-taking power. Help me humbly to take it and to use it wisely. Amen.

AFFIRMATION FOR THE DAY: *I have the noblest of callings: to be an extension of the incarnation of Jesus Christ in my situation.*

294

PRAYER IS COMMITMENT

Second, *Prayer is commitment.* We don't merely co-operate with God with certain things held back within. We don't merely co-operate with God with our actions. We, the total person, co-operate. This means that co-operation equals commitment. And commitment means self-commitment. Prayer means that the total you is praying. Your whole being reaches out to God, and God's whole Being reaches down to you.

I have mentioned that the central thing in the Incarnation is this phrase: He "emptied himself" (Phil. 2:7, Moffatt). And the corollary: "Therefore God raised Him high" (v. 9). Here is a law that is effective for God and man: you find your life by losing it! Amazing that even God obeys this law—He loses His life and finds it again; He empties Himself and is raised high, high to the very throne of the universe. So it's an unbreakable law for God and man. You don't break it; you break yourself on it.

Prayer, then, true to the deepest law of the universe—saving your life by losing it—means primarily self-surrender. I found myself at an Ashram communion praying this prayer: "Take me as I am, and make me as Thou art."

When we lose our lives in self-forgetfulness, we find them again. The Japanese as conquerors were usually hard. But there were kindly spots. A missionary friend visiting the Pescadores, belonging to Formosa, found a god shelf with a Japanese policeman among the gods. Asked why the policeman was there, the owner replied, "This policeman was very kind to us. And when he was taken away, I placed him on my god shelf as a god." He lost himself in self-forgetfulness and found himself—a god!

Jesus said: "If any man serve me, let him follow me." Is it possible to serve Him and not follow Him? Yes, we often offer our service in lieu of offering ourselves. The self lurks behind the service, intruding itself again and again into that service.

Prayer is demanding—it demands you, the total you.

Dear Father, take me as I am, and make me as Thou art; and the "me" means the total me—body, mind, spirit, possessions. Amen.

AFFIRMATION FOR THE DAY: *Prayer demands that I pray with my life. I'm praying with my life behind my prayers.*

PRAYER IS COMMUNION

We have been looking at prayer as commitment. Mary sums it up in these words: "On that particular evening my heart was just a humble empty manger, instead of a busy inn, and since that time all life has been transformed." In prayer we are open and surrendered as the humble empty manger—ready to receive Christ and be the setting of His birth in the hearts of those around us.

This leads to the third step in prayer. Third, *Prayer is communion.* Prayer is a means, but often it is an end in itself. Like the little boy who came into his father's study and when asked what he wanted, replied, "Nothing. I just want to be with you." There are times when your own wants and the needs of others drop away and you want just to look on His face and tell Him how much you love Him.

I have often said that the phrase I most often repeat to the Father is this one: "Lord, you've got me." That phrase is still basically there and is repeated again and again, but there is another one that is in ascendancy, being repeated oftener: "Lord, I love you, I love you, I love you." It has become a refrain. I open my eyes in the early morning often repeating it to myself the first thing—the subconscious must have been repeating it through the night hours. I've found myself going through a railway station in Japan amid the throngs of hurrying people, talking to myself: "Lord, I love You, I love You, I love You." And what a sweetness it leaves within the breast! So much so you feel drunk with love and stagger under the weight of glory.

Oxenham puts it in these lines:

> A little place of mystic grace,
> Of sin and self swept bare,
> Where I may look into Thy face
> And talk with Thee in prayer.

Then the heart becomes a moving shrine from the altar of which arises the continual incense of love and adoration. You are always at home in God and never alone.

Dear Christ, Thou art my Home. In Thee I'm never alone. In Thee I'm at home anywhere, everywhere, and at all times. Amen.

AFFIRMATION FOR THE DAY: *Today, again and again I shall drop into the silence of my heart and there commune face to Face.*

A PEG ON WHICH TO HANG MY GRATITUDE

When we have prayer as communion, we can fill in the hours and moments with quiet peace. I've learned the habit through long practice of dropping into the heart in prayer whenever I'm compelled to wait for an elevator, a friend, or an engagement. I head off the possible resentment and impatience by forestalling it with prayer. I occupy the conflict moment with a communion moment. The destructive is pushed out, and the constructive comes in.

A man was riding with a friend and spoke to him at a traffic light and thought it strange when he got no reply. Afterward he asked his friend about it and got the reply, "Oh, I really didn't hear you, for I've made a habit of dropping into my heart and praying at traffic lights." It saved him from being tense, and it made him calm and receptive, and ready for the run to the next light.

Yesterday I had an interesting request from a Japanese lady asking me to get the opera singer Traubel to send her the rose named after her. And her reason was that she was so impressed by the famous opera star's pausing in prayer before each performance. More than her singing did that simple act of prayer impress this Japanese lady.

And that communion, often wordless, more often turns to thanksgiving. Yesterday I thanked the Father for a peg on which to hang my coat. And then I said to myself, "I'm always hunting for pegs on which to hang my gratitude, and I find so many." I find myself thanking Him for everything, for everything furthers you deeper into God if you will let it. As someone has said, "Never face a trouble without first thanking God for it." And then the trouble is no longer a mere trouble; it is an opportunity for victory through the trouble. Paul puts it this way: "Rejoice at all times" (I Thess. 5:16, Moffatt). And the secret of rejoicing at all times is the next: "Never give up prayer" (v. 17). And the outcome is: "Thank God for everything" (v. 18). If you are in a constant state of prayer, you can "rejoice at all times" and "thank God for everything." Your heart is a fountain of thankful rejoicing.

O Christ, Thou hast taught me a secret—the secret of the quiet, thankful, rejoicing heart. I'm impervious. Amen.

AFFIRMATION FOR THE DAY: *Every event shall shake the gratitude out, but the depths will be undisturbed.*

PRAYER IS COMMISSION

We have been looking at prayer as communion. This communion is intimate and tender and personal. A little fellow in New Haven expressed it, though he didn't intend to, when he repeated the Lord's Prayer thus: "Our Father, who art in New Haven, how'd you know my name?" He does meet us where we are, and He does know our name, and deeper—He loves us in spite of knowing us entirely.

This inner communion becomes the source of our strength. I have quoted before: "Your life is hidden" (Col. 3:3, Moffatt). I looked down from a plane over Burma and saw a series of long lakes. But they were not lakes; they were patches left when wet-weather rivers ran dry. They had lost contact with the eternal snows and were simply drying up little by little. That is a picture of life that has lost communion with God—slowly drying up.

Fourth, *Prayer is commission.* Out of the quietness with God, power is generated that turns the spiritual machinery of the world. When you pray, you begin to feel the sense of being sent, that the divine creative compulsion is upon you. As Mary says, "When you pray, you no longer have a chip on your shoulder; you have a Hand on your shoulder."

A young woman stood in one of our meetings and said, "I said to the Lord, 'I do wish I could feel this way all the time.' And He replied, 'You haven't seen anything yet.'" And yet she had seen a very great deal. She was a Christian only six months when she went to her pastor and said, "The people in my community won't go to church, but I think they would come to my house. Would you be willing to lead an 'abundant living group' in my house if I got them together?" He agreed. She got a Sunday-school class as a nucleus, but she said they couldn't come unless they brought a pagan as the ticket of admission. Soon she had seventy-five. In a year fifty people had been won to Christ and the church through that group. A Christian of six months had a sense of commission when she listened to God in prayer. And out of that listening a living movement came.

Father, help me to know how to listen and then to go forth from that listening with Thy hand on my shoulder. Amen.

AFFIRMATION FOR THE DAY: *"He that sent me is with me: the Father hath not left me alone."*

A SENSE OF COMMISSION IN ALL OUR FACULTIES

The account says: "After that, as Jesus knew that everything was now finished and fulfilled, he said . . . 'I am thirsty'" (John 19:28, Moffatt). After His commission was finished and fulfilled, He thought of His own thirst. His thirst was subordinate to His mission. Prayer puts our commission in the first place and our thirsts in the second place. Many put their thirsts first, and their commissions fit into their thirsts. But prayer puts first things first—revalues our values. A Belgian pastor during the German occupation read a statement regarding the political situation: "I would rather that our relations to Germany should deteriorate than that our relations to Christ deteriorate." He was shot on the road. The next day every book seller had an open Bible in the window, open at a verse so passersby could read. The pastor, though dead, yet spoke through that verse to the whole nation. He kept his commission first, his thirst for life second.

Prayer puts all our powers at the disposal of God—puts a sense of mission into all our faculties. Paul says: "My aim is to make the Gentiles an acceptable offering, consecrated by the holy Spirit" (Rom. 15:16, Moffatt). The Holy Spirit is received by consecration and faith, and then He turns and consecrates the offering. He continually dedicates the powers and talents to higher purposes. This is more than sublimation; it is sublimation to the Sublime! If we had to do the perpetual consecrating, then the offering would not stay consecrated. But if the Holy Spirit has charge of our motives in the subconscious, then He has charge of our day-by-day dedications. This means that the Holy Spirit is the Sanctifier—the Cleanser—yes, but He is also the Consecrator. We consecrate everything to Him, and He in turn perpetually consecrates our powers and our very selves to God and His service.

Consecration is "holy with," "sacred with." "May the God of peace consecrate you through and through!" (I Thess. 5:23, Moffatt). You are holy when you are "holy with" Jesus—when your purposes and His are aligned. You are holy when you are wholly His. Those who are aligned to Him are alike to Him.

O Holy Spirit, I consecrate myself and my powers to Thee. Take them in turn and consecrate them perpetually. Amen.

AFFIRMATION FOR THE DAY: *I do not nervously have to hold my offering on the altar. The Holy Spirit consecrates the depths.*

"THOU ART THE BREEZE—BLOW ON"

In order to grow in prayer set a framework of devotional life. Set aside a certain amount of time for prayer each day. Pray by the clock. If you say, "I'll pray everywhere at all times, but at no specific time," my prediction will be that you'll probably end by praying nowhere at any time. You'll not be able to sustain the "everywhere" except by a "somewhere," nor "all times" except by a specific time.

Take your Bible into your prayer time. A picture in a missionary home depicted a little boy holding up before the blind man a flower, so that the first thing he will see will be the flower as Jesus lays His hands upon his eyes. The Word of God will let you look into the face of Jesus as the first thing you see in beginning your prayer time. Then become silent before Him and let Him speak. Repeat the Chinese hymn: "I am the grass, Thou art the Breeze—blow on." Then pour out your unfinished business into His lap and ask for guidance. And believe the guidance will be given.

Then rise up from the hour to project it into the day. You have prayed somewhere; now you can pray everywhere. Now you can repeat the words "Forget, forgive, for God." And go out to do everything for the love of God. And now there will be no strain through the day. A telegraph wire expends more energy when it is idle than when it is carrying a message. Now your life is co-ordinated—all of one piece and not a bundle of remnants.

As the camel kneels before his master to have him remove the burden at the end of the day, so kneel each night and let the Master loose the burdens of the day. And as the same camel kneels before his master at the beginning of the day to receive a load for the day, so kneel each morning and let Him lay on you the responsibilities for the day. "And as thy days, so shall thy strength be."

The prayer climate will be the climate of the day. You will be like the captain who had navigated the Mississippi for many years, and when a friend commented, "You must know where all the shoals are," replied, "No, but I know where the channels are."

Dear Lord and Master, help me this day to begin and end this day with Thee and have Thee throughout the day. Amen.

AFFIRMATION FOR THE DAY: *My prayerful heart shall be the repository of His love and goodness as the hours drop them in.*

ON PRAYER VIGILS

We have talked about organizing personal prayer life. We must now talk about prayer groups and prayer vigils.

Get a "prayer partner" and start a group, maybe with only two, and then enlarge as kindred spirits come in. Learn to have corporate silence so that no person but the Holy Spirit will assume the leadership. No sermons, but seed thoughts and ideas may be passed on as they come to you in prayer. Confess your faults to one another if you feel impelled. Bring into the prayer group the needs gathered from many hearts. Let the group be "on tap" so that a telephone message can be passed around and you can pray for specific things that arise in a crisis. Keep out the "queer" and marginal. Hold it to the redemptive movement in Christ. Then the prayer group can become a power group.

Prayer vigils can be organized on a one-day or seven-day basis. Select a quiet place, a chapel or a room fixed up as a chapel. For a seven-day vigil divide the time in shifts of an hour. Make a chart with squares representing an hour, and have people put their names in the hour they will take. It will take only 168 people for a seven-day vigil, and some people will take more than one hour. No leading is necessary. The one responsible may simply sit, or kneel, in silent prayer. Have a prayer-request book prepared, and requests may be put in before and during the vigil. Some devotional books may be near at hand. Vocal prayer may be used, but usually the vigil is carried on in silence. The one who is responsible should stay until the next person responsible takes over, so that the vigil will not be broken. Prayer suggestions with Scripture references to prayer can be drawn up before the vigil begins so they can be available to each participant. A central theme may be chosen, but other requests, personal and corporate, can be added.

People who have never prayed an hour continuously in their lives find the hour slip by quickly as Eternity invades them in the silence. A prayer vigil can be used of God to spiritualize a church, a city, a nation. It is power.

Father, help me to learn how to pool my prayer life with others so that my personal life may be heightened by the rest. Amen.

AFFIRMATION FOR THE DAY: *My heart shall have a prayer vigil going on all the time as the hours come and go.*

GROWTH IN SOCIAL CONSCIOUSNESS

We have been considering prayer as the outreach of man's spirit to God and man. We come now to consider growth in social consciousness.

The question of expanded social consciousness can best be raised by the question "Who is my neighbor?" This question was asked by a lawyer when Jesus approved of his answer that one must love God totally, and "Also your neighbor as yourself." The Jews had defined the "neighbor" as a Jew. That clipped the wings of this command so it could not fly beyond the Jewish fence. Jesus sent His command soaring when He defined the neighbor as a man of another race in need. In other words, everybody is your neighbor—literally everybody.

Growth, then, is a growth in our conception of "Who is my neighbor?" And an appreciation of and care for that neighbor.

And this is scientifically sound. For basically humanity is one, modified slightly by local environment and customs. A Westerner who has spent his life among the Japanese people and has made their life his own says: "There is no such thing as Japanese psychology—it is just human psychology." They are the same basically as other people—modified by a Japanese past and present culture. The brain of humanity is one. We have set up a psychiatric center in Lucknow, India, and our psychiatrists there report that the basic mental and emotional problems are the same as those in the West, caused by slightly differing environmental conditions. This is most important. It shows a basic humanity, one and the same. A white teacher in a college in Africa said to me that he had taught students in Europe, and that these Africans have as good brain power as students in Europe. This was corroborated by a missionary who had taught in Africa and Japan. She adds: "We had a boy in Africa, right out of the Bush, who got 100 per cent in all his mathematical examinations." There are no permanently superior and no permanently inferior races. There are only developed and underdeveloped races.

Father, we thank Thee that we are one humanity. Help us then to act that way and build our future upon it. Amen.

AFFIRMATION FOR THE DAY: *Every man of every race and class is my neighbor. I have resolved to be neighborly.*

"IN HOT WATER"

We are studying growth in expanded social consciousness. The Bible says: "[God] hath made of one blood all nations of men for to dwell on all the face of the earth." Is this true? Yes, there is one blood in humanity, the microscope being witness. There are four types of blood, and these four types run through all races. It may be that my type of blood is better matched by a man of another race than by my own blood brother, so that if I want a blood transfusion, I am nearer in blood to a man of another race than to my own blood brother.

It is simply prejudice that sets up barriers. A little auburn-haired white girl blew a kiss to me and then one to my Japanese interpreter as the train pulled out of a station. Her soul and sight had not been corrupted by prejudices imposed by culture.

All races have these imposed prejudices. An African in Africa said to a Burmese friend of mine: "White man no good, you Burmans no good. White man get in sun, his color change to red; you Burmans get sick, your yellow color change to white. No fast color. But African get in jungle in shade, still black; get into sun, still black. Fast color." Another African put it this way: "God made the African, and He made the white man. But He put the white man in hot water, and his skin came off." There is some truth in the statement that the white man is in hot water—he is because of his color prejudices. Witness South Africa and the United States. In a daily paper in Japan a Japanese Communist was attacking America because of its treatment of the Negro as an inferior being. Much of the account was twisted, but there was enough truth in it to put us "in hot water" over it.

The South, from which I come and which I love, has a policy of "segregation." Results? It has adopted a social pattern that can't be universalized in our country, so the South simply cannot elect to the Presidency any man from its section holding those views. The country won't adopt them. So the South in its policy of segregation simply segregates itself from national leadership—from the Presidency. And resentments boiling down underneath are making the situation hotter and hotter. God is making us uncomfortable, to make us a family.

O Father, Thou art disturbing us to deliver us—to deliver us from our impossible ways of life. Make us a brotherhood. Amen.

AFFIRMATION FOR THE DAY: *I shall so live today that if my acts and attitudes were universalized, we'd have the answer.*

303

"WHO IS MY NEIGHBOR?"

Africa is the battleground for human rights. There the whole continent is astir and resentful. An African studying in India came to our Sat Tal Ashram and said a very bitter word and yet said it very quietly: "I am a Christian, and I don't like Communism. But I wouldn't mind if Communism came into Africa if it would wake up the white man to give us human justice." No more ominous word could have been spoken. Of course, his remedy is wrong, for basically Communism is as intolerant of difference in idea as the white man is intolerant of difference in color. Both attitudes will break down—will have to if we are going to have a brotherhood world.

I was in a city formed around an atomic plant in America. On a billboard was a notice headed: "How we protect our neighbors." It told what precautions were being taken to protect life and property, chickens, animals, crops, and plants from the effects of atomic radiation. It was done thoroughly and carefully. As I stood reading the heading, I could not suppress the question: "And who is my neighbor?" The answer was of course: "Americans surrounding the atomic plant." And there in that protected area bombs were being prepared to drop on whole cities to destroy them in a ghastly flash. And who are the people in those cities? Well, they're not our neighbors. So we say. But Jesus keeps asking, "Who is your neighbor?"

This is being written in Hiroshima, Japan, where the first atomic bomb was dropped. Yesterday I stood at the spot where the bomb fell and bowed in prayer with several Japanese praying that no Hiroshima should ever happen to anyone anywhere again. We dedicated ourselves to peace. I saw a spot on the granite steps of a bank, outlining the body of a man who was sitting there when the bomb fell. The granite all around him was bleached by the flash, but his body protected the spot, and it was the original dark shade. Was that man my neighbor? I inwardly cried out against this thing called war—the monster that turns all our neighbors into enemies. No time now to apportion blame. The thing itself—war—must be abolished.

O Father of us all, forgive us that we haven't been able as yet to abolish war from the earth. Forgive us, forgive us. Amen.

AFFIRMATION FOR THE DAY: *As far as I am concerned, war is at an end. I am armed with love and peace.*

WAR MUST BE ABOLISHED

After the visit to the spot where the bomb fell, we went to a civic reception at which the mayor and his officials received us. After the formalities were over, the first question by the mayor was, "How can we get peace?" He said that of the present population of Hiroshima—320,000—about 90,000 had gone through the explosion. The 90,000 to a man all vote against rearming. They had had their bitter, blinding, blistering experience. No more war for them under any circumstances.

Will the expanding consciousness of neighborliness look back one day on war as we look back on this inscription on the tombstone of an Indian fighter in New England: "He took eighty-two scalps and hoped to live to have a hundred. But he fell asleep in Jesus" on such and such a date? We recoil at that, and yet one day that was acceptable and Christian. Then this story: A New England minister who was an Indian fighter wanted to kill an Indian standing beside the water. But it was the Sabbath, and he debated whether it should be done on the Sabbath. Finally he decided that it was a good deed, so it could be done on the Sabbath. So he killed the Indian. Will we recoil at this mass killing called war the way we recoil at such individual killing—done even in the name of our holy faith?

I believe we will. The conscience of humanity is slowly expanding to include war in its central repudiations. For we are being pushed into this position by the very weapons we use. If war comes again, it will be fought with atomic energy, and no one will win an atomic-energy war. Both sides will be ruined in perhaps twenty-four hours. No one will be victor. One side may crawl out as survivor, but no one as victor. God is almost coercing our consciences into repudiation of war. We have relied on force in human affairs, and now God has let us see into the heart of an atom. He points to it and says, "You have believed in force. There it is in an atom! But if you use it, both sides will be ruined. Now choose." And we are in the hour of fateful choice. Have we attained sufficient moral maturity to choose wisely?

O Father, help us to make the right decision lest the ages pronounce that we were too immature to handle mature forces. Amen.

AFFIRMATION FOR THE DAY: *I shall handle no explosive material of temper and power in an explosive way.*

A GROUP THAT CARES, SHARES, AND DARES

Growth in the Christian spirit means the enlargement of our social awareness. We become conscious of people as people and not people as foreigners, or of this class or that, or of this color or that.

A good description of a church in this regard is that a church is a group that cares, shares, and dares. But first it cares. Von Hugel's definition of "a Christian is one who cares" is a profound one. And the more Christianized, the wider and deeper the caring. The real Christian cares for everybody, even for enemies.

James emphasizes this growth in social consciousness—a growth that wipes out distinctions of class. He says: "Are you not drawing distinctions in your own minds?" (James 2:4, Moffatt). He insists that Christianity produces a classless society. "If you pay servile regard to people, you commit a sin, and the Law convicts you of transgression" (v. 9). Then again he says: "If you really fulfill the royal law . . . , You must love your neighbour as yourself." This gives us a new royalty—the royalty of every person. Every person is infinitely precious in the sight of God and must be in the sight of men.

A native of the Tonga Islands in the Pacific told me that the queen, who is a Christian, considers all her subjects as her Christian brothers and sisters while they are together in the church. There they are free to speak to her without hesitation or inhibition. But outside the church the distinctions are set up again, and queen-and-subject relations begin again—a striking example of the influence of Christianity in leveling up every man.

Fosdick defines Christianity as "an ethical adventure into new human relationships and dynamic spiritual power for new life." The young missionary who drove me on an evangelistic tour in Okinawa had an elder brother who was killed in the fighting on the island. Instead of being embittered, he felt he wanted to do something positive for the Okinawan people. As we passed along, a little Okinawan girl ran out and waved her hand to him. "She was my best little friend when I took a vacation here for a week." His is an ethical adventure in human relationships.

Father, I pray Thee that this day I may look for an opportunity for ethical adventures in human relationships. Amen.

AFFIRMATION FOR THE DAY: *Life for me shall be one long ethical adventure in love—love for everybody.*

INFERIOR STATUS OF WOMEN

Growth in social consciousness should wipe out of our civilization all remnants of social inferiorities which are still there, sometimes consciously and sometimes subconsciously.

For instance, Paul gave the Christian position regarding the structure of a Christian society thus: "In it there is no room for Greek and Jew [social distinction], circumcised and uncircumcised [religious rite distinction], barbarian, Scythian [cultural distinction], slave, or free man [social, economic distinction]; Christ is everything and everywhere" (Col. 3:11, Moffatt). And in Gal 3:28 he adds: "There is no room for male and female [sex distinction]; you are all one in Christ Jesus." That is the Christian position—clear, positive, sweeping. And in Peter's speech at Pentecost he said: "Your sons and daughters shall prophesy"—note "and daughters"—(Acts 2:17, Moffatt).

But in I Cor. 14:34 (Moffatt) Paul enjoins something else: "Women must keep quiet at gatherings of the church. They are not allowed to speak; . . . as the Law enjoins." Note that he appeals to "the Law" for authority. Is he falling into the very thing he told the Galatians they were doing? It seems so. Every time Paul tried to put woman in a subordinate position, he appealed to the Old Testament, not to Jesus. Note: "but woman represents the supremacy of man. (Man was not made from woman, woman was made from man; and man was not created for woman, but woman for man.)" (I Cor. 11:7-9, Moffatt). Here he turns back to the first creation for corroboration for his position—the first creation, not to the new creation in Jesus where "there is no room for male or female." Again in I Tim. 2:12-14 (Moffatt) he says: "I allow no woman to teach or dictate to men, she must keep quiet. For Adam was created first, then Eve; and Adam was not deceived, it was Eve." Here he turned to the first Adam for the sustaining of his position—the first Adam, not the Second Adam, Christ. His Christianity slipped a cog. And that slipping back to the pre-Christian has caused much confusion. Paul says that sometimes he was not inspired—he was speaking on his own. This was one of the times. And the ages have suffered because of it.

Dear Father, forgive us when we limit Thy love and thus limit its operations in human relationships. Help us to follow Thee. Amen.

AFFIRMATION FOR THE DAY: *My love shall overflow the narrow channels of race and class and inundate all hearts I meet.*

"WE ALL SHED THE SAME TEARS"

Unexpectedly I had to take off my shoes and enter the pulpit of a cathedral in India in my socks. I saw a little boy on the front seat obviously embarrassed because he had a torn place in his short trousers. I had a deep fellow feeling for him, for I had a hole in my sock which I too was trying to hide! We were brothers in embarrassment! Down underneath throughout all races are the same inner failings, which we are trying to hide in various ways.

At the close of the war a German lady sought employment from an American woman, who, when she found out the other was German hesitated. The German replied, "Madam, we all shed the same tears." A Japanese president of a college said to me, "When the stunning news of the surrender came, my wife and I stood and held hands, and our teardrops silently fell as the awful meaning dawned upon us." Those silent teardrops were shared by the South when the news of Lee's surrender came. We all shed the same tears. When I was in Russia, I was looking for someone who knew English. I tapped a young man on the shoulder and asked, "Are you a student?" And he replied, "I am an aspirant." He too was an aspirant—an aspirant for knowledge and a fuller life. I felt he was wrong in his ideas and his methods as a part of an oppressive system, but along with youth around the world, he too was an aspirant. And we have to feel that sense of solidarity if we are going to get out of the mess we are in. Paul says: "I feel myself under a sort of universal obligation. I owe something to all men" (Rom. 1:14, Phillips). "Universal obligation" —that's it! We grow as we grow in awareness. When that awareness takes in all men as men, then we are truly growing. We grow as we go over all barriers of race, class, and color. This prayer expresses it: "And may the Lord make you increase and excel in love to one another and to all men" (I Thess. 3:12, Moffatt).

When the great-souled Helen Keller was asked what she wanted most in life, she replied: "I want people in the world to live like brothers and sisters." Her soul had grown out of the shell of blindness, deafness, and dumbness to reach every human being.

O Father, take my little loves and enlarge them into Thy loves, my little sympathies and expand them into Thy sympathies. Amen.

AFFIRMATION FOR THE DAY: *I shall push out the area of awareness today to territories I have not taken in.*

GROWING IN AND THROUGH OLD AGE

On the tombstone of an Alpine climber was this inscription: "He died climbing." That should be on the tombstone of every one of us. I have often said that if people don't quite know what to put on my tombstone, I'd like to so live and die that this would be fitting: "He died learning." Thirty-five years ago a missionary friend overheard another missionary say, "Stanley Jones has shot his bolt." I laughed then, and I laugh now and hope to laugh up to the very end, by learning from everybody I meet and everything that happens and from everything I hear and read. And especially from what I hear from God at the Listening Post.

I saw a sign on a hill: "Don't coast"; and I said to myself, "Yes, don't coast on past achievements; climb! Climb by making everything that happens further you." I saw also on a road a sign: "End of reconstruction." When you get to the end of reconstruction, you are getting near the end. For life should be a constant reconstruction. I often say, "I'm only a Christian-in-the-making," and I expect this to be true to the end. I expect to be in the process of being made until I awake in His likeness—and beyond! I believe in an eternal growth.

This might well be on the Golden Text of this book: "He who has begun the good work in you will go on completing it until the day of Jesus Christ" (Phil. 1:6, Moffatt).

And another verse may be added: "Now to him who is able to keep you from slipping and to make you stand unblemished and exultant before his glory" (Jude 24, Moffatt). Is He able to keep us from "slipping"—mentally, spiritually, physically? Yes, I believe He is. He guarantees us against decay—real decay.

An Indian paper made the announcement: "An elderly man of forty-seven died." Here is what Dr. Alexander A. Bogomoleto says: "A man of sixty or seventy is still young. He has lived half his normal life. Old age can be treated just as any other illness, because what we are accustomed to regard as normal old age is actually an abnormal, premature phenomenon." It is, and most of it is in the mind.

Dear God and Father, prod me from within when I begin to settle down. Let me die learning. In Jesus' name. Amen.

AFFIRMATION FOR THE DAY: *I am as old not as my arteries, but as my attitudes.*

"HE IS ALWAYS GROWING"

A man introducing a speaker paid this lovely compliment: "I have known him for thirty years. He never changes except upward. Many speakers lose their fire as they get older. This speaker never does. He is always growing." And why not?

As you climb the steps of a tower, the horizons widen and the view becomes clearer and wider. So should life be from youth to old age and beyond.

Longfellow gives us this possibility:

> How far the gulf stream of our youth may flow,
> Into the arctic regions of our lives—
> For age is opportunity no less
> Than youth itself, though in another dress,
> And as the evening twilight fades away
> The sky is filled with stars, invisible by day.

But if old age is to be beautiful, we must bring to it something that makes it beautiful. We don't grow old, we get old by not growing. If we obey the laws of growth, then these laws will operate clear up to the end of life—and beyond. But you can't keep from getting old by various subterfuges of dress and paint. Age stares through this flimsy stuff. Painting a dead tree with green paint doesn't make it living. The life has to come from within or not at all.

An old man runs away from an old people's home periodically and is brought back by the police. He was overheard telling the rest of the old folks there about his return: "I came back to the home with two uniformed chauffeurs driving me. I was seated in the back seat of the car with my legs crossed, smoking a cigar. I was escorted up the steps by the two uniformed chauffeurs." He basked in this world of make-believe greatness. But no one was fooled—not even himself. You're happy in old age or you're not. You can have "the unfading loveliness of a calm and gentle spirit" (I Pet. 3:4, Moffatt), but if you do, then you will bring that unfading loveliness into old age. And it must be real.

O Jesus, I thank Thee that the touch of Thy creative spirit can be upon my life, inwardly and outwardly, forever. Amen.

AFFIRMATION FOR THE DAY: *My adventure in God is young. I have had only a running start—the course is forever.*

GROWTH AFTER PHYSICAL GROWTH CEASED

We saw yesterday that if we are to have a beautiful old age, we must decide that it will be so. It won't just happen by circumstances, however pleasant they may be. We must grow from within out. We must be so reinforced from within that this reinforcement may push out the wrinkles and counteract decay.

What Paul calls "a growth divine" is a growth that makes growth possible after physical growth has ceased. It is the growth of the mental and spiritual which makes possible growth continuously and eternally. The grave and fatal mistake is to assume that the end of physical growth is the end of growth. I can only testify, but this year has been the greatest year of growth I've known in my sixty-nine years!

Sometimes God allows the pain of a slight ailment in old age in order to make us more careful of larger issues. We become more disciplined—disciplined in our general habits to take care of the slight ailment and thus tone up our general health and thus live longer. The little is the agent of the larger better.

A French philosopher has said: "To exist is to change, to change is to mature, to mature is to go on creating oneself endlessly." But not only creating oneself, but others, endlessly. We are contagiously creative.

This tips life forward, not backward. We are the people of expectancy, not of reminiscence. But some of us are like "the rod of Aaron that once blossomed" (Heb. 9:4, Moffatt)—"once blossomed" —it was a remnant of the past, instead of a reminder of the future, a "has-been" instead of a "to-be."

But with the impact of Life upon life there is constant stimulus toward expectancy. "Something momentous is going to happen today," wrote Mary. "I feel it." But the momentous is always happening to her, for she puts the meanings of eternity into the passing hours. This verse expresses it: "He shall blossom like a lily, and strike roots down like a poplar" (Hos. 14:5, Moffatt). "Like a lily"—beauty; "like a poplar"—strength. Strength and beauty combine to make old age glorious.

O Father, make my old age tender with love and strong with Thy strength and growing with Thy life. Amen.

AFFIRMATION FOR THE DAY: *Old age shall not creep on like a dread disease. I shall meet it with a cheer, for I am ageless in God.*

GROWING OLD GRACEFULLY AND GROWINGLY

It is a beautiful thing to grow old not only gracefully but growingly. But it is an awful thing to come to old age frustrated. Here was a man who had difficulties in getting along with his wife. Her sharp tongue made him retreat into apparent insanity when dealing with her, but with others he was perfectly sane. He became a dual personality in old age. He escaped the sharp tongue by retreating into imbecility and yet retained his self-respect when dealing with others. Christ could have gathered that sundered personality and made it into wholeness by giving him power to use the sharpness of his wife's tongue to prod him forward into God and victory.

In contrast to the above:

A gold medal for distinguished service to humanity has been awarded to Dr. Lillian M. Gilbreth—engineer, psychologist and author—by the National Institute of Social Sciences. Dr. Gilbreth is in her seventies. She is an engineer, psychologist and professor, also mother of twelve children, author of ten books, recipient of nine academic degrees and an industrial consultant presiding over her own corporation.

Many in old age are religious but soured. They seem to have read the Bible called "the Vinegar Bible"—a Bible where "vineyard" was printed "vinegar." Many seem to have nourished their souls on "the Vinegar Bible." Many live in the Old Testament more than the New. They nourish their souls on a sub-Christian conception of life. Hence they have a sub-Christian type of life. They haven't "a New Testament face." They are grouchy and frustrated. A professor asked some college students the definition of "pious" and got the answer: "One who is difficult to get along with."

But a religion that makes old age beautiful by ripening the character and disposition is the most beautiful thing in the world. When someone asked Frank Wright, the famous architect, now eighty-three, what he would select as his masterpiece, he replied: "My next one." He was right—it should be for us all.

O living Christ, keep the stimulus of Thy Spirit within me so that I shall be inwardly reinvigorated up to the end. Amen.

AFFIRMATION FOR THE DAY: *There is no end to the Christian, only eternal beginnings; and old age can be one of them.*

OLD AGE THE MOST FRUITFUL

It is possible to make old age the most fruitful part of our lives. *Sunshine Magazine* reports that an examination of the careers of some four hundred men, the most notable of their time and outstanding in many activities—statesmen, painters, warriors, poets, writers—shows that the decade between sixty and seventy contained 35 per cent of the world's greatest achievements; between seventy and eighty, 23 per cent; after eighty, 8 per cent. In other words, 64 per cent of the great achievements have been accomplished by men who have passed their sixtieth year.

A lady in charge of a school she had built up through the years saw it burn when she was seventy-six. She rebuilt it. And then at eighty-one she fell and dislocated her spine. She has recovered and at eighty-two runs her school and is radiant.

Here is another woman who at seventy-six went to college. She teaches during the winter and goes to summer school during the summer. She is now eighty and will soon graduate.

A Portland lawyer is still practicing at ninety. His formula for living long is "light eating and as little worrying as possible." He remarked, "I'm ready to go when my time comes, but in the meantime I don't intend to worry myself into the grave."

Winston Churchill, speaking of his seventy-seventh birthday, said, "We are happier in many ways when we grow old than when we were young. The young men sow wild oats. The old grow sage."

Some of the old Quakers, when they had a good year of spiritual growth, were allowed to add one fourth of an inch to the brim of their broad hats. Among the American Indians of the west coast there is the custom that when they have had a good week spiritually, they sit on the front seat in church; if a bad week, at the rear; and if a mediocre week, then halfway back. The pastor can glance over his audience and see what kind of week they have had. But the best indication of growth is not broader brims on hats or front seats, but an expanding mind and a front-seat soul, eager for truth.

O Father, I thank Thee for the years that come and go and leave enrichment and growth and peace and poise. Amen.

AFFIRMATION FOR THE DAY: *Since creation is at work within me, I shall be creative up to the end of my earthly existence.*

"NOBLE JO"

A few days ago I was in the town where Dr. Kagawa was born. When someone asked Dr. Kagawa if he knew Dr. Logan, he smiled a broad smile and said, "He was the one who first showed me the blueprint of love." It was Dr. Logan who led Kagawa to Christ. When Dr. Logan retired from Japan by reason of the age limit, he went to America and established four new churches.

I had the privilege of seeing and talking with one of God's noble-women a few days ago—Mrs. Nobu Jo. She is eighty-two and stone deaf and lame, but she came to my service and had someone write what I was saying. She is affectionately called "Noble Jo," and rightly. She put up a sign near a place famous for suicides: "Wait a moment! God is love! Anyone contemplating suicide may come to Mrs. Nobu Jo, and she has help for you." Over five thousand would-be suicides, see-ing that sign, have come to her for help and have found it. Her greatest work began when an old farmer in America, hearing of her work, sent her five yen, saying it was small, but he hoped it would help her in her work. She felt the responsibility and spent three days and three nights in prayer and then came down with a sense of mis-sion. And how mightily she has carried out that mission! When her whole plant was destroyed by the bombing, she began all over again at seventy-six to rebuild it. And she did! When a Buddhist offered to rebuild it for her if she would leave out the name of Christ, she refused. She was made permanently lame by an injury in running away from the fire which destroyed her plant. And now at eighty-two she is responsible for four hundred women under her charge. While talking to me she emphasized a point by banging her fist into a tray of teacups which was being offered but which she didn't see. She wiped off the scalding hot tea and without wincing went on with her story. She had been in hot water before! Eighteen times she has been attacked seriously by ruffians. For she knows how to fight crime, and she fights it righteously and successfully. "Noble Jo," those who love courage and admire dedicated lives salute you!

O Father, we thank Thee for those who have fought a good fight and have kept the faith and of whom the world is not worthy. Amen.

AFFIRMATION FOR THE DAY: *Old age is just a new page upon which you can write life's noblest chapter.*

STEPS IN GROWTH IN OLD AGE

We come to consider the steps by which we can make old age a blessed period.

First, *Don't retire. Change your occupation.* After a few months of retirement you'll get restless. Change your occupation to something you have always wanted to do. We are made for creation, and if we cease to create, we cease to live.

Second, *Learn something new every day.* Someone has said, "The sense of drift, which is the passive way of feeling the loss of the *élan* of growth, is one of the most powerful of the tribulations that afflict the souls of men and women who live in an age of social disintegration." To keep free from this "sense of drift," mark out lines of study and fulfill the marked out portion each day.

Third, *Set yourself to be gracious to somebody every day.* You will find life worth living if you make it worth living for someone else.

Fourth, *Don't let yourself grow negative; be positive.* A very successful chaplain dealing with tragic cases of amputation in hospitals got the amputees to undertake to cheer up the others. He got them to wheel themselves around to other cots and tell the men how many possibilities are open to amputees. They pushed out the negative by the positive.

Fifth, *Look around you to find something for which to be grateful every day.* And as you look for things for which to be grateful, they will pop up everywhere. And the spirit of gratitude will grow the more it is exercised. Gratitude will become a settled habit.

Sixth, *Now that your bodily activities are slowing down, let your spiritual activities increase.* As life becomes more inward, make that inwardness an increased opportunity for prayer. You can gather the world to your heart and broaden your influence through prayer.

Seventh, *Keep laying up as the years come and go "the good store" of which Jesus spoke.* This "good store" is the depository of every thought, motive, action, attitude, which we drop into the subconscious mind. It can be the deep subsoil into which we can strike our roots in old age and blossom at the end like a night-blooming cereus.

O Father, "Thy years shall not fail," nor shall mine, for my life is rooted in Thee, not in years—I'm yearproof. Amen.

AFFIRMATION FOR THE DAY: *I am young in God, therefore young in myself, therefore young in years.*

GROWTH IN SPIRITUAL CONTAGION

We come now to an important area of growth—growth in spiritual contagion. Christianity is catching, and if people aren't catching it from us, perhaps we haven't a sufficiently valid case of Christianity.

Christianity is not merely a conception; it is also a contagion. And when the contagion is lost, then the conception too is lost. For you cannot long be evangelical if you are not evangelistic. It is a law of the mind that that which is not expressed dies. And if our Christianity is not expressed in evangelism, it soon dies as a fact within us. Nothing is really ours unless we share it. For the moment someone else shares our faith, then that faith means something more to us.

Evangelism is not then an imposition into particular days and weeks and periods; it is part and parcel of our Christian faith. Paul puts it this way: "You have contributed to the gospel from the very first day down to this moment; of this I am confident, that he who has begun the good work in you will go on completing it until the day of Jesus Christ" (Phil. 1:5-6, Moffatt). From the very day they stepped into the Kingdom of God they began to contribute to it—to spread it. It was not something they learned; it was instinctive. It was as natural as a baby's cry at birth.

The four words making up the Christian gospel are: "Come . . . see . . . go . . . tell" (Matt. 28:6, 7). We get a firsthand knowledge— we "come and see"—and then the instinctive impulse is "go and tell." And if there is no "go and tell" impulse, then the "come and see" experience has never been ours. Or if it has been ours, it has faded out.

A Jewish rabbi says: "All religions are glad to have inquirers come to them, but this Christianity is different—it seeks out the lost, it goes to the lowly, the undeserving, the sinful." And if it doesn't do so, then it sinks back into the Judaism out of which it came. When it loses the fervor, it loses the fact.

Evangelism, then, isn't something that we can take or leave and nothing happens; it is something which, if we don't take, we lose the very faith itself. For the expression of the faith is of the essence of the faith.

O Christ, I thank Thee that the moment we see Thee we want to share Thee. Then help us to see Thee anew. Amen.

AFFIRMATION FOR THE DAY: *I am contagious with contagion, loving with love, and redemptive with redemption.*

"MY BUSINESS IS WITNESSING"

Yesterday I went around the circle of Japanese pastors and laymen at a luncheon party and asked each man to tell his profession or business. One old man of eighty-two, with a very radiant and intelligent face, said: "My business is witnessing for Christ." And it was! And an interesting story lay behind it all. He had been the town roughneck, a seller of fish. He came to a church and as he lifted up a long pole, said: "You kill the devil in me, or I'll kill you and the devil in you too." (It was the day in which the Christians were supposed to be possessed of devils.) That night he was soundly converted—the devil was killed in him. And now he and a lady of sixty-four are prayer partners and go out together to win people. And they do! That town roughneck is an honored, respected citizen of the city.

Here is a blind man who sits at a busy intersection and reads aloud from his Braille Bible to the passersby, dropping into their busy hearts the words of eternal life.

And here is a young man afflicted with tuberculosis who read in the paper about newspaper evangelism and was converted by correspondence. His brother was the priest of a Buddhist temple, and the young man asked to be baptized in the temple. The brother prudently stayed away, but the mother met the pastor and the missionary and said, "I consent to his baptism because since he has adopted his new faith, his spirit has changed. He used to be angry and bad-tempered when his meals did not arrive exactly on time. Now he is sweet-tempered —something I'm sorry to say our faith could not produce in him. So baptize him in the temple." They did. And the young man lay on his bed and painted cards with texts of scripture and hung them in his window so the passersby could read. He changed them every few days. A number around him were converted.

These were in the authentic tradition of the Christian faith, which Harnack says "won all its early conquests through informal missionaries." On the other hand, a woman writes, "I had a real experience of God, and I did nothing about it, so it died."

O Father, help me to have an experience of Thee and to do something about it—and do it today. Amen.

AFFIRMATION FOR THE DAY: *I am a Christian, and I'm going to do something about it, and I'm beginning today.*

"A PROVEN ASSEMBLY LINE"

Christ said: "Ye are my witnesses." What does that mean? It means that Jesus is on trial again before the world, and every one of His disciples is called in as a defense witness. Suppose we refuse to say a word on His behalf; then by our silence we join the prosecution, for He said, "He that is not with me is against me." Or suppose that when called, we talk about ourselves and our achievements instead of talking about Him—then? Or suppose we mumble and apologize and talk in two directions—then? We let Him down—and badly.

And in the process we let ourselves down. Rev. 12:11 says: "They overcame him by the blood of the Lamb, and by the word of their testimony." They overcame by what He did—the blood of the Lamb—and by what *they* did—the word of their testimony. And if the word of our testimony is silent, then the blood of the Lamb is silenced too and does not speak in our behalf. We cut ourselves off from His cross if we do not take ours. We cancel its power for ourselves unless we pass on its power to others.

An amazing thing has happened in Korea. The Christian church in South Korea has doubled its membership from five hundred thousand to a million during the war. Part of this is due to immigration of Christians from the North, but most of this is from the Christians' witnessing wherever they were scattered and winning others. There was the custom of not baptizing a person unless he had first won someone else—that proved he was a Christian.

This verse is to the point: "Though by this time you should be teaching other people, you still need someone to teach you" (Heb. 5:12, Moffatt). The sign of real growth was that they were teaching others.

In a non-Christian paper in Japan was a cartoon with the title: "A Proven Assembly Line." It was the figure of a woman putting a garment around the shivering body of a little girl, and behind the woman stood Christ throwing a cloak around her shoulders. It is a proven assembly line—give out to others, and it will be given to you, pressed down and running over—especially running over!

O Christ, I reach one hand to Thee for grace and the other to those struggling in life's tempestuous sea. Amen.

AFFIRMATION FOR THE DAY: *I'm no choked channel of redemption. I'm open Godward and manward.*

"TO KNOW HIM, TO HELP OTHERS TO KNOW HIM"

I was in the most effective church I've seen in America, the Hollywood Presbyterian Church, a church which is organized for evangelism down to the last man of its 6,500 members. In the youth hall up in front was this motto: "To know Him, to help others to know Him." This sums up the Christian faith—to know Him ourselves as personal Saviour and Lord and to help others to know Him as personal Saviour and Lord. These two constitute the alternate beats of the Christian heart—the intake and the outgo, receptivity and response. And if both sides are not in operation, the Christian heart ceases to beat. Then we settle down to dead forms and dead attitudes and dead prayers—not prayers *for* the dead, but *of* the dead. "What do you do when you kneel in prayer as you enter the pew?" was asked of a church member, and the reply came: "I count forty." Really the whole thing counted for nothing.

This verse goes to the point: "Land which absorbs the rain that often falls on it, and bears plants that are useful to those for whom it is tilled, receives a blessing from God" (Heb. 6:7, Moffatt). Here are the two things so vital to Christian faith: receptivity—"absorbs the rain"; and response—"bears plants that are useful." This type receives a blessing from God. But if it only receives and never produces, then a curse falls upon it.

This passage is luminous: "He Who gives the seed to the sower" (II Cor. 9:10, Phillips). He gives seed to the sower—to the one who uses it. He gives it only to the sower. If you don't use the seed, then you won't get it. Your mind will dry up.

A man was talking about the glory of the church of Westminster Abbey. A little woman spoke up and said, "Wait a minute. Has anyone been saved here lately?" It was a good question to be asked of any institution and of any life. For "no heart is pure that is not passionate, no virtue is safe that is not enthusiastic," and no life is Christian that is not Christianizing. Save and be saved.

O Christ, give to me the heart that cares and shares and dares. And let me never be ashamed of Thee, my Saviour. Amen.

AFFIRMATION FOR THE DAY: *I am asking for seed, for I intend to be a sower today, sowing beside all waters.*

"I AM AT HAND"

When we have the will to evangelize and dedicate our powers to Him, then He takes over and gives them a plus. We become a surprise to ourselves—and others.

Mary writes:

I have noticed one thing—always when I come to the part of asking them to come to Jesus and walk His way and share the blessedness and glory of it, I quit and the Spirit takes over; for it sounds so good to my own ears I want to kneel at the altar and say "Lord, you've got me!" It is the Spirit, because I couldn't very well be evangelizing my own self! The rest of the talk may be stupid and full of flaws and bad grammar and all, but that part is flawless. That proves He takes over and does His own calling, and His sheep know His voice, not mine, and they respond accordingly.

Starr Daily tells of a prostitute, just converted, who stood on a street corner and poured out a perfect stream of scripture which she and others did not know she knew. It was apparently stored up in her subconscious mind in the pre-fallen days, and the Holy Spirit tapped that hidden reserve and let it pour forth in converting power. She was a surprise to herself—and others.

Someone asked a lady who was one of the most useful persons in the community how it was that she was so useful to God, and her reply was: "I suppose I am at hand." That's it—be at God's hand, and He'll use you.

Your powers are dead or dedicated. If they are dedicated, they are alive with God and tingle with surprising power. If they are saved up, taken care of for their own ends, they are dead.

A good word to a pastor concerning his laymen: "If you don't use them, you lose them." And they lose themselves.

We are made for creation, and the highest creation is in the realm of creating new lives, new hopes. If we are not creative there, then we are not fulfilling the highest ends of our being. Hence we are frustrated and unhappy. To be used in helping others to Christ is to be fulfilled at the highest.

O Spirit Divine, take over my powers and add a plus to them, turning me from ineffectiveness to effectiveness. In Jesus' name. Amen.

AFFIRMATION FOR THE DAY: *Remember*: *When you begin to witness, the Spirit takes over—He always does a good job.*

INWARDLY MADE FOR THE GOSPEL

As "prospect cards" were being considered, one card was about to be thrown into the wastebasket when a deaconess objected, saying that everybody should be visited. But this card was of a lawyer who had been untouched by any approach. The weakest team was sent to him and came back with three cards—the man, his wife, and his daughter. The lawyer himself went out in the next campaign of visitation evangelism.

Two laymen went out in a visitation evangelism campaign rather scared, for they had never done this work before, and they were especially shaky when they found that the first man on their list was a leading lawyer. They began, "We have come to ask you to join the church." The lawyer replied, "Is that all you want of me? If so, I'm not interested. Lots of people have asked me to join the church through the years, and if that's all you want, I'm not interested." "Well," they replied, "there is this other side about surrender to Christ, but frankly we don't know much about that ourselves. So we have begun on the only level we know—church membership." "Well," said the lawyer, "I am interested in this other side. Haven't you a commitment card?" (He had read something about it in the paper.) They fished one out of their pockets and handed it to him, and he slowly read it, took his pen and signed, and said, "I've always wanted to do that." And then he added, "Where do you go next?" They told him, and he said, "I'd like to go with you." He went through the whole of the campaign, and his conversion created a sensation. When couples would come to him for a divorce, he would hand them a copy of *Abundant Living* and would say to them: "Read that for a week, and then if you are still interested in a divorce, come back and I'll talk to you." He just needed that last push, and frightened men gave it—and won him!

Among the head-hunters of Formosa a tattooed old woman, affectionately called "Grandmother," persecuted and hunted by the then Japanese government, won a thousand people to Christ. She began a movement in which thousands have been won.

O Jesus, I do love you, I do love you. And I would sell this glorious product this day to someone who needs it—desperately needs it. Amen.

AFFIRMATION FOR THE DAY: *If I am available, God will send someone in need across my pathway today.*

"WILL YOU?"

When the minister pointed to where I sat with some young men in the gallery and said, "Young men, Jesus said, 'He that is not with me is against me,'" it went straight to my heart. I turned to a chum and said, "I'm going to give myself to Christ. Will you?" He replied, "No, I'm going to see life first." My first impulse as I turned toward Christ was to share it—"Will you?" That invitation was turned down, for he saw no "life" in me, so he sought it elsewhere. But when I found "life" for myself, the invitations began to be accepted.

A salt manufacturer in Japan found himself the only Christian in his city. He might have felt that the only thing to do was to play safe. But he didn't. He started in to win others. In six years he has been responsible for winning 265 people. He called a pastor and now has a church meeting in his office rooms on Sunday. He invited our mission there, and in one meeting there were 130 decisions. He said, "I have a passion to make my city a Christian city."

A doctor found a little dog by the roadside with a broken leg, had compassion on him, took him home and put the leg in splints, and kept him until he was well. Then the dog began to run around the house. But in a few days he disappeared. "That's gratitude," thought the doctor. "As long as he needed me he stayed, but when he didn't need me, he ran away." But the next day there was a scratching at the door, and here was the little dog back again. And he had another little dog with him—and the other little dog was lame!

A woman and her husband were arguing and drinking their way to the divorce court. Then the woman and I knelt, and she became profoundly changed. Each day she wrote in her book a letter to God, telling Him everything. Her little girl of nine asked if she could write something to God in the book. So she wrote, "Dear God, I'm thankful to You for making such a great change in Mummy. I hope you'll make the same change in Daddy." The impulse to share is inherent. John Wesley summed up his life impulse when he said: "I commend my Saviour to you."

O Christ, who can look into Thy face and not want to share Thee? Forever I shall cry: "I commend my Saviour to you." Amen.

AFFIRMATION FOR THE DAY: *If I am a Christian, I am inherently an evangelist. I shall not choke the impulse.*

322

THE WAY OF THE FIGHTER

This week we will look at five ways to face life—and then the Way.

What happened around Jesus seemed not just local happenings; they seemed seed happenings—happenings with a universal significance. Men are reacting to life now in almost the exact way they reacted to life then. They take the roads to the same dead ends, trying to make life work in the same impossible ways.

This thing called life is our problem and our possibility. How we react to it determines whether we exist in the frustration of life with a dead end or whether we live in the fruitfulness of life with an open end. In Jesus' day there were five groups who reacted in five ways to the pressure of life.

The first way was the way of the Zealot. The Zealot was the fighter. He wanted to stand up and fight Roman domination, whatever the consequences. Jesus had one of these among His twelve disciples. He converted his pugnacious attitudes into construction for Kingdom purposes.

We have many today who are Zealots. They usually fight with those who do not agree with them and their doctrinal viewpoint. One such minister advertised that he was attacking me. I saw him the next day and asked how many were converted to Christ by his exposure of my many faults. I told him that I had had twenty-five people converted at the very time he was exposing me—what was his count? I asked him whether his gospel was the gospel of the weaknesses of Stanley Jones or the gospel of the strength of Jesus Christ? "I'm out to fight the devil," he replied, unconscious that the devil was invading him—his clouded, tense face being witness.

If we are in the prosecution stand, we are not in the witness box. If we are talking about the badness of others, we are not talking about the beauty of Jesus.

In the book of Revelation, Satan is given an interesting name—"the accuser of our brethren." That seemed to be his chief business—to tell what was wrong with "the Brethren." I wonder why those who echo that chief business don't see the relationship?

O Father, keep me from seeing the faults of others and not Thy saving beauty. Help me to see Thee and not them. Amen.

AFFIRMATION FOR THE DAY: *I shall be a Zealot for the finding of the good and appealing to it.*

THE WAY OF THE ESCAPIST

We are thinking about the five ways to get into dead ends.

The second is the way of the Essenes—the way of retreat. The Essenes were a group that withdrew from the strain and turmoil of life into monastic quietism. Life was too much for them, so they retreated out of it.

The modern counterpart of this attempt to escape from life and its responsibilities is the escape into illness and the escape into drink. A doctor in India told me of Hindu and Mohammedan purdah women who develop illnesses in order to get the freedom of the hospital from purdah (the veil). Here was a girl in India who was very active in public affairs, but after marriage was put into a family system where she was "under" the mother-in-law. She developed something like epilepsy to gain attention and sympathy. Another girl to gain attention vomited everything, even water, and had to be fed with a tube. Tests showed there was nothing physically wrong.

Some try to escape from life and its responsibilities and sorrows through drink. I took up a wine list in a diner by mistake, and at the bottom of the list I read: "Aspirin 25 cents." Someone has called this age "the age of aspirin." We get headaches to cure heartaches.

Others try to escape through diversions. A craze for slot machines has swept Japan. Nine hundred thousand slot machines for the playing of pachinko have been installed in about four years—one for every eighty persons in the country. Eleven per cent of the national budget now goes into these machines. Why this craze? To escape the awful spiritual emptiness caused by the defeat and the announcement of the Emperor that he was not divine. A philosophy of life broke down and left an inner vacuum. Into that vacuum are rushing all sorts of things to take over the lost loyalty. A Japanese doctor told me that tuberculosis had been displaced as killer No. 1 by circulation diseases, especially high blood pressure. "Why high blood pressure?" he was asked. And the reply: "Spiritual uneasiness." Many belong to the Essenes in their modern flight from life.

O Father, help me not to run away from life, but to run into the arms of Life. Then I can face life, whatever happens. Amen.

AFFIRMATION FOR THE DAY: *I have stricken escapism from my acceptable attitudes. I'm out for Life and more Life.*

THE WAY OF THE SELF-RIGHTEOUS

The third way is the way of the Pharisees. They stayed in life, but they inwardly stepped within themselves in the proud consciousness of superiority. They were the separatists. They were different—and superior, morally superior. That too was an escapism—an escape upward, supposedly, into an aloofness from the ordinary.

Those who take the way of the Pharisee are legion. "I thank God I am not as other men" resounds in varying accounts from many types of Pharisaism. Jesus said to His disciples: "Beware of the leaven of the Pharisees." It must have sounded absurd to tell a semicultured, semieducated group of disciples to beware of the leaven of the Pharisees, a group educated, proud, supercilious, and morally superior to the common herd, so they thought. But Jesus was right, as always. The leaven of the Pharisees has invaded us. And subtly. We are superior because we have a superior religion. Superior because our country is superior. Superior because our group is superior. Superior, because our denomination is superior. We get our superiority by proxy. But it is Pharisaism nevertheless.

This pride can be pride of lace—our clothes; pride of face—our looks; pride of race—our country; pride of grace—our brand of religion. It is all the same outcroppings of Pharisaism. And it is usually an inverted sense of inferiority asserting itself as superiority.

Only those who are truly great can afford to be humble. "Jesus knowing that the Father had given all things into his hands . . . took a towel . . . and began to wash the disciples' feet." The secret of His humility—His taking a towel—was His consciousness of His greatness—all things had been delivered into His hands. The Pharisee has to keep up a pretense of superiority, for he is inwardly not sure of that superiority. The truly great has nothing to keep up, for he knows that he is up—inherently. He isn't trying by taking thought to add a cubit to his stature, for he is sure of that stature. The Pharisee tries to escape from life and its realities by escaping upward into supposed superiorities—a road with a dead end.

Dear Father, save me from Pharisaism—my particular brand, and make me real—real in the fiber of my thoughts and actions. Amen.

AFFIRMATION FOR THE DAY: *I shall tolerate nothing on the outside that is not an expression of the inside of me.*

THE WAY OF THE MATERIALIST

The fourth way is the way of the Sadducees. The Sadducees were the materialists. They believed in no future life—"neither angels nor spirit." "The Sadducees, who were annoyed at them teaching the people and proclaiming Jesus as an instance of resurrection from the dead" (Acts 4:2, Moffatt). The crux of that objection was the phrase "as an instance"—they didn't mind so much the idea, but "as an instance"—that hit them hard, for they were the supposed realists, and here was "an instance." So they did what all materialists try to do—settle things by force: "They laid hands on them and . . . put them in custody" (v. 3). As if you could put an idea, and especially an incarnate Idea, into custody!

Here was the head of a well-known industrial empire who, when he found he had an incurable malignancy, committed suicide—a physical remedy for a physical malady. He knew no other remedy, for his values were all material.

In the world situation the materialists think that the only remedy for Communism is to put it down by force, not seeing that the thing that produces Communism is the uprising of the depressed portions of humanity who feel out of things and exploited. And they are! The only way to defeat Communism is to lift the exploited, depressed masses and let them share our lot—economically, socially, politically, culturally. The remedy is partly material and partly spiritual, for the disease is partly material and partly spiritual. But the materialist, like blind Samson, blindly pulls down the temple of civilization by precipitating war in order to get rid of a spiritual malady.

The blindness of the materialist is to be seen in the fact of the leaders of the Jews giving the soldiers money to say that the disciples had stolen the body of Jesus. They tried to stop the resurrection of Jesus by money—"a considerable sum"! The peoples of the world are rising from dead submission and are asking for equal rights and privileges. And giving money for rearming of nations won't stop them. You have to help that rising by going out to give "liberty and justice for all."

O Father, help me to believe in the rising of the people, and help me to help them to a fullness of life in Thee. Amen.

AFFIRMATION FOR THE DAY: *I shall accept the ferment of ideas and action as the new wine which must be put into new wineskins.*

THE WAY OF THE COMPROMISER

We come to the next way men tried in those days to face life: *Fifth, the way of the Herodians.* This group too felt the pressure of life and its demands, and they devised a method of meeting it—they allied themselves to power. Herod was in power, so they allied themselves to Herod and were called Herodians. They were the "yesmen" of that day. They were the compromisers, ready to do anything that furthered their ends. The Herodians are still with us.

Many are of the type who try to be ingratiating to everybody. If the crowd drinks, they drink too. "You must stand in," even if "standing in" means standing in moral mush, or worse, moral mud. "You don't expect me to stick my neck out, do you?" Well, if you don't stick your neck out on some issues, there will not be an idea in your head worth sticking out. Government officials during the war came to the principal of the Kobe College, Japan, and told him to take the Bible off the pulpit in the chapel. "Do you want me to close the college?" he quietly replied. And then they insisted that the constitution of the college be changed and the Christian dedication part be left out. And again he replied: "Do you want me to resign?" They backed down on both counts. And this man who refused to be a Herodian instead of a Christian is now the respected head of a flourishing college. The government officials have disappeared from sight.

The spirit of Herodianism persists in the world today in people who are followers of policy instead of principle. To find an exception is refreshing. A member of the Japanese Parliament dared oppose the regime about the war. He was thrown into prison. There he got hold of a Bible, was converted, and on release became a pastor. Then while a pastor he became mayor of the city. He chose principle, so the people chose him. Some Hindu merchants voting for Congress Party also sent contributions to the Communist Party with the request that they be marked "Anonymous," thereby hoping that if the Communists came to power, they would "stand in." But Herodianism is a dead failure. It is backed by nothing real in the universe and becomes nothing. It is a dead end.

O Father, I thank Thee that everything is doomed to failure but Thy way. Help me to take it—at any cost. Amen.

AFFIRMATION FOR THE DAY: *I shall ally myself with no authority save only with the Throne of the universe.*

THE WAY OF THE CHRISTIAN

We have seen five powerful classes of people take five different ways of facing life—the way of the Zealots, the Essenes, the Pharisees, the Sadducees, and the Herodians. Each as a group passed away and left deep disillusionments. But another way remained.

Sixth, the way of the Christians. When the pressure of life came upon them, they turned to Christ and fastened their allegiance upon Him. It seemed so risky, for the gathering storm told that He would be crucified. But they risked their all upon Him. And won! The other five groups have passed away, but these Christians live on! And how! Jesus said to the little group around Him: "Fear not, little flock; for it is your Father's good pleasure to give you the kingdom." It seemed absurd! This little group of nobodies to rule—to have the Kingdom? But that statement, so absurd then, has become literal fact. The idea and principles and spirit which they embodied have become the ruling ideas of civilization. They have ruled and still do rule the development of civilization. To the degree that civilization has been built upon their ideas, to that degree has civilization flourished; to the degree it has rejected those ideas has civilization floundered. The Kingdom has been given to them. They are the real rulers. Why?

Well, for one thing, they surrendered to the right Person and accepted the right principles of life. Everybody surrenders to something—each group did. The Zealots to resistance, the Essenes to retreat, the Pharisees to incasement, the Sadducees to materialism, the Herodians to power. The Christians surrendered to Christ. But having surrendered to Christ, they surrendered to nothing else. Low at His feet, they stood straight before everything else. Having run into His arms, they ran away from nothing else. They faced everything and they used everything—sorrow, loss, opposition, life—everything—and made something else out of it. The cross became their one dear symbol, and it stood for the worst becoming the best, the darkest becoming the lightest, and the cruelest becoming the most contributive. There they set their pains to music, turned their Calvaries into Easter mornings. Life was not dodged; it was developed.

Dear Lord and Saviour, I thank Thee that I need be conquered by nothing save by Thee. There I want to be conquered. Amen.

AFFIRMATION FOR THE DAY: *I am a Christian and therefore unconquerable save by love.*

"PREDESTINED TO OBEY JESUS CHRIST"

We have found that the Christians were not running into roads with dead ends, except as they deviated from the way of Jesus. They were on the Way with an invincible certainty. They felt that the sum total of reality was sustaining them.

They felt the truth of this statement from the Wisdom of Solomon: "For the creation, ministering to its Maker, straineth its force against the unrighteous for punishment." They felt that creation was not only straining its force against unrighteousness; it was also backing them.

They also knew that life now added up to sense and not nonsense. They felt a pattern being worked out and that they were a part of that pattern. They knew that the Kingdom would come no matter how many setbacks there might be. A Jewish rabbi unconsciously witnessed to this ultimacy of Jesus and the Kingdom: "I don't believe Jesus is the Messiah. I don't believe the Messiah and His Kingdom will ever come. But if it should come, I couldn't think of anything higher and more beautiful than that it should embody the spirit of Jesus."

They knew the truth of what Jesus said: "Inherit the kingdom prepared for you from the foundation of the world" (Matt. 25:34). This Kingdom was "prepared," built into the foundation of the world. It formed the structure of reality. And this Kingdom was prepared for them. The laws of the Kingdom were the laws of their own beings. So when they obeyed the Kingdom, they obeyed the thing for which they were made—they were obeying themselves. Hence freedom.

Life was not now a bundle of remnants; it was all of a piece. There was a wholeness—a wholeness that became a holiness. All life had meaning, was sacramental.

These people felt they were destined for this, "predestined . . . to obey Jesus Christ" (I Pet. 1:2, Moffatt). And that destiny was written into the fiber of their beings, in their nerves, their blood, their tissues. The Way was in them, and they were on the Way.

O Christ, I'm predestined to obey Thee. I can live against that destiny —and get hurt. Help me this day to fulfill my destiny. Amen.

AFFIRMATION FOR THE DAY: *I am destined to be a Christian. I shall work out that destiny with joy.*

GROWTH IN BALANCED VIRTUES

We now turn to growth in balanced virtues. Sometimes we are growing but growing lopsidedly, with virtues out of proportion.

A French philosopher once said that "no man is strong unless he bears within his character antitheses strongly marked." Each virtue must be balanced by its opposite virtue and held in a living tension. This tension makes a growing point.

One can see these antitheses strongly marked in Jesus. He was militant and passive—militant in that He was projecting the most redemptive movement, the Kingdom of God, into the total life to affect a total change; passive in that He unresistingly went to a cross without a murmur or complaint. He was world-renouncing and world-participating—world-renouncing in that He could say: "I am not of the world"; world-participating in that He lived His life out in intimate human relationships and finally died for the world.

He was tender and He was terrible—tender in that He wept over a city and at the grave of His friend; terrible in that He drove the usurpers out of His Father's house with whipcords of tongue and lash. He had the strength of the man and the qualities of the woman—the strength of the man in that Pilate could cry: "Behold the man," the qualities of the woman in that He could say: "As a hen gathereth her chickens under her wings." He was a man of prayer and a man of action—of prayer in that He spent whole nights in prayer; of action in that "He went about doing good." He was self-renouncing and self-asserting—self-renouncing in that He "emptied himself" (Moffatt), and self-asserting in that He said: "I am the way, the truth, and the life."

There is a leaning tower in China built by a ruler who saw in a dream a spirit who was lame and therefore crooked. We always make our earth in the image of what we see in the sky. "Show me your gods and I'll show you your men." We become like that which we worship. If our God is unbalanced in character, we become unbalanced. We can be grateful, very grateful, that the center of our faith and our loyalty was the most balanced Character ever seen on our planet.

O Christ, take the chisel and make me into Your image. Help me not to wince when You cut and cut deep. Amen.

AFFIRMATION FOR THE DAY: *I am God's workmanship. He will not botch His job unless I wince and pull away.*

SELF-CRITICISM AND OTHER-CRITICISM

It was said of Moses that he was "a strong man in speech and actions" (Acts 7:22, Moffatt), and of Jesus it was said He was "strong in action and in utterance" (Luke 24:19, Moffatt). Moses was strong in speech first, then action. This is interesting, for he told God he was "slow of speech," but when he once got started, he made a speech that covered the whole book of Deuteronomy! In Jesus it was the other way around—"strong in action" was first. The content of His actions went into His words—and what a content!

In some of us the two have gone out of balance—our words have outgrown our actions. We talk more than we do. And very often the talking substitutes for the doing. And we are building a crooked tower, leaning wordward. On the other hand, there are those who are strong in deeds and weak in words. They cover up their lack in winning others by substituting deeds. Both are wrong. Deed and word should be the alternate beats of the Christian heart. And each beat should equal the other.

Someone has defined piety as "the art of right growing." But if the growing is "right," it must be balanced growing.

There is another way in which we must grow symmetrically—in self-criticism and other-criticism. In Rev. 4:6 (Moffatt) are these words: "Four living Creatures full of eyes inside and outside." They had eyes on the "inside" to see themselves, and eyes on the "outside" to see others. But the "inside" was first. And both are necessary. If you turn your eyes always on the inside, you become morbidly introspective; and if you continue doing so too long and too intensely, you become neurotic. On the other hand, if you look at others too much and not at yourself, you become critical and a motepicker. If some people were as good in telling what is wrong with themselves as they are in telling what is wrong with others, they would be wonderful Christians. Now they are only wonderful Pharisees. Some have cataracts on the "inside" eyes and powerful bifocals on the "outside" eyes. As we go periodically to an oculist to get our glasses adjusted, so we must go to the great Oculist and have our "inside" and "outside" eyes corrected.

O Father, take away my tendency to look one way or the other, and help me to see my life steadily and see it whole. Amen.

AFFIRMATION FOR THE DAY: *I shall see myself through the eyes of Christ, and then I'll see others with love-anointed eyes.*

331

THE KINGDOM AS GRADUAL OR SUDDEN?

Are we to "build the Kingdom of God," or are we to await the return of Jesus to set up the Kingdom?

We might point out first of all that we are not taught in the pages of Scripture to "build" the Kingdom. To "receive" the Kingdom, to "proclaim" the Kingdom, to "suffer for" the Kingdom, but not to build. This Kingdom is built—"built from the foundation of the world." It is the absolute Order ready to break into our relative order if we submit and "receive" the Kingdom. "Let us be grateful for receiving a kingdom that cannot be shaken" (Heb. 12:28, R.S.V.). Note "receiving."

While we don't build the Kingdom, nevertheless we can be the agents of its coming—it can come through us. We receive it and we transmit it. The Kingdom is to come through us by gradualism. The Kingdom of God is "like a grain of mustard seed" that grows into a great tree. The Kingdom of God is "like unto leaven" which leavens the whole lump. These and other passages teach that the Kingdom will come by gradualism—heart to heart, clime to clime. When we pray "Thy Kingdom come," it literally means, "Let thy Kingdom come through me; I surrender to it to be the agent of it—now."

But there is another set of passages which teaches that the Kingdom will come by apocalypse with the return of Christ. The Kingdom of God is like unto a man who "went into a far country to receive a kingdom, and to return," evidently referring to Jesus' going to the Father to receive a Kingdom and to return to set it up.

Some take only the gradualism; some take only the apocalyptic. But you can't take one or the other without disrupting the account, for both are integral parts of the account. Each without the other is a half-truth. The gradualism gives us a task—to be the agent of the coming of that Kingdom *now*. And the apocalyptic, or sudden coming gives us a hope—that the last word will be spoken by God and suddenly when we least expect it. So Europe with its major emphasis on the apocalyptic and America with its major emphasis on gradualism are both living on half-truths and growing lopsidedly.

O Father, save us from lopsided emphases and hence lopsided personalities. Help us not to separate what Thou hast joined. Amen.

AFFIRMATION FOR THE DAY: *I shall endeavor to produce the new man out of both parties in every situation.*

"WISDOM AND REVELATION"

We come now to see another pair of opposites which must blend. "May the . . . glorious Father, grant you the Spirit of wisdom and revelation" (Eph. 1:17, Moffatt).

Note the two: "wisdom" and "revelation." Some emphasize the "wisdom"—man's coming to his own wise conclusions by trial-and-error test and the accumulated wisdom of the past. This, says John Dewey, "is the only revelation"—the slow unfolding of verified experience—wisdom. It is from man up.

On the other hand, there are those who say that the only way to learn is from God down—from "revelation." They despise all this manside of wisdom through accumulated knowledge and experience. Nothing can come to us except it come through the Book. It cancels out the whole scientific approach. A tension is set up between man's approach and God's revelation through the Book.

This is a false antithesis. The God who put the facts within nature and unfolding human experience is the same God who reveals Himself finally and perfectly in Christ. And as we work up from the facts and down from revelation, we come out at the same place—Christ.

During the 1948 crisis, Warren Austin, United States representative to the UN, urged Arabs and Jews to get together and settle their problems "in a true Christian spirit." That was put in the *Reader's Digest,* under the caption "Tripping Tongues." But that wasn't a bad break. It would be accepted as sense by Hindus and Mohammedans. "I hope I showed the true Christian spirit toward him," said a Hindu to me. A Hindu showing to a Mohammedan the true Christain spirit! Mixed up, but true. They saw this was the ultimate spirit. The facts of life drove them to that place.

Humanists look only for wisdom, and it turns out to be of the earth, earthy. The ultra divine-invasionists see only revelation. But the Christian position is wisdom and revelation. The Christian sees God supremely invading us in Christ and also pervading us and the universe.

O Father, I thank Thee that Thou art pervading me and invading me. I accept both joyously and gladly. Amen.

AFFIRMATION FOR THE DAY: *If my wisdom has no sense of revelation in it, it is less than wise.*

THE AGGRESSIVE SPIRIT AND THE YIELDING SPIRIT

We come to another pair of opposites—the aggressive spirit and the yielding spirit. One of the problems of life is to know when to yield and when to stand and be aggressive.

Wesley translates this passage: "Let your moderation be known unto all men" (Phil. 4:5), as "Let your yieldedness be known to all men." But all yieldedness would make us everybody's door mat, and all aggressiveness would make us everybody's thorn in the flesh. We must grow in yielding aggressiveness and in aggressive yieldedness. We must learn when yieldedness should operate, and when aggressiveness. Perhaps the principle that would be the right one is: Yield in small matters where no principle is involved, but stand up and be aggressive where big matters involving principle are concerned.

Sometimes we become aggressive over little things that don't matter and miss the really important things. A night watchman was instructed to watch carefully the tools of a contractor, and in the morning he triumphantly checked over every small tool and showed they were all there. But the steam shovel was gone—stolen! He gave his time to the little and missed the big! There is the story of an outfielder in an important series in baseball who was running to catch a fly, lost his cap, turned back to get it, and missed what ought to have been an easy out but became a two-base hit and decided the series! He made an issue of the little—a cap—and missed the big—the catch!

Some of us can't distinguish between shovels and steam shovels, between caps and catches. We exhaust ourselves in skirmishes and lose the battles and the wars. I know a man whose life is a failure as a whole. The reason is that he is always getting tangled up over little issues of personal prestige and small hurts and resentments. He is not aggressive at the place that counts—big issues, where principle is involved.

When we are wholly yielded to God, we don't mind yielding to men in little matters. For the center is secure. But the man who is not wholly yielded to God, not sure of the big, makes an issue of every little thing.

Dear Father, wash out my eye so I can see the big things as big and the little things as little. In Jesus' name. Amen.

AFFIRMATION FOR THE DAY: *No false prestige shall keep me from yielding in matters where I ought to yield.*

UNION AND FREEDOM

We come to a pair of opposites which, when not put into a living blend, cause a great deal of havoc—union and freedom.

The collective life of the churches of the world is being rent asunder because we don't know how to put these two things together. And the unionists and the freedomists are about equally to blame. The unionists insist that all denominations as such should be wiped out and with them, of course, all freedom of such bodies. On the other hand, the freedomists insist on freedom completely, and all union is wiped out. Both groups are unhappy, for they add to our "unhappy divisions." The monolithic unionists are just as responsible for division as the denominational freedomists. Both are existing on a half-truth.

The unionists must see that there must be freedom under the union, and the freedomists must see that there must be union. For there are two apparently contradictory urges within us—a desire for union and a desire for local freedom. Federal union puts these two urges into a living blend—there is real, organic union, and yet there is freedom under that union, local self-government, state's rights within the branches of the federal union. If the desire for freedom under the union is not satisfied, then one of two things will happen. Either the union will tend to become sterile and atrophy, lacking drive, or, if dynamic, it will break up into its constituent elements again.

Bishop Temple put it thus: "The united church must bring together all the elements of truth in all the several traditions, each unblunted as regards its definition and consequently as regards its cutting edge." But the traditions are "blunted" under monolithic union, and the cutting edge is gone, as experience has proved and is proving. This is true except where the monolithic union involves only one tradition in the uniting bodies. Where it involves several, the cutting edge is blunted. We will have to harness the drive of denominational loyalty to the collective good, to the union. Federal union would give the branches the sense of union and the sense of drive. It is therefore the union of the future. For it joins together what God has joined together in us—a desire for union and a desire for freedom.

O Father, help us to bring Thy people, sundered by half-truths, into the union around Thy principles of union and freedom. Amen.

AFFIRMATION FOR THE DAY: *We need to be completed in one another in order to be complete in God.*

SATISFACTION AND UNSATISFACTION

Here is another pair of opposites—satisfaction and unsatisfaction. Can they be put together?

There is a sense in which the Christian is a truly satisfied man. He feels that the center of his life has found its Center. This is "It"! He knows that he is "complete in Him." He doesn't need anything to piece out his life satisfactions. He has found them in Jesus. "Jesus satisfies" is simple and profoundly true.

But there is a sense in which the Christian is forever an unsatisfied man. Not dissatisfied, but forever unsatisfied. He doesn't want *other* than he has, but he does want *more* of what he has. And the moment we become satisfied with our satisfactions, then we are on the point of losing those satisfactions. My first public testimony, given a few days after I was converted, was this one: "There is only one thing better than religion—and that is more religion. I want more." I came into the Kingdom crying, "More." When I arose from knees after making my surrender to Christ, I took hold of a man beside me and said, "I've got it." What did I mean by *"it"*? Well, everything I wanted—reconciliation with God, myself, and life—yes, everything I wanted. But, strangely enough, that very satisfaction created within me an unsatisfaction. He touched me into satisfaction and unsatisfaction at one and the same time. Only God could do that!

And you want this new satisfied unsatisfaction to spread to all areas of life. If you are satisfied with it personally, you are not satisfied with its social application. We were talking to a group in Travancore, India, where Communism was a pressing problem, particularly as it related to land for the landless. A missionary spoke up: "The Christian is a satisfied man. He is saved by the blood of Christ. That is all he needs." If the missionary exchanged his spacious house for the grass hut of his outcaste converts and lived in their economic surroundings, would his satisfactions hold then? The outcaste convert's central satisfaction in Christ should drive him to be unsatisfied with his surroundings and improve them. And we should be driven to help him, or else his and our satisfactions are simply stagnations.

O Christ, satisfy me and stir me. Give me a content and a divine discontent. Thus I shall have peace and progress. Amen.

AFFIRMATION FOR THE DAY: *I am content with a divine content, I am discontent with a divine discontent.*

ON BEING ONE HUNDRED PER CENT

We come now to study our growth in percentage. Are we twenty-five, fifty, seventy-five, or one hundred per cent Christians?

There is a difference in trying to be one hundred per cent Christian and "perfectionism." In perfectionism you are striving for something that cannot be and therefore are frustrated when you attain less than perfection. Michelangelo, after he had produced "Moses," looked at it and said, "Thou canst not speak," threw down his chisel, and never looked at the statue again. That is perfectionism.

But being one hundred per cent Christian is different. That means that as of this moment you are one hundred per cent Christ's. It may be that the next moment you'll see areas of life which need yet to be surrendered, for surrender is once-and-for-all and yet continuous.

Look at the progressive surrender of the disciples: (1) They dropped their nets (Matt. 4:20). (2) Then they left the boats (v. 22). (3) And then their father (v. 22). And finally themselves. But the nets, the boats, the father, all went before they came to the final thing—themselves. And they didn't let go that last thing, themselves, until the day of Pentecost. There they offered their all, and God gave His all—the Holy Spirit. But even after that their "all" was an unfolding "all," and they found more and more meanings and applications in that word. But at any one period they could say, "He has my all up to this point, and according to my present light." That is what we mean by being one hundred per cent Christian.

All of us—the best of us—are only Christians-in-the-making. We are never "made." But at any given moment the surrender and the obedience should be one hundred per cent. Not like that of Johnny, who climbed on a chair, took the cookie jar down, slapped his hand, and said, "Johnny, don't," but took the cookie! He tried to satisfy the moral law by slapping himself and then tried to satisfy himself by taking the cookie! He was fifty per cent good. He was akin to the man who stood up in a testimony meeting and said, "I'm sinning on a progressively higher level." Which was a doubtful progression! We must be one hundred per cent good.

Dear Father, help me to be all-out. I've seen the Best in Jesus and now I cannot rest this side of that Best. In His name. Amen.

AFFIRMATION FOR THE DAY: *All my buds shall become flowers, all my flowers fruit, all my fruit seeds of the future.*

KNOW CHRIST; LOVE CHRIST; OBEY CHRIST

Bishop Sinker, of India, calls our attention to these passages of Scripture: "One thing I know"—the mind, "one thing have I desired"—the emotions; "one thing I do"—the will. To know, to love, to obey—these are the three steps in Christian living. To know Him more clearly; to love Him more dearly; to obey Him more nearly—these sum up the total growth in the total man.

"One thing I know." The enemies of Jesus tempted Him "to speak of many things," hoping to trip Him up in one of the many things. The devil tempts us as ministers "to speak of many things," to try to be an oracle in matters outside our sphere. But we must resist and say, "This one thing I know," and then point to the Redeemer.

"One thing have I desired." The enemy will try to introduce many desires into our lives—desires incompatible with the controlling love of Christ. Choke them. One psychiatrist said that half his patients were minister's wives. Why? Well, one reason was that they couldn't school themselves not to try "to keep up with the Joneses." They began to desire "many things," instead of "the one thing."

Paul could say, "This one thing I do." Many of us could say, "These forty things I dabble in." He left a mark; we leave a blur. He broke open a civilization; we don't make a dent. The world remembers him; it will forget us.

So these three things: "One thing I know"—know Christ; "One thing I desire"—love Christ; "One thing I do"—obey Christ. Then you can say with Paul: "For to me to live is Christ." And as you give a whole allegiance, you get a whole Christ.

Mary writes of going to church in a hurry and finding when she got up to sing that

I had forgotten to wear the belt to my dress. Three years ago that would have embarrassed me, but to my surprise I just smiled all over and sang louder and didn't even try to hide the fact. It made me feel grand to know I still do stupid things and that I can laugh now and not get upset over trifles.

Father God, I thank Thee that Thou art making me more and more single-minded, single-hearted and single-willed. Amen.

AFFIRMATION FOR THE DAY: *I'm on the Way with both feet, and I'm all out, inside and out and forever.*

THE HOLY SPIRIT IN THE SUBCONSCIOUS

If we are to be one hundred per cent Christian, then our subconscious must join the joy of being Christian. Can it be Christianized? If not, we can be only fifty per cent Christian—the conscious mind Christian and the subconscious mind unchristian.

A thirty-seven-year-old Sicilian had his legs atrophied by squatting thirteen years in a cellar where his mother had confined him to hide his madness from the neighbors. He was a medical student but developed schizophrenia, brought on by thwarted love for a baroness. When his whole condition was brought up and faced, he began to get well again. He is now learning to walk. Often we repress our conflicts and put them into the cellar, our subconscious, for we are ashamed to have ourselves, or our neighbors, know about them. The first thing to do is to bring them up and face them before God and ourselves. The second thing is to surrender the subconscious to God. Then the Holy Spirit, who fathoms the depths of God and the depths of us, moves in and cleanses and takes control of the subconscious and co-ordinates it with the conscious. Then we move from the fifty per cent to the one hundred per cent class of Christians.

Don't try to suppress the subconscious; it will only fester. And don't try merely to mop up the overflowings of a bad subconscious. Get to the very depths of it by surrender and acceptance of the Holy Spirit. I was trying to mop up the water in a cellar. But as the water did not diminish, I concluded that it was coming under a partition and filling in as fast as I could mop. I went behind the partition, and sure enough, there was a deep reservoir of water. I tackled it, and then the necessity of mopping on the other side ceased.

The area of the work of the Holy Spirit is behind that partition that separates the conscious from the subconscious. Some of us are worn out mopping up the overflowings of the subconscious into the conscious. There is an easier and more effective way. Don't mop up the subconscious as it flows into the conscious, but surrender your very all, including the subconscious, and believe that He undertakes where you can't touch.

O Holy Spirit, I am designed for Thy operation, and Thou art designed for my need. Move into the depths and cleanse and control. Amen.

AFFIRMATION FOR THE DAY: *With my subconscious mind Christian I can be Christian with all the stops out.*

GROWTH IN THE FAMILY SPIRIT

There is another area of growth where we must be one hundred per cent—the home.

Some of us are Christian in our public relations but unchristian in our home relationships. We may even class ourselves as one woman classed herself, "a street angel and a house devil." A wife tells of how her stomach turns over when she hears the sound of her husband's car coming up the driveway. What spleen will he take out on his wife which he didn't take out on his business associates? Or it may be the other way round—what nagging will he get from the dammed-up resentments of his wife?

As one wife wisely says, "The wife and mother usually hoists the sails of the family ship every day. We determine whether those sails shall catch the breezes of God's love and understanding, or the winds of bickering and discord." This gracious wife and mother adds, "When a man succeeds, he does so by climbing a ladder steadied by a woman who believes in him."

If the family group is to develop and grow as a group and as individuals, I would suggest two things: First, family worship—if not before breakfast, then at the breakfast table. The various books on devotion help those who are not trained to conduct or carry on devotions on their own. There the individual and the group get resources for the day. An Alcoholics Anonymous worker tells me how he carries around with him cut flowers to illustrate to the alcoholic how the flowers will soon wither because they are cut off from their roots. So one cut off from the resources of God withers.

Second, Let there be a Family Hour, preferably after supper, where family problems are brought up and faced and discussed in love, and suggestions entertained which are made for the improvement of the family life. This Family Hour will train the family group in group thinking and in co-operation. In our Ashrams the Family Hour is a safety valve when all questions and complaints and suggestions for improvement are brought up and cleared day by day. Thus they grow and grow together.

O Father, from whom every family derives its name and nature, help us to live together this day as a family of God. In Jesus' name. Amen.

AFFIRMATION FOR THE DAY: *I shall do my part in helping the family show the family likeness of the Father.*

APPLYING CHRISTIANITY TO BUSINESS RELATIONS

We come to another area into which we must extend our Christianity and become one hundred per cent. This area is our business or occupation.

A civilization is to be judged as Christian or not by the way it earns its livelihood. If our Christianity does not function there, it functions only marginally and does not affect the roots, therefore not the fruits.

Can capitalism be Christianized? I am convinced that it can be, provided it extends its benefits to the workers—its full benefits. This would mean a labor-capital management and an equitable division of the profits and losses. Sharing of losses takes place now in a brutal manner—unemployment. It would be far better for labor to share the losses when they come in a proportional cutting of their profits and their wages. To share profits should give a new incentive to labor. Production should automatically go up.

But I'm told by a big cotton manufacturer that this is not true unless profit sharing is coupled with labor-capital management. The laborer is not certain whether it is profit sharing or a bonus. Since he is not represented in the management, he is not sure about the profits —the books are not open to him or his representative. He looks on it as paternalism at its best, and that best is not good enough. If he hasn't a part in management, then he will be susceptible to the temptation of the Communist when he offers the laborer the control of the factory itself. The way to beat Communists is to beat them to it by making labor an integral part of capitalism.

A friend took over the management of a business in the red. He put in profit sharing the first thing and was soon in the black. The worker had a stake in the business, and he showed his appreciation by added production. This is good for capital, not only economically but morally and spiritually. The capitalist then feels he is working not only for himself but for others. This gives him a sense of loving his neighbor as he loves himself, therefore a sense of being more Christian —a higher percentage.

Dear Lord and Father, we pray Thee to make us Christian this day in all our relationships, especially the economic. Amen.

AFFIRMATION FOR THE DAY: *The acid test of how Christian our civilization is, is at the place where we earn our daily bread.*

CHRIST GIVES FLAVOR TO ALL LIFE

When we speak of being one hundred per cent Christian, there are those who have an inner question as to whether Christianity should claim our all. Can't we have too much of it? We certainly can have too much of offbrands of Christianity, centered in off-center emphases. But you can't have too much of Christ. For He is Life and gives flavor to all life.

A grocer told a friend of mine that he couldn't give him a fruit cocktail, for he had no pineapple. If pineapple were not put in, the pear would permeate the whole and turn the rest of the fruit into a pear taste. But pineapple gives its own flavor and in addition brings out the flavor of each constituent fruit. It augments the flavor of each.

Christ is that way. He adds His own flavor to life, but He also brings out the distinctive flavor of every right human quality and relationship. Our work is given an added zest and flavor, our homes are homes instead of houses, the stars twinkle as they never did before, sex becomes a sacrament instead of a sacrilege; we do everything for the love of God, and the love of God glorifies everything. You can't have too much of *that!*

This man was looking at another Jesus, not the real Jesus, when he wrote: "Now my taste for Jesus study has left no room for my professional work. I do not feel interested in my day-to-day office duties. As a result my health is going down gradually." He saw a Jesus who was calling him out of life—a false Jesus. The real Jesus makes all life vital and adventurous and sacramental. Then all work becomes "fun." When Mary wrote: "Have fun with Jesus," she was expressing a profound truth. Life is fun with Jesus. If it isn't, then life is no fun at all. It is a dull drudgery, instead of a dancing delight.

The song that says that "the things of the world grow dim when the face of Jesus I see" is questionable. The things of the world grow vivid and beautiful and attractive when I look into the face of Jesus. For He made those things, and when I see Him, I see them. And anything He makes is bound to be beautiful if I can see it with His eyes. Jesus puts taste into life—and what a taste!

O Christ, my Lord, Thou art the flavor of all that Thou dost favor, and Thou dost favor all real life—only on the false is Thy frown. Amen.

AFFIRMATION FOR THE DAY: *My Christianity shall be the flavor that brings out all the right flavors of life.*

"GEE-UP, GEE-UP"

All half-obedience brings a half-Christ with a half-result. Full obedience brings a full Christ with a full result. A village Christian in India had up a Christian flag in his compound. The Congress Nationalists asked him if he would put up a Congress flag. And he replied that he would. "Will you take down the Christian flag?" And he replied, "No." He was put in jail. When he came out, he won a number of villages to Christ. They listened to a man who was one hundred per cent. And there was a hundred per cent result.

A half-obedience ties us up to being a half person with half contribution. A man in a mental hospital who had large areas of sanity wrote a novel that was a masterpiece in the first half. The head of the institution read it with admiration and astonishment. It was really great. But the second half of the novel was nothing but a repetition of the word "Gee-up. Gee-up." When the superintendent asked the author why he filled the second half of the book with that phrase, he answered, "Well, you see, the hero had not untied his horse from the hitching post, so 'Gee-up' is all he could say for the rest of the book." The author was rather sane in his insanity—he saw that if you don't cut loose from certain things, from some hitching posts in life, then you'll spend the balance of your days in a futile cry of "Gee-up!" It was probably his own life history. He was caught by a certain futile idea, and he couldn't unhitch from it. Many a Christian is caught in futility by a half-surrender and spends his days nagging at a nag called life that won't go anywhere.

An absent-minded don of an English university spoke in the chapel on the Ten Commandments and then, forgetting that he was not in an examination hall, said absent-mindedly, "Only five should be attempted." Many of us look on the Christian way as a relative way of life and ask ourselves for a fifty per cent obedience, forgetting that the Christian way is an absolute way demanding a total obedience in the total life. Jesus is Lord of all or not Lord at all. Anything less than a hundred per cent allegiance is bound by its very nature to be a disappointment. Jesus gives His full power to those who are fully His.

O Jesus, since Thou hast given Thy All for me and to me, help me this day to give my little all for Thy great All. Amen.

AFFIRMATION FOR THE DAY: *I have untied my life from all hitching posts that hold me up. I'm free to live!*

GROWTH IN FREEDOM

We come this week to consider growth in freedom. Everyone wants freedom. A little Filipino boy was taking an examination before the Philippines got their freedom. The subject was a cow, and he described the cow as follows: "A cow is an animal that stands upon four legs, fastened at the four corners. A cow gives milk, but as for me give me liberty or give me death!"

We all want freedom, but so few know how to get it. They seek it first, and if you seek freedom first, you'll miss it. We are made not primarily for freedom, but for obedience. Freedom is a by-product of obedience. If you put freedom first, it will be the freedom to get tied up with yourself and others. Some try to get freedom by doing as they like; others try to get freedom by doing as they ought. Only the latter find freedom. The first freedom turns to futility. The second freedom turns to fertility.

The first lie that was told was about this matter of freedom. Satan said to Adam and Eve, if you do as you like, "ye shall be as gods." More people get hooked on that bait than on any other. Satan is a skillful player and lets you take the first few tricks in the game of freedom, and then he cleans you out.

But Satan isn't quite so clever as he seems. In reality he is a fool. For everything he brings on others comes on him. When he prepares a hell for others, he himself has to live in it. He seems to have a freedom to ruin, but it only turns out to be a freedom to ruin himself.

There is only one way to be free, and that is through obedience. But this must be qualified thus: obedience to the right thing. You can obey and end in bondage if you are obeying the wrong authority. The center of your obedience must be set straight.

There is nothing more fallacious than saying, "Any faith is good, provided you are sincere." You may sincerely follow the wrong thing to a wrong destination. Sincerely sitting in a railway train, believing you are on the right train, won't get you to your destination if it is actually the wrong train. So freedom comes only through obedience to the right thing.

O Father, teach me to get this straight, for if I go wrong here, all life will go wrong with it. Help me to see straight. Amen.

AFFIRMATION FOR THE DAY: *I am free to choose, but not free to choose the results of my choosing. They are in hands not my own.*

"THE GOD THAT FAILED"

We ended yesterday by asking the question, What is the right thing to obey? James puts the matter thus: "Whereas he who gazes into the faultless law of freedom and remains in that position, proving himself to be no forgetful listener but an active agent, he will be blessed in his activity" (James 1:25, Moffatt).

What is this "faultless law of freedom?" What is the "law" that turns out to be a "law of freedom," and a "faultless" one to boot? Some would say that the center of obedience is the Pope as "the vicar of Christ." But all leaning upon "infallible" human authority lets you down—ultimately. "My religion has weakened me," said a Latin American youth to me. And he could have added, "Yes, and it has weakened a whole continent along with me." For it has. There is nothing infallible in the Pope except that he's infallibly fallible like the rest of us.

A friend of mine was an ardent Communist in India. The actions and attitudes of the Party members were decided by the Politburo, a group of nine men. He was assigned to wreck a train. The remnants of his Christian conscience, suppressed through the years in absolute obedience to the party behests, revolted. He resigned. They turned on him like a pack of wolves and tried to wreck him and his home. He said, "They had no respect for my personality. I was a cog in the party machine—or nothing." The perfect obedience was perfect bondage. A group of literary men, once enamored of Communism, wrote a powerful book entitled *The God That Failed,* telling the pathetic story of their obedience to a totalitarian system and then their disillusionment. Their initial freedom turned into ultimate bondage.

On the other hand, to make "the American way of life" an absolute is to commit the same blunder in another form. "The American way of life" is a compound of elements from Christianity, democracy, individualism—sometimes selfish and anti-social—and gadgetism. Any blind leaning upon it will result in disillusionment and bondage to a relativism. The god will fail us if we make it a god. "The American way of life" is valid to the degree that it fits into the Kingdom of God.

O Father, help me not to let my whole weight down on anything this side of Thee. In Jesus' name. Amen.

AFFIRMATION FOR THE DAY: *The half-gods inevitably let us down if we try to make God out of them.*

"THE FAULTLESS LAW OF FREEDOM"

Some make society the absolute and give it absolute obedience. How many things we do because others are doing them is obvious. A friend took twelve small boys aged three to six and looked after them while their fathers were at a banquet. One boy wanted a drink; all twelve had to have one! One boy wanted to go to the toilet; all twelve had to go! Up to a certain point this following of the herd gives freedom. You are not fighting the herd; you catch step and fall in. You are free—to follow.

But this lock-step mentality soon becomes an absolute, and you are in bondage. You are free only to conform, and a freedom to conform is a freedom to go into deeper and deeper bondage.

Some people just succumb to noise to give themselves release from themselves. Worshipers in some Buddhist temples strike the huge gong rhythmically and sway, singing with the noise. In this way they are supposed to be healed of mental and spiritual and physical diseases. The noise does draw them out of themselves and does make them forget themselves and to that degree is healing. A man back from a vacation in the quiet of the Adirondack Mountains stepped out of the train in New York, and amid the roar of trains and travelers put up his arms and said, "This is the life." The quiet of the mountains bored him; the roar of New York make him forget himself. Noise detracted him from his own self and his own problems. It is the Western equivalent of the Buddhist gong. The ritual and the results are the same—temporary freedom and then the moments when the facts of self in bondage intrude again.

All these are faulty laws of freedom. They crack under the pressures of life. Then where is "the faultless law of freedom"? It is not really a "law"—it is a Person. That Person is Christ. It is a strange and incredible thing, but the more we belong to Him, the more freedom we enjoy. And I mean "enjoy." It is freedom without a "catch" in it. You are not always waiting for the blow to fall. It is what Jesus meant when He said: "If the Son . . . shall make you free, ye shall be free indeed."

O Christ, the moment I step into Thee, that moment freedom pervades me to my fingertips. I thank Thee. Amen.

AFFIRMATION FOR THE DAY: *I am as free as the birds that fly and as bound to the goodness and bounty of God.*

"GRACE AFTER GRACE"

We saw yesterday that "if the Son . . . shall make you free, ye shall be free indeed." The "indeed" freedom distinguishes it from all other freedoms, supposed or real. It frees the total person, in his total relationships, for the total duration of his existence.

It covers the total person. The total person is attached to a Person in love. The code becomes a Character. You are not obeying a set of laws and regulations. That would produce a legalism, a meticulous obedience to a set of imposed laws for which we are more or less made —mostly less. The product is a very good Pharisee or a very good Brahmin. And the mentality is a legalistic righteousness that has pride of attainment at its core. It stands in the Temple and thanks God that he is "not as other men." But attachment to a Person makes love the outstanding characteristic and humility the outcome. For the relationship is that of grace, and one can never get over the wonder of that grace. It sends you to your knees in humility and lifts you to the highest heaven in rapture. He fills our boat with overwhelming blessings, and instead of feeling our importance as a result of our possessions, we fall at His feet and cry with Peter, "Depart from me; for I am a sinful man, O Lord." He gives something that can't be given except through grace, namely, a sense of abundant possessions and a sense of humility at one and the same time.

Therefore He doesn't have to limit our possessions in order to limit our pride. For the more He gives, the more we are overwhelmed by a sense of unworthiness. Hence the door is open for freedom to give infinitely and to receive infinitely. God's hands are untied because our pride is tied and our receptivity is therefore untied.

Therefore John could say: "For we have all been receiving grace after grace from his fulness" (John 1:16, Moffatt). We are scarcely over the surprise of one grace when another comes—it's "grace after grace." So life becomes one long growing in gratitude and one long growing in humility. Out of those two roots deeper and deeper love springs. The more He gives, the deeper the roots of gratitude and humility go, and the deeper they go, the more the fruits of love appear.

O Christ, my gracious Lord, your grace is so overwhelming that my love grows and grows but cannot keep up with it. Amen.

AFFIRMATION FOR THE DAY: *Today my hands shall be alternately opened to receive and folded to thank the Giver.*

THE ETERNAL CRY IS "MORE"

We looked yesterday at the freedom "indeed" and how God can give freely and how man can receive freely. And now we add another word: forever.

This freedom to give and this freedom to receive are limitless as to time—and eternity. For in giving ourselves to an infinite Person we are free to grow infinitely into the likeness of that Person. We soon outgrow rules and regulations. A religion founded on rules comes up against two inexorable alternatives: Either the people in growing break the rules, or the rules are so strong they break the people. A religion founded on rules produces a resistance from the growing, or a restriction of the growing. But not so in the Christian faith. For here the Character, who is our Code, is infinitely unfolding.

He is static in history—fixed in an account written in the New Testament. Something to which we can always refer, not as idea, but as fact. The standard is fixed as a norm in history, something to tie to. But not too tightly. For this goal is a flying goal. It is something fixed and yet unfixed. It is behind you in history and ahead of you now. The more you see, the more you see there is to be seen. No one can ever rest and say, "Now I'm completely Christian." For the definition of a Christian grows the more you see of Him who is the standard of what a Christian is.

That makes you free to grow and to grow forever. For the finite will approach the infinite and approach it forever but will never arrive at infinity. The eternal cry is "more." And the giving of "more" means more growth in gratitude and humility, therefore a safe growth. No fruitless sucker growth here. It is all solid, substantial, fruit growth. On the lowest branches is the low-hanging fruit of humility, and on the uppermost branches is the fruit of rapturous thankfulness.

We are grafted with a branch from the Tree of Life, and the Tree of Life is eternal in quality and quantity. You can't have too much of Life. So the vistas beckon, and Life within us urges us on to more abundant life and to endless growth in the image of the Divine. What a destiny!

O Christ, my Lord, I've come under continuous redemption and continuous release and freedom. I'm grateful. Amen.

AFFIRMATION FOR THE DAY: *This is the way to live, and I'll be a fool, a stark fool, to try to live any other way.*

"ALL COHERES IN HIM"

We have looked at "the faultless law of freedom" as being faultless in that it will never be outgrown. It is faultless again in that though it is a law seemingly imposed upon us, it is really the very law of our being. So it is not imposed; it is exposed as the thing for which we are made. So the revelation which Jesus gives of God turns out to be a revelation of us, since we are made in the image of God. The God-man reveals both God and man. He reveals man's sin as a fallen being. But even in the fall he retains the law of his being. As a fallen being he is living against himself as he lives against God. He is so fallen that he thinks that the laws of his being revealed in Christ are a foreign imposition. He revolts—against himself. A civil war ensues.

Hosea expresses this revolt against what are truly the laws of our being: "I have written to him the great things of my law, but they were counted as a strange thing" (8:12)—"a strange thing"—foreign and alien to his own nature. This is the central heresy—God's laws are not our laws!

But in Jesus we see ourselves writ large—in possibility. And when we accept His love as our discipline, we find that for the first time in our lives we're free—free to fulfill the very laws of our being, therefore "free indeed."

This verse expresses it: "For it was by him that all things were created both in heaven and on earth, both the seen and the unseen. . . . All things have been created by him and for him; he is prior to all, and all coheres in him" (Col. 1:16-17, Moffatt). Two startling things: all things are created *by* Christ and all things are created *for* Christ. The touch of Christ is upon all creation, and all creation, including us—and us especially—is made *for* Him, finds its meaning and completion in Him. Or as it is put here, "all coheres in Him"—holds together in Him. We find a coherent universe in Him. Out of Him it is all incoherent, adds up to nonsense. In Him life makes sense. Our sums are all adding up to the right answers. We are free to be sensible, to be coherent, to walk ways into opening vistas of integration and wholeness. We are free, free, free!

O Christ, I thank Thee for this amazing freedom to be myself, to know that in finding Thee I'm finding my very own. Amen.

AFFIRMATION FOR THE DAY: *A Christian is free to be what God intends him to be. The shackles are off.*

"BITTER TO DIGEST"

The final thing in the "faultless law of freedom" is the faultless way in which it is executed.

There are loopholes in every man-made law. Lawyers are often experts in finding those loopholes for their clients. A prominent lawyer who was in charge of the war-guilt prosecution in a certain country remarked to a friend of mine: "Laws are made to entangle people." The result is that many innocent people languish in jails along with the guilty. The execution of laws made and executed by man is faulty.

But this faultless law of freedom is perfect in its execution. For the moment you break the faultless law of freedom, you automatically go into bondage. The law is self-executing. You get tied up with yourself the moment you break connection with Him. "He went away sorrowful" is the history of every single person who gives up Christ for something else.

There is a passage to the point: "It will taste sweet as honey, but it will be bitter to digest" (Rev. 10:9, Moffatt). Evil has an initially sweet taste; then it is bitter to digest. The system is not made for it, cannot assimilate it. To lie, to steal, to commit adultery, to get revenge on enemies, to criticize others, all these are sweet to the taste, but they are bitter to digest. The soul rejects them, for the soul and evil are allergic to each other.

On the other hand, goodness tastes bitter, but it is easy to digest. To begin goodness you have to repent, and repentance is a bitter pill. But once you swallow it, it is easy to digest. The system accepts it as its own. And when Christ comes in, the every fiber of our being receives its very own. He is an affinity. All coming to Him has the feel of a homecoming upon it. "Now I can breathe as deep as I want to," said a soul who had surrendered to Him.

And this freedom is not precarious. It is as sure as a law. Fulfill the condition—obedience—and the law will work with a mathematical precision. So you are "free indeed," for you are free in fact, a permanent fact.

O Christ, my Lord, I accept Thee as my faultless law of freedom. In Thee I shall live and move and be free forever. Amen.

AFFIRMATION FOR THE DAY: *Living now under "the faultless law of freedom," one day I shall stand "faultless before the presence of his glory with exceeding joy."*

"BARRING THESE CHAINS"

We come now to study growth in convictions.

One of the most inspiring verses ever written about any man is this one concerning Paul as he stood before Agrippa about to be sent to Rome to undergo his execution. "I would to God that not only you but all my hearers today could be what I am—barring these chains!" (Acts 26:29, Moffatt). The grand old warrior was nearing the end of his course, and injustice was piled on injustice to crown his career. But the core held secure, so he could say to a king who sat as his judge: "I would to God that . . . you . . . could be what I am"—I do not pity myself; I pity you that you are not sharing what I am sharing, and knowing what I know, and realizing what I realize. His life convictions held. Not one iota was shaken! That is one of the noblest scenes in human history. And to that amazing strength is added this graciousness: "barring these chains!" I wouldn't want you to have them, but I feel sorry for you that you haven't the rest!

It is a great thing to have the years as they come and go deepen your life convictions so that they really become you. Paul didn't say, "I want you to believe what I believe"—he wanted that, but he wanted more; he wanted them to be what he *was!* The life convictions had become him. They were one. That is growing in convictions—life and convictions grow into a living unity and harmony.

On the other hand, nothing is more pathetic than to see a man as the years come and go have his life convictions fall apart. The years have battered them to ruins. They were not big enough to stand up under life.

I sat in a train at evening time having my Evening Quiet Time and asked myself this question: "Stanley Jones, you have walked with Christ through half a century in many climes, under many circumstances, often very stumblingly, but what have the years taught you? What do you really believe? What holds you? What are the basic convictions of your life?" So I took out my pen and wrote down twelve basic life convictions. I do not hold them any longer; they hold me. These convictions have become part of my life—they are me.

O God, I thank Thee for the coming and going of the years that leave a deposit of conviction within. I thank Thee. Amen.

AFFIRMATION FOR THE DAY: *Since my life convictions are becoming me, I had better take stock of them—minutely.*

TWELVE LIFE CONVICTIONS

The first life conviction that I noted was: *That there is a moral universe which always has the last word.* That moral universe is built into the nature of things. No one gets past it. You have to come to terms with it or get hurt. No one gets away with anything. The moral universe has the last word, whoever has the first or the intermediate word. And that last word is inexorable. No individual, no group, no nation, escapes. We reap what we sow, somewhere, somehow. "There is nothing covered, that shall not be revealed; or hid, that shall not be known." Life ultimately reveals reality, however we may dress it up in make-believe. The goodness and the badness all shine through all make-up of character and action. It is the very nature of life to reveal itself. So the very concealings become the revealings.

Anyone who thinks he can cheat a moral universe is a moral imbecile. "The mills of God grind slowly, but they grind exceeding small"—nothing escapes. The moral universe doesn't have a payday every Saturday night, or at the end of every month, or at the end of every year. But everybody pays and is paid in exact coin.

This moral universe is not built up by mores, customs; it is built into the nature of reality. Therefore the moral universe is not subject to man's vetoes or abrogations. It stands. You don't break its laws; you break yourself upon them. And those laws are color-blind, class-blind, religion-blind, race-blind.

And this moral universe is ubiquitous. You cannot run away from it. For it is within you. The laws of your being are a part of the moral universe. And those laws are self-executing.

Are we caught, then, in a web of circumstances and past deeds—caught like a rat in a trap? Are we doomed to eat the bitter fruit of our doings? Is the law of Karma—the law of sowing and reaping—the law of the universe? Yes. Except for one thing, and that is a very important thing—grace. The door of grace is the open door—the only open door—out of our tragic dilemma. Those who do not take this only open door sink back into the inexorable consequences of their own doings. The moral universe closes in.

O Father, I thank Thee that Thy moral universe is Thy preventive grace —preventing me from getting mortally hurt. Amen.

AFFIRMATION FOR THE DAY: *The moral universe guarantees the stability of right living and the instability of wrong living.*

JESUS, THE PERFECT BUT UNFOLDING REVELATION

The next life conviction which I hold is this: Second, *That the revelation of God to man is progressive, appearing in varying degrees among all races and culminating in the final and perfect revelation in Jesus Christ.* God apparently intends to redeem the race of mankind, for wherever the mind of man is open and receptive, God has revealed Himself in varying degrees. "He has not left himself without witness in any nation." In the Hebrew people He found His best, though imperfect, medium, through which the final revelation should come. But the Old Testament, which is the period of preparation for Christianity, is not Christianity. It is pre-Christian and sub-Christian. Christianity is Christ. Christians are people who believe in God and man and life through Jesus Christ.

In Jesus Christ we see what God is like and what man can be like. He is the revelation of both God and man. And He is the final revelation. "Beyond that which is found in Jesus of Nazareth the human race will never progress," said Coleridge. And the years and the centuries say a resounding "Amen."

But if He is final, He is also unfolding. New meanings are constantly breaking out from Him and will continue to do so. He is on the other side of our twentieth century beckoning us into the new day. Surprises and new, scintillating meanings break out of His person. Such infinity of revelation could come only from the infinite.

Third, *The deepest place of that revelation is the Cross.* There God let us see His heart through the broken heart of Jesus. There was illustrated on a cosmic scale what takes place in a home where pure love meets sin in the loved one. At the junction of that love and that sin a cross of pain is set up. For it is the nature of love to insinuate itself into the sin and sorrow of the loved one and make them its own. All love has the doom of bleeding upon it as long as there is sin in the loved one. The Cross is the meeting place where the pure love of God meets sin in the loved ones, in us. And there that pure love bore in its own body our sins on a tree. God being what He is and we being what we are, the Cross was inevitable. It was inherent.

O God, my Father, the Cross breaks me down and lifts me up. It sends me to my knees and lifts me to highest heaven. Amen.

AFFIRMATION FOR THE DAY: *The Cross is the ground plan of the universe. I'm making it the ground plan of my life.*

THE KINGDOM WRITTEN INTO US

My next life conviction is: Fourth, *The Kingdom of God is written not only into the Bible, but into the nature of reality and into us.* The Kingdom is the revelation of what heaven's order is and what earth's order ought to be. It is the way men are to live individually and collectively and is therefore the Way. This passage confirms that; "Then Paul entered the synagogue . . . arguing and persuading people about the Reign [Kingdom] of God. But as some grew stubborn and disobedient, decrying the Way" (Acts 19:8-9, Moffatt). Here the Kingdom of God and "the Way" are used synonymously.

And the Kingdom of God and Life are used synonymously: "better be maimed and get into Life," "better get into God's Realm [Kingdom] with one eye" (Mark 9:43, 47, Moffatt). Then the Kingdom of God and Life and the Way are the same. But these terms are used of Jesus: "I am the Way, . . . the Life." Then Jesus and the Kingdom are one. The absolute Order—the Kingdom—and the absolute Person —Jesus Christ—are the same. God redeems through Christ, and God reigns through Christ.

Fifth, *The Christian Way is the natural way to live.* I am convinced that sin and evil and every other way are unnatural ways to live. Inquity is literally "missing the mark." The "mark" is the Kingdom, the Way. So all living against that Way is a living against yourself. For the Kingdom is the "mark" within us—the way we are made to live. To live against yourself is impossible, not only foolish but impossible. So sin and evil break down the self. The self disintegrates under it—"perish" is the word Jesus uses.

But to find Christ is to find yourself at home, harmonious, integrated, built up, happy, natural. You smile—naturally; you enjoy life—naturally; you work—naturally; you grow—naturally; You are a freeborn citizen of your Homeland. You walk the earth a conqueror. You breathe deeply. You look upon life with dancing eyes watching the unfolding drama of redemption. You trip along life's way, sure that this is the Way. You feel yourself expanding to meet expanding meanings. Deep down you say, "This is It!"

O Christ, I thank Thee that in Thee I am at Home. I am where I was made to be. I have arrived. I am myself. Amen.

AFFIRMATION FOR THE DAY: *"If the natural will not submit to the Supernatural, it becomes the unnatural."*

THE KINGDOM IS GOD'S TOTAL ANSWER

We come now to the next conviction. Sixth, *The Kingdom of God is God's total answer to man's total need.*

The rise of modern totalitarianisms is a symptom of man's felt need for something to totally command him, to bring life into integration under a single control and direct it toward a single end. Without this, life is at loose ends. Hence in religion the totalitarian church—the Roman Catholic Church; in political life the totalitarian state—the military nationalism of Germany, Italy, and Japan, as seen in Nazism and Fascism; in the totalitarian dictatorship of the proletariat—the communist society: all these are symptoms of an inner disease—the lack of total meaning felt by modern man. These half-answers let men down. When you totally obey them, you find total bondage.

But has God no total answer to man's total need? He who put order in the lowest cell, has He left unplanned the most important portion of life on our planet—the total life of man? No! The total answer to man's total need is the Kingdom of God. When you totally obey it, you find total freedom.

Seventh, *The way to meet unmerited suffering and injustice is not to bear them, but to use them.* When I saw that possibility years ago through this verse, "That will turn out an opportunity for you to bear witness"—the unjust bringing of you before judges and governors to be tried (Luke 21:13, Moffatt)—an entirely new world opened before me. I had been trying to explain suffering, and now I saw that we are not to explain it, but to use it. Everything that happens to you —good, bad, or indifferent—can contribute to you if you know how to use it. Everything furthers those who follow Christ—provided they know how to set their sails. All winds blow you to your goal. It is the set of the soul that does it. When you know this secret, you are afraid of nothing, because you can use everything. That makes you march up to every human happening, with the possibility tucked away in your mind of plucking a blessing out of the heart of everything.

Dear God, how grateful I am for this possibility. Help me to use it to the full and to use it always in everything. Amen.

AFFIRMATION FOR THE DAY: *If Jesus turned the worst thing that could happen, namely the Cross, into the best thing that could happen, namely redemption, then He can help me to do the same.*

THE HOLY SPIRIT, BIRTHRIGHT OF BELIEVERS

We come now to the next great conviction: Eighth, *That the Holy Spirit is the birthright of believers.* I am persuaded that the Holy Spirit is the applied point of redemption. He brings redemption where it counts, namely, down among the basic springs of life. Psychologists tell us that the subconscious mind really determines the conscious. If this is true, then it is of the first importance to human living that something very redemptive control the subconscious. This need is supplied by the Holy Spirit. If we turn over to Him all we know—the conscious mind—and all we don't know—the subconscious mind, then the Holy Spirit takes over the control of the driving urges—self, sex, and the herd—and cleanses and redirects them and dedicates them to the purposes of the Kingdom of God.

This takes the precariousness out of the spiritual life, for the depths —the deepest depths—are held by the Divine. Therefore fears and anxieties drop away.

The Holy Spirit is possessed by all who truly believe in and follow Christ, but when there is complete surrender to Him, we not only possess the Spirit; He possesses us. That change is important—very. You do not work so much as you let Him work through you.

This leads to the next conviction: Ninth, *That the way to live is by grace and receptivity.* To know how to receive is the most important lesson of life. It is the first lesson that the newborn child learns—to receive air into its lungs and to receive nourishment from the mother's breast. Spiritually we do not live unless we learn how to receive the grace of God and to live by its resources. As you grow strong by that grace, you also grow humble. For your very life depends on being able to receive. But it does something else: it takes out all the strain and tenseness of living. It makes us calm and assured—and adequate. We have enough to live by—enough and to spare. And it is out of that "enough and to spare" that we give out to others. Work is not then work; it is sharing—a sharing of what has been shared with us. This takes fussiness out of our work and gives a sense of quiet adequacy. We are afraid of nothing, for we can meet everything.

O Father God, I thank Thee for the beauty and the bounteousness of living by Thy grace. We have nothing and yet possess everything. Amen.

AFFIRMATION FOR THE DAY: *Living by receptivity makes one a little child in the Father's House—free to receive everything.*

THE CHRISTIAN WAY WORKS

We come now to our next conviction: Tenth, *That Jesus Christ will have the last word in human events.* It sounds an incredible thing to say, but events all point to one thing, namely, that the Man who walked our dusty roads is now on the throne of the universe and will have the last word in human affairs. This sounds absurd. And yet human affairs are working out just that way. Everything that embodies His will survives, and everything that goes against that will perishes. Jesus is the rock upon which we build or upon which we go to pieces. And there are no exceptions. He is the Alpha—the Christ of the beginning—and the Omega—the Christ of the final word.

Eleventh, *That Love is the strongest force in the universe and will finally prevail.* Hate seems strong but its strength is only seeming. It has the seeds of its own destruction within it. Love seems weak, but its weakness is only seeming. It has the seeds of construction within it. And construction will outlast destruction. The men of hate have gone down like tenpins in human history as they created the forces that destroyed them. Jesus, the Man of love, stands up under every tempest and emerges stronger at the end. Love will wear down all hate. And because I believe in the power of love, I believe that war will be banished from the earth.

Twelfth, *That the Christian way works.* It will work to the degree that we work it. I know of no other way that does work. All alternatives to the Christian way turn out to be alternative ways to ruin. There are many wrong ways; there is only one right way. And Jesus always turns out to be that Way—always. Life to me is one long corroboration of that fact.

These are the twelve life convictions that have now become axiomatic to me. I expect these convictions to grow through the coming years. They are pressing me forward with an almost irresistible compulsion. They are so many hands reaching out of the past and pushing me forward on this Way. If life had meanings other than these, it wouldn't be life. It would be death.

O Father, I thank Thee that this is Life—Life abundant, free, and victorious. I am on the Way with a singing heart. Amen.

AFFIRMATION FOR THE DAY: *Every day I'll say: If I want to live, this is the way. If I don't want to live, then I'll live some other way—and get hurt.*

AN INDUSTRIAL CHECK-UP

As we come down to the last week of our quest for growth, we will check up to see how we have been getting on. A friend who is an engineer in human relations has a system whereby men in a plant can check up on themselves as to their growth in human qualities necessary to success in that particular situation. The man checking himself rates himself as A, B, or C to the following statements:

(1) He is liked. (2) He is kind. (3) He is a good listener. (4) He controls his temper. (5) He is patient. (6) He develops men under him. (7) He is fair and sincere. (8) He is a self-starter. (9) He is creative in his work. (10) He is enthusiastic about his job. (11) He finishes what he starts. (12) He works well with people. (13) He accepts responsibility and takes the consequences. (14) He is not the Big "I." (15) He is not self-centered.

You might go over this list for your particular situation in which you work. Your ability to look at your self objectively without attempting to defend yourself, or excuse yourself, will be the measure of your growth and maturity. If you find yourself defending or excusing yourself, then you had better mark yourself down accordingly.

You might take your list and its grading to a trusted friend, or to a group, and get the judgment of that friend or the group on your own grading. To get the judgment of a friend or a group is to see ourselves as others see us. They may rate us higher or lower than we do ourselves.

Some years ago when I first made a recording for a broadcast, the man in charge warned me as he played it back that I wouldn't recognize my own voice. He told me of a little girl who, when she heard her own voice played back, burst into tears saying, "That's not my voice." Your voice sounds more resonant to you than it does to the other person and not nearly so flat. So when you test yourself on these fifteen points, be sure to check it up with others.

Father, I want to grow. I do not want a pat on the back. I want to add a cubit to my spiritual stature. Help me. Amen.

AFFIRMATION FOR THE DAY: *I will be as honest as truth, as open as sunlight, and therefore free to grow.*

A GENERAL CHECK-UP ON GROWTH

We saw yesterday the marks of a successful person in an industrial situation. Today we must apply these tests to ourselves as persons. We have suggested twenty-five marks of a growing Christian and a place where you can mark your percentages as you see him and others see him.

My appraisal   *Others' appraisal*

1. He is self-surrendered.
2. He is free from resentments.
3. He is harboring no guilts.
4. He is free from fear and
     anxiety and tensions.
5. He is not a stagnant personality.
6. He knows how to receive grace.
7. He reacts in a Christian way to what
     happens to him.
8. He is characterized by love.
9. He is a person of joy.
10. He is a man who knows peace within.
11. He is a man of good temper.
12. His outlook is kindliness.
13. He is a man of generosity.
14. He is trustable—a man of fidelity.
15. He is adaptable.
16. He has self-control.
17. He has a wide and deep social awareness.
18. He has a prayer life that is transforming.
19. He is a steward of time, money, and talents.
20. He is growing in good family relations.
21. He is growing in spiritual contagion.
22. He is a growing, balanced personality.
23. He is growing in simplicity of life.
24. He is learning more and more to
     take resources.
25. He is becoming a Christlike person.

O Father, I am under the stimulus of Thy Son. And I am being made in His likeness—and what a likeness! Amen.

AFFIRMATION FOR THE DAY: *Growth is written in my make-up. I am intended to grow. I accept and co-operate.*

WILL THERE BE AN ETERNAL GROWTH?

We will spend these last few days together in considering whether this growth of our personalities will cease at death, or whether we will have an eternal growth. This is important.

We have said that the goal of life was a perfected individual in a perfected society. But suppose that perfected individual and that perfected society are earth-bound, environed by nothing eternal. Then both your perfected individual and your perfected society begin to shrink. They have no meanings beyond this earthly life. That does something to your perfection—it isn't perfect! It is a striving after wind, or more accurately, after dust. For it all ends there.

It is not enough to say that we live on in our descendants and in the society we help to influence. Is that all? I sat on a prayer knoll in Sat Tal, India, and on the tree above, the large pods, about six inches in length, would burst with the sound of a firecracker and in the bursting would fling their seeds at a distance from the tree, and then the two sides of the pods would fall to the ground together—their lifework done. Is that all human life is? Does the explosion called death throw our children on their own and leave us to drop into the silence of oblivion—our work done?

If that be true, then the most precious thing on our planet—human personality—has no ultimate meaning and therefore no ultimate value. Life is fundamentally cheapened. And the universe, which conserves energy, so that no energy anywhere is lost, fails to conserve value, human character, and when a human character has lived out its earthly life, it is not conserved—it is thrown on the dump heap. Such a universe would add up not to sense, but to nonsense. And the personality would be scrapped just when it is most valuable—with all the years of accumulated experience and growth at their very best. What is the use of order and law in the cell and the atom if, at the place of greatest value, at the very epitome of life—human character, there is nothing but disorder and lawlessness? Death explodes all, leaves a rotting heap.

O Father, I feel beating within me the pulse beats of eternity. How then can I die eternally? I cannot—Thou art alive. Amen.

AFFIRMATION FOR THE DAY: *I am alive with God, God is alive forever, therefore I am alive forever!*

"PLUS ULTRA"

If there is no eternal significance to human character, human life is automatically cheapened.

A devoted missionary lady found the lepers of a certain government leper asylum committing suicide, a dozen a month, for nobody cared. Then she began to show she cared and demonstrated it in a wonderful way—she organized a church for them, work classes, training in various skills, recreation, choirs, etc. The suicides stopped. Then she asked a United States government official operating a cultural center for some films for the lepers and got this reply: "We are here for political purposes, and frankly, lepers are not politically important." He was right, if life is bounded by political horizons. Within that framework lepers don't count. But suppose the leprosy of the mind, which this official showed, is more devastating than the leprosy of the body which the patients showed; then our values must be reversed in the light of eternal meanings. If immortality goes, then immorality comes. A man is not "a man for whom Christ died"; he is a man of no political or any other consequence.

I saw a man in China, obviously a pagan, carrying out a dead child for burial. He walked along carrying the child by the arm, the body dangling as he walked. It was only a dead child. It was not one of "these little ones" whose angels always see the Father's face.

But set death in the center of the Christian conception of life with an eternity of growth stretching beyond, and death really has no sting.

There was a sign at Gibralter with the words *"Ne Plus Ultra"* ("Nothing beyond") on it. That was before the new world was discovered. Then when it was discovered, they had to change it by rubbing out the *"Ne"* to *"Plus Ultra"* (Everything beyond). Before Jesus rose from the tomb, over the portals of death was written, "Nothing Beyond"; after He arose, it had to be written "Everything Beyond." For in Jesus death is not even an interruption; it is a larger beginning.

O Father, I thank Thee that I cannot be stopped by death, for eternal Life is my possession now—and forever. Amen.

AFFIRMATION FOR THE DAY: *I am a child of eternity. I must lift my sights and put eternal meanings into now.*

"TELL THEM WE'SE RISIN"

Someone has defined this life as "a vale of character making." If the end of this life is not happiness, but character, then when the character is made in the years of maturity, is it made to be canceled or continued? The question of whether there is a good God, and intelligent, hangs on the answer to that question. If the universe can't answer that question intelligently, then all the other seeming wisdom written into things is more than doubtful; it is damnable—damnable in that it is utterly careless, or worse, ruthless at the place where it matters most—human personality.

The statement of Jesus is important: "And your reward will be great, and you will be sons of the Most High" (Luke 6:35, R.S.V.). The reward is in a quality of being—"You will be sons of the Most High." Does the Most High become the Most Low in snuffing out His sons just when they are most mature? He couldn't be the Most High unless we could share with Him our most high aspiration, namely to share with Him an eternal fellowship.

Eternal growth is a "must" for God and man. When General Armstrong, friend of the Negroes, went to the South after the Civil War, he asked a crowd of Negroes just out of slavery what message he could take back to the North from them. At the back a Negro boy called out: "Tell them that we'se risin." Wonderful message! And true! And will that "risin" be for eternity, or will it cease at death? Such "risin" has the leaven of eternity in it and will rise forever.

A missionary went back to the head-hunters of Formosa after the war. Food was scarce in Formosa and scarcer in the hills where they lived, and they were semi-starved. He expected them to ask for food, first of all, but their first question was not food, but: "Are there any Bibles in America? Please get us some." Thousands had become Christians through their own people's spreading the gospel. I would like to ask this question: Is there not to be an eternal "risin" for these who had such little opportunity in this life? And are there no Bibles in heaven from which these can learn eternally the meaning of grace?

O Christ, Thou hast shed a shaft of light into the darkness of death— and beyond. I belong to the Beyond. Amen.

AFFIRMATION FOR THE DAY: *I have a running start for eternity, and now for the real race!*

ANY PRODS TO PERFECTION THERE?

We are now being compelled to look for an eternal growth. Everything sensible points in that direction.

I believe that we begin in heaven where we leave off here. This means that rewards in heaven are not arbitrarily given for faithful service to God. The reward is in the quality of being we take with us. We will start in heaven with the capacity for the enjoyment of God we have developed here. The greater the capacity we take with us, the greater the enjoyment of God, hence the greater the reward. Each will be enjoying God with the capacity he brought with him. Hence there can be no jealousy of another's greater reward. We won't even know he has a greater reward—only God and he will know that. Hence there can be no asking for bonuses or jostling for rewards.

There will be no first seats or peanut galleries; everyone will take from the Infinite what his capacity for taking will allow. Everyone's cup will be full, but some cups will be larger. They made them so through the years.

Will heaven provide incentives to growth? In a perfect environment where is the stimulus? Toynbee tells of the herring fisherman of England who found that the catch of herring deteriorated in the tank in the hold of the ship, their flesh getting soft and flabby by the time they got to port. To overcome this tendency to soft flabbiness, they introduced huge catfish among the herring. The herring were always running away from the catfish, so they kept in firm condition until the end of the voyage. Earth provides us with many catfish that prod us into firmness of character. But has heaven any catfish? Are there any prods to perfection there? I do not know. Perhaps the prods are within us. We are made for perfection, and that inward prod will be eternally with us.

But the greatest prod will be the sight of God. When we see Him as He is with the veils off ourselves and off Him, we will be so overwhelmed with longing to be like Him that we will need no prods—this pull will be sufficient. Love will love us into its likeness.

Father, I see Thee now, and my heart is on fire to be like Thee. What will it be when I see Thee face to face? Amen.

AFFIRMATION FOR THE DAY: *Love is loving me into its likeness now. Today I shall let that love have full sway.*

"WE SHALL BE LIKE HIM"

We come now to our last day together. Will there be tasks in heaven? If not, how could we grow? In almost all the Japanese schoolyards there is a statue of a boy with a load of wood on his back walking along reading an open book. Is that boy the eternal pilgrim? We will never cease to be like that boy. In our hands there will eternally be the Book of Life and on our backs will be the eternal burdens to bear. Will there be no kindergartens in heaven where we will be able to teach the beginners in the Way? And no postgraduate courses for us to take? And are there no other worlds to be evangelized? Give me twenty-four hours of rest in heaven, and I'll ask for an assignment to one of those worlds! The call of the Beyond is upon me now. And then?

Will we ever grow and grow until we become God? I think not and I hope not. In Ps. 8:5 we read: "Yet thou hast made him little less than divine" (Moffatt). That "little less" is important. We are finite and He is the Infinite. The finite will infinitely approach the Infinite, but we will never become the Infinite. In that growth of the finite in the image of the Infinite will be our eternal happiness.

But I don't want to be God. I just want to love God. And I couldn't love God if I were God. To love God is enough for time and eternity. I want nothing else. I don't want to be lost in the Ocean of Being. I want to be myself, a redeemed self—that will produce humility; and yet I want to look at my Saviour—that will produce the incentive for growth. For when I see Him, I see what I am and what I can be in Him.

I saw a number of ropes going out from big trees in the forests of Japan to the little trees around. It meant that the big trees were pulling the little trees around them, which were inclined to crookedness, into straightness.

Jesus is the Big Tree—planted in eternity. I am bound to Him by cords of love, and He is pulling me into straightness and will do so both now and forever. I'm out for eternal growth.

O Father God, I'm a pilgrim of the Infinite. I love the Way. For I know the Way is leading me to His likness. Amen.

AFFIRMATION FOR THE DAY: *"What we are to be is not apparent yet, but we do know that when he appears we are to be like him"* (I John 3:2, Moffatt).